STRANGE
REVOLUTION

Exploring the Life of Jesus

TREVOR PETTY

Wanderhome Publishing Company

Originally published in paperback by
Wanderhome Publishing Company, March 2018

ISBN-13: 978-0-9997473-7-7

to Lincoln,
may you cherish the wonder

TABLE OF CONTENTS

ILLUSTRATIONS

PROLOGUE (Start Here)

I WAS PROBABLY ABOUT twelve the first time that I picked up a Bible to read. One night in bed, I started at the beginning, as I would have with any other book. It didn't take long for me to realize that this wasn't the kind of book I was used to. The chapters were only about a page each, and the text was organized into columns with verses. On top of this, there was little explanation about the author or how the book was structured. And there were long lists of people's ancestors, called genealogies.

Encountering an ancient world much different than my own, I thought the stories got kind of weird pretty quickly. It wasn't quite the divine instruction manual I had anticipated, though I'm not sure what exactly I was even looking for at the time. Instead of bringing clarity to my questions about God, this book just gave me more. Dismayed, I soon lost interest.

A few years down the road, I picked up the mammoth of a book again. I was in high school now and plenty curious. I had encountered part of one of the letters from the Bible and was surprised by the way it seemed to speak to me. Someone encouraged me to try beginning with the New Testament (the smaller, second portion of the Bible). So, taking the advice, I naturally started again at the beginning of this second part, in the gospel of Matthew. As before, I found a genealogy. Once the stories got started, they tended to be much shorter than before (often only a few paragraphs). Jesus seemed nice, but much of what he said just confused me. And the story was still set in a drastically different culture, making it hard to follow. I decided that reading the Bible was a pretty frustrating endeavor. I remained curious about Jesus, but my questions continued to pile up.

A GOOD STORY

I've always been someone who wanted to understand things. As a student, it left me with a natural affinity for English classes. Reading comprehension was actually one of my worst subjects, but I loved the discussions we had about books and life in class. Eventually, this brought me to study literature in college. I enjoyed the big questions and deep conversations, and my classes were built around these. We'd read and dissect. We'd walk through characters and themes. We'd explore history, draw comparisons, and reflect on our own lives in the process. And, of course, we'd debate.

Many of our conversations about books ultimately came back to the simple question, "Is this any good?" This question popped in and out of our discussions (and often our frustrations), simmering beneath the surface of our analyses of characters and themes. What exactly makes a good book, anyway? One of the ways we would talk about this was through the magical "test of time." Does what we were reading still matter? Does it still have something to say? Or should it just be filed away and forgotten?

A good story is able to transcend time and place to express something basic about our human experience. It moves us as if we are humming along with a song or tapping our foot to the beat as we step into a setting, a struggle, an idea or emotion. It tells us something about who we are and what it means to be human. It tells us that we're not alone and are part of something much bigger than ourselves—that we're part of a broader narrative at work in history. When we read, it's like we are constantly asking, "Is this me? Does this tell my story? Does this tell our story?"

Naturally, we share what we think are good stories. It's why we pass along our favorite movies, television series, songs, and books. It's our way of saying, "Yes, this is me," and then asking those around us, "You too?" We want to know that we aren't alone. Retelling a story is like saying "Amen." It's a way of saying "Me too," and asking, "Do you understand?" And so, good stories get retold. They get passed along generation after generation as if to say,

"Indeed, this is who we are." They teach us. They remind us. They unite and guide us.

But there's a problem.

As things are handed along, time passes. Places change. People change. The question "Does this still speak?" is interrupted by "What's this even saying? Is it worth all this work?" This is the struggle of every student trying to read Shakespeare. This is the struggle of reading. This was my struggle with the Bible.

THE "GOOD BOOK"?

As with Shakespeare and other classics, the Bible is a story that's been retold and passed down through the ages. It's been carried along because on some level people have continued to say, "Yes, me too" because they believe it sheds light on who we are and why we are here. Yet, like other ancient books, there are numerous obstacles to reading it. Considering how hard it is to read Shakespeare (just a few hundred years old), it's no surprise that the Bible (a couple thousand years old) can be difficult. Have you encountered this? For many, the obstacles pile up and the story is over before it ever really starts.

Yet the Bible is a story. Well, it is a *long* story, or maybe more of a catalogue of episodes and literary works that fit together to form an enormous collection. It only seems fitting that as we approach it, we would ask some of the very same questions that are so natural to us and that we would apply to other literature. Does it still speak? Is it worth all the work? Is there a broader narrative shaping history? This is part of why Christians treat the Bible as scripture. It means Christians believe this book contains God's essential message for humanity. If it is the "Bible" or "divine library" as claimed, then it actually *should* speak to our most basic human experience and struggle. It must. If it doesn't, then what's the point?

HERE LIES THE PURPOSE OF THIS BOOK

While churches and Bible studies try to help people understand the Bible, they can present a number of additional challenges. Will I fit in? What's expected of me? What is everyone doing and why? What if I don't agree? Can I just stand back and watch? Will people notice if I don't participate? Will people think badly of me?

For a lot of folks, this is a terrifying option.

Besides, the Bible can be intimidating on its own. It's huge. It's old, and at times it gets used more like a weapon than a book. It gets some bad press and is carried around by some real basket cases. People make a huge deal out of it. It's risky as a reader. People think, "What am I getting myself into?"

Maybe that's where you're at. Maybe you've never been able to get much past the cover and you find Christians (or Christianity) a little intimidating, but you still want to explore. Maybe you've felt overwhelmed by the people, the traditions, the opinions, and the headlines. You aren't comfortable with the available options of studies and gatherings, but you are still curious about who Jesus is and what it's all about.

This book is for you.

In what follows, I'll do my best to help navigate different obstacles as we follow a basic story line through the life of Jesus. This book is a collection of several stories from the Bible that I attempt to frame and connect. I invite you to listen to the story and ask the same basic questions we asked in my college English classes: Does it still speak today? Is it worth the effort? Does this tell my story? Maybe you'll find places where you say, "Me too." But even if you don't, I hope you'll at least walk away with a better understanding of what all the fuss is about.

Or, maybe you've been through all of this. You know the basic story but are still searching. You're familiar with Christianity but still want more.

This book is for you too.

I've met a lot of Christians who are surprisingly unfamiliar with stories about Jesus beyond his crucifixion and resurrection. There's a lot more depth and significance to these other stories than is often explored. So, let's dig in and see what we can find.

I should warn, though, if you've picked up this book searching for fuel for debates about the Christian faith, you've come to the wrong place. While some of the content will no doubt relate to that subject matter, this book isn't so much an argument or defense as it is an exploration of the story central to Christianity. Who is Jesus and what does it have to do with me? Why is it so important to so many people? While I am a Christian, I've tried my best to not assume any kind of agreement and to anticipate different kinds of questions and skepticism. For the most part, what follows will navigate things in a way consistent with Christianity throughout history across the predominant movements within the faith.

Now, a couple decades down the road from my first attempt at reading the Bible, I stand full of wonder at the incredible story that continues to leave me saying, "Amen," and I can't help but get excited to share it with you. So please, come join me. Wherever you are as a reader, my hope is that what follows will help you on your own journey of discovery.

A ROAD MAP

There are a few things that I should explain before we get started. As I've written, I've tried to approach this as if speaking with someone that has no familiarity with the Bible whatsoever. I hope you aren't bothered by this, and I hope that it's helpful. I've basically collected stories from the Bible and combined them with some commentary to help connect them and explore what is happening. Most of these stories (with the exception of the first and last chapters) are from the first four books of the New Testament, which are called gospels. These books are something like ancient biographies written by some of Jesus' pupils and others in their community.

Interestingly, Jesus' pupils were storytellers and really good ones. At a time when books were uncommon (expensive and time-consuming to produce), they travelled around telling these stories until it was finally necessary to collect and record them because the primary sources (Jesus' students and other eyewitnesses) were passing away. Some of these witnesses were even getting executed because of the content of their stories. I've tried to include what I believe to be some of the stories basic to these books as well as to utilize some portions from each writer: Matthew, Mark, Luke, and John. While it's difficult at times to know the precise order of events, I've done my best to construct a general chronology and to keep things in an order consistent with that is presented in the gospels as we weave between the different authors.

After beginning with the first story of the entire Bible, the story of the Garden of Eden, we will work our way through the life of Jesus before finishing with a chunk from the end of the New Testament (the end of the Bible) to see if it all fits together or not.

It's also necessary for me to acknowledge the "elephant in the room" here. As we walk through this first story, the creation story, I will be focusing primarily on the who and why rather than the how. I think it's important to mention this because of the raging arguments surrounding our origins. While I do believe these discussions are significant, they often overwhelm the creation story and distract readers from all sorts of important stuff. So, in what follows, don't expect me to make any arguments about the age of the earth or anything like that.

I should also mention that about 2/3 of the Bible is located between our first story and the gospels. Chapter 2 is devoted primarily to summarizing some of the significant elements from these stories as well as some relevant historical information. If it seems a little dense and information heavy, don't fret, it doesn't last too long. Elsewhere I will summarize some of these skipped stories and occasionally refer back to events as needed (they come up often in the stories we'll read). For our purposes, though, I've focused on what I believe to be the best place to start.

I've arranged things in the familiar chapter format and have included any portion of biblical text necessary as we go. At times, I combine multiple accounts of a story in order to provide more detail. I've left citations at the beginning of each section for the passages in case you would like to look them up on your own, but I didn't want to otherwise require you to constantly flip back and forth. For the quotations, I've used a translation of the Bible called the New International Version. While different folks have their preferences, I've selected this one simply because it is one of the most common and at a pretty accessible reading level. If you have a Bible somewhere, there's a decent chance it will be this translation or something close to it. These citations will look like this: John 3:16.

The Bible is actually a collection of many books. Near the beginning of any Bible, there should be a table of contents listing these books and the corresponding pages. Books are divided into chapters and verses. The first word of the citation is the book. The citation above is from the gospel of John. If you'd like to find a passage that we look at, grab a Bible and check the table of contents for the page where the chapter begins. Once you find the book, the first number in the citation will tell you which chapter. Here, it's chapter 3. The number following the colon will tell you the verse. Here, it's verse 16. The top outer corner of any page will tell you the book, chapter, and possibly verse, on the pages before you. This is useful because Bibles come in various shapes and sizes, so it can be hard to find your place.

To be clear, there is plenty of commentary between quotations in this book that *is not in the Bible*. And while I hope to help provide a basic understanding of what is happening, this commentary is just a beginning. There is much more to be mined from these passages. To help distinguish between my comments and these passages, quotations from the Bible will always be...

> *in a block quote and in italics.*

For more information, I've included a few notes at the bottom of pages[1] as well to reference other passages of interest that may not be included or to share other beneficial information. Each chapter also has a corresponding FAQ section online at strangerevolution.com. There you'll also find the work of some different artists and musicians who have collaborated with me on this project. They have joined me in retelling some of these stories through the lenses of their own skill sets.

Well, that's all for now. I'm excited that you are here, and I hope that you'll find the journey well worth the trouble as I pass along what I've found to be a beautiful treasure.

---

[1] You've probably seen something like this before. Not too complicated.

Part I

Beginnings

ONE
Setting the Stage

E VERY STORY HAS A beginning. One way or another, the pieces have to come into view. Characters and settings must be introduced. The Bible is no different. Before we can dig into the life of Jesus, we need to understand some more about what frames his story and about the Bible as a whole. For this reason, we will start with the Bible's beginning and the creation story. Pretty quickly we are brought to some themes that will continue through the rest of the book.

CREATION
Genesis 1:1-2:3

> *In the beginning God created the heavens and the earth.*

Almost immediately, we have our first character or *the* character behind it all. We have a grand architect who crafts the stage for the story, a God who sounds something like a mind or will preceding the existence of the cosmos. With little explanation, we are given a couple of distinguishable stages where the action will play out: the heavens and the earth. Are these two things separate like different doors in a hallway, or are they rather two dimensions of the same stage? So far, not so sure.

> *Now the earth was formless and empty, darkness was over the surface of the deep, and the Spirit of God was hovering over the waters.*

It's a strange beginning.

Things exist yet are still formless. Something is missing. There is a void. There is depth and darkness, and this is where God's spirit waits, gliding over the waters as if peering into a blank canvas. It's an eerie and mysterious scene.

I've heard that even today we actually know more about the surface of the moon than the depths of the oceans. By and large, the seas remain an unsearchable enigma to us. Yet this is where God moves, dancing elegantly over the depths like a mist in the breeze. It sounds mystical and magical, but it won't remain this way for long.

And God said, "Let there be light," and there was light. God saw that the light was good, and he separated the light from the darkness. God called the light "day," and the darkness he called "night." And there was evening, and there was morning—the first day.

And God said, "Let there be a vault between the waters to separate water from water." So God made the vault and separated the water under the vault from the water above it. And it was so. God called the vault "sky." And there was evening, and there was morning—the second day.

And God said, "Let the water under the sky be gathered to one place, and let dry ground appear." And it was so. God called the dry ground "land," and the gathered waters he called "seas." And God saw that it was good.

And God said, "Let the land produce vegetation: seed-bearing plants and trees on the land that bear fruit with seed in it, according to their various kinds." And it was so. The land produced vegetation: plants bearing seed according to their kinds and trees bearing fruit with seed in it according to their kinds. And God saw that it was good. And there was evening, and there was morning—the third day.

There is action, but to whom is God speaking?

God is beginning with something that is shapeless and chaotic (like the waves of the sea) and bringing it form. This says something about our primary character. God doesn't just create things for pandemonium but instead provides order and function. Amid the darkness and disorder, God brings structure, purpose and meaning.

God begins organizing, distinguishing, and naming things. It appears God is arranging a setting for some plan. Through God's word, it is so. God separates the light from darkness. God parts the waters, perhaps separating the fresh waters above (rain) and the salt water below (the ocean and seas). Then, God shapes a space for life to spring forth. We suddenly have the skies, lands, and seas that will serve as a dwelling for all that lives. Here, vegetation flourishes. There is a rhythm developing, a refrain as work is done with each day. There is a quality to things. At the end of the third day God is pleased and proclaims, "It is good."

And God said, "Let there be lights in the vault of the sky to separate the day from the night, and let them serve as signs to mark sacred times, and days and years, and let them be lights in the vault of the sky to give light on the earth." And it was so. God made two great lights—the greater light to govern the day and the lesser light to govern the night. He also made the stars. God set them in the vault of the sky to give light on the earth, to govern the day and the night, and to separate light from darkness. And God saw that it was good. And there was evening, and there was morning—the fourth day.

And God said, "Let the water teem with living creatures, and let birds fly above the earth across the vault of the sky." So God created the great creatures of the sea and every living thing with which the water teems and that moves about in it, according to their kinds, and every winged bird according to its kind. And God saw that it was good. God blessed them and said, "Be fruitful and increase in number and fill the water in the seas, and let the birds increase on the earth." And there was evening, and there was morning—the fifth day.

And God said, "Let the land produce living creatures according to their kinds: the livestock, the creatures that move along the ground, and the wild animals, each according to its kind." And it was so. God made the wild animals according to their kinds, the livestock according to their kinds, and all the creatures that move along the ground according to their kinds. And God saw that it was good.

Then God said, "Let us make mankind in our image, in our likeness, so that they may rule over the fish in the sea and the birds in the sky, over the livestock and all the wild animals, and over all the creatures that move along the ground."

With each day, the refrain continues. Now lights cover the skies, with two designated specifically to govern day and night. Things are being appointed roles with purpose. The waters, skies, and lands are now teeming with life. Things multiply "according to their kinds," bearing categorical resemblance, and things again are *good*. After filling the earth with all kinds of creatures, God finally arrives at humanity, who will also have a special purpose in creation.

But this time something is different. When God makes humanity, it is in "our image, in our likeness." This is new and different. What exactly does it mean? Also, why is God speaking in the plural? And is humanity's given role as ruler of other creatures a part of humanity's intended resemblance to God?

So God created man in his own image, in the image of God he created him; male and female he created them.

God blessed them and said to them, "Be fruitful and increase in number; fill the earth and subdue it. Rule over the fish of the sea and the birds in the sky and over every living creature that moves on the ground."

Then God said, "I give you every seed-bearing plant on the face of the whole earth and every tree that has fruit with seed in it. They will be yours for food. And to all the beasts of the earth and all the birds of the sky and all the creatures that move on the ground—everything that has the breath of life in it—I give every green plant for food." And it was so.

God saw all that he had made, and it was very good. And there was evening, and there was morning—the sixth day.

The complexity, uniqueness, diversity, beauty, and design are all structured around the existence and abundance of life. We have our stage. Thinking of the way that a work of art reflects the artist, it seems fitting that creation likewise speaks something of its creator. Yet among all of creation, humanity, including both men and women, uniquely expresses God's character. Maybe this is something like a child's resemblance to its parents.

God is building a world. As life flourishes, a society is developing, and humanity has an important role in the process. Man and woman will be a part of the shaping of this domain as they too fill it with life. For now, there is order and harmony. Things are in their designated places, and the scene is set.

But the refrain changes.

As if through the climax or the icing on the cake, this time God steps back and proclaims creation *"very* good." Interestingly, God doesn't say that it is finished. But God is especially pleased with the wholeness of things, enough so that next we even see some new behavior on God's part…

Thus the heavens and the earth were completed in all their vast array.

By the seventh day God had finished the work he had been doing; so on the seventh day he rested from all his work. Then God blessed the seventh day and made it holy, because on it he rested from all the work of creating that he had done.

Once again we see the heavens and earth mentioned together as though completed simultaneously. Today, the heavens can refer to something above like the skies or outer space, though it often carries the sense of something beyond, something transcendent like the dwelling or resting place of God. Here we are told that this great beyond (heaven) has been finished in conjunction with the earth as though they are linked, two related yet distinguishable realms of existence. While shaping one, God has also been forming the other. This seems fitting considering that God just finished crafting what we could call a kind of heaven on earth. Could it be that God has just constructed his own dwelling place as an intersection between the transcendent heavens and the earth?

Ceasing from work (at least for now), God stops to rest. Resting often means a few things. For one, of course, it means no longer working. Instead, it is delighting in the present and celebrating what has been accomplished. It could involve some sort of leisure activity. This could be as simple as spending time at one's home or taking a little excursion to delight in some beauty (like a vacation). In the ancient world among nomadic peoples, resting meant pitching your tent somewhere along the journey and setting up camp, preparing a home base to stay for a while.

Here, we see God take time to relax after the work of putting things together. He is going to soak things in and celebrate the quality of what's been done. God even enters into his creation (something we will see in the next scenes). He's pitched his tent and set up base. Where God previously stood back to direct, he will now be present and engaging from within his creation.

God is pleased enough by what's been done that he makes a special occasion of this time, and he calls this seventh day holy. Holiness is a quality of goodness, beauty, and wholeness derived from likeness to God. It is special. This day becomes known as the Sabbath. This rhythm of days and weeks continues today in our own lives. Work naturally leads us to rest. God leads us to rest. Could the purpose of all of God's labor actually be the construction of a home to enjoy?

As this first scene comes to a close, all things have progressed to this special rest. There is wholeness, perfection, peace and harmony, pleasure and delight, and God residing in and with his creation.

A REMIX IN THE GARDEN
Genesis 2:7-10, 15-25

So far, things sound pretty majestic and wonderful. We've only just begun, though. The stage is set, but the plot has yet to be framed.

There are still more characters to develop and much to happen. This next scene rewinds a little, zooming further into the scene where humanity was made.

Then the Lord God formed the man from the dust of the ground and breathed into his nostrils the breath of life, and the man became a living being.

This is a neat scene. God doesn't just make things out of nothing, he also shapes things from what already exists. God turns dirt into a living person. It's weird to imagine this first person as a hunk of clay, formless and void, resting limp in God's hands until filled with God's breath, the wind of life. The name Adam, in fact, the Hebrew word for "man," actually resembles the word for ground.

Now the Lord God had planted a garden in the east, in Eden; and there he put the man he had formed. The Lord God made all kinds of trees grow out of the ground—trees that were pleasing to the eye and good for food. In the middle of the garden were the tree of life and the tree of the knowledge of good and evil.

A river watering the garden flowed from Eden...

The Lord God took the man and put him in the Garden of Eden to work it and take care of it. And the Lord God commanded the man, "You are free to eat from any tree in the garden; but you must not eat from the tree of the knowledge of good and evil, for when you eat of it you will certainly die."

Having played the part of a potter, the Lord God is now a gardener as well. He's present on the ground and getting his hands dirty. We catch a glimpse of a special place that the man will tend. Like additional characters, a couple of specific trees are mentioned. They are beautiful and fruitful. One is the source of life. The other is a source of knowledge. As his teacher, the Lord gives man one specific instruction. While the man has an appointed role, this sounds like a reminder that he isn't the supreme authority. That position belongs to God alone. God is still the great master, and people are his appointed servants.

We are left with an ominous sense of where this story is headed. The one tree is to be his source of life. Eat of it, and man can flourish and live forever. The other offers understanding of good *and* evil. If he eats of it, it will be his undoing. Instead of the flourishing of life it will bring... death? What is this thing? Creation is full of contrasts (dark and light, day and night), and now we have one more: life and death. There are two potential paths. Will the man trust God as his teacher, or seek his own way?

Next, for the first time we are told of something that *isn't* good...

The Lord God said, "It is not good for the man to be alone. I will make a helper suitable for him."

Now the Lord God had formed out of the ground all the wild animals and all the birds in the sky. He brought them to the man to see what he would name them; and whatever the man called each living creature, that was its name. So the man gave names to all the livestock, the birds in the sky and all the wild animals.

But for Adam no suitable helper was found.

God's work for this day isn't done yet (remember, we pressed rewind). Human beings were designed for relationship, so God does something about it. The word translated "helper" here isn't something demeaning. It is actually the same word used elsewhere[1] in reference to God as a liberator. This helper is someone who brings freedom and life. This companion will bring a fullness and presence to the great void of loneliness. But where is this helper to be found?

God starts the search by bringing the wild animals to man, "to see what he would name them." Surrounded by wild beasts, man is suddenly mimicking God's own behavior as one who names things. These friendly animals also demonstrate Eden's unique quality of peace. In this scene, too, we see man interacting with the Lord on a person-to-person basis. God behaves like parents sitting around and

---

[1] Psalm 60:11

16

cooing while watching their kids play on the floor with the toys the parents provide. Parents love and delight in their children. Like a parent, God delights in the man. Like a child, the man mimics God. But man's companion is still nowhere to be found. Man has a relationship with other creatures, but something is still missing.

> *So the Lord God caused the man to fall into a deep sleep; and while he was sleeping, he took one of man's ribs[1] and then closed up the place with flesh. Then the Lord God made a woman from the rib he had taken out of the man, and he brought her to the man.*

> *The man said, "This is now bone of my bones and flesh of my flesh; she shall be called 'woman,' for she was taken out of man." That is why a man leaves his father and mother and is united to his wife, and they become one flesh.*

> *Adam and his wife were both naked, and they felt no shame.*

Rising from his deep slumber, Adam awakens to find a new flesh, a new creation, his beautiful bride. Where Adam was made from dust, the woman is made from the flesh of his side. From his side, she will stand by his side as an equal. The void is gone. The awaited companion has finally arrived, and it is very good.

We were made for relationships. We hunger for communion with others. Sexuality is an extension of this longing for companionship and oneness. Through this act of oneness comes new life, a departure from an old identity to enter a new one together. This unity can bring the fruitfulness of new life (a child) in likeness to its origins (parents), a further reflection of the unity and intimacy of the mysterious "us" behind all of creation that cooperates to bring forth all that lives.

The creation story is actually that of a great wedding banquet. Marriage is a covenant relationship, meaning that it is built around a pledge or a vow that defines the parameters of the commitment. This covenant requires faithfulness to the pledge. In Genesis 2, we actually see two covenants take shape. Before Adam became a husband, he was invited into a special relationship with God and was

---

[1] Or *took part of the man's side*

given an instruction that would shape his identity and the direction of his life. Will he choose the path of life or death? Will he remain faithful to this covenant?[1] The marriage between man and woman parallels the covenant formed between God and humanity. Will the man remain true to his marriage?

Where the first chapter moved thematically toward home, this second creation story builds toward a harmony of relationships, a covenant that shapes the quality of a presence that constitutes a "home." There is nakedness—vulnerability, trust, and intimacy. There is complete harmony between creation, humanity, and God. It is enjoyable, and it's all very good.

THE PLOT THICKENS
Genesis 3

But of course, it won't remain this way forever. There must be some struggle. As the third scene begins, we find that there is another character present in the Garden, and we are about to be introduced.

Now the serpent was more crafty than any of the wild animals the Lord God had made. He said to the woman, "Did God really say, 'You must not eat from any tree in the garden'?"

The woman said to the serpent, "We may eat fruit from the trees in the garden, but God did say, 'You must not eat fruit from the tree that is in the middle of the garden, and you must not touch it, or you will die.'"

"You will not certainly die," the serpent said to the woman. "For God knows that when you eat from it your eyes will be opened, and you will be like God, knowing good and evil."

We've met our bad guy.

We see that Adam has relayed the Lord's command to his wife, but he appears to have added something. "And you must not touch it." Where did this come from? Maybe he thought, "Better safe than

---

[1] Hosea 6:7 refers to this relationship between God and Adam as a covenant.

18

sorry. Surely another rule couldn't do any harm." Man has mimicked God as a teacher. But is this a good thing? Does the man know best?

The serpent smoothly enters the conversation as if innocently curious about God's teaching. Beginning with a simple question, the serpent weaves its way into a lofty claim that is in conflict with what the Lord has said. "You will not certainly die," it says, quoting God's command and even adding a word that God had used but Eve had left out. Beyond this bold claim, the serpent accuses God of evil motivations. Is God cruelly keeping something good from Adam and Eve? Who is truly the deceiver, God or the serpent? And could humanity really play the role of God? There is much at stake in this temptation.

When the woman saw that the fruit of the tree was good for food and pleasing to the eye, and also desirable for gaining wisdom, she took some and ate it. She also gave some to her husband, who was with her, and he ate it.

Unsure who to believe, the woman reconsiders and examines the fruit. She's hungry, and it looks not only delicious but, suddenly, *attractive.* She takes it in her hands, and nothing happens. Did Adam lie when he said she shouldn't touch it? Maybe Adam has been keeping things from her all along. Or did God lie to Adam? Suddenly, Eve's world is falling apart. Has she been betrayed by the one she loves? He existed first, so she trusted him. Was this a mistake?

The more she thinks about it, the better the fruit looks and sounds. What if this fruit is the key, and she could actually be the one in charge? Then she could be free from relying upon her silly husband and his unnecessary rules.

Meanwhile, apparently Adam has been standing by the whole time. He has to be facing his own dilemma. What should he do? He wasn't trying to deceive her but to protect her because he loves her. Now, she is holding the fruit and discovering that he was wrong about not touching it. Should he admit that God didn't actually tell him not to *touch* the fruit? Now, she is eating it! What's going to happen? Will she be taken away? He has experienced the longing of loneliness before. Will he stand by and risk it again? Must he really choose between Eve and God?

Yet, as she eats the fruit, nothing seems to happen.

Has God tricked him? Could the serpent be right? Can Adam and Eve cultivate their own world without God? Think of all that power! They wouldn't just be *like* God, they could *be* God.

The temptation to eat the fruit is built upon several questions. Who or what is God? Is God actually good or evil? Is God a deceiver? Is he an evil tyrant subjecting man and woman to his will? God and the serpent stand opposed, but which is to be trusted? Also, who or what do man and woman think they are? Can they be the Lord and master of creation? Surely they won't die. God needs them! They are central to creation, right?

Sure enough, they break the covenant with God. They feast on the serpent's words instead of God's. They've appointed a new master, and it will cost them dearly. Instead of remaining cultivators of life, they have now opened the door to the cycle of death.

Then the eyes of both of them were opened, and they realized they were naked; so they sewed fig leaves together and made coverings for themselves.

Was the serpent right? Their eyes open, and immediately they see things differently, but not as they expected. There's a surprising sting to it. The peace that previously existed within them is gone. What is this new knowledge? Is this punishment? They become self-conscious, and it is uncomfortable. They quickly search for a covering, making do with the leaves of a fig tree.

This is the power of shame. It is embarrassment. It makes us feel naked and exposed. It is discomfort with our identity or quality of being (our likeness to something that isn't good). It is concern about how others see us. It drives us to cover ourselves in an effort to hide our discomfort.

Then the man and his wife heard the sound of the Lord God as he was walking in the garden in the cool of the day, and they hid from the Lord God among the trees of the garden. But the Lord God called to the man, "Where are you?"

He answered, "I heard you in the garden, and I was afraid because I was naked; so I hid."

We see God out for a little stroll through the garden in the "cool of the day." Is this all on the Sabbath? Is it possible that mere moments after finishing his work, God has arrived on his day off only to find this mess? What will God do? The man and the woman have never felt this way before, and they are terrified. They are afraid of dying. They can feel it coming, and it drives them out of the open spaces and into the cover of darkness. They want to escape what has happened and avoid what will happen. The peace that existed between them and God is now gone.

This is the power of fear. It's the concern for evil and an awareness of something more powerful than ourselves. It is discomfort about the identity and quality of other beings, and it leads us to flee even the presence of God.

Having given them freedom and responsibility, God now invites them to tell the truth, to take responsibility for their actions. Will they confess to what has happened?

And he said, "Who told you that you were naked? Have you eaten from the tree that I commanded you not to eat from?"

The man said, "The woman you put here with me—she gave me some fruit from the tree, and I ate it."

Then the Lord God said to the woman, "What is this you have done?"

The woman said, "The serpent deceived me, and I ate."

God already knows what happened. It's like a parent entering after a loud crash to find a broken lamp and the kids hiding with their feet sticking out from behind the couch. There's no mystery here, and the answer is painfully simple. Yes. They have eaten from the tree and disobeyed God. But Adam doesn't just admit to it. There has to be some justification, a reasonable excuse that will free them from this mess of discomfort, he thinks. Adam points the finger at someone else. This is hypocrisy—duplicity and deceit.

This is the power of guilt. It's the sting of responsibility and accountability. If shame is feeling bad about who I am, guilt is feeling bad about what I've done. It's related to the harm I've inflicted upon the world around me.

Both Adam and Eve try to deflect attention from their own deeds. Explain myself? No, attack! It's someone else's fault. Adam not only blames Eve, he also blames God for putting the woman with him. The woman does something similar and points to the serpent: "It tricked me, and you put it here." God gets blamed. Eve gets blamed. The serpent gets blamed. They try to hide behind their words, but it doesn't work. Their words can't cover them.

They've trusted the wrong teacher. Instead of resembling God, they've become deceitful like the serpent. Where they were meant to be cultivators of life, they have instead opened the gates of destruction. As they ignored God's command, they have destroyed the peace within them, between them, with God, and with creation (as we will see). The order and design of creation has been polluted. The fabric of abundant life has been tarnished, and things are about to begin a new course as creation takes on a new normal: death. And so begins a cosmos shaped by the forces of entropy and disarray, a harsh world to be molded by natural selection and the violent struggle of the "survival of the fittest."

The interrogation is over and it's time for the verdict.

So the Lord God said to the serpent, "Because you have done this, 'Cursed are you above all livestock and all wild animals! You will crawl on your belly and you will eat dust all the days of your life. And I will put enmity between you and the woman, and between your offspring and hers; he will crush your head, and you will strike his heel.'"

After politely questioning the man and woman, God blames the serpent and begins explaining the consequences of what has happened. It sounds as if these two characters already know each other. Is it possible that something like this once happened before with the serpent? Misery loves company. Perhaps the serpent knew what was happening and wanted to kill them. This was its plan, and death was the aim all along. Or was this a jealous attempt to steal their authority and role? Or does the serpent believe that it can actually win this battle and overthrow God?

Because of what it did, the serpent will now be lowly in stature and reduced in capability. It has been demoted, humiliated. It has attempted to take authority but has instead lost something. It will now exist to be a nuisance to Eve's children and their descendants, cursed to strike their heels, only to meet a fatal end with its head crushed. Where God organizes, gives, and brings life, the serpent distorts, steals, murders, and destroys.

But who is this "he" that will crush the serpent? Is this predicting a specific person?

To the woman he said, "I will make your pains in childbearing very severe; with painful labor you will give birth to children. Your desire will be for your husband, and he will rule over you."

Having sought to rule, Eve will now be ruled. Producing life from her flesh and bones will be much, much more painful. In addition, having sought to create a new identity, she has lost hers, now looking to her husband for her lost peace. Instead of the intimacy, unity, and trust that once existed, one partner will now rule over another. It's a distortion of God's original design for relationships. There will be inequality, exploitation, and abuse. People will seek to rule over others, and it will bring destruction.

To Adam he said, "Because you listened to your wife and ate from the tree about which I commanded you, 'You must not eat of it,' cursed be the ground because of you; through painful toil you will eat fruit from it all the days of your life. It will produce thorns and thistles for you, and you will eat the plants of the field. By the sweat of your brow you will eat your food until you return to the ground, since from it you were taken; for dust you are and to dust you will return."

Adam could have eaten from any other tree and been nourished. But, because he ignored God, the ground will now resist him. His relationship with creation has just changed drastically. There will be "thorns and thistles." Crops will fail. His labor will bring pain and suffering. He will struggle against futility and depression, a longing for purpose and satisfaction as existed in the garden, but he will be left wanting. Instead of a lush garden, he will live in a wilderness. He will work with his hands to prove himself, to seek a new identity, to hide and cover himself, but it will not satisfy. Covered in dirt, he will become dirt. From dust to dust, we all die.

Invited to be a part of developing God's society on earth, the man and woman have chosen a new path independent from God. Instead of cooperating with the designer, they have sought to do things by their own power. They have rebelled against the true king and appointed another in God's place. Yet in the enveloping darkness, there's a glimmer of light. They aren't dead yet. God has graciously permitted their lives to continue for the time being, but in a very different direction. What will they do? Where will they go? As if giving them what they sought, God will permit their decision to play out in the world. He will let them try to do things themselves. They will taste and know evil in a way that only God did before.

Adam named his wife Eve, because she would become the mother of all the living.

The Lord God made garments of skin for Adam and his wife and clothed them. And the Lord God said, "The man has now become like one of us, knowing good and evil. He must not be allowed to reach out his hand and take also from the tree of life and eat, and live forever." So the Lord God banished him from the Garden of Eden to work the ground from which he had been taken. After he drove the man out, he placed on the East side of the Garden of Eden cherubim and a flaming sword flashing back and forth to guard the way to the tree of life.

Adam returns to naming again. It was his first task, a rhythm from something familiar and past—a purpose. But is this good? Or is this the first manifestation of the curse, a distortion of God's authority? Previously, naming the animals was an exercise of dominion over them. Has he now begun to exert that cursed dominion over his wife as he attempts to play the role of God?

Then, God does something interesting. He covers them. Their little fig leaves, the work of their hands, just won't do. They need something else. So there is a death, an animal, and from it God shapes clothing. From flesh, God makes an appropriate covering. Because Adam and Eve have become uncomfortable in their own skin, God responds by providing them with new ones.

What does this mean?

God says life won't go on like this forever. They aren't going to keep eating of this tree and remain endlessly in this sad condition, so he kicks them out of the garden. They are exiled, never to return this way again. Cherubim are angels, guards standing at the entrance with flaming swords. If Eden was an intersection between the heavens and earth, this connection has been fractured. There is now a distinct separation, an impasse dividing Adam and Eve from what was. They no longer live in God's realm and won't experience his presence in the same way any longer. The relationship has been broken. They've been driven out of their home with God and into a different world. They wanted to run the show, and so God has allowed it. There is a new stage, and they appear to be left to their own devices.

Adam and Eve still live, whether they should or not. They must be wondering what "death" is. Is it the same as being driven out of Eden? When will it happen? They will continue in a world driven by the conditions of fear, shame and guilt, and shaped around the curse of suffering, oppression, toil and death. Will God ever work to create again? As for the serpent, he will crawl around as a nuisance. The struggle with the deceiver will continue. But who is the "he" that God mentioned of Eve's offspring? Will a "son of man" arise one day to redeem them? In this gloom, we are left with the vague promise of a coming savior. But who exactly, and when, and…

How?

Two

Out of Eden

THE ELEMENTS OF THE curse (suffering, toil, oppression, and death) and the experiences of fear, shame, and guilt continue to shape the world. Medicine, technology, insurance, financial planning, injustice, inequality… all linked to these influences. What's interesting is the way the story has identified the source of the problem. What we have so far is the claim that all of these things are the result of a broken relationship with God.

As for our story, many years pass and history takes its course. Much happens, but God doesn't abandon humanity. Numerous tales of God's generous involvement are gathered over time, and a story line develops following this relationship with a specific family—that of a man named Abram (later renamed Abraham) from Hebron (a Hebrew).[1] These stories get passed along, recorded, and become known as the Hebrew scriptures. These stories comprise what Christians today commonly refer to as the Old Testament, the larger of the two portions of the Bible.

All together, these stories resemble something like the story we saw in Genesis. God is again creating, or re-creating, a dwelling place on earth and establishing a covenant relationship (like a marriage) with people and restoring the harmony of the garden. Re-working God's order and design upon the earth, humanity again has a role to play. There are instructions and more disobedience until

---

[1] Genesis 12:1-25:11

people are eventually exiled again as the cycle repeats itself. Revival, restoration, disobedience, destruction… there are numerous tales spread over a thousand years of lengthy journeys, battles, migrations and deportations, renovations and demolitions, but we will have to save those for another time. Before we can return to our story, though, we need to go over some basics from these events.

THE PEOPLE OF ISRAEL

Where the story of Eden ended with a curse, Abraham's story begins with a blessing.[1] As if counteracting the curse, God makes promises[2] to Abraham regarding a home (instead of exile), a community of descendants, and a gift of provision and security (not suffering, oppression, and toil). This man is told that it is through his son Isaac that his "offspring will be reckoned,"[3] and that his family will be a conduit of God's kindness to all peoples.[4] It sounds like the offspring of Eve (through Abraham) will indeed restore things as foreshadowed in Eden.

Isaac has a son named Jacob who is later renamed Israel.[5] Israel has twelve sons that form the "nation of Israel" and eventually become an enormous population enslaved in the powerful nation of Egypt.[6] Through a leader named Moses and a spectacular turn of events,[7] God sets the people free from this captivity and teaches them how to be a nation, inviting them to be a people reflecting his character and design as a Godly society on earth. As in the garden with Adam, he again invites their trust and commitment to a special relationship, an appointed role as his servants and mediators to the rest of the world.[8] They are to follow God for abundant life and not the other ways of the world (the path of the serpent), which will only lead to death.[9]

His instructions (laws) address all areas of life:[10] diet, public health, farming, sanitation, civil disputes, morality, justice, a court system, and even worship. As in Eden, God pitches his tent among his people in a physical structure where the nation can interact with

---

[1] Genesis 12:1-4   [2] Genesis 15:1, 5, 18-21   [3] Genesis 21:12   [4] Genesis 22:17-18
[5] Genesis 32:28   [6] Exodus 1:1-14   [7] Exodus 7:8-11:10   [8] Exodus 19:3-6   [9] Leviticus 26; Deuteronomy 28   [10] Exodus 20-23, 25-31; Leviticus 1-7, 11-25; Numbers 15, 18-19, 28-30; Deuteronomy 4-6, 11-19, 21-26

him personally through the assistance of numerous guidelines. A sort of moveable temple (this is an ancient nomadic community), this tent structure is called the tabernacle, and there are special mediators called priests who are appointed to serve the people before God. This location serves as a sort of storehouse and community center as well as a place of healing, forgiveness, and worship. It is a place designed for restoring relationships and cultivating life. While the relationship between the heavens and earth is still fractured, the law establishes a system through which people can interact with God and flourish.

The law sets up a system of sacrifices and offerings (animals and crops) that function to make amends for the mistakes of the people, a temporary "covering" for their wrongs like the clothing provided in the garden. There are prescribed responses for various offenses. This relationship, like a marriage, requires faithfulness (obedience) to these laws and becomes the foundation of their identity as a people. It also allows for continued peace among people, God, and his creation. They are told that their faith and obedience will lead them home to peace and rest (not oppression), health (not suffering), long life (not death), and prosperity (not toil). Disobedience, however, will only bring terrible destruction.

As this lineage of Abraham, Isaac, and Jacob eventually becomes a large nation[1] with a homeland[2] and monarchy in place,[3] they build a more stationary dwelling for God (or so they think) in Jerusalem.[4] Located in the capital, this temple is known as the "house of God" and is at the center of the life of the people. The nation experiences a sort of glory days during the rule of a king named David and his son Solomon. During this time, the nation flourishes like never before, and God makes some more special promises to David about an everlasting kingdom and an eternal home that will come through his descendants.[5] Yet these things never quite come to fruition.

THINGS FALL APART

After some initially encouraging developments through David's son Solomon, things seem to take a turn for the worse. Within a few decades the complications of kingly succession divide the nation in

---

[1] Numbers 1:44-46   [2] Joshua 12   [3] 1 Samuel 8-10   [4] 1 Kings 6, 8   [5] 2 Samuel 7:12-16

two: a northern kingdom (10 tribes referred to thereafter as Israel or Ephraim—the largest tribe among them) and a southern kingdom (2 tribes and the line of priests referred to as Judah—the largest and strongest tribe of them all).[1] It isn't long before the people begin to worship other gods and violate the parameters of their covenant relationship again. As the two kingdoms feud, the northern kingdom seeks to distinguish itself from the religion and culture of its southern rivals and begins to mix in various components of other religions and cultures to the point of outright rejection of the covenant with the God of Israel.[2] At one point, they even go so far as to kill God's appointed leaders (prophets and priests) and set up altars to other gods. They build a new capital in Samaria, a temple, and with it they forge a new identity rejecting that of their neighboring kin.[3]

Eventually a similar disobedience comes to plague the south as well,[4] and they too violate their covenant with God.[5] Like a bitter divorce, battles between the two nations continue for hundreds of years until both nations fall into disarray. Through numerous leaders called prophets, God warns the people that they need to change their ways or face destruction at the hands of their enemies.[6] Sure enough, both nations fall to foreign invaders[7] as they are confronted again with the harsh realities of oppression and exile.

The people of Israel become entangled in a lasting power struggle that reshapes much of the globe as conquering kingdoms get progressively larger and stronger. First, the Assyrians overtake the North in 722 B.C., then the Babylonians conquer both Assyria in 612 B.C. and Judah in 586 B.C., destroying Jerusalem's temple in the process. The Persians aren't far behind (538 B.C.), and before long the Greeks (Alexander the Great) and Romans arrive on the scene.

Each kingdom (or ruler within a kingdom) imposes its own restrictions upon the various nations under its rule. Some deport people, destroy city structures, and initiate new ways of life. Others are more lenient and allow the previous cultures to continue as long as there aren't problems. Bit by bit, the people of Israel and Judah are scattered across the globe. There is a massive blending of

---

[1] 1 Kings 11:26-12:24   [2] 1 Kings 12:25-33; Hosea 6:7, 8:1-6   [3] 1 Kings 16:24, 29-33, 18:4, 19:9-10   [4] 2 Kings 8:18, 25-27, 16:1-4, 21:1-6   [5] Jeremiah 11:1-10; Malachi 2:8
[6] Isaiah 1:18-20; Jeremiah 3:11-13; Amos 5:1-15   [7] 1 Kings 17, 21:10-15, 25:1-21

languages (Aramaic, Greek, and Latin), religion (polytheism and emperor worship), and culture.

Following the disintegration of the relationship surrounding the laws of God, countless questions remain. Will God follow through with his promises to Abraham and David, or are things beyond repair? In the absence of the temple that provided people a place to interact with God, there is confusion over how to continue to pursue this relationship. However, amid the broken record of disobedience, God continues to give the people of Israel glimmers of hope. The prophets teach that God isn't giving up, but things must change. As God rebukes his people, he leaves them mysterious descriptions of a coming restoration.[1]

Among these many prophesies are numerous descriptions of a leader known as the Christ or the Messiah (which means appointed or anointed one)[2] predicted to arrive and be "cut off" at a specific time.[3] This special person, a king[4] and priest[5] from the tribe of Judah,[6] and more specifically, the line of the King David (a "Son of David"), will establish an everlasting kingdom, and it will be *good*.[7] He will be born in Bethlehem[8] and work in the region of Galilee.[9] He will gather and reunite the scattered tribes[10] and lead the people to freedom as Moses did previously.[11] He will be a great teacher and miracle-worker.[12] God will forgive people's sins[13] and establish a new covenant relationship[14] that will extend to all nations[15] as once promised to Abraham. There will be a new temple[16] far greater than what they have ever known,[17] and God's presence will reside with people in a new way.[18]

Beyond these things, there are many other titles and descriptions used to detail additional figures and themes. One of these figures, the "Son of Man," is described as full of God's power and ruling a

---

[1] Hosea 2; Amos 9:11-15   [2] Psalm 2, Isaiah 61:1; Daniel 9:25   [3] Daniel 9:25-26
[4] Jeremiah 23:5; Zechariah 9:9-11   [5] Psalm 110:1-4; Jeremiah 33:17-18; Ezekiel 45:17; Zechariah 6:11-13   [6] Genesis 49:10   [7] Isaiah 9:6-7, 11:1-5; Jeremiah 23:5-8   [8] Micah 5:2
[9] Isaiah 9:1   [10] Ezekiel 20:41, 34:11-16, 36:24; Zephaniah 3:20   [11] Isaiah 52:1-12; Hosea 2:15; Micah 7:15   [12] Psalm 78:1-2; Isaiah 29:13-14, 18, 35:5-6, 50:4; Jeremiah 33:6; Micah 7:15   [13] Jeremiah 33:8; Ezekiel 36:25; Micah 7:18-19; Zechariah 13:1   [14] Isaiah 42:6, 55:3; Jeremiah 31:31-34, 32:40; Ezekiel 37:26-27   [15] Isaiah 2:2-4, 11:10, 25:6, 42:6, 49:6, 22, 56:3-8, 66:19-21; Daniel 7:14; Hosea 2:23   [16] Zechariah 1:16, 6:12-13   [17] Ezekiel 40-43; Haggai 2:6-9; Zechariah 2:4-5   [18] Isaiah 7:14; Jeremiah 31:32-33; Ezekiel 36:26-27

kingdom that extends to the ends of the world.[1] Other passages describe a great servant figure who will suffer on behalf of the people to bring about forgiveness.[2] There's also mention of a messenger,[3] one of their great prophets, named Elijah,[4] who will return to prepare the nation for God's arrival. But there is much debate about who exactly these figures are and how the passages relate. On top of this, there are numerous passages describing things like death being removed[5] and people coming back from the dead,[6] topics that become heavily debated among the Jewish people. Sure enough, during Persian rule the Jewish people are allowed to rebuild a temple in Jerusalem known as the "Second Temple,"[7] but many people who visit weep when they see it for the first time.[8] With many promises unfulfilled, there is confusion about what exactly God has in store and when he will return.

After the death of Alexander the Great around 323 B.C., his kingdom is too large to maintain itself. What follows is a frenzy of ruling powers struggling to establish regional control. The Hebrew people find themselves caught geographically between the Ptolemaic Kingdom (Egypt) and Seleucid Kingdom (Syria), who are both attempting to take the region. Around 166 B.C., the Jewish people have had enough and successfully revolt, beginning a period of independence. During this time of independence, Judah's borders are expanded beyond the area of Galilee and what used to be the northern kingdom. The temple in Samaria is destroyed by the Judeans, which only further perpetuates the already severe historic tension between the two regions.

Not quite fitting the prophesied events, this time just adds to the number of questions. After years of oppression, how should the nation be structured? This period continues to be a time of turmoil as several different factions within the nation struggle for power. In one of these revolts, 50,000 people are killed, and 800 of the surviving rebel nationalists (known as Pharisees) are crucified along the road to the capital of Jerusalem, which has come under the control of a

---

[1] Daniel 7:13-14   [2] Isaiah 42:1-9, 49:1-6, 50:4-9, 52:13-53:12   [3] Isaiah 40:1-11;
Malachi 3:1   [4] Malachi 4:5   [5] Isaiah 25:8, 28:18; Hosea 13:14   [6] Job 14:11-17, 19:25-27,
33:23-28; Psalm 16:10-11, 49:15; Isaiah 26:19, 53:8-12; Ezekiel 37:1-14; Daniel 12:2; Hosea
6:2   [7] Ezra 1, 3, 6:13-18   [8] Ezra 3:12

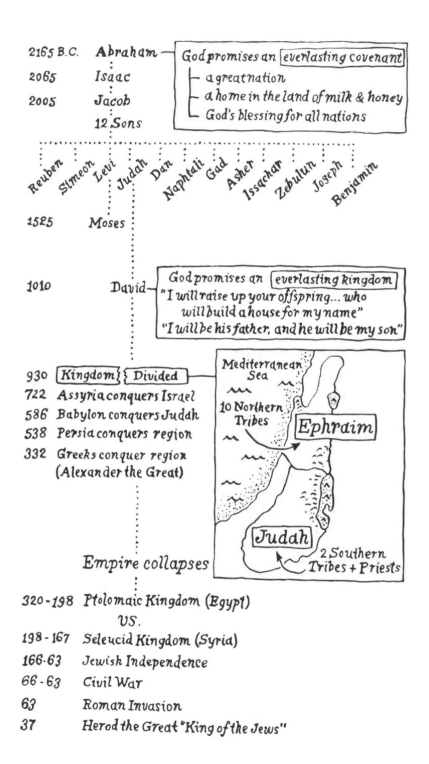

2165 B.C. **Abraham** — God promises an [everlasting covenant]
2065 **Isaac** ⎡ a great nation
2005 **Jacob** ⎢ a home in the land of milk & honey
 12 Sons ⎣ God's blessing for all nations

Reuben Simeon Levi Judah Dan Naphtali Gad Asher Issachar Zebulun Joseph Benjamin

1525 **Moses**

1010 **David** — God promises an [everlasting kingdom]
 "I will raise up your offspring... who
 will build a house for my name"
 "I will be his father, and he will be my son"

930 [Kingdom] [Divided] Mediterranean Sea
722 Assyria conquers Israel
586 Babylon conquers Judah 10 Northern Tribes
538 Persia conquers region **Ephraim**
332 Greeks conquer region
 (Alexander the Great)

 Judah 2 Southern Tribes + Priests
 Empire collapses

320-198 Ptolomaic Kingdom (Egypt)
 VS.
198-167 Seleucid Kingdom (Syria)
166-63 Jewish Independence
66-63 Civil War
63 Roman Invasion
37 Herod the Great "King of the Jews"

movement of priests and the aristocracy (called the Sadducees). In the ongoing struggle, both sides make overtures to the Romans (Pompey) for assistance, and the period of independence lasts only until 63 B.C.

During the turbulence of the next few decades, the Romans work with a particular family known as the Herods to establish order. Over time, one of these men, named Herod the Great, is viewed increasingly well by the Romans as he effectively quashes revolts and collects taxes. A lover of both Greek and Roman culture, he is appointed over the regions of Judea (the south), Samaria (central), and Galilee (the north). Much to the chagrin of the general populace, he is eventually awarded the title "King of the Jews" by the Romans. Herod comes to be reviled by the people as an extension of their foreign (and former) oppressors, and he develops a reputation for being especially ruthless. Viewed as Rome's puppet, he had travelled a long and bloody road to power that included numerous executions. As a peaceful gesture later in life, Herod initiates some massive renovations to the temple in Jerusalem that take nearly 50 years to complete. However, in the eyes of many, the temple authorities are illegitimate and tarnished by compromise and the politics of Rome.

By the time Jesus is born, the Roman Empire dominates the landscape of the globe, reaching into North Africa, Europe, the Middle East, and even Asia. At the time, it is the largest kingdom known. After endless tensions between regions, its ruler Augustus Caesar (originally named Octavian, the adopted son of Julius Caesar) is able to unite the empire under one banner and establishes a time of peace and prosperity known as Pax Romana. The Roman "Prince of Peace," he is viewed by most as the ruler of the world and worshiped in some places as a god. Near the beginning of his reign, he even added the phrase, "Son of the Divine" to his title, and we have found an inscription referring to Augustus as a god, savior, and the bringer of good news.[1] His domain includes the province of Judea and the multiple factions of Hebrew people.

Part of what remains of the northern kingdom is now the region called Samaria, previously its capital, and the people are referred to

---

[1] If you've got a minute, look up the *Priene Calendar Inscription.*

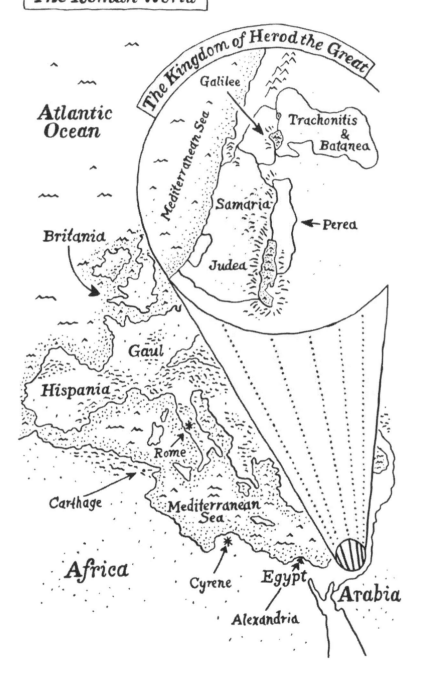

The Roman World

The Kingdom of Herod the Great

Galilee

Trachonitis & Batanea

Atlantic Ocean

Mediterranean Sea

Samaria

Perea

Britania

Judea

Gaul

Hispania

Rome

Carthage

Mediterranean Sea

Africa

Cyrene

Egypt

Alexandria

Arabia

by this name (Samaritans). Further north is the region of Galilee, a blended area of settlements with people from a variety of nationalities and beliefs. What was once the southern kingdom is now called Judea. Its capital, Jerusalem, is still a significant city and central to the people identifying with the religious, cultural, and geographical heritage of Judah (known as the Jews).

This complexity provides us with a backdrop, and it is amid this rich tapestry of tension and struggle that a particular baby finally enters our story.

AN UNEXPECTED PREGNANCY
Luke 1:5, 26-35, 38; Matthew 1:19-21

In the time of Herod king of Judea...

...God sent the angel Gabriel to Nazareth, a town in Galilee, to a virgin pledged to be married to a man named Joseph, a descendant of David. The virgin's name was Mary. The angel went to her and said, "Greetings, you who are highly favored! The Lord is with you."

Mary was greatly troubled at his words and wondered what kind of greeting this might be. But the angel said to her, "Do not be afraid, Mary; you have found favor with God. You will conceive and give birth to a son, and you are to call him Jesus. He will be great and will be called the Son of the Most High. The Lord God will give him the throne of his father David, and he will reign over Jacob's descendants forever; his kingdom will never end."

Our story begins again with mention of a number of significant details. Galilee, a descendent of David, a son, a throne, a never-ending kingdom... these are surprising declarations. But for Mary, this news might be better described as a startling interruption than a fresh start. We have a young woman likely 12-14 years old, pledged to be married, who has just been informed that she is pregnant. In a situation like this, pregnancy may not seem like such good news to this young lady.

During this time of betrothal, Joseph (18-20 years old was considered the ideal age for a man to marry) would be working to build a new home for them as they prepared to begin their new life together, and any sexual relations are forbidden. Such a discovery would surely upset Joseph and be grounds to terminate the engagement. What would he think? What would he do? What would other people think? A gift from God? It would be humiliating. But all of these descriptions are incredible. The name Jesus means, "the Lord saves," and is one of the Hebrew words for "help."[1] Is this the child to accomplish God's salvation? Has God finally sent a helper to save people from this mess? This must be good news but…

"How will this be," Mary asked the angel, "since I am a virgin?"

The angel answered, "The Holy Spirit will come on you, and the power of the Most High will overshadow you. So the holy one to be born will be called the Son of God."

"I am the Lord's servant," Mary answered. "May your word to me be fulfilled." Then the angel left her.

The "Son of God."

This is no ordinary birth, and this is no ordinary child. The course of Mary's life is about to change drastically. As if anticipating a grand wedding with God, her people have been expecting and waiting for this day for a *long* time now. Like Adam, they have been waiting for the arrival and company of their great helper. They have been longing and preparing for the restoration of this special covenant relationship. Yet as exciting and terrifying as it is, Mary isn't going to defy God. She understands that she is God's *servant*. Where Eve once rejected such a role, Mary embraces it. And so she will be a new Eve, the one who bears the promised offspring that will finally defeat the serpent. Just as in the beginning, the spirit of God will overshadow the waters again, this time bringing life to a human

---

[1] Yeshua, or "Joshua," translates as "Jesus."

womb, the offspring of Eve. But it may not be quite so simple. There is still Joseph to worry about....

Because Joseph her husband was faithful to the law, and yet did not want to expose her to public disgrace, he had in mind to divorce her quietly. But after he had considered this, an angel of the Lord appeared to him in a dream and said, "Joseph son of David, do not be afraid to take Mary home as your wife, because what is conceived in her is from the Holy Spirit. She will give birth to a son, and you are to give him the name Jesus, because he will save his people from their sins."

Things get a little uncomfortable when Joseph learns Mary is pregnant. He is understandably confused and angry. This is not what he had in mind. Here they were to be married, and now she is pregnant? He is a religious man, but this strange tale is still a bit much to believe. In disbelief, he decides not to be too hard on her, but it's time to part ways. The wedding is off, or so he thinks, until Joseph has a little visit of his own. An angel appears and confirms everything she had said. Mary hadn't lied to him. This strange thing is true. He and Mary will have an important role to play in what comes. They are the appointed cultivators of a human life, and they will have to endure the public shame and difficulties that may accompany her abrupt pregnancy.

This is great news and an incredible honor. The angel is reporting that salvation has finally come, and it has arrived in the unexpected form of an "illegitimate" child who will restore humanity again to the likeness of God. God has finally come to save people as he promised. This child will free them from the destruction of *sin*. Sin is the mark of the serpent, human resemblance to something other than God. It is the brokenness that changed everything. While we aren't told how, God is at work to fulfill his promises of old. Joseph decides to stay with Mary and raise the boy as his own, a decision that will undoubtedly prove to be quite difficult.

THE LITTLE TOWN OF BETHLEHEM
Luke 2:1-20

In those days Caesar Augustus issued a decree that a census should be taken of the entire Roman world. (This was the first census that took place while Quirinius was governor of Syria.) And everyone went to their own town to register.

So Joseph also went up from the town of Nazareth in Galilee to Judea, to Bethlehem the town of David, because he belonged to the house and line of David. He went there to register with Mary, who was pledged to be married to him and was expecting a child. While they were there, the time came for the baby to be born, and she gave birth to her firstborn, a son. She wrapped him in cloths and placed him in a manger, because there was no guest room available for them.

Again, we are given several details that give us clues about the timing of this child's birth. Augustus is emperor and has demanded a census. Such a census was a sour reminder of oppression to the Jewish people, who knew that it likely preceded taxes. To most, taxes resembled slavery (or even a kind of forced worship) and were to be reviled and even resisted. Forced by the authorities to travel the country, Joseph and Mary set out for his hometown, where he would likely get to reconnect with many of his relatives (those from the family of David). From Galilee, this unborn child is suddenly on his way to another noteworthy location—Bethlehem, the prophesied birthplace of the Messiah.

Hospitality is of great significance to these people, and homes were often opened to travelers. Unfortunately, the census has left the town overwhelmed with people. Likely arriving in the company of several family members, Mary and Joseph find shelter from the elements in what may be a barn or a cave,[1] where they can set up camp among the animals until able to get settled elsewhere. These are strange and humble beginnings for the birth of a king. Instead of

---

[1] Some theorize that Jesus was born specifically in a cave used by shepherds for birthing lambs at Migdal Eder (which means "watchtower of the flock"), a location mentioned in Micah 4:8.

a palace, he will arrive to the company of beasts (much like Adam once arrived to the company of animals in Eden) in their rugged and natural setting. Swaddled in linens, he is placed in a manger, which is essentially a food troth for animals. It isn't long before some company arrives to join them.

And there were shepherds living out in the fields nearby, keeping watch over their flocks at night. An angel of the Lord appeared to them, and the glory of the Lord shone around them, and they were terrified. But the angel said to them, "Do not be afraid. I bring you good news that will cause great joy for all the people. Today in the town of David a Savior has been born to you; he is the Messiah, the Lord. This will be a sign to you: You will find a baby wrapped in cloths and lying in a manger."

Suddenly a great company of the heavenly host appeared with the angel, praising God and saying, "Glory to God in the highest heaven, and on earth peace to those on whom his favor rests." When the angels had left them and gone into heaven, the shepherds said to one another, "Let's go to Bethlehem and see this thing that has happened, which the Lord has told us about."

So they hurried off and found Mary and Joseph, and the baby, who was lying in the manger. When they had seen him, they spread the word concerning what had been told them about this child, and all who heard it were amazed at what the shepherds said to them. But Mary treasured up all these things and pondered them in her heart. The shepherds returned, glorifying and praising God for all the things they had heard and seen, which were just as they had been told.

The occasion is quickly celebrated by a crowd of shepherds who join the scene. Of all people, this is a strange group for angels to notify. Shepherds, among the poorest of their society, were generally reviled and distrusted by the religious populace. These shepherds, located just outside of Bethlehem, may very well have been tending the flocks to be used as sacrifices by the thousands in religious ceremonies in Jerusalem (just six miles to the north). In fact, in the final year of the temple several decades later, we are told by one Jewish historian that around 270,000 lambs were slain at the temple.[1] While these shepherds' work served the activities of the temple, it also frequently prevented their participation in religious festivals (part of why they were frowned upon).

Yet here, it pleases God to announce the birth of his king to *this* population. Plus, as confirmation of these things, they are told to look for some particularly strange details—a baby *swaddled in a manger*. This is not something they'd expect to find. Who would put a baby in an animal's food trough? This is an unlikely occurrence, yet sure enough it is exactly what they find.

God has entered the story as the child of a poor family announced to the poorest of workers, the surprisingly reviled servants of the house of God. This group goes on to be the first messengers of what has happened. Apparently God isn't too concerned with class or social status. This child will be good news to even those most insignificant and despised by the world.

AN ANCIENT BABY SHOWER
Matthew 2:1-5, 7-11, 13, 16, 19-23

Faithful Jews, Mary and Joseph will raise Jesus in the traditions and practices of their religion and culture. The family probably remained in Bethlehem for an extended period and found work and better shelter (remember, Joseph has roots in the area). If the earlier events didn't stick out as already unique, there would be more to come. Eventually, still others arrive for another surprising and strange visit.

After Jesus was born in Bethlehem in Judea, during the time of King Herod, Magi from the east came to Jerusalem and asked, "Where is the one who has been born king of the Jews? We saw his star when it rose and have come to worship him."

---

[1] Flavius Josephus is one of our more significant sources of information about the time. His two works *Jewish Wars* and *Antiquities of the Jews* provide all sorts of insight into various people and events.

When King Herod heard this he was disturbed, and all Jerusalem with him. When he had called together all the people's chief priests and teachers of the law, he asked them where the Messiah was to be born. "In Bethlehem in Judea," they replied...

Then Herod called the Magi secretly and found out from them the exact time the star had appeared. He sent them to Bethlehem and said, "Go and search carefully for the child. As soon as you find him, report to me, so that I too may go and worship him."

After they had heard the king, they went on their way, and the star they had seen when it rose went ahead of them until it stopped over the place where the child was. When they saw the star, they were overjoyed. On coming to the house, they saw the child with his mother Mary, and they bowed down and worshiped him. Then they opened their treasures and presented him with gifts of gold, frankincense and myrrh....

Mary and Joseph must be chuckling in delight by this point at the absurd and diverse encounters their son has already brought. First shepherds come to give praise, and now these men arrive, showering their poor family with priceless gifts? These are two extremes. Where shepherds were poor and disliked, Magi are a group of scholars and astrologers of notable prestige coming from afar. But why exactly? There were no dreams or angelic visitors mentioned this time. Instead, these sojourners took note of some strange occurrences in the sky.[1] Awaiting a sign from God, the Magi discovered that he kindly spoke their language as even the heavens proclaimed the good news of this special child. The stars, coordinated like clockwork since the beginning of time, have led them to this very event.

---

[1] There are some fascinating theories about what star or planet movements and constellations these men may have seen. One of these includes a "king" star (a planet that moves irregularly) circling Leo the lion (sign of the tribe of Judah) before passing through Virgo (the virgin). See the documentary *The Star of Bethlehem* for more.

Some speculate that these men may come from one of the schools of the East in Babylon once led by the prophet Daniel,[1] who once shared visions of the "Son of Man" figure that would rule in the authority of God to the ends of the earth.[2] Is it possible that through this distant school even foreigners learned the prophecies and faithfully kept close watch? Whoever they are, they have an interest in this child and desire to *worship* him—like a God. At a time when Augustus is worshiped as a God, they've come to honor a Jewish baby. Suddenly, the birth of this child has already united both foreigners and locals, wealthy and the poor, intellectuals and the uneducated. It is a peculiar scene and just a taste of what will follow in the life of this unique child.

There is a problem, though...

Out of respect to the local authorities, they first arrive and meet with Herod to see what they can learn. They ask about one born as "King of the Jews," which is an unpleasant surprise to Herod's ears. He is the appointed "King of the Jews," and he hasn't just had another son. In fact, he has already faced several assassination attempts on his own life as his days seem to be coming to an end. One of these attempts even claimed the life of his brother, and he's already executed members of his own family out of suspicion.

He quickly fetches some religious scholars to inquire about the Messiah and uncovers that the Magi's expectations are in line with ancient prophesies, a startling discovery to say the least. He speaks with the Magi deceitfully and sends them as an envoy to find the baby as though he too will pay his respects to the child. They are welcomed guests from a foreign land, and he's not about to do anything to harm them and strain any relations with their homeland. They know of his intentions, though. Instead of reporting back to Herod, they return home by a different route.

When they had gone, an angel of the Lord appeared to Joseph in a dream. "Get up," he said, "take the child and

---

[1] Carted off to Babylon during the exile (Daniel 1-2), Daniel went on to lead a school of magi.
[2] Daniel 7:13-14

*his mother and escape to Egypt. Stay there until I tell you,
for Herod is going to search for the child to kill him."*

*...When Herod realized that he had been outwitted by the
Magi, he was furious and he gave orders to kill all the boys
in Bethlehem and its vicinity who were two years old and
under, in accordance with the time he had learned from the
Magi.*

Warned of Herod's malice, Mary and Joseph flee, and the child
is kept safe.

These are tense times. In brutal desperation, Herod orders the
murder of a population of children thinking that surely this will
prevent any potential king from rising against him. This also hints at
the large amount of time that might have already passed since Jesus'
birth (killing kids up to a couple of years old). As described before,
his paranoia takes him to extreme measures. Can Herod prevent this
promised King from rising?

*After Herod died, an angel of the Lord appeared in a dream
to Joseph in Egypt and said, "Get up, take the child and his
mother and go to the land of Israel, for those who were trying
to take the child's life are dead."*

*So he got up, took the child and his mother and went to the
land of Israel. But when he heard that Archelaus was
reigning in Judea in place of his father Herod, he was afraid
to go there. Having been warned in a dream, he withdrew to
the district of Galilee, and he went and lived in a town called
Nazareth.*

Herod's days were numbered. While he may have remained a
king during his life, he couldn't avoid his coming death. Wary of the
violent rule of Herod's son Archelaus, Joseph thinks it best to settle
somewhere other than the region of Judea (which includes
Bethlehem). Instead, Joseph and his family make their way back to
the small town of Nazareth. Here, the son of a carpenter, Jesus will
grow until it is time for the real excitement to begin.

JUST A SMALLTOWN BOY

From what we can gather through the dating of different rulers and events, Jesus was likely born between 6-4 B.C.[1] Not a lot is known about his childhood, but some brief details and historical events leave us with a number of intriguing possibilities about his youth.

Herod's death in 4 B.C. leaves the nation in upheaval as complications abound. He had several children through a number of wives and leaves a mess of wills upon his death. Eventually, his kingdom gets divided between 3 of his sons (Archelaus, Herod Antipas, and Phillip), but it takes some time before there is much stability. To the Jewish people, Herod's sons are foreign oppressors like their father. Their appointments are especially disappointing because one of Herod's executed wives had actually been a Judean. As the people call for social reform, there are several revolts during this transition and insurgents attempt to overthrow these "foreign" heirs. Hiding in the rough terrain of surrounding hillsides, numerous collections of bandits appear and become particularly common to the region of Galilee. Employing the tactics of guerilla warfare, the groups prove difficult to remove at times.

In the city of Sepphoris, one of the largest of Galilee, a man named Judas (son of Hezekiah) raided the palace and seized its weaponry with a multitude of brigands. These bandits then led a number of attacks on the authorities before the Governor of Syria (Quirinius) marched in to restore order (which may have destroyed the city). Around the same time, one of Herod's former slaves named Simon of Peraea also revolted. Leading a rebellion, he destroyed the palace in Jericho along with several other structures before also falling to a legion of Roman soldiers. Elsewhere in Judea, a shepherd named Anthronges led a rebellion with his four brothers as each directed a company of rebels. They attacked both Herod's forces and Roman soldiers alike for a year or two before they were defeated.

Considering the tumult of assassination attempts on Herod, his execution of several of his own family members, the murder of

---

[1] The dating assumes that Herod's death is in 4 B.C. There are some who argue Herod died as late as 1 B.C., which would place Jesus' birth in 3-2 B.C.

countless infants, and the chaos of revolts following his death, it is understandable that Mary and Joseph fled the region and resettled elsewhere. As these revolts subsided, the restored "order" under Herod's sons still left many concerned. In the character of his ruthless father, Archelaus would later massacre thousands of religious pilgrims due to social unrest during the Passover festival, a decision that would contribute to his removal from his post. Around this same time, one of Herod's other sons, Herod Antipas, decided to rebuild the city of Sepphoris (the entire city had eventually been destroyed) as his new regional capital. Since this city was located just 5 miles from Nazareth (about an hour's walk), its reconstruction may have provided a great opportunity for Joseph's craftsmanship as a carpenter. Learning the family trade, Jesus would have grown up witnessing firsthand the destruction of these violent revolutions.

Carpenters weren't the poorest of people, but they were by no means wealthy. As artisans, they were a sort of ancient lower-middle class at a time when the general populace was overwhelmingly poor. Located in the region nicknamed "Galilee of the Gentiles," Jesus would have been raised encountering people from a diversity of backgrounds. The area had a reputation as a mixing pot of numerous cultures, something less characteristic of Judea and especially of Jerusalem. As a carpenter, he would have grown accustomed to life on the road as he travelled the region for projects. His work would have further exposed him to people of varying classes, nationalities, religions, and political backgrounds. Near Sepphoris, he would have been very familiar with the abuses of both the regional authorities (Herod's sons) and the overshadowing Roman powers.

A village of a few hundred, Nazareth was not held in high regard. Travelling yearly to Jerusalem to celebrate the Passover, Jesus likely experienced some degree of social prejudice related to his upbringing in the north (Galilee), especially coming from a small town like Nazareth. We later hear this prejudice as someone discovers his origins. They ask what good can come from a place like Nazareth.[1] To many, even social encounters (particularly meals) with gentile people were contemptible and left one unclean before God. The

---

[1] John 1:46

religious culture generally reviled the basic lifestyle of their foreign neighbors, and Jesus may have been associated with such things due to his home and work in such a gentile area, especially as someone laboring in the reconstruction of a gentile city.

While soaking in every opportunity to learn from the fine teachers at festivals in the big city, Jesus would have received most of his education at the local synagogue. Synagogues functioned as community centers spread across the countryside. The synagogue would have also provided him a place to study the scriptures as a young man. Here he would have learned to read and write and heard lectures from guest teachers as they travelled through the area.

Jesus probably spoke multiple languages during his life. Aramaic was still the most common language spoken in this particular region from centuries past. However, Greek had grown more common in larger cities outside of Palestine, and Latin was the language of the Roman elite. As a Jewish boy, Jesus may also have learned some Hebrew. While not the common language, it shared many roots with Aramaic and was held in high regard as an important part of Jewish heritage. It may also still have played a role in religious liturgies (prayers and songs) as they worshiped.

Because Archelaus proved particularly inept for rule, a delegation of both Jews and Samaritans travelled to Rome to plead for his removal and a restored autonomy. He was deposed by Roman authorities in 6 A.D. Instead of self-rule, the area once under his control was reorganized as a Roman province and placed under the authority of a Roman governor given the title of "Prefect." The first governor responded to his appointment in a way that would seem obvious to any Roman—by establishing new taxes in the region. Up to this point, the people had been exempt from paying such tributes, which were seen by most Judeans as a form of emperor worship. Another revolt ensued led by a man named Judas the Galilean. Judas spearheaded a group of zealots known especially for their interest in regaining national independence. Decades later, his grandson would one day lead another significant rebellion in Jerusalem (which we will discuss later).

Once the insurrection by Judas was resolved, several other prefects took turns ruling in place of Archelaus, and his brothers

(Herod Antipas and Phillip the Tetrarch) remained in their respective positions for the remainder of Jesus' life. The region of Galilee, however, continued to be a notorious hotbed for insurgents.

Around the time of Judas the Galilean, we are told of a particular visit[1] by Joseph's family to Jerusalem for the Passover (story not included here). Jerusalem, a city of probably 80,000 and the hub of social and political activity, would have been bustling with pilgrims each year for the festival. These journeys (about 3 days to travel) were expected of anyone able to travel. Entire villages are even known to have journeyed together. Staying with friends of family in the area upon arrival, Jesus would also have been quite familiar with all that took place at these temple celebrations. With the region of Samaria standing between Galilee and Judea, the journey would have included a lengthy and necessary detour to avoid conflict in Samaria. As a young man, Jesus would have been reminded regularly of these tensions between Samaritans and Jews.

HEAD OF THE HOUSEHOLD

From what we gather, Joseph passes away in the years following the temple story because he is never mentioned again. We later learn that Jesus has several siblings[2] (4 brothers and some sisters), and as the oldest son Jesus would have been responsible to support the family at a potentially young age. A builder working with wood and stone, he would have continued the family trade. This responsibility would have given him an interesting perspective on the treatment of women in his world. As a young man, he would have witnessed the difficulty and desperation widows and divorced women faced to care for their families in complicated circumstances such as his own.

Jesus' role as the man of the house leaves us with some interesting questions. Given the strange events surrounding his birth, would there have been any remaining questions of his mother's fidelity once they returned to Nazareth? Could there have been some questions among his brothers or Joseph's family about his legitimacy as an heir? In such a small town, it isn't difficult for rumors to spread. Also, what about his brothers and the strange stories surrounding his birth?

---

[1] Luke 2:41-52   [2] Mark 6:3; Matthew 13:55-56

Would there have been some jealousy or resentment toward this special son? We will later witness tension between Jesus and his brothers;[1] could this stem from these early years?

Augustus Caesar passes away in 14 A.D., and with it the season of Rome's peace begins to fade. His adopted son Tiberius (who married Augustus' daughter) takes over the reins of the empire. It is during Tiberius's reign that Rome mints what is known as the *tribute penny*, a coin with his image and an inscription that read, "Tiberius Caesar, August Son of the Divine Augustus." Meanwhile, the province of Judea continues to churn through prefects. Not long before the beginning of Jesus' ministry, a man named Pontius Pilate is appointed prefect in 26 A.D. More of a warrior than a politician, Pilate is quickly introduced to the complications of his new position. After placing a statue of himself at the temple (again, standard behavior for a Roman official), he faces protests. In response, he sends his troops to spread quietly among the crowd, and when the troops draw their swords the crowd responds boldly and surprisingly by baring their necks. Well aware that a public massacre isn't the best way to keep his position (the case with Archelaus), Pilate removes the statue without further altercation. His aggressive tactics, however, continue. He is known later to have hidden troops among another crowd with instructions to begin clubbing as protests broke out. Such brutality was normal for an empire known for terrorizing its subjects.

The colorful influences shaping Jesus' youth leave us with an intriguing portrait of an individual with a keen understanding of a variety of social dynamics. He would have had exposure to prejudice of all sorts, classism, sexism, religious moralism and conceit, and most any other form of oppression or inequality imaginable. He would have seen the exploitation of power, anger over taxes, debates over wages, arguments over religious freedoms, political campaigning and recruiting, protests, violent rebellions, the privilege of wealth, the abuses of sexism, the refinement and leisure of the religious elite, the rugged life of laborers, disregard of the poor and sick, and ethnic contempt for foreigners. Might he have been present

---

[1] Mark 3:20-21, 31-35; John 7:3-5

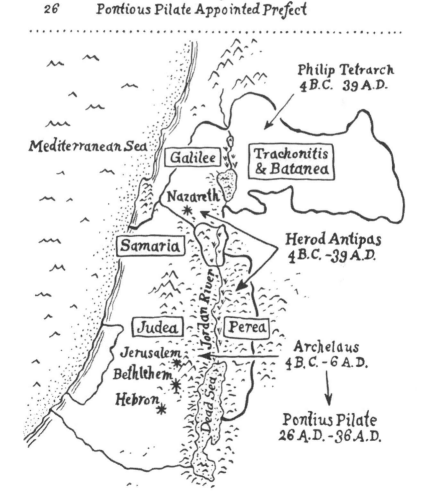

The Rule of Herod's Son

37 B.C.	Herod the Great "King of the Jews"
27	Augustus Caesar Emperor
7/6	John the Baptist born
6/5	Jesus born
4	Herod dies (Kingdom split between sons)
6 A.D.	Archelaus replaced by Roman Prefect
14	Tiberius Caesar Emperor
26	Pontious Pilate Appointed Prefect

Philip Tetrarch
4 B.C. 39 A.D.

Mediterranean Sea

Galilee

Trachonitis & Batanea

Nazareth

Herod Antipas
4 B.C. -39 A.D.

Samaria

Jordan River

Judea

Perea

Jerusalem

Bethlehem

Hebron

Dead Sea

Archelaus
4 B.C. - 6 A.D.

Pontius Pilate
26 A.D. - 36 A.D.

to witness the non-violent protest about Pilate's statue? These things would one day provide fuel for his ministry as he would engage most of these tensions and the stereotypes surrounding them. What remains to be seen is how.

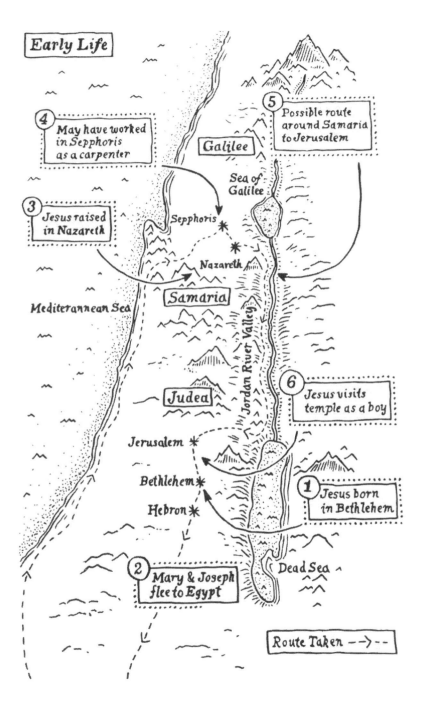

Early Life

4 May have worked in Sepphoris as a carpenter

3 Jesus raised in Nazareth

5 Possible route around Samaria to Jerusalem

Galilee

Sea of Galilee

Sepphoris

Nazareth

Mediterannean Sea

Samaria

Jordan River Valley

Judea

6 Jesus visits temple as a boy

Jerusalem

Bethlehem

Hebron

1 Jesus born in Bethlehem

Dead Sea

2 Mary & Joseph flee to Egypt

Route Taken → --

THREE

Something is Brewing

THE FOUR ACCOUNTS THAT we have of Jesus' life are called gospels. A commonly used term in the ancient world, a *gospel* is a proclamation or announcement of good news. Gospels informed people of significant things that had just happened—for example, that a new king was enthroned, a great battle had been won, or peace had returned. For the writers of the Bible, that long-awaited news was the life of a person named Jesus. He was the king to be enthroned and the message of peace and victory related to the long-desired kingdom of God. For the Jewish people, the word gospel carried even more significance. One of the prophets used this word to describe the time when God would return to his people.[1]

Of the four accounts of Jesus' life, two begin with his birth. The other two jump straight into his adulthood. One of these, called the "Gospel of John," picks an interesting way to introduce Jesus before moving into his ministry. Instead of the birth of a baby, John recalls a period before the birth of *the whole world.*

IN THE BEGINNING, A REMIX
John 1:1-4, 10-14

> *In the beginning was the Word, and the Word was with God, and the Word was God. He was with God in the beginning.*

---

[1] Isaiah 40:9, 52:7-12

"In the beginning," this is like Genesis, and we are back to our first story. Poetically (and maybe somewhat confusingly), John directs our attention to the way things began. For John, these two stories are unavoidably linked. To talk about Jesus is to talk about the story of everything.

We saw in our first chapter that things began with God speaking the world into existence. The world came to be through God's language. By his instruction (words) came all of life. Here we see John speaking as if God's language were an unnoticed character, a "he" present from the start. Not only was this "he" present, "he" is actually God. Suddenly the strange "us" behind creation makes a little more sense. To whom was God speaking in the beginning? Oddly, himself.

In Greek, the original language of the New Testament writings, the word *logos* (translated as "word" here) holds a little more meaning than it does in our language. It refers to a thought, spoken instruction, or wisdom. Philosophers debated which came first. Was it the material world, or the idea or essence (*logos*) behind the material things. John steps into the argument, saying that it was the *logos* that came first, and that essence is actually God who has now come to earth in the form of a human being. The design behind our world is actually the eternal God through whom all things were made.

In ancient Jewish thought, word/wisdom was often personified.[1] One writer even described wisdom as a person, present from the beginning of creation, calling out to people in the streets.[2] Elsewhere in Jewish writings, God is described as creating with and through his word/wisdom, which is a sort of blueprint or plan behind all things.[3] It is said that creation can't stray from these purposes or design (God's "word"), which will ultimately bring about God's intended aim.[4] John cleverly ties these thoughts together in his introduction to the life of Jesus as though this very person, Jesus, is that eternal blueprint and destiny present and involved from the very beginning who has now arrived to bring about God's original aim.

---

[1] Psalm 18:30, 33:4, 107:20   [2] Proverbs 1:20-33, 8:1-9:6   [3] Psalm 33:4-9, 104:1-24; Proverbs 3:19-20; Jeremiah 10:12   [4] Isaiah 55:11

Through him all things were made; without him nothing was made that has been made. In him was life, and that life was the light of all mankind. The light shines in the darkness, and the darkness has not overcome it...

He was in the world, and though the world was made through him, the world did not recognize him. He came to that which was his own, but his own did not receive him. Yet to all who did receive him, to those who believed in his name, he gave the right to become children of God—children born not of natural descent, nor of human decision or a husband's will, but born of God.

The Word became flesh and made his dwelling among us...

Now, God is at work speaking and creating again. This "he" is the wisdom and instruction of God intertwined with the fabric of the cosmos from the beginning. He who was involved in the birthing of all creation has now come to earth born as a man to continue work in the *rebirthing* of all creation. Could this be the same "he" that God spoke of in Eden[1] who would crush the serpent's head?

In Eden, God's instruction was the key to life. Disobedience was the advent of death. Now, that life (or light, as John says above) is living again in the world. He is the instruction that will somehow renew life, the means through which God will recreate. God has just entered the story covertly as an ordinary person. In surprising fashion, he will walk among his creation and interact with humanity on a person-to-person basis as before in Eden. God has pitched his tent and moved into the neighborhood. The author has written himself into the book. This time the dwelling isn't a sacred garden, it's a sacred body. There is a new strange and profound mingling between heaven and earth, and God is about to get his hands dirty.

---

[1] Genesis 3:15

A STRANGE MAN IN THE DESERT
Luke 3:1-2; Matthew 3:1-2, 4-7; Mark 1:7-8; Matthew 3:14;
Mark 1:10-13

Although foreign powers ruled the land, there was still a council of Jewish leaders called the Sanhedrin that oversaw the courts and dictated a good deal of the nation's direction when it came to religion and culture. This council was influenced heavily by its presiding officer, called the High Priest. This wasn't an elected position. Appointed by the Roman authorities, the High Priest came from the lineage of priests. For most of Jesus' adulthood, a man named Caiaphas was the appointed high priest. Legal matters were then filtered through questions of jurisdiction. Was something a matter for the Jewish courts (the Sanhedrin), the client kings and their regions (the Herods) or the Prefect of Judea (such as Pontius Pilate)?

Beyond these leaders, various cultural movements sought to bring about the laws and practices that they believed would bring the people prosperity and freedom. People longed for change and struggled to understand where to turn. Should the Jews mix and mingle with the Romans while embracing the Hellenistic (Greek) culture, as the Sadducees claimed? Or, as the Pharisees taught, should they separate and distinguish themselves as the people of God once again through a revival of religious behavior and devotion? Some (later called zealots) desired the overthrow of ruling powers to restore something like the independence that existed before Rome entered the picture. Still others (called Essenes) wanted to scrap the current religious institutions (the priest and temple corruption) altogether, retreating to the desert to pursue a monastic lifestyle and community of devotion until the Messiah finally arrived. While these movements were influential and shaped much of their culture, a large portion of their society didn't identify particularly with any of them and instead simply remained loyal to the basic observance of the law, worship at the temple and their unique identity and story as the chosen people of God.

During Jesus' lifetime, the two dominant movements were called the Pharisees and the Sadducees, and it was the Sadducees who controlled the Sanhedrin and the temple. The Sadducees, most of them priests and members of the aristocracy, were much wealthier than the Pharisees. Although they embraced a more literal interpretation of the law, they believed that the future of Judaism depended upon its ability to adapt to the surrounding world, not on waging a continual war against outside influences. So they readily took on many of the manners of Greek culture. When it came to the scriptures, they viewed only the Torah (the books of Moses or "the law") as authoritative and rejected the prophets and other writings and so had little or no hope in a coming Messiah. They rejected the idea of a general resurrection at judgment (that God would one day raise the dead) as well as belief in any kind of spiritual beings like angels or demons.

The Pharisees contrasted with this group in a number of ways. Historic enemies of the Sadducees (they had actually fought and lost to them in the war that ended with Roman occupation), this group was larger and more diverse. They may have gotten their name from the word for "separatist" and were known for their piety and patriotism. Unlike the Sadducees, this group reviled anything resembling the broader pagan culture and sought to distinguish themselves from the surrounding world as God's holy people. They believed that in order for God's favor to return, all citizens needed to adhere again to the basic laws of scripture in addition to those laws that otherwise applied only to priests. Then, as a loyal "nation of priests," they believed God would fulfill his promises to them. This strict adherence extended beyond the laws of scripture (which were also embraced by the Sadducees) to incorporate teachings known as the "tradition of the elders" as a supplement of equal authority to the law. The Pharisees also viewed the prophets and other writings as a part of scripture and maintained the hope of a Messiah. They believed in an immortal soul, a coming resurrection of the dead, and the existence of other spiritual forces like angels and demons.

The Essenes (often associated with the community that left us the Dead Sea Scrolls) stood as an outlier to the others. A small community of just a few hundred, the Essenes rejected the nation's authority structures during the brief period of Jewish independence and retreated to the desert. There they established a monastic community known for radical devotion (even more so than the Pharisees) and asceticism. With a strong emphasis on purity (washings and diet), they were known for being fairly apocalyptic and believing that the prophecies of scripture were coming to pass in their day. They believed that heredity wouldn't protect anyone from God's judgment and saw the groups leading the temple as the corrupt enemies of God. They also expected the coming of *two* messianic figures: one as a priest, and one as a king.

Beyond these groups, there were other folks commonly referred to as the "scribes" or "experts in the law." This was more of a profession than a movement, though it appears that there were many scribes involved with the Pharisees. As a result of their profession, scribes were often well versed in various legal matters as well as the interpretation of the scriptures and stood at the center of the debates between these different parties. In a world where many were illiterate and the process of transcribing documents (like the scriptures) was lengthy and expensive, scribes had a unique skill set. In many ways, they were like the academics or librarians in their society.

For the most part, these groups defined the cultural landscape of their people, but things were beginning to change. Around AD 28, a new movement began to take shape behind a unique figure named John the Baptist. This John (different from the gospel writer) was in many ways an outsider. While we know that he was the son of a priest,[1] he doesn't appear to have been raised working in the temple. We are told instead that he was raised under a particular religious vow (the Nazarite vow)[2] which would have exempted him from temple service. Such a pledge would have meant John the Baptist was raised with a number of additional restrictions surrounding his diet and general lifestyle (which fits what we know of him).[3] Could his father, a priest, have embraced this as a way to remove his son from the corruption at the temple while still honoring God?

Born when his parents were quite old, John may have matured fatherless (or even parentless) like his cousin Jesus. If so, this may have strengthened the bond we will see between John and Jesus in their adulthood. They would both have been fatherless sons thrust into independence and responsibility at a young age, young men forced to rely radically upon God's guidance and provision. It's

---

[1] Luke 1:5-25 [2] Numbers 6; Luke 1:15 [3] Matthew 3:4; Luke 7:33

possible that John was raised by the Essenes, who were known to take in orphans. This could explain his unusual appearance and behavior, similar to members of the strict Essene community. Regardless, John the Baptist was a truly unique individual.

In the fifteenth year of the reign of Tiberius Caesar—when Pontius Pilate was governor of Judea, Herod tetrarch of Galilee, his brother Philip tetrarch of Iturea and Traconitis, and Lysanias tetrarch of Abilene—during the high priesthood of Annas and Caiaphas, the word of God came to John son of Zechariah in the wilderness.

In those days John the Baptist came, preaching in the wilderness of Judea and saying, "Repent, for the kingdom of heaven has come near."

John's clothes were made of camel's hair, and he had a leather belt around his waist. His food was locusts and wild honey. People went out to him from Jerusalem and all Judea and the whole region of the Jordan. Confessing their sins, they were baptized by him in the Jordan River.

John the Baptist would be a funny name today, but in those days people didn't have last names, and titles like this were often used to clarify who one was referring to. They'd use professions (carpenter, tanner, tax collector), cities (from "so-and-so"), and even family members ("son of" or "brother of"). Sometimes an individual would pick up a nickname or some transliteration of their name to another language. Recognized for his peculiar behavior, John became known for what he did. John immersed people in water, so he became known as "the Baptist."

John was not some young guy groomed for the political spotlight. He didn't mesh well with the activities at the temple, the Sanhedrin or the movements of Pharisees and Sadducees. In fact, we will see later that his work seems to outrightly reject them. Regardless, the spotlight shone on him. At a time when people were starving for something new, John stood out as someone heading in a different direction. That's actually what "repent" means, to turn around as if otherwise going the wrong way.

Instead of the city, Jerusalem, the center of all political and religious life where people flocked to worship, his place was the desert. Eating locusts and honey (part of the Nazarite vow) and wearing strange garments made of hair (similar to a noteworthy prophet named Elijah),[1] John the Baptist worked out in the barren landscapes. In many ways, his mission resembled the work of the ancient prophets, and it just so happens that these are the landscapes described in passages about the Messiah's predecessor.[2]

As people confronting the wrongs of their day, prophets were known for their strong rebukes of both religious and political figures. Similarly, John the Baptist spoke as one bringing a message from God and told people that they had taken a wrong turn. He spoke of a kingdom, God's kingdom, a new order to things that was about to arrive, and he gave little heed to the dominant kingdom in their midst. He spoke as if God was about to do what he'd promised long ago to put things back in their right place again. So he baptized people in the Jordan river.

To baptize means "to immerse." We still immerse ourselves in water on a regular basis. We baptize often, we just don't call it that. We bathe. Daily we shower, shampoo, condition, deodorize, and scrub. Soaps and cleaners boast things like "purification," "revitalization," and "energizing power," and who doesn't want that? We can't get away from the dirt of our world. We are covered in it, and one some level we all want cleansing from it. This is our condition, our curse, and we are stuck trying to deal with it.

These people also longed for cleansing. Except this wasn't just about dirt on the skin, it was about revival and the fulfillment of God's promises. John the Baptist wasn't scrubbing people with soap, he was calling people to be purified by God. People need renewal. Baptism was a natural expression of this.

The people understood this. In fact, ceremonial washing was a basic religious custom. Through the laws of scripture, people were required to wash in various ways before entering the temple to worship. The temple was thought to be the place where God communed with people. It represented a sort of heaven on earth, a

---

[1] 2 Kings 1:8   [2] Isaiah 40:3

sacred or holy space in a dark and corrupt world. Washing was a way of acknowledging the separation from God, our unacceptable dirtiness that stood in contrast to God's holiness (a quality of purity, goodness, and perfection). If you wanted to be with God, you needed to be clean. But John the Baptist wasn't baptizing at the temple…

But not only does John appear to reject the legitimacy of the temple as the special dwelling place of God, he also appears to be rejecting its appointed authorities, the priests, who were baptized at the temple as part of their ordination. It's as though John the Baptist was anointing a new group of godly mediators. John's baptisms represented cleansing to enter God's presence, repentance, and the ordination of priests… all functions that took place otherwise at the temple. It's as if the temple wasn't accomplishing its purpose of bringing people to God. It had become sick and corrupted. It was going in the wrong way, and God was doing something new. So instead of Jerusalem, John met people in the desert. Instead of the temple, John baptized them in a river.

But this wasn't just any river.

The Jordan River held great historical significance. It was a natural boundary to the land that was once crossed as the people saw some of God's promises fulfilled. And here, still longing for a home and the fulfillment of these promises, people came to pass through the waters once again with John. By baptizing in the Jordan, John was pronouncing that the time of fulfillment had come, and it wasn't through the religious structures or cultural movements with which they were familiar. As foretold, he was the one to prepare the way for the arrival of God's kingdom.

He also had some sharp words for the movements of his day…

But when he saw many of the Pharisees and Sadducees coming to where he was baptizing, he said to them: "You brood of vipers! Who warned you to flee from the coming wrath?"

He even calls them snakes! And what coming wrath is he talking about? Is he associating them with the serpent's promised doom? You wouldn't want to be wrong about such things. Such comments could get someone in serious trouble or even killed. Not surprisingly, people began to wonder if John the Baptist was in fact the Messiah.

"...After me comes the one more powerful than I, the straps of whose sandals I am not worthy to stoop down and untie. I baptize you with water, but he will baptize you with the Holy Spirit."

They know something special is going on, and so does John. But John isn't the one they are looking for. While they think John the Baptist is a big deal, he says that he isn't even worthy enough to be this person's servant. John uses water, but this person will immerse people in the Spirit of God. They will be washed in the holiness of God's presence. God will be among them in a new way, and they will reflect his image again.

Much to the surprise of John the Baptist, Jesus arrives one day to be baptized as well.

But John tried to deter him, saying, "I need to be baptized by you, and do you come to me?"

John the Baptist knows that Jesus is this very person God has promised, but he is confused. How can Jesus need change? He's the one to bring the change! But Jesus' baptism isn't about repentance like everyone else's is. Something different happens.

Just as Jesus was coming up out of the water, he saw heaven being torn open and the Spirit descending on him like a dove. And a voice came from heaven: "You are my Son, whom I love; with you I am well pleased."

At once the Spirit sent him out into the wilderness, and he was in the wilderness forty days being tempted by Satan...

This didn't happen the last time John baptized someone. The heavens have torn open, and God's Spirit has descended upon Jesus to anoint (think accompany or empower) him. That's what *Messiah* actually means, anointed one. The great mediator has finally arrived. Jesus is the Messiah. God is present and active in a new spectacular way, and it isn't through the temple. It's through a person.

This person is the temple.

Jesus identity has now been revealed. It is through this person that one day others will be immersed in the presence of God. He is connected to all that is happening with John the Baptist. They are a part of the same mission, and it isn't going to sit well with the other leaders of their day. The son of a priest and the son of a carpenter are about to change the social landscape.

Like John the Baptist, as his ministry begins, Jesus doesn't head to Jerusalem but the desert. He's ready for a showdown with the enemy. Things are about to get interesting, and Jesus isn't going to seem so ordinary anymore.

WELCOME TO PALESTINE

The land of ancient Israel, or the "Kingdom of Herod" as we've discussed, is the region otherwise known as Palestine. This terrain is an interesting combination of extremes, and its geography, weather, agriculture, and prominent features serve as a vital backdrop to the stories in the gospels.

To the West lies the Mediterranean Sea, which extends as a barrier between North Africa and Europe. Rising slowly out of the Mediterranean are some coastal plains that steadily turn into a rugged hill country. This hill country includes a notable collection of mountain peaks ranging from around 2,000 to 4,000 feet tall, stretching from the south along the Dead Sea to beyond the Sea of Galilee in the north. Ultimately these ranges extend to the high peaks of Lebanon and Syria, which tower around 10,000 feet above sea level. To the east beyond this string of mountains, the terrain descends quickly into the dry depths of the Jordan River Valley. This valley runs north to south for 65 miles, descending from the Sea of Galilee to the Dead Sea. Across this valley to the east rises another range that plateaus into an eastern tableland consisting mostly of harsh deserts.

The Dead Sea (or Salt Sea) gets its name from its unique concentration of salt in the water. This intense concentration prevents the growth of plants and animals (hence the name) and makes the water incredibly buoyant. Almost 1,400 feet below sea level, the dry and salty shores of the Sea include the lowest point on the earth and

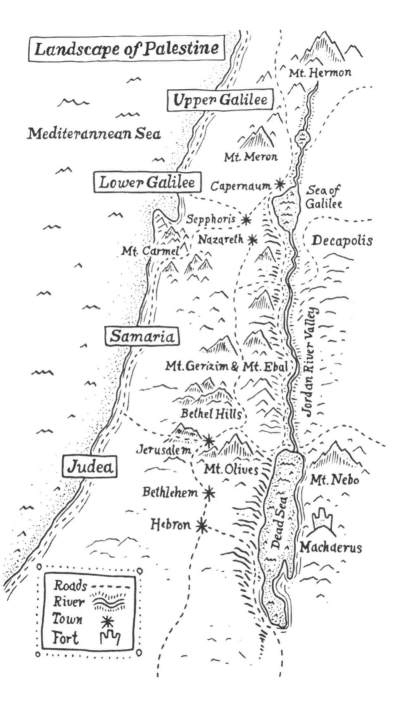

stretch about 50 miles long and 10 miles wide. Nestled in the hills along its shores are the cities of Hebron, Bethlehem, and Jerusalem, a "city on a hill" which lies somewhat hidden behind the Mount of Olives. Along the road descending from Jerusalem into the valley is Jericho, at nearly 850 feet below sea level. Looking across the Dead Sea is Mount Nebo (2,700 feet tall), not far north of one of Herod's fortresses, called Machaerus.

Just north of Jerusalem are the Hills of Bethel and some of the higher summits in the range. Beyond these hills is Samaria and the twin peaks of Mt. Gerizim (the former location of the Samaritan temple) and Mt. Ebal. Further north begins the region of Galilee, which stretches along the western shore of the Sea of Galilee. This region can be divided into two parts. Lower Galilee, the southern portion, is somewhat flatter and includes Nazareth, the hometown of Jesus. Upper Galilee stretches to the north in more rugged terrain and includes the significant city of Capernaum along the northern shore of the Sea of Galilee. Among the high peaks of this region is Mt. Meron, towering above at almost 4,000 feet.

The Sea of Galilee, which goes by many different names, stands in stark contrast to the Dead Sea. It is much smaller at about 13 miles long and 8 miles wide, but was teeming with life. At almost 700 feet below sea level, it was a deep lake surrounded by ports and full of fish. The region was lush and green, known for its groves and vineyards. Just to the southeast was the "Decapolis," a diverse region of independent gentile cities. Still further north, a sort of wall separating the region from Europe, towered the great mountains of Lebanon and Mt. Hermon in Syria to the Northwest. With summits around 10,000 feet, these mountains served as a sort of backdrop to the region most heavily travelled by Jesus and his followers.

LET THE GAMES BEGIN
Matthew 4:1-10; Luke 4:13

We all face death. It is our curse. What better place to reflect on the curse, death, than the dusty and lifeless desert overlooking the Dead Sea? What better place to remember the chaos and void of creation than the formless spaces of the wilderness? Led by the same

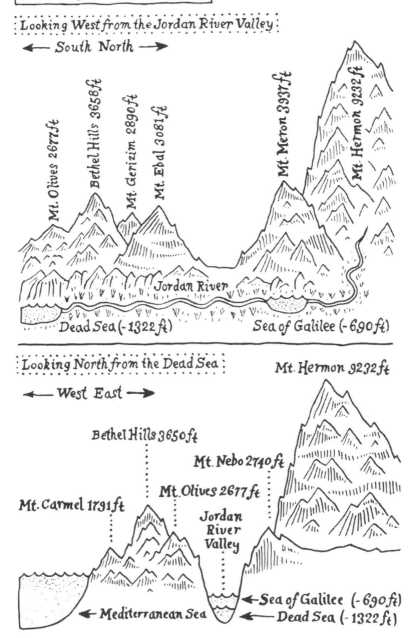

View of the Horizons

Looking West from the Jordan River Valley

← South North →

Mt. Olives 2677ft
Bethel Hills 3658ft
Mt. Gerizim 2890ft
Mt. Ebal 3081ft
Mt. Meron 3937ft
Mt. Hermon 9232ft

Jordan River

Dead Sea (-1322ft)

Sea of Galilee (-690ft)

Looking North from the Dead Sea

← West East →

Mt. Hermon 9232ft

Bethel Hills 3650ft

Mt. Nebo 2740ft

Mt. Olives 2677ft

Mt. Carmel 1791ft

Jordan River Valley

← Sea of Galilee (-690ft)
← Dead Sea (-1322ft)

← Mediterranean Sea

Spirit that once hovered over the shapeless waters in the beginning[1] and descended upon him at his baptism, now Jesus too will stare into these formless depths of the sandy water-like landscape. He has stepped into these distorted landscapes in an act of solidarity. His work will not be in the flourishing locale of the garden, but in the absent spaces of the desert.

Then Jesus was led by the Spirit into the wilderness to be tempted by the devil. After fasting forty days and forty nights, he was hungry. The tempter came to him and said, "If you are the Son of God, tell these stones to become bread."

In the scriptures, the number 40 comes up in some interesting places. The people of Israel wandered the desert for 40 years,[2] and Moses spent 40 days on the top of a mountain[3] before returning with the law, the parameters of his people's relationship with God. Has Jesus now entered into this trial that he might finally lead his people home with the new parameters to a restored relationship with God?

Generally, to fast is to abstain from something (like food) for a given period in order to devote oneself to some aim—social change (as with hunger strikes), spiritual growth (self-discipline), and or prayer. In Jesus' time, it was a basic religious practice and played a part in various celebrations and festivals. A "cleanse" like many people use today for health reasons may be the closest example in practice, though it is very different in motivation. Besides fasting for particular religious events, people would fast in times of great preparation and to focus in prayer under other special circumstances. It could be for a big decision or to prepare for a new stage of life, which seems to be the case here. Fasts were often accompanied with a retreat (solitude) as a way to remove distractions. Obviously, 40 days is a serious fast. It pushes the body's limits to the extreme.

But, why do it?

While fasting may seem like self-torture, that isn't the point. Think of an athlete running to get ready for a big race. Someone who's not an athlete might view running and various other forms of exercise as torture, but it strengthens and conditions. Similarly,

---

fasting is a way of preparing for life's struggles and utilizing the experience of hunger to focus and fuel prayer. It's also a discipline and a meditation on longing. It's a way to step back from something to see the bigger picture. It sets aside some time to reflect and prioritize, an attempt to keep things (usually passions or behaviors) in their right place.

Fasting seeks to redirect these passions and actions back toward God as first intended in the Garden. As pilgrims, the world outside the garden is our home. It is the desert, the wasteland shaped by the influences of death, suffering, toil, and oppression. Experiencing the pains of hunger for food, we are reminded that there are greater things for which we long that are left unsatisfied in this world. We remember that the garden is gone and the story isn't finished. We long for healing and renewal from the influence of this brokenness upon us and within us. We hunger for God, our real food and the true source of life and goodness, to fulfill his promises.

This is why Jesus fasted.

Jesus is preparing to address the core of this struggle, all that took place in the garden. He's meditating on his purpose and this basic struggle of humanity. He's understandably hungry. Jesus isn't alone. This is starting to sound familiar. We've met this character before. We see the "tempter" begin by questioning his identity. Do you really believe what God said moments ago at your baptism? "If you are...," prove it. To me. To yourself. Test it and see. You are hungry, why not turn a rock into bread? Listen to your desires...

Jesus answered, "It is written: 'Man does not live on bread alone, but on every word that comes from the mouth of God.'"

This is the point of the fast, to rely on and be sustained by God. Eating would interrupt his focus and would be a frivolous use of his authority. Jesus quotes a passage from scripture to say this. His miraculous power isn't a toy. Jesus trusts God and will feast on his word,[1] not the tempter's. Jesus won't be deceived by the false promises of his passions.

---

[1] Job 23:10-12

Then the devil took him to the holy city and had him stand on the highest point of the temple. "If you are the Son of God," he said, "throw yourself down. For it is written: 'He will command his angels concerning you, and they will lift you up in their hands, so that you will not strike your foot against a stone.'"

Again, the devil challenges his identity as the Son of God. The tempter may also be trying to lure him into rejecting the humbling qualities associated with his humanity. Will Jesus take the bait? Is Jesus indispensable?

The devil takes him to the city and shows him something special, and he's catching on. Jesus quoted scripture, so the devil gives it a shot. That's right, even the devil quotes scripture. It's possible to use (well, misuse) scripture to accomplish evil. The devil says, you trust what God has said, do you? Well here's a passage, says you can jump off this building and not die! You are invincible. Surely God wouldn't actually let you die, right? But the tempter is distorting God's words again. This passage is not actually about jumping from buildings, and the devil's intent here is clear. The devil wants to kill Jesus. It worked before in Eden, will it work here?

Jesus answered him, "It is also written: 'Do not put the Lord your God to the test.'"

Foiled again. Jesus still refers to scripture. This is part of his purpose, to teach and clarify the true meaning of God's instructions. He again refutes the devil. Are we so important that God can't let us die? You're not gonna catch some loophole as if God is a fool. Don't try to force God's hand. Why would Jesus be exempt from this? Jesus isn't going to try to rival God's plans or power. He is here for a purpose, not the flippant abuse of his appointed role.

Again, the devil took him to a very high mountain and showed him all the kingdoms of the world and their splendor. "All this I will give you," he said, "if you will bow down and worship me."

Once again, identity is the issue. Who is God? Who are you? Whose are you? The devil is all in now, and these are pretty high stakes. Power, kingdoms, splendor, what more could a person want? Will Jesus reconsider? What is it he really wants? He's been raised by a single parent and led a life of manual labor. Surely this is his weak spot. Besides, what has God ever given him? Poverty? Loneliness? Oppression? The insignificance of a common life from a small town? The devil can give him control, power, significance, and leisure, but what does it mean that the devil has power over all of this? How did the devil come to be in charge here?

We've seen this before.

Jesus said to him, "Away from me, Satan! For it is written: 'Worship the Lord your God, and serve him only.'"

Satan resembles the Hebrew verb for "to obstruct, oppose, accuse." It's the opposite of help. This name seems appropriate. Jesus knows his purpose, and this isn't it. Satan is getting in the way in an attempt to derail the plan. Jesus won't have it. He hasn't come to rule over people but to serve. It is his purpose. Pursuing another life would be rebellion. Speaking from scripture, Jesus declares that only God is to be worshiped and served, one of the most basic commands. Get out!!

Jesus' experience in the desert is the story of the garden all over again. The tempter is using the same tricks as before, though the scenery has changed considerably. Instead of a lush garden, we are in a desert. Instead of a place of harmony, the world is in constant battle and disarray. But the tempter uses the same old arguments. Just as with Adam and Eve, the serpent strikes the desires of the flesh, our pride, and our vanity. Who are you? Whose are you? Who is in control? Who will you trust? Who will you be? Make yourself, prove yourself, give yourself a new identity, be a God on earth! Are you really going to be God's servant, or do you want to rule?

Jesus already has all that Satan could offer and more at his disposal, and he has forsaken it to enter our story. He has entered into our exile to bring us out. He has stepped into our desert to replant a garden. While he is here to install a kingdom, it's not the kind of kingdom that Satan knows, and it's not like the kingdoms of this world obsessed with exerting power *over* others. Jesus is here to bring a new way unlike anything the world has ever seen. He's here as a servant, the role humanity was originally given in Eden and the opposite of what Satan offers. Same scenario, different result. Where Adam and Eve failed, Jesus prevails. As humanity distorted the harmony of creation in the attempt to rule, Jesus has embraced the role of a servant. The serpent has struck, and Jesus is crushing him.

When the devil had finished all this tempting, he left him until an opportune time.

The battle is on, and it sounds as though we haven't seen the last of this devil. Defeated for the moment, the serpent slithers away until the time is right for another showdown.

FOUR

The Life of the Party

RETURNING FROM THE DESERT, Jesus gets things started with a visit to his hometown of Nazareth. Visiting town one Sabbath, Jesus seizes an opportunity to re-introduce himself. As we will see, things don't go quite as one might expect...

THE HOMETOWN HERO
Luke 4:16-22, 24-30

> *He went to Nazareth, where he had been brought up, and on the Sabbath day he went into the synagogue, as was his custom. He stood up to read, and the scroll of the prophet Isaiah was handed to him. Unrolling it, he found the place where it is written: "The Spirit of the Lord is on me, because he has anointed me to proclaim good news to the poor. He has sent me to proclaim freedom for the prisoners and recovery of sight for the blind, to set the oppressed free, to proclaim the year of the Lord's favor."*
>
> *Then he rolled up the scroll, gave it back to the attendant and sat down. The eyes of everyone in the synagogue were fastened on him. He began by saying to them, "Today this scripture is fulfilled in your hearing."*

The Sabbath, God's day of rest from Genesis, is each Saturday. The synagogue was a local gathering place for the Jewish people that served as a community center. It functioned as a place for celebration and participation in various elements of their religious life, which included prayer and the preservation and teaching of scripture. Synagogues were different from the temple. There was only one temple, and that was in Jerusalem. It was the special place of God's presence where people traveled for festivals and to offer sacrifices.

Here at the local synagogue on the Sabbath, as was custom, Jesus is asked to read something. As an adult, Jesus might have regularly been involved in these gatherings. He is handed the scroll of Isaiah, one of the prophets. He reads aloud from an exciting passage. It's a section about the Messiah, the "anointed one," and what he would accomplish. It's an important passage. It explains why Jesus has come. It's like a mission statement. He's calling his shot, and there are multiple layers to each line he reads.

We've already seen from his baptism that he is "anointed," and God's Spirit is on him. The passage talks about one who has come "to preach good news to the poor." Poverty is need. Jesus is here because of need, and not just the financial kind. He has good news for anyone that lacks. This includes the outcasts, the overlooked, those trampled upon by the world. He's also here to bring "freedom for the prisoners" and "set the oppressed free." Prisoners to what? Oppressed by whom? People can be held captive by a lot of things. Addictions, sickness, our self-perception, a reputation, inequality, fear, guilt, death—all imperfections which are a result of the curse. Jesus has come to address all of these problems.

In addition to this, he's come to restore "sight for the blind." Jesus will go on to help people who are physically blind. But that isn't all. Like Adam and Eve when tempted, people have fallen under the cloak of deceit from the serpent and fail to see things as they truly are. Just because people have sight doesn't mean that they see. Just because someone is blind doesn't mean that they can't see. We are blind to who God is and who we are. We've tried to cover ourselves with new identities (good deeds, nice belongings) as if these things can hide our shame or eliminate our guilt. We are blind to the world around us and our place in it. Jesus has come to give us sight that we might see truly again.

Finally, Jesus has come to proclaim that a special time has arrived, the "year of the Lord's favor." This refers to an ancient practice from their law[1] every fifty years when slaves were set free, debts were forgiven, and land was redistributed to its original owners. It was a massive restructuring of society and a re-enfranchisement for all sorts of people. It leveled the playing field and settled all accounts. It was an enormous equalizer. Understandably, it was called the "Year of Jubilee" (which means celebration). Jesus came here to set things straight. He's going to clear the books, erase debts, accomplish forgiveness, and bring justice and equality in a way that has been distorted since exile from the garden. He's going to restore the harmony between people again. He's going to restore peace with God.

This is good news for everybody. It's encouraging to hear, but that's not what gets a stir from this particular audience. After reading the passage, Jesus claims it has been fulfilled in their hearing.

All spoke well of him and were amazed at the gracious words that came from his lips. "Isn't this Joseph's son?" they asked.

At first, what he says sounds really nice, but is he saying *he* is the Messiah? Almost immediately, they doubt whether this is possible. This is just Jesus, Joseph's son, the kid that grew up down the street. My sister used to babysit him. His family is poor. His dad was a carpenter. This can't be right. Jesus is quickly written off as foolish, which incites a rather scathing response from him, one that will bring serious consequences.

"Truly I tell you," he continued, "no prophet is accepted in his hometown. I assure you that there were many widows in Israel in Elijah's time ... Yet Elijah was not sent to any of them, but to a widow in Zarephath in the region of Sidon. And there were many in Israel with leprosy in the time of Elisha the prophet, yet not one of them was cleansed—only Naaman the Syrian."

All the people in the synagogue were furious when they heard this. They got up, drove him out of the town, and took

---

[1] Leviticus 25:8-55

him to the brow of the hill on which the town was built, in order to throw him off the cliff. But he walked right through the crowd and went on his way.

Rebuking their disbelief, Jesus reiterates that he has been sent by God to them and even speaks of himself as a prophet. He claims that if they won't listen to him then he's happy to go elsewhere. He points out where this has happened previously with other prophets (Elijah and Elisha) who were rejected by their people and went on to perform miracles and help Israel's pagan enemies. He even mentions a specific story about a Syrian, the ethnicity of some of their despised former rulers. This proves to be too much. How could he speak such condemnation of them? Who does he think he is? Is he really saying that God would prefer evil, sinful, and irreligious people over them? The group is outraged and runs him out of town, apparently intending to have him killed.

It's possible that Jesus' own brothers and sisters may have been present. This would have humiliated their family. As we will later see, even they seem to reject him as the Messiah during his life, so it isn't hard to believe that they might have been a part of this crowd. In a society build around honor and shame, this may actually describe an attempted "honor killing' aimed at restoring honor to the family.

It's not quite the response you'd hope for after your first sermon. But it isn't too difficult to imagine something like this happening. Their reaction is fueled by all sorts of anger and a painful history. It's easy to become so absorbed in one's own struggle that such a rebuke would certainly be offensive. It can be even harder to imagine God being generous toward people who have done great harm to you, particularly an oppressive enemy. However, where the townspeople of Nazareth had great hope of a day when God would save them, they seem to have forgotten that God actually promised to do much more. Where some were waiting for a "Savior of the world," this crowd seemed much more interested in a "King of the Jews."

Jesus quickly becomes an outcast as he is driven out of town. Adam and Eve were once kicked out of their hometown, the garden of Eden, because of the wrong they had done. Now, Adam's descendants have built their own cities across the globe in a corrupted world, one shaped by sin. Jesus has come to the scene as a good man calling out this evil and gets kicked out, exiled from his own home. He simply doesn't fit the system.

WEDDING CRASHER
John 2:1-11

Run out of his hometown, Jesus begins travelling and teaching people in the area. Like John the Baptist, he begins to gather followers of his own. For the next few years, he will be moving from town to town and sharing his teachings with crowds. But just as things get started, he makes his way to Cana for a special occasion.

...a wedding took place at Cana in Galilee. Jesus' mother was there, and Jesus and his disciples had also been invited to the wedding. When the wine was gone, Jesus mother said to him, "They have no more wine."

"Woman, why do you involve me?" Jesus replied. "My hour has not yet come."

Hour has not yet come? For what?

Weddings can be an exciting occasion. They represent a uniting of people that follows a long period of anticipation. After much waiting, there is rejoicing as two people are joined and take on a new identity together.

Jewish weddings were a grand celebration. The reception would take place at the home of the groom, and the best man would act as master of the banquet. The celebration could last for up to a week depending on the family's finances.

Cana was a region known for its wine. Imagine if you invited friends for a feast in a place known for fine cuisine and then ran out of food. You definitely don't want to host a formal event like a wedding only to run out of drinks in the middle of the reception. This would have been humiliating for the groom.

In the moment of distress, Mary steps in expecting that her son can do something. She knows he's the Messiah and is ready to see what he can do. But it sounds as if Jesus doesn't intend to make a big splash quite yet.

His mother said to the servants, "Do whatever he tells you."

Nearby stood six stone water jars, the kind used by the Jews for ceremonial washing, each holding from twenty to thirty gallons.

In that motherly way, Mary gets things moving. These large jars were used to hold the water to clean people before the meal. Jews had a great concern for what was "clean." It wasn't just about dirt. They didn't want to consume things (food, behavior) that would make them unclean (destructive to the body or spirit and dividing people from God). It was customary for Jews at this time to rinse themselves before meals, maybe something like the way we wash our hands before a meal today but a little more ritualistic. A good host would have water basins available. These jars (or tubs) would have held that water and all together could contain 120-150 gallons. This would have been pretty gross stuff. Think of the bathwater after you've finished with the tub.

Jesus said to the servants, "Fill the jars with water"; so they filled them to the brim.

Then he told them, "Now draw some out and take it to the master of the banquet."

They did so, and the master of the banquet tasted the water that had been turned into wine.

At Jesus' word, something filthy is made into something wonderful. The water used to clean becomes the wine used to celebrate. Jesus turns their dirt into the substance of their dancing, their filth into fuel for the party. Where there could have been great shame and humiliation, Jesus intercedes so that the feast can continue.

He did not realize where it had come from, though the servants who had drawn the water knew. Then he called the bridegroom aside and said, "Everyone brings out the choice wine first and then the cheaper wine after the guests have had too much to drink; but you have saved the best till now."

Behind the scenes with a few friends and servants present, Jesus performs the first of his miracles. Not even the banquet master knows what has happened. Jesus is full of surprises, and he is just getting warmed up. God's kingdom is coming, and it will be something like this wedding. After much waiting and anticipation, Jesus is initiating a reunion and giving people a new identity. There is much to celebrate. His mother knew it, and now these servants know it too. He turns dirt into something sweet that people might rejoice together. He changes humiliation into a celebration. He steps in so that the party might go on, providing something better than what the guests had otherwise. Jesus is the true life of the party. He is the substance of real celebration.

However, it isn't quite time for all that yet. There's still something bigger to come. God has saved the best for last, and the party has only just begun.

A STRIKING RESEMBLANCE
John 3:22-30

As Jesus continues travelling from place to place and teaching, his following grows. People notice the way he resembles John the Baptist. Is he upstaging the one who baptized him? Shouldn't he be honoring his predecessor as other rabbis do? Who is the greater teacher, Jesus or John? It isn't long before John the Baptist is asked this very question.

After this, Jesus and his disciples went out into the Judean countryside, where he spent some time with them, and baptized. Now John also was baptizing at Aenon near Salim, because there was plenty of water, and people were coming and being baptized. (This was before John was put in prison.) An argument developed between some of John's disciples and a certain Jew over the matter of ceremonial washing. They came to John and said to him, "Rabbi, that man who was with you on the other side of the Jordan—the one you testified about—look, he is baptizing, and everyone is going to him."

*To this John replied, "A person can receive only what is
given them from heaven. You yourselves can testify that I
said, 'I am not the Messiah but am sent ahead of him.' The
bride belongs to the bridegroom. The friend who attends the
bridegroom waits and listens for him, and is full of joy when
he hears the bridegroom's voice. That joy is mine, and it is
now complete. He must become greater; I must become
less."*

Using some interesting language, John is quick to clarify things.
We learn that Jesus (or his disciples) are baptizing in the same way
John is, which obviously links the two, since no one else is doing
such a thing. John's disciples aren't sure if this is ok or not, especially
when Jesus seems to be growing more popular. Shouldn't John the
Baptist, who started all this, be getting the attention? John points out
the real "originator" of these things, and it isn't him. This is God's
work, and he is simply a servant. He reminds them what he'd taught
them previously, that he is simply working to prepare things for the
coming of the Messiah. Like the "best man" at a wedding, he has
been waiting for the groom. Now, that groom has arrived, and John
the Baptist couldn't be happier. It is time for him to step into the
background as Jesus takes center stage. As we will see, this indeed
happens as John the Baptist gets caught in some sad circumstances.

Jesus' popularity in Judea grows and it is soon time for him to
move along to other places, a decision that leads us to an interesting
location for our next story.

RISKY TERRITORY
John 4:1-34, 39-42

*Now Jesus learned that the Pharisees had heard that he was
gaining and baptizing more disciples than John – although
in fact it was not Jesus who baptized, but his disciples. So he
left Judea and went back once more to Galilee.*

*Now he had to go through Samaria. So he came to a town in
Samaria called Sychar, near the plot of ground Jacob had
given to his son Joseph. Jacob's well was there, and Jesus,*

tired as he was from the journey, sat down by the well. It was about noon.

This is a journey that Jesus would have been quite familiar with as he travelled back to Galilee (north) from Judea (south). Smack dab in the middle was Samaria. To the Romans, Samaritans may have been seen as a faction of the Jewish people. However, Judeans would have scoffed at such an association. Tensions between Judea and Samaria had continued for centuries and were further heightened when Judeans destroyed the temple in Samaria during the brief period of Jewish independence. Samaritans were ridiculed for intermarrying with other nations and also for rejecting worship at the temple in Jerusalem. Travelling through Samaria on the way to worship at the temple could lead Judeans into serious trouble. As a result, people went out of their way to avoid the region. But here, Jesus seems perfectly happy to travel right through the area and stops by a significant well in the heat of the day (around noon). It is here that we meet our next character.

When a Samaritan women came to draw water, Jesus said to her, "Will you give me a drink?" (His disciples had gone into the town to buy food.)

The Samaritan woman said to him, "You are a Jew and I am a Samaritan woman. How can you ask me for a drink?" (For Jews do not associate with Samaritans.)

So begins what will be an interesting conversation that will challenge several different social stigmas at once. Women would typically travel in groups to draw water early in the morning in order to avoid the heat. This woman's arrival at the well around noon is peculiar and betrays what we will soon discover is her poor reputation. Also interesting in the interaction is that Jesus doesn't offer to draw the water for her but instead asks for her help. It's as if he stands back to see if she will be generous enough to help a Judean or will be distracted by prejudice.

Most Jewish men would have completely avoided such an interaction for a number of reasons. For one, such intimate interactions, even in broad daylight, were viewed as scandalous.

Also, as the woman is aware, Jews would have considered even her dishes "unclean" to drink from. Is he irreligious or just plain ignorant? Immediately, the woman draws attention to his ethnicity. Perhaps Jesus' clothing or accent indicates to her that he is a Jew. She's shocked that he would speak to her.

Jesus answered her, "If you knew the gift of God and who it is that asks you for a drink, you would have asked him and he would have given you living water."

"Sir," the woman said, "you have nothing to draw with and the well is deep. Where can you get this living water? Are you greater than our father Jacob, who gave us the well and drank from it himself, as did also his sons and his livestock?"

The volley has begun. Jesus' response immediately touches upon the tensions between their regions. When he speaks of the gift of God, it would have sounded like he was highlighting God's favor for his people over hers. She would have been used to such talk related to views about what was true and acceptable worship at the temple in Jerusalem (where her people refused to worship). In fact, within view of Jacob's well was Mt. Gerizim, the former location of the Samaritan temple and the sacred place of worship for her people. Does this strange man really think so highly of himself? Is he to be her mediator before God because he is a Judean?

But that isn't really what he's saying. She hasn't caught it yet, but he's actually emphasizing his special identity, not some prejudice against Samaritans. In response to his apparent arrogance, she questions his greatness by pointing out that this not-so-living-water that he seems to think of as sub-par is actually from their shared forefather. Both of their peoples come from Jacob's line. Has he overlooked this? Does he view Samaritans as only "half-breeds" as so many others do? Does he really think that he is greater than Jacob who built this well himself? Besides, to point out the obvious, Jesus doesn't even have a bucket. How on earth could he give her something to drink?

Jesus answered, "Everyone who drinks this water will be thirsty again, but whoever drinks the water I give them will never thirst. Indeed, the water I give them will become in them a spring of water welling up to eternal life."

The woman said to him, "Sir, give me this water so that I won't get thirsty and have to keep coming here to draw water."

The conversation has just gotten much more complicated. Jesus isn't just here for a sip of water. He's actually come to offer something special. We constantly hunger and thirst for things, a process that never ends. It's as if Jesus sees these basic elements of the human experience as symbols of a far greater truth. He isn't speaking about the thirst for well water to just delay death, he's offering something that brings abundant life. In simple terms, yes, he is greater than Jacob.

He is also highlighting the repetitive nature of ceremonial cleansing that was so basic to worship at the time. Navigating a world tarnished by death and all things "unclean," people were constantly in need of water for cleansing. Yet Jesus here describes something that puts an end to this need. Prophets once spoke of something like this when describing a future temple, a time when God's healing presence would be poured out like living water upon the people, [1] but that never quite happened.

She doesn't seem amused by his comments and mocks his strange claim. While he speaks about eternal life, she hears an absurd comment about no longer needing to draw water from this well in the heat of the day. Either she's completely missed what he's said, or she thinks he's ridiculous. She responds as if to say, "You'd save me a bunch of work if such a thing were true!"

He told her, "Go call your husband and come back."

"I have no husband," she replied.

Jesus said to her, "You are right when you say you have no husband. The fact is, you have had five husbands, and the

---

[1] Isaiah 32:1-2, 15-20, 41:17-18, 44:3-4, 55; Ezekiel 47:1-12; Zechariah 12:10, 13:1, 14:8-9

*man you now have is not your husband. What you have just
said is quite true."*

If this wasn't strange enough already, things just got even more
complicated. He could be pointing out the way she seemed angered
by his comment, as if to say, "Why don't you go get your husband
and we will sort this out." She answers directly that she has no
husband. He then speaks of her with a familiarity that had to be
uncomfortable. How could he know this? Sure, maybe he could have
discovered her reputation somehow, but he even knows of her
present relationship (which is probably a secret affair).

She is shocked.

He's starting to connect the dots to his previous comments. She
has been returning repeatedly to a well thirsting for redemption, a
love that will set her free. She has been looking for satisfaction in a
man that she has not found. Or, as God once described to Eve, her
desire is for her husband who rules over her. She has been longing
for a relationship that will endure and restore. Ironically, she has just
found the answer in the man standing before her. But this is no
ordinary man.

He has her attention now. He is different from other Jews she has
known. She wants to know what he has to say, but not before
conveniently moving away from the topic of her sex life.

*"Sir," the woman said, "I can see that you are a prophet.
Our ancestors worshiped on this mountain, but you Jews
claim that the place where we must worship is in
Jerusalem."*

*"Woman," Jesus replied, "believe me, a time is coming
when you will worship the Father neither on this mountain
nor in Jerusalem. You Samaritans worship what you do not
know; we worship what we do know, for salvation is from
the Jews. Yet a time is coming and has now come when the
true worshipers will worship the Father in the Spirit and in
truth, for they are the kind of worshipers the Father seeks.
God is Spirit, and his worshipers must worship in the Spirit
and in truth."*

She now understands that he is something special, so she brings up what continues to be a point of confusion and debate. How is she to worship God? Jews claim that the Samaritans must travel all the way to Jerusalem (rejecting their Samaritan heritage) for worship at the "true" temple. Is this true? Jesus acknowledges the issues though he doesn't speak in support of the view that everyone must worship in Jerusalem. As if pointing to the prophet who once spoke of the special and new temple that would come,[1] he speaks of something *not confined in Jerusalem*. At the same time, he acknowledges the prophets who spoke of a Messiah who would come from the line of Judah and bring about this reconciliation between people (salvation is from the Jews). In further resemblance to the prophets, he goes on to speak of authentic worship that goes beyond the basics of time and place common of the time when God would pour out his Spirit upon people.[2] Instead, God seeks authenticity, not vain appearances or empty traditions. God wants people who genuinely humble themselves before him. This new people will not just be Jewish, but of all nations.

The woman said, "I know that Messiah" (called Christ) "is coming. When he comes, he will explain everything to us."

Then Jesus declared, "I, the one speaking to you – I am he."

She seems to understand him now. At the very least, if she is still confused, she professes the belief in the coming Messiah who will teach everyone the true ways of God again (as he is describing). Little did she know that this figure stood before her as she confessed this faith! Not long after a conversation about going to other peoples (while in Nazareth), Jesus has just invited faith and offered salvation to one of his people's most despised enemies—Samaritans. On top of this, he is speaking with a woman of low moral status. Already he's bringing sight to the blind, good news to the poor, and releasing the oppressed. His mission is well underway, and the disciples return just in time to find out about his fruitful conversation with this woman.

---

[1] Zechariah 2:4-5   [2] Isaiah 32:15-18, 44:3-4; Zechariah 12:10, 13:1

Just then his disciples returned and were surprised to find him talking with a woman. But no one asked, "What do you want?" or "Why are you talking with her?"

Then, leaving her water jar, the woman went back to the town and said to the people, "Come, see a man who told me everything I ever did. Could this be the Messiah?" They came out of the town and made their way toward him.

The passage highlights the obvious taboos that Jesus has violated. It isn't acceptable for him to be speaking with a woman like this. What would people think? Their skepticism is immediately contrasted then with the woman's great faith. "Leaving her water jar," the woman runs off to share the exciting news. God has finally come to reunite his people, and it doesn't matter whether one is a Jew or Samaritan. All are invited to worship God in truth again. The Messiah has finally come to restore things. As a result, she will no longer need this water jar. She can leave this old way of life behind (seeking the attention of men to "save" her). She has found what she was looking for. Sure enough, just like the shepherds at Jesus birth, God has again chosen a unique messenger to share his good news. We've seen Magi, shepherds, and now this Samaritan woman proclaiming the arrival of the Messiah while even Jesus' closest relationships (his family and hometown) have denied it.

Meanwhile his disciples urged him, "Rabbi, eat something."

But he said to them, "I have food to eat that you know nothing about."

Then his disciples said to each other, "Could someone have brought him food?"

"My food," said Jesus, "is to do the will of him who sent me and to finish his work..."

Many of the Samaritans from that town believed in him because of the woman's testimony, "He told me everything I ever did." So when the Samaritans came to him, they urged him to stay with them, and he stayed two days. And because of his words many more became believers.

They said to the woman, "We no longer believe just because of what you said; now we have heard for ourselves, and we know that this man really is the Savior of the World."

Concerned for his wellbeing (and maybe their own hunger), his followers offer Jesus some food. After a conversation about water that wasn't really about water, he now has a similar conversation with the disciples about food. While they are busy thinking about their next meal, there is much good work to be done. They are about to be presented with an opportunity too great to overlook. Soon after, many more Samaritans arrive because of the woman's story. Curious to see this man for themselves, they too come to put their faith in him and make an interesting proclamation—not that he is the "King of the Jews," but something far greater. They believe he is the "Savior of the World."

After a couple of days reaping and sowing in this little town in Samaria, a strange place for a group of Jewish men to stay, it is time for Jesus to move on. It is around this time that he receives some sad news about his comrade.

BAD NEWS ARRIVES
Matthew 4:12; Mark 6:17-20; Matthew 4:13, 17

When Jesus heard that John had been put in prison, he withdrew to Galilee.

For Herod himself had given orders to have John arrested, and he had him bound and put in prison. He did this because of Herodias, his brother Philip's wife, whom he had married. For John had been saying to Herod, "It is not lawful for you to have your brother's wife." So Herodias nursed a grudge against John and wanted to kill him. But she was not able to, because Herod feared John and protected him, knowing him to be a righteous and holy man. When Herod heard John, he was greatly puzzled; yet he liked to listen to him.

Leaving Nazareth, he went and lived in Capernaum, which was by the lake in the area of Zebulun and Naphtali...

From that time on Jesus began to preach, "Repent, for the kingdom of heaven has come near."

These are tense times.

Given the various political tensions, Herod's reputation, and John the Baptist's message, it's not surprising that John is finally arrested. In relation to this event (and likely his own homecoming), Jesus relocates to Capernaum, which is in the region of Galilee, and picks up where John the Baptist left off by preaching of God's coming kingdom. Times are changing, and his ministry is about to change as well.

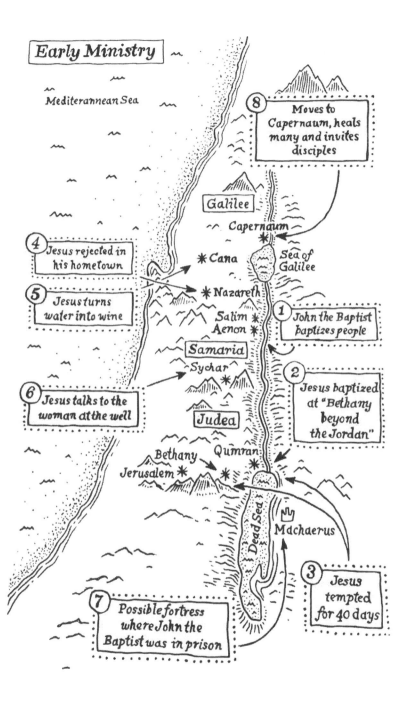

Early Ministry

Mediterannean Sea

Galilee

Capernaum

8 Moves to Capernaum, heals many and invites disciples

Sea of Galilee

Cana

4 Jesus rejected in his hometown

Nazareth

5 Jesus turns water into wine

Salim
Aenon

1 John the Baptist baptizes people

Samaria

Sychar

6 Jesus talks to the woman at the well

Judea

2 Jesus baptized at "Bethany beyond the Jordan"

Qumran

Bethany

Jerusalem

Dead Sea

Machaerus

3 Jesus tempted for 40 days

7 Possible fortress where John the Baptist was in prison

Part II

A Growing Movement

FIVE
Turning Heads

GALILEE COVERED ABOUT 25 miles in diameter and could be travelled in a few days' journey to most locations. The region likely had a population somewhere between 200,000-300,000 people. One of its prominent features, the Sea of Galilee, was known for its fishing industry. Elsewhere, the region was known for exporting olives, wheat, and wine. This allowed for a decent amount of wealth, but this wealth was unevenly distributed and the majority of people were of the lower class and working poor (laborers and farmers).

As Jesus continues to travel around teaching, he begins to perform public miracles and his following grows. Along the way, he has also begun to specifically invite some people to be what are called disciples. In doing so, he's inviting them into a different relationship than that which he has with the crowds. He's inviting them along for the journey and to eventually do just as he is doing. It was common for rabbis, which means "teachers," to have disciples. A disciple not only heard lectures but was expected to pay close attention to every detail of what the teacher (rabbi) would do. It was a way of life. They would follow, and, people said, were to "not let a word fall to the ground." It was an intense calling.

These will be Jesus' pupils, like apprentices on job training. The closest thing we have today might be something like an internship or studying for a graduate degree under some professor, just a little more involved. Those he invites will go on to spend the next several years with him. It's a new direction and a different vocation than what they otherwise knew.

This process begins one day while he is teaching in Galilee...

NO MAN IS AN ISLAND
Luke 5:1-10; Mark 1:17-18

> *One day as Jesus was standing by the Lake of Gennesaret, the people were crowding around him and listening to the word of God. He saw at the water's edge two boats, left there by the fishermen, who were washing their nets. He got into one of the boats, the one belonging to Simon, and asked him to put out a little from shore. Then he sat down and taught the people from the boat.*

Jesus teaches people in all sorts of places (not just synagogues). Here he's at the water's edge, a boat yard. There are fishermen finishing up their work as they clean their nets. These are common folk, the laborers, the blue-collar construction worker or farmer types of their day.

They didn't have microphones back then, so as people gather around he gets in a boat. Jesus isn't being pushed in or something, this is just a practical way to magnify sound. Have you ever noticed how voices carry over water? It's also a clever way to involve someone. There's a lot of interest in Jesus, and suddenly he's asking Simon (later known as Peter) if it's ok to use his boat for a few minutes. Simon cooperates, and they put out a bit in the water.

There's no mention of what Jesus actually teaches them. This is kind of funny. We will get more of that later. It isn't what he says that was most noteworthy here. It's what happens after...

> *When he had finished speaking, he said to Simon, "Put out into deep water, and let down the nets for a catch."*

> *Simon answered, "Master, we've worked hard all night and haven't caught anything. But because you say so, I will let down the nets."*

Simon is a fisherman, and Jesus is not. This is an awkward situation. You don't walk up to someone and tell them how to do their job. Simon knows what he's doing, and he's been toiling all night and caught nothing. He's a pro, and here Jesus expects to walk up and just magically know what to do? There's no good reason this will work. But Jesus is a respectable person and everybody is watching. Simon is put on the spot. Should he get into a weird argument or just do what the guy says? Simon makes it a point to explain that they aren't going to catch anything, maybe hoping to change Jesus' mind. But since he respects Jesus, he will do as he's told. This is the *only* reason though. So he drops the nets (the ones he had just cleaned) even though it's sure to fail.

When they had done so, they caught such a large number of fish that their nets began to break. So they signaled their partners in the other boat to come and help them, and they came and filled both boats so full that they began to sink.

This is excessive, even embarrassing. You don't just miss a bunch of fish like this. It's the catch of a lifetime. How could Jesus know? Simon had doubted Jesus in front of everyone, and Jesus didn't even have to lift a finger. The struggle of fishing which has cost Simon so much time and effort was nothing to Jesus. Jesus just speaks, and it is. Who does that? Who can take empty waters and fill them with life?

Simon knows this isn't possible.

When Simon Peter saw this, he fell at Jesus' knees and said, "Go away from me, Lord; I am a sinful man!" For he and all his companions were astonished at the catch of fish they had taken, and so were James and John, the sons of Zebedee, Simon's partners.

They know they've just witnessed something special, and Simon Peter is overwhelmed. Who is this guy? He can't help but bow to his knees and even addresses Jesus as "Lord"! Simon's understanding of who Jesus is has just changed. He's encountered something incredible, and he and his companions all know it. Surely he doesn't deserve this. Jesus is clearly special, a man of God, anointed, something *other* than what he is. Peter has been put in his place. Jesus is better, greater, more, and like God.

As if naked, Simon Peter is suddenly self-conscious and squirming in discomfort as he tries to send Jesus away. Surely Jesus wouldn't want anything to do with him. He's a lowly peasant who has done terrible things. There is no reason Jesus would want his company. Surely if Jesus really knew who he was, how he lived, all that he had done wrong, there would be no place for them to be friends. Simon doesn't deserve God's kindness. Simon is lacking. Maybe Jesus will just spare him the humiliation and leave. He's made his point already. Or has he?

"Come, follow me," Jesus said, "and I will send you out to fish for people."[1]

What?

Simon Peter is the last person that should make the cut, and yet he's the one that's invited? He's doubted Jesus. He's uneducated. He's made mistakes. He's not a "good" man. He's not qualified.

Yet unfazed, Jesus invites him and makes a promise.

Stuck in all of his inadequacy, exposed, embarrassed, afraid of what's to come, squirming from the filth of his past, Jesus comes specifically to *him* and invites him to something new. Leave it all behind. I'll take care of everything. I will make something of you.

He doesn't say, "No Simon, I think you're great! You're so smart and handy! You're better than everyone else!" His lack of correction acknowledges, "I know. I know who you truly are and what you've done, except it doesn't have to stand in the way. Trust me, and I'll make you something new."

Simon Peter was stuck in the curse. This is a story of the daily grind of toil and the weight of guilt, but Jesus interrupts all of that and invites him out of it. Where Simon was cursed, Jesus is something else. He is blessed, and the one with power over this curse.

Given the choice, what would you do?

At once they left their nets and followed him.

This is getting exciting.

---

[1] Jeremiah 16:16 describes a time when God would send fishermen out to gather his people to teach them.

A DIRTY MAN
Mark 1:35-45

As word spreads about him, Jesus frequently takes time to step back and pray. It's like he's getting recharged and focused again for his mission as he reconnects to his time in the wilderness.

Very early in the morning, while it was still dark, Jesus got up, left the house and went off to a solitary place, where he prayed. Simon and his companions went to look for him, and when they found him, they exclaimed: "Everyone is looking for you!"

Jesus replied, "Let us go somewhere else—to the nearby villages—so I can preach there also. That is why I have come." So he traveled throughout Galilee, preaching in their synagogues and driving out demons.

Jesus' disciples are surprised that he's ready to pack up and go. But Jesus is a man on a mission. He knows his purpose, and it isn't simply to please the crowds. He's not going to forsake the bigger picture of why he has come.

We've already seen a couple of his miracles, but over time these occurrences, intentionally or not, become more and more public. At times this spotlight will even get in the way as he is bombarded with people. But one day, while he is away from all the fuss, he is visited by a man with a special request.

A man with leprosy came to him and begged him on his knees, "If you are willing, you can make me clean."

The word here used for leprosy could actually refer to a number of different skin diseases. Leprosy itself is a serious condition that still exists in our world today in regions of poverty dealing with malnutrition and often poor water sources. Leprosy is a chronic infection caused by a bacteria that works on one's nervous system over time to numb the sense of touch and the ability to feel pain. It's weird to think that the ability to feel pain can actually be a good thing. These numbed areas lead to various other problems as cuts or injuries go unnoticed and can worsen until extreme enough that someone might even lose extremities from repeated injury and infection. It's a really sad condition. While it is only mildly contagious, the various social stigmas surrounding such a visible disease were severe.

In the ancient world, victims of this sort of disease would basically get quarantined outside of town to prevent the spread of the disease. In Jewish culture, such a person would periodically check in with the priest to assess if the condition was improving. There were various practices (according to law)[1] used to determine one's condition. With some skin diseases, things would improve, and eventually the person could re-enter society. For others, as with lepers, the condition could persist until death.

Aside from concerns about the spread of the disease, there were a number of other social stigmas attached to leprosy. Among Jewish people, the law was seen as a protection and source for healthy living in all areas of life. As a result, a diseased person was viewed as cursed by God, punished for some action or violation of God's law. The sick or lame were often labeled as "sinners." They were stigmatized as "dirty" (or unclean) and a risk to others' own health and standing before God.

Being a leper meant being an outcast, excluded from the community with only the company of other similar outcasts while relying on the generosity of others to survive. Being a leper meant being untouchable. This man was trapped within a condition where it appeared as if he was decaying from the outside in. To everyone, he was visibly "unclean." He was covered in death. With no remedy at hand and a gruesome death looming overhead, being a leper meant being hopeless.

Yet this man had the hope to approach Jesus.

As if Jesus was somehow in control and with power over this affliction, the man asks Jesus if he is "willing." Isn't God the one behind this supposed punishment or curse? Isn't it God's will that is the real thing in question here?

---

[1] Leviticus 13

Jesus was indignant. He reached out his hand and touched the man. "I am willing," he said. "Be clean!" Immediately the leprosy left him and he was cleansed.

Jesus' response is shocking. He reaches out and *touches* this man. This is all backwards. Instead of the leper making Jesus unclean, Jesus makes this man clean. Jesus reverses the process.

I wonder how long it had been since someone had touched the leper. Though he may have been numb, I wonder if he felt this touch upon his skin. Again, at Jesus' word, what was dead, dirty, infected and dying is immediately healed and fully alive.

This is remarkable.

Who can reverse a curse like this? Who can reverse *the curse* like this? Who can bring life to what is dead with just a few words?

As people at the time understood it, the law was necessary to mitigate the effects of the curse upon them. The law was a kind of fence that kept the destruction and death of sin at bay, necessary to navigate life and live in a way pleasing to God. This dance required constant caution because at any turn one could be touched and made unclean, a process that no individual could overcome by his or her own power. Only God, as prescribed in his laws, could restore someone from such a state. Yet here Jesus acts as though God, restoring as though he were a new kind of law now at work in the world, and no one has seen anything quite like it before.

Jesus sent him away at once with a strong warning: "See that you don't tell this to anyone. But go, show yourself to the priest and offer the sacrifices that Moses commanded for your cleansing, as a testimony to them." Instead he went out and began to talk freely, spreading the news. As a result, Jesus could no longer enter a town openly but stayed outside in lonely places. Yet the people still came to him from everywhere.

There is a protocol to follow to verify this man's healing so that this man can enter into relationship again with his community. He's been restored. But why should the man be silent? Jesus is going to have some trouble blending in anymore, and he will go on to spend a lot of his time in these lonely places as his fame grows. This will be his home as the sick, the lame, the poor, and the needy flock to the one who gives them hope. There is something bigger to be done and Jesus hasn't forgotten that. He isn't here to just travel everywhere and heal everyone all over the world one miracle at a time. There's something else that has to happen.

But what?

RAISE THE ROOF
Mark 2:1-12

A few days later, when Jesus again entered Capernaum, the people heard that he had come home. The gathered in such large numbers that there was no room left, not even outside the door, and he preached the word to them.

News spreads quickly once he's back in town and there's a heck of a turnout. The house is exploding with people as the crowd spills out the door. Once again, we aren't told what he teaches them, but "preached the word" implies that he's speaking the very words of God as though a prophet (or even God). Everyone is listening until there is a surprising interruption.

Some men came, bringing him a paralyzed man, carried by four of them. Since they could not get him to Jesus because of the crowd, they made an opening in the roof above Jesus by digging through it and then lowered the mat the man was lying on.

We don't know why this man is paralyzed. It could be from an accident of some kind, or maybe he was born this way. Either way, part of his body simply isn't working, and he requires the assistance of others to even get around. He's stuck. But, he has four incredible friends. Not only are they all completely confident in Jesus' ability to heal their friend, they will go to absurd lengths to see it happen. They'll even climb on top of someone else's home when there is no room inside to dig a hole in the roof so that they can put their friend directly in front of Jesus. This had to be messy! I can't imagine the awkwardness of trying to lower someone from a ceiling on a mat without dropping him.

When Jesus saw their faith, he said to the paralyzed man, "Son, your sins are forgiven."

There's that *sin* word again. It's the problem. It's separation from God stemming from the disobedience in the garden. It's the brokenness behind the "offness" of our world. But great! I mean, this has to be good news. Who wouldn't want their sins forgiven, right? This has to be a little surprising though, maybe even a little disappointing. After all, that's not why the man's friends went through all this trouble. They didn't tear a hole in the roof so that Jesus would forgive his sins. It's wonderful but a little abstract. Besides, they regularly go to the temple for that. They brought their friend so that he'd be able to walk again. There seems to have been a mistake.

But, that's not the only issue…

Now some teachers of the law were sitting there, thinking to themselves, "Why does this fellow talk like that? He's blaspheming! Who can forgive sins but God alone?"

Some teachers catch on to what Jesus has just said. Jesus isn't forgiving them for disrupting things or breaking a roof as if they just offended him, he has made a grand pronouncement as if clearing the man's record before God entirely. He's wiping the slate clean. Sure, you can forgive someone for what they do *to you*, but how can you forgive someone of their sins which stand between them and God? Only God can do that. In fact, there's an entire system of laws that God established about what people are to do when they sin. There are sacrifices that must be made. Here Jesus just tosses it all aside as if it's nothing?

He's speaking as if he is God.

Immediately Jesus knew in his spirit that this was what they were thinking in their hearts, and he said to them, "Why are you thinking these things? Which is easier: to say to this paralyzed man, 'Your sins are forgiven,' or to say, 'Get up, take your mat and walk'? But I want you to know that the Son of Man has authority on earth to forgive sins."

So he said to the man, "I tell you, get up, take your mat and go home." He got up, took his mat and walked out in full view of them all.

The "Son of Man" is one of the titles describing the time when God's kingdom would come to earth,[1] and not usually associated with forgiveness but judgment. Here, Jesus uses this title to refer to himself and wants to make clear that this prophetic figure is also able to forgive sins. While prophets elsewhere referred to a time when God would ultimately forgive the sins of the people,[2] this isn't something that they expected from the "Son of Man." As he speaks, Jesus knows their hearts. He can read the room and understands exactly what is going on around him. Which is more difficult, forgiving sins or healing someone?

This is awkward.

Both? It's not like the audience could really do either—forgive his sins, or heal him. Here Jesus has made light work of both as if they are interchangeable. He is connecting the two actions. Who is this that forgives sins? Who is this that can just tell someone to walk, and by his words it is so? Whose power is at work here?

Only God could do such a thing.

Now that the man is healed, they are stuck. Clearly, God's power is at work here. They can't really deny it. How could Jesus blaspheme God in one sentence by presuming to forgive sins, and then heal by God's power in the next sentence? Surely God wouldn't let such a blasphemer heal someone, right? They are understandably confused. Who is this person that can heal *and* forgive one's sins against God? They are seeing without seeing. The answer is staring them in the face—this only makes sense if Jesus is God. It's just not what they expected.

This amazed everyone and they praised God, saying, "We have never seen anything like this!"

---

[1] Daniel 7:13-14   [2] Jeremiah 33:8; Ezekiel 36:25; Micah 7:18-19; Zechariah 13:1

While they don't really get it yet, it's clear to them that Jesus has God's stamp of approval to heal the sick, and apparently it's ok for him to forgive sins too. Jesus brings life to something lifeless and makes it completely functional again. He restores this man. Even greater than this, though, he also restores this man before God.

A DINNER WITH A SINNER
Luke 5:27-31; Matthew 9:13

> *After this, Jesus went out and saw a tax collector by the name of Levi sitting at his tax booth. "Follow me," Jesus said to him, and Levi got up, left everything and followed him.*

Things are moving quickly. There are crowds, confrontations, and miracles. To top it off, Jesus is now forgiving sins as well. I wonder if Levi (identified elsewhere as Matthew,[1] the gospel writer) witnessed what just happened. He's at work and appears to know who Jesus is. Did he see one of the other miracles or hear him teach?

The Romans collected a few different kinds of taxes. They would sell the rights to collect these taxes to the highest bidder. The tax collector, paying up front for the rights to this debt, could then go and do what was necessary to collect the funds. Think of some mix between the IRS and a collecting agency. These guys could be ruthless and held all the power. It took money and a lot of gall to be a tax collector. It meant being hated by the general public, though it could pay a handsome reward if someone was willing to put up with the rejection.

Tax collectors were viewed as sell-outs who had forsaken their Jewish heritage and identity for the money of the enemy, and they were notorious for abusing their power and exploiting people. For the most part, Rome didn't care what the tax collectors did so long as it got its money. Having such wealth and only the company of others similarly reviled by the community (especially the religious), the group wasn't exactly known for its moral standards.

So why does Jesus choose Matthew (Levi)?

Apparently he saw something, and he chose well. At the drop of a hat, Matthew leaves this way of life behind. Maybe he felt stuck

---

[1] Matthew 9:9-13

with a reputation. Maybe he bought into the trade with high hopes only to later regret the path he'd taken with its shame and troubling status. Maybe he felt tricked, guilty about the things he'd done and wanted a way out. Maybe Matthew just wanted a clean slate. This was it. Jesus just so happens to be a man that can forgive sins.

Without hesitation, Matthew jumps into action. Next thing you know, he's throwing a party, and Jesus is the honored guest.

Then Levi held a great banquet for Jesus at his house, and a large crowd of tax collectors and others were eating with them. But the Pharisees and the teachers of the law who belonged to their sect complained to his disciples, "Why do you eat and drink with tax collectors and sinners?"

It isn't surprising that this would raise some eyebrows. Table fellowship carried significance unmatched today. It represented intimacy and unity between those eating together. In a religious climate shaped by the Pharisaic obsession over ritualistic purity (priestly laws and other traditions) even in home settings, eating with the company of "undefiled hands" was of utmost importance. There were a variety of customs that needed to be observed. Who made the meal? What was in it? Were these people "clean"? Who else would join in eating it? What was their standing before God? Dinners were a daily expression of all kinds of social boundaries (race, class, and lifestyle) thought to be sanctioned by God. Here, Jesus' radical inclusion openly defies this behavior.

It's a remarkable scene.

Jesus is at a dinner surrounded by what may be the most loathed population of the entire city. What is he doing? People start talking.

This can't be a good idea.

But Matthew is rejoicing, and he invites everyone he knows to join him. All these "enemies" of the general populace come to hear the man that has changed everything. Jesus is good news even for a tax collector.

He also has a message for his critics. As if it should be obvious.

On hearing this, Jesus said, "It is not the healthy who need a doctor, but the sick. But go and learn what this means: 'I desire mercy, not sacrifice.' For I have not come to call the righteous, but sinners."

This is a slap in the face. Jesus quotes one of the prophets.[1] The Pharisees and teachers of the law prided themselves on knowing scripture backwards and forwards, and here Jesus tells them to go study some more. It's like telling a pastor to go read the Bible.

They've missed something.

Sacrifice means doing something to cover your back. It means that you've made a mistake and need God to forgive you for it. It's paying a price to make amends. This could obviously be abused. Someone might willingly do wrong knowing that they could simply pay for it later with the inconvenience of a sacrifice. Think that's what God wants?[2]

Mercy is a display of kindness. It's generosity. Instead of simply making sure I've covered my back, mercy is about my actions toward others. It reflects God's patience with everyone because God is merciful.

Who is behaving more like God here, Jesus or his critics?

Jesus isn't interested in the people who don't think they need help from God. He isn't interested in the "righteousness" of someone who thinks they are perfect or have it all taken care of and don't need to be saved from anything. They've got it under control (or can just deal with the necessary sacrifices later). Why would he waste his time with them?

Jesus has come for those who are stuck and understand that they need a hand because they've gone astray. He's come for those who don't seem to have a way to reconciliation. He's here for those who know that they are lacking, like Simon Peter and Matthew (Levi). He's here for those that have made mistakes and want to take a different path. He's here so that sinful people can walk with God.

It looks like Matthew's thick skin may come in handy some day. He knows what it's like to be hated, and from the look of things this might be great preparation for what lies ahead if he sticks with Jesus.

---

[1] Hosea 6:6   [2] Proverbs 21:3

A SABBATH SHOWDOWN
Mark 3:1-6

> *Another time he went into the synagogue, and a man with a shriveled hand was there. Some of them were looking for a reason to accuse Jesus, so they watched him closely to see if he would heal him on the Sabbath.*

We have another person with some kind of paralysis. There's already enough recent tension that people expect Jesus to defy their customs yet again. He's touched a leper (unclean), forgiven someone's sins (blasphemy), and now how will he regard the Sabbath—or at least their application of the idea? I can't help but wonder if they might have even brought this guy out just to see what would happen, like he's a toy.

You may remember, the Sabbath is a holy day, the seventh day when God rested. He ceases to work and instructed us to keep this day special. Because of this, the people went to great lengths to ensure that they didn't do anything that could be considered work on the Sabbath. Beyond any laws from scripture, they had built all sorts of other traditions around this idea in order to be extra cautious. What's the harm of a little extra caution? Rather be safe than sorry, right? Here, it seems they expect that Jesus will have a problem with their safeguards around this idea.

> *Jesus said to the man with the shriveled hand, "Stand up in front of everyone." Then Jesus asked them, "Which is lawful on the Sabbath: to do good or to do evil, to save life or to kill?" But they remained silent.*

> *He looked around at them in anger and, deeply distressed at their stubborn hearts, said to the man, "Stretch out your hand."*

This is confrontational. He's not beating around the bush or avoiding their attention. This is gonna go down so that everyone can see it happen. And the answers to his questions are painfully obvious, yet no one will speak. Of course, do good and save life—heal on the

Sabbath. But admitting such would mean acknowledging that they were wrong.

It's hard to admit when you're wrong.

In fact, it would mean that a great deal of what they have held so dear in their devotion to God not only was wrong but actually stood in the way of their doing the right thing. Their "righteous" acts were actually quite the opposite.

They've been tricked.

Like Adam and Eve, what they thought was good was actually evil. They've been so busy trying to cover themselves and be good that they've missed God's desire for the Sabbath—to bring people life. In all their fervor, they've actually ignored God altogether. They have become blind.

He stretched it out, and his hand was completely restored. Then the Pharisees went out and began to plot with the Herodians how they might kill Jesus.

This is severe.

Yet again, Jesus restores something to life. He is healing what is broken. He is revealing God's truth and putting things back in place. He is reordering the way they have structured their lives and reforming the way they understand what it means to follow God.

We don't want to think we are ever wrong. We don't want to admit what we've done. We can't handle our nakedness before God, so instead we blame others. It has to be more complicated. There has to be another explanation. Like Adam, we blame someone instead. It's Eve's fault. Let the axe fall on her. Here, Jesus is upsetting a delicate balance. What will they do? Should they admit to their mistake, or blame him? Let the axe fall on him.

Kill him.

This is political, and this sounds like the attempts of another antagonist we've seen.

We don't know much about the Herodians, but as you can guess it's pretty clear that they are affiliated with Herod—the "King of the Jews." The dynasty already tried to kill Jesus at birth, and now it has arrested John the Baptist, his affiliate. It's not hard to speculate about their interest in what is happening here with Jesus. He's challenging their system of authority. He's challenging their ways of life. He must be removed. Jesus is a wrinkle in their plans. He is a threat to their power.

He is a threat to their kingdom.

MEETING AT MIDNIGHT
John 3:1-12, 16-21

Jesus is becoming a well-known figure, and the tensions around his actions and teachings are building. What exactly is he doing, and who does he think he is? Various groups are understandably getting flustered as they try to sort through his apparent opposition to their ideals. What are you to do with a man like this? He doesn't fit the present molds or leadership profiles of the time.? We've seen people approach him to be healed, but now we are going to see different people coming to feel him out. Given the recent turmoil, it isn't surprising that people of any prestige might be cautious about being seen with him in broad daylight...

> Now there was a Pharisee, a man named Nicodemus who was a member of the Jewish ruling council. He came to Jesus at night and said, "Rabbi, we know that you are a teacher who has come from God. For no one could perform the signs you are doing if God were not with him."

It's interesting that Nicodemus is a Pharisee. He identifies with one of the groups that have been challenged the most by Jesus thus far. It's easy to fall into generalizations at times when talking about Jesus that leave us favoring one group over another as somehow his favorites, but it isn't accurate. Here, Jesus receives even one of his likely opponents. In the dark of night, this man is curious and afraid. He knows that something special is happening that he and his companions don't understand. It's hard to overlook the significance of all these miracles. But how does Jesus do it? Jesus doesn't fit what they think about God. He doesn't fit their understanding of what is good. After all the gossip, Nicodemus has come to ask the source. So Nicodemus begins by stating the obvious. Surely Jesus has come from God or he wouldn't be able to perform these miracles.

Jesus replied, "Very truly I tell you, no one can see the kingdom of God unless they are born again."

Excuse me? Nicodemus came pointing out the obvious about the miracles but the conversation has just headed a different direction. This isn't adding up. It's as if Jesus is of God, but how could he be given the way he defies common religious traditions and the teaching of the elders? Because they are blind. They don't have the eyes they need. If they want to understand, something radical must happen. Nicodemus has gone the wrong way and must begin again. No one can see truth unless...

"How can someone be born when they are old?" Nicodemus asked. "Surely they cannot enter a second time into their mother's womb to be born!"

Jesus answered, "Very truly I tell you, no one can enter the kingdom of God unless they are born of water and the Spirit. Flesh gives birth to flesh, but the Spirit gives birth to spirit. You should not be surprised at my saying, 'You must be born again.' The wind blows wherever it pleases. You hear its sound, but you cannot tell where it comes from or where it is going. So it is with everyone born of the Spirit."

Nicodemus doesn't get it. Incredulous, he points out the awkwardness of Jesus' statement. What does it mean to be "reborn?" What does any of this have to do with birth?

Jesus moves full speed ahead with the idea and speaks of two births. There is the flesh, and then there is the Spirit. We are born of flesh (bodily) but have not all been born of the Spirit. This is referring to the Spirit of God that hovered over the waters in Genesis. Without God's spirit, things won't make sense.[1] Without this spirit, we will not enter God's kingdom. Against popular opinion, Jesus is saying that people aren't naturally "children of God" but quite the opposite. As descendants of Adam, we now bear likeness to a different master. As a result, things must be changed. There's something still to happen, a necessary and impending birth that still awaits us. It gives

---

[1] Job 32:8

sight, and it sounds something like baptism. John the Baptist said that the one to come would baptize with the Spirit, and that one to come is Jesus.

We need baptism. In a way, we are already dead, and we need to be made alive. There is a sort of spiritual birth waiting in the needed waters of forgiveness (as Jesus described to the Samaritan woman). We must pass through these waters. We need to be cleansed and brought to life. On our own, we will never enter God's kingdom. We need renewal. We need rebirth. We need God's Spirit. It restores and reconnects us. It opens our eyes and ears to something we haven't understood. It puts us in tune with the sounds of a new song that we couldn't hear before. While we could observe the Spirit's effects, like the wind, we won't understand what God is doing unless we return to him.

"How can this be?" Nicodemus asked.

"You are Israel's teacher," said Jesus, "and do you not understand these things? Very truly I tell you, we speak of what we know, and we testify to what we have seen, but still you people do not accept our testimony."

Nicodemus is blown away. This is big stuff, heavy stuff, and it isn't where he thought the discussion would go. Jesus has just confused one of his people's brightest teachers and now speaks of himself in the plural. In what follows, Jesus shares what includes one of the most quoted passages of the Bible in our time. We aren't going to read it all, but he goes on to say a great deal.

"I have spoken to you of earthly things and you do not believe; how then will you believe if I speak of heavenly things?...

For God so loved the world that he gave his one and only Son, that whoever believes in him shall not perish but have eternal life. For God did not send his Son into the world to condemn the world, but to save the world through him. Whoever believes in him is not condemned, but whoever does not believe stands condemned already because he has not believed in the name of God's one and only Son. This is the verdict: Light has come into the world, but people loved darkness instead of light because their deeds were evil. Everyone who does evil hates the light, and will not come into the light for fear that their deeds will be exposed. But whoever lives by the truth comes into the light, so that it may be seen plainly that what they have done has been done in the sight of God."

There is another kind of life that doesn't perish. The flesh decays. It has been corrupted since the garden. It cannot last. We've been bitten by the snake, and its poison works to our destruction. There is a solution though, something that can endure. This second birth of the Spirit brings a new kind of life that will not decay. It has come from God and through God in the form of his one and only Son. This Son has come to save the world. When we embrace the Son, we embrace God and his work in us and in our world. When we reject the Son, we reject what God is accomplishing in our world. It's a matter of life and death. It's day and night, light and darkness. God is separating what is light from what is dark. But like Adam, we are evil and hide. We don't want to acknowledge our imperfection. We have loved the wrong things and so hate what is actually good. Will we embrace the truth? Can we acknowledge our brokenness and come into the light?

We aren't told what happens next. As this story closes, we don't know exactly how Nicodemus responds, but this won't be the last we will see of our late-night visitor.

Six

A Voice on the Mountain

THE GROUP OF PEOPLE following Jesus grows as word spreads. At this point, Jesus has attracted a lot of followers, and it's time to narrow things down. He can't be with everyone all of the time. It's hard to travel with such a large group, and he can't effectively continue his mission with an enormous mass of people following him everywhere he goes, let alone be a mentor to so many at once. He's going to have to spend some intimate time with his pupils, significant time, if he's really going to train them. He's got some decisions to make, so he takes some time to pray.

THE GOOD LIFE
Luke 6:12-16; Matthew 4:23-5:20

> *One of those days Jesus went out to a mountainside to pray, and spent the night praying to God. When morning came, he called his disciples to him and chose twelve of them, whom he also designated apostles: Simon (whom he named Peter), his brother Andrew, James, John, Philip, Bartholomew, Matthew, Thomas, James son of Alphaeus, Simon who was called the Zealot, Judas son of James, and Judas Iscariot, who became a traitor.*

Jesus gathers the people in order to appoint some of them specifically as his apprentices. There are twelve of them in all. This group becomes known as apostles (which means "sent ones") and will play an important role in all that is to come. They will need to be with him constantly. It is expected. They will spend the next few years of their lives travelling with him, emulating all that he says and does and even teaching and performing miracles as he does along the way. By his side through thick and thin, they will be prepared to continue the mission that he's begun. From the beginning, it is understood that one day he will send them off to do as he does with them now. It's the whole point of discipleship. His purpose is theirs. These twelve eventually become known as "The Twelve," or "The Apostles" (capital A) because of all that will follow.

Almost immediately, we see some significant differences from the practices of other rabbis of his time. For one, he hasn't sought out the best and brightest students. Instead, he's approached working men, ordinary common folk. This isn't about how much they know. Also, in a society where students selected teachers and became pupils based on their own preferences, here Jesus is the one doing the choosing. They haven't selected him, he has chosen them, behavior that resembles the way God once chose the people of Israel to be his "followers" in the ancient world.

It is interesting that he chooses this number of disciples. Ancient Israel was made of 12 tribes of people. It was believed that the Messiah would reunite the tribes and gather those that had been dispersed. We've already seen Jesus engaging Galileans, Samaritans, Judeans—people in areas historically populated by several of the tribes. Now, these 12 disciples are symbolic of the reunification which his work will bring.

It's also an interesting group of people. There are some familiar names here. We've already heard of Simon (Peter), James, and John (sons of Zebedee) from the story about the great catch of fish. We've heard of Matthew (Levi) from the calling of the tax collector. Among the others, we are given tidbits of information here and there, but we don't know all of their back stories and are left making educated guesses. What we can tell, though, is pretty intriguing.

They come from a variety of backgrounds and likely span a significant age range. There are a couple pairs of brothers (Peter and Andrew, James and John). There are fishermen (common laborers), and there are wealthy professionals (a tax collector). There are adults and teens. Tax collecting is a job that may have taken some time (and wealth) to arrive at, which puts Matthew well into his adulthood and among the older of the group. Meanwhile, other stories give the impression that John (brother to James, a son of Zebedee) is likely among the youngest of the group. He is listed after his brother which means he is the younger of the two, and we know that he later becomes the last surviving member of the Apostles. He may be just into his teens when he begins to follow Jesus.

There is also some serious political diversity among them. Tax collectors were viewed as greedy people who had sold out to join the ranks of the ruling powers that oppressed the Jewish people. This is in stark contrast to Simon the Zealot. His name may refer to a political affiliation. He might have been a nationalist seeking a revolution (a connection historically to the Maccabean revolt and one of the insurrections during Jesus' childhood). Needless to say, there would have been some lively conversation among them all.

But why such diversity?

In the way he mixes so many groups, he clearly isn't identifying with the dominant movements of his day. Instead, God has come to re-unite people in the midst of their divisions. He's come to restore their relationships with each other even across what were some massive social boundaries. This group will be an example of the unity he has come to restore. His selection also emphasizes his reliance on the power of God—that he can use anyone. He's inviting people from a variety of backgrounds because his call is one of repentance. He's asked them to leave their previous ways to join him. In some way or another, they are all wrong. If they will simply follow Jesus, he will make them all that they need to be. It's not about where they come from—their qualifications or heritage. It's not about how good they are, their age, class, affiliations, money, prestige, or education. No particular background is necessary, only faith in him. If they will trust him, this is the perfect group.

And so he continues on his way with his fellowship of apprentices.

Jesus went throughout Galilee, teaching in their synagogues, proclaiming the good news of the kingdom, and healing every disease and sickness among the people. News about him spread all over Syria, and people brought to him all who were ill with various diseases, those suffering severe pain, the demon-possessed, those having seizures, and the paralyzed; and he healed them. Large crowds from Galilee, the Decapolis, Jerusalem, Judea and the region across the Jordan followed him.

Now when Jesus saw the crowds, he went up on a mountainside and sat down. His disciples came to him, and he began to teach them.

He's drawing the attention of folks farther and farther away. Now that he has gathered a specific group and made his intentions clear with them, it is time to sit down and teach them. He's going to set some ground rules, setting the course for their time with him and explaining what is expected as his disciples—what life in the "Kingdom of God" is all about. It's a foundation, discipleship 101. What he's about to outline isn't like anything these men have heard before. Life in this kingdom is nothing like the kingdoms most familiar to them. This is something different than the world has known. Jesus wants to be sure they hear it and understand. He's going to flesh it out for them up front even though they will probably hear these teachings repeatedly over the course of his ministry.

What follows is one of the largest chunks of Jesus' teaching that we have. People have written entire books and courses over its content. The sermon has remarkable symmetry. There's a poetic introduction, two sections of the body, and a conclusion. Here, we are going to dip our toes in the water and see what sense we can make of things.

And so it begins…

"Blessed are the poor in spirit, for theirs is the kingdom of heaven. Blessed are those who mourn, for they will be comforted. Blessed are the meek, for they will inherit the earth. Blessed are those who hunger and thirst for righteousness, for they will be filled. Blessed are the merciful, for they will be shown mercy. Blessed are the pure in heart, for they will see God. Blessed are the peacemakers,

for they will be called children of God. Blessed are those who are persecuted because of righteousness, for theirs is the kingdom of heaven.

These are known as the Beatitudes. This part is actually a poem with a meter and rhythm in the original language along with a repetitive structure. It serves as a kind of introduction to the rest of what he'll teach, ideas that will come up throughout. Each sentence begins with the word "blessed." Outside of church talk, this word isn't very common today. Here, "blessed" means something along the lines of "salvation has come to" or "happy are those who." The disciples would have been familiar with blessings and curses from the scriptures.[1] Who do you think of today as blessed or favored by God? The wealthy, the healthy, maybe the intelligent? The attractive, the athletic, the popular? The disciples' expectations might have been similar. But Jesus' list is a little odd. The people he describes as blessed would seem like anything but that to most of his listeners.

He begins with "the poor in spirit." This is an odd place to start. We usually praise things like independence, not need or humility. As Jesus said before at Matthew's dinner, he says now that this kingdom belongs to those who know their need, not those who think that they have it all together on their own. The folks who think they are hot stuff? Well, they're in for a surprise. That's what Adam and Eve thought when they ate the fruit. That's how our world came to be corrupted. The kingdom Jesus talks about is instead for those that recognize that something is wrong and beyond their power to correct, like Simon Peter. This is consistent with what we've seen so far. It's what Jesus was telling Nicodemus. And then Jesus follows this up with mention of God's kingdom—it's already theirs, like an inheritance awaiting them.

The second line has a similar form. It again gives an example of blessed people that doesn't fit what we'd expect. To mourn means to experience loss or pain, to be left longing. How is this a blessing? Surely being comfortable and safe, healthy, and struggle free—that's the real blessing, right? It's also possible that the word "mourning"

---

[1] Genesis 12:1-3, 27:27-29, 49:1-28; Numbers 6:22-27; Deuteronomy 28; Psalm 1, 32, 128; Isaiah 44:3-5

is describing regret, the tears of those who have made mistakes and are sorry. This time, Jesus follows up with mention of something still to come. It's not possible to undo what's been done, but the story isn't finished yet. There is comfort on the way. [1] What hurts will be mended, and what's lost will be restored. Will we still suffer? Will we still experience the loss of loved ones? Yes, but not forever.

The next several sentences follow this same pattern: a blessed group with something promised that is yet to come. We would think of power as the blessing, but here the power is meekness—self-control in the face of an offense like oppression. To be meek means to taste struggle. It means experiencing exploitation, abuse, neglect, false accusation, injustice, inequality... and, instead of erupting with anger in response, holding one's tongue and choosing words wisely. It means resisting the urge to scream, break things, or throw words and punches. Which is real strength, controlling someone else or controlling yourself? This is not how we typically think of power.

And again, meekness is attached to a promise of something still to come.[2] This time it's an inheritance of *the whole earth*. Kind of puts things into perspective. Imagine being an oppressed people, a minority that has lost its home, been exiled and transported in a world of harsh rulers, tyrants, taxers, withholders, restrictors, abusers, murderers and more. Jesus is encouraging them to know real strength, and one day that oppression will end. They will have a home again, the entire world. It will all be theirs, as it was in the beginning. This isn't just some spiritual paradise, it's all of creation restored in its entirety.

Next is those that hunger for what is good and just. In a world full of evil, injustice can be infuriating. Massive problems that plague the globe—starvation, disease, abuse, poverty—and for those who long to see things done right? Jesus says they are blessed, because one day *it will happen.* It isn't always going to be this way. This hunger for justice will be satisfied.[3]

"Blessed are the merciful." To show someone mercy often means to have experienced wrongdoing. Mercy is an act of kindness that forgives. It's sparing someone and letting them off the hook. It's

---

[1] Isaiah 25:8   [2] Psalm 37:10-11   [3] Psalm 17:14-15

forgiving a debt or wrong to set someone free. In Jesus' time, the word was also used generally to describe unwarranted kindness or compassion. Jesus says that God will mimic the behavior of the merciful. Forgivers will be forgiven. Those who are kind will be shown kindness. The givers will be given to.

Those who are pure in heart? They'll see God. But what does pure in heart mean? Being authentic and genuine. It's not hiding behind masks or pretending to be something or someone else. Here, it's like that straightforwardness is matched by a God who will be seen face to face, exposed and plain to us. Who hasn't called out to God wondering where he went? Who hasn't felt like God was nowhere to be found? One day, there will be no more obstacles, veils, or barriers. For those who are raw and honest, God's presence will be known fully, and he will be seen plainly.

The people who make peace will be called God's children. They are the reconcilers, the menders, the restorers, the healers of relationships and communities. This will be recognizable because they resemble their father. That's what he is like. That is who Jesus is. They are reflecting that image from which they were created, and it will be seen. What more could someone want than to be *like* God, to be known as one of God's children?

And finally, Jesus addresses the persecuted, people who are slandered and suffer as a result of doing good. Like the people in the first Beatitude (poor in spirit), theirs *is* the kingdom. Rejection and exile lead to the promise of a home with God. Somehow, these persecuted ones have staked a claim. In the face of suffering or loss, these people are given a guarantee. It will all be worth it in the end.

At this point, Jesus has finished the Beatitudes by coming back around to the start again. The first and the last speak of a kingdom belonging to people in the present, while those in between speak of things still to come. This kingdom of heaven is both now and later. It's present and tangible for some, but hasn't completely arrived. This story isn't over yet, and it isn't what most would expect.

And if the Beatitudes weren't surprising enough, they are just the introduction of the sermon.

"Blessed are you when people insult you, persecute you and falsely say all kinds of evil against you because of me. Rejoice and be glad, because great is your reward in heaven, for in the same way they persecuted the prophets who were before you.

Jesus repeats himself but this time connects persecution to what has happened in the past. If people are facing such hardships, they aren't alone. In fact, such struggles were common among the great spiritual leaders who came before them. Those who are treated in this way are taking part in the very same story and can rejoice because of faith in what will come. They aren't alone. Their experience is shared with many of those they revere.

"You are the salt of the earth. But if the salt loses its saltiness, how can it be made salty again? It is no longer good for anything except to be thrown out and trampled underfoot. You are the light of the world. A town built on a hill cannot be hidden. Neither do people light a lamp and put it under a bowl. Instead they put it on its stand, and it gives light to everyone in the house. In the same way, let your light shine before others, that they may see your good deeds and glorify your Father in heaven.

This is pretty direct. Jesus is addressing a group of unimpressive people here and claiming that they are like salt and light to the world around them. Does he remember to whom he is speaking? These people are nobodies. They are commoners. They are failures, under-qualified and inadequate as disciples. So what is he trying to say? Salt enriches and preserves. Light allows people to see. In the listeners' landscapes, cities were often located on the tops of hills. At night, the city lights were often the only lights that people could see. But what good is salt once it goes bad, or light if it's under a bowl? These people are asked to preserve and enrich something, God's goodness in the midst of a decaying world.

Somehow, this strange audience is to be these things, like a light in darkness, standing out and not shy about it. They aren't to hide or separate themselves. They are to interact with the world in the open so that people may see what's happening and recognize God in it, even thanking God for it. Living this way reveals the character of God to the world at a time that he is otherwise somewhat hidden. This is central to their purpose in the world, mirroring and continuing God's goodness as light in dark and rotting places, because God is coming back. God is at work again. Can you imagine leading a life that leads people to thank God for your presence?

"Do not think that I have come to abolish the Law or the Prophets; I have not come to abolish them but to fulfill them. For truly I tell you, until heaven and earth disappear, not the smallest letter, not the least stroke of a pen, will by any means disappear from the Law until everything is accomplished.

The "Law and the Prophets" is a way of referring to portions of the Hebrew scriptures. He's making it clear here that he hasn't come to do away with all that. At the same time, this seems to set up where he's about to go next. He's going to address their understanding of God's laws, and some will likely question if he's throwing all the laws away. His answer is no. He's coming to fulfill them, not throw them out. He's the next piece, moving the story towards its completion. In fact, he is the culmination of things up to this point. It's all connected and has been building throughout the ages for this special time and particular climax. Nothing will be thrown away until all of heaven and earth disappear.

"Therefore, anyone who sets aside one of the least of these commandments and teaches others accordingly will be called least in the kingdom of heaven, but whoever practices and teaches these commands will be called great in the kingdom of heaven.

Having already asserted the significance of the Hebrew scriptures (that won't pass away), he is now going to show them real "greatness" as if his own words are on par with God's commands in the law or even surpass them. His teaching is the path and the way to live in this kingdom. His teaching is now the standard by which one will be measured. This is a HUGE claim and would have caught his listeners' attention. They have only ever seen the laws of Moses as this standard. How can Jesus say that he is greater than Moses? It's no wonder that people thought that he was trying to "abolish" these laws. But, as we will see, Jesus doesn't throw them out but explains them to encompass the real intentions behind these teachings, taking them far deeper than understood before. This isn't about making some cut or determining who is "in" and "out" of the kingdom. Rather, Jesus is about to reveal the path to what really is "great" and "least" in the eyes of God, and it will contradict much of what they have heard.

> *"For I tell you that unless your righteousness surpasses that of the Pharisees and the teachers of the law, you will certainly not enter the kingdom of heaven.*

Now this would have been a little shocking. The Pharisees as a group were known for their extreme devotion to the law. The idea of surpassing their "righteousness" would have seemed absurd. Even more shocking, Jesus is saying that if someone isn't *better* than the Pharisees then they won't enter the kingdom. If this is true, how can anyone enter? A second ago, it sounded like various groups (poor in spirit, persecuted because of goodness) already belonged to the kingdom. Now, he's talking about three groups: people outside of this kingdom, the least in it, and the greatest in it. And the Pharisees, commonly viewed as the most "righteous" people, are outside.

This is scandalous. Good is not what it seems.

He's saying they've got it wrong. Want to know what truly is good? Want to know real greatness? In the midst of numerous differing ideologies about what people should do so that God might be pleased and restore them, Jesus claims to have the real answer. It isn't what everyone else has been saying (including the Pharisees). Remember Nicodemus—one must be born again. Something is dead. Everyone is in need, and this is the foundation of Jesus' teaching, not our believed goodness or purity (the approach of the Pharisees). Once someone understands this, with God's help they can begin to do something beautiful and good. Once someone embraces this truth, they can begin the journey of participation in God's kingdom.

Ready to see what that looks like?

MISINFORMED
Matthew 5:21-48

In the beginning, God's word separated darkness from light. Here, Jesus is going to do the same. He's going to explain what is good and what is bad, separating and distinguishing between darkness and light. The next section of the sermon begins the body of the teaching. Jesus is going to use the different things people often said in order to change the way they understand and apply a number of laws from the scriptures. He's going to call attention to some things that have fallen by the wayside and call out the way that some of these laws have been altered and abused. Jesus is about to set the record straight. These six chunks that follow all begin with, "You've heard it said... But I tell you." In this way, Jesus is speaking as if he holds the same authority as the laws of scripture, the very words of God. At the same time, he is expanding these laws as if he knows the true understanding of their original purposes. He speaks as if he was the one behind all of these laws to begin with.

> *"You have heard that it was said to the people long ago, 'You shall not murder, and anyone who murders will be subject to judgment.' But I tell you that anyone who is angry with a brother or sister will be subject to judgment. Again, anyone who says to a brother or sister, 'Raca,' is answerable to the court. And anyone who says, 'You fool!' will be in danger of the fire of hell.*

He starts by quoting a passage of scripture[1] and then gives its true meaning. It's from one of their most basic and familiar passages—the Ten Commandments. Where they were most concerned with the action, he highlights motives—one's internal disposition toward someone, such as malice, anger, or holding someone in contempt. He then connects this internal motive to slander, another form of action it often takes (besides murder). "Raca" is a term of contempt that was viewed as wrong and punishable in their courts (though not in the law of Moses). But Jesus takes it further. Our language isn't just to be grouped as good and

---

[1] Exodus 20:13

118

bad words. It's not just a matter of what word is used. It's a matter of motive, an attitude of the heart. While today we have all sorts of "bad words" that will raise eyebrows, Jesus says someone shouldn't even call another person a fool. Why? Holding someone in contempt is a poison that leads to things like murder and slander.

> *"Therefore, if you are offering your gift at the altar and there remember that your brother or sister has something against you, leave your gift there in front of the altar. First go and be reconciled to them; then come and offer your gift.*

> *"Settle matters quickly with your adversary who is taking you to court. Do it while you are still together on the way, or your adversary may hand you over to the judge, and the judge may hand you over to the officer, and you may be thrown into prison. Truly I tell you, you will not get out until you have paid the last penny.*

It's not just about your contempt toward someone, but another's anger with you. Don't slander, but if someone is at odds with you, take the initiative to mend that bridge. In fact, this is of such importance to God that if you think of this while in the middle of worship, stop. Go and take care of it. Be peacemakers. This is true worship and of more importance than your offerings. God wants reconciliation, and we are to reflect that priority in our lives. In the present day, this teaching is actually the foundation of greeting times in church services (which used to be called "passing the peace"). It is a chance for people to mend bridges before the service begins. God's reconciliation with us is to propel our unity with others. The example he uses of being handed over to the judge highlights the risk of delaying resolution.

> *"You have heard that it was said, 'You shall not commit adultery.' But I tell you that anyone who looks at a woman lustfully has already committed adultery with her in his heart. If your right eye causes you to stumble, gouge it out and throw it away. It is better for you to lose one part of your body than for your whole body to be thrown into hell. And if your right hand causes you to stumble, cut it off and throw it*

away. It is better for you to lose one part of your body than for your whole body to go into hell.

Again, this is from the Ten Commandments.[1] They know this, it's wrong to have an affair. But he goes further and connects this external action to the internal heart condition, lust. Their law also condemns being covetous (jealous) of a neighbor's wife,[2] but this was apparently getting ignored. Jesus says lust is a form of adultery. How serious is it? Important enough to cut off or remove part of a body. To our knowledge, none of the disciples mutilated themselves. The example Jesus gives, though, makes it clear that sin is a big deal. It's destructive and needs to be addressed. If not, it can damage and consume us. Delaying or avoiding things only risks greater harm in the end. We need to hunger for what is good, not what is destructive. We need to have self-control. Even though it's easier to recognize actions than thoughts, our hearts need to be pure.

"It has been said, 'Anyone who divorces his wife must give her a certificate of divorce.' But I tell you that anyone who divorces his wife, except for sexual immorality, makes her the victim of adultery, and anyone who marries a divorced woman commits adultery.

This is confrontational. Like today, divorce was pretty common in their society. In Jesus' time, men were the ones that initiated divorce, and a man could divorce a woman for most any reason. This left women incredibly vulnerable.

Jesus connects adultery with divorce, but he flips the responsible party. Doing so, he acknowledges the union that occurs in marriage but claims that men are *making* women commit adultery through their flippant approach to divorce by preventing women the possibility of following through with their marriage vows. It's as if the marriage union still remains even when someone is divorced, and men are causing their ex-wives to violate the marriage covenant as they are remarried (and sexually united with someone else). The exception to Jesus' statement is the woman who is already an adulteress because she has already committed the sin on her own

---

[1] Exodus 20:14   [2] Exodus 20:17

120

accord. Focusing on the legal parameters of divorce, Jesus' listeners had lost sight of God's designs in marriage and neglected the condition of the heart (the union that occurs through sex and marriage).

> *"Again, you have heard that it was said to the people long ago, 'Do not break your oath, but fulfill to the Lord the vows you have made.' But I tell you, do not swear an oath at all: either by heaven, for it is God's throne; or by the earth, for it is his footstool; or by Jerusalem, for it is the city of the Great King. And do not swear by your head, for you cannot make even one hair white or black. All you need to say is simply 'Yes' or 'No'; anything beyond this comes from the evil one.*

The quotation he uses seems to differentiate between types of oaths (to people, and to God) and the way people placed priority on the oaths made to the Lord. The saying he quotes about oaths doesn't occur in scripture. It must have been a common phrase from their day. Although the significance of oaths was emphasized in the law (being faithful and trustworthy),[1] in practice, apparently people could break promises if oaths weren't explicitly to God. Jesus says, is there a difference? Is any oath not taken before God?

Jesus uses some examples of things they were swearing on to point this out and arrives at an interesting conclusion—why make oaths to begin with? Does the truth of the promise depend on what is being sworn upon? It's absurd that we would swear by one thing, like God's temple, as if it's ok to break that *kind* of oath. Be truthful. Follow through. Don't lie. Any perversion of this is from the devil who is the deceiver. Want to be like him or like God? We need to be genuine and honest, pure of heart, not deceitful.

> *"You have heard that it was said, 'Eye for eye, and tooth for tooth.' But I tell you, do not resist an evil person. If anyone slaps you on the right cheek, turn to them the other cheek also. And if anyone wants to sue you and take your shirt, hand over your coat as well. If anyone forces you to go one*

---

[1] Numbers 30

mile, go with them two miles. Give to the one who asks you, and do not turn away from the one who wants to borrow from you.

This may be the most difficult and controversial passage of the teaching. There's a lot of debate about these verses and what Jesus means. The standard of "eye for an eye" comes from scripture.[1] In the ancient world rife with revenge killings where a rape could lead to the slaughter of an entire city,[2] God gave them a standard for what was fair punishment. God brought order to the chaos. Instead of limiting revenge, however, "an eye for an eye" appears to have been used to justify it at times. Have you ever thought, "well they did so-and-so, so I will also in return," as a reason for doing something you knew otherwise was wrong? Fair punishment, not revenge, was the purpose of this law. Unfortunately, in the Roman Empire, the Jewish people were an oppressed minority ruled by foreigners who had rights and privileges that Jews lacked. This "eye for eye" passage may have fueled Jewish people's hatred of the authorities and even led them to justify crimes against the ruling powers.

When struck, we naturally want to hit back. This is pretty dangerous, especially when you are an oppressed people. Instead of fighting, Jesus says, present your other cheek. This doesn't pretend nothing happened, it draws attention to the fact that you won't be drawn into a fight. Why not just diffuse the situation? Don't participate in destruction or abuse. It's hard to pick a fight with someone who doesn't fight back.

If someone is trying to take the clothes off your back? Just hand the clothes over. It's absurd to leave someone standing naked. This isn't referring to theft, but a courtroom setting to enact just payment for something. Arguments can escalate and get ridiculous as people try to reason about restitution. Why not just cooperate peacefully? If things have gone too far, cooperate and draw attention to the absurdity of the situation.

As for being forced to walk distances, Roman soldiers could legally interrupt someone and require them to carry their gear (weighing about 50 pounds) for up to a mile. This privilege was

---

[1] Exodus 21:23-24; Leviticus 24:17-20   [2] Genesis 34

certainly abused. Jesus says, instead of arguing about carrying supplies, go an extra mile. It wasn't legal for soldiers to require people to haul their gear for two miles, so walking an extra mile would call out the ridiculousness of the law. It's harder to exploit someone who goes to such extreme ends that it makes you uncomfortable (and that may get you in trouble). All this kindness also spares the person committing these offenses such as hitting or stealing from being guilty any more of the crime. Is it stealing when the "victim" willingly gives to you? Is it abusing power when someone willfully serves you?

Jesus connects this standard for fairness to generosity and grace. We need to be cautious of the way that our desire for justice, when fueled by anger, can turn into revenge. Instead of retribution, why not peacefully call out the injustice and turn it into a gift with kindness? These actions draw attention to something absurd, and then overwhelm the offender with obscene generosity. Acting in this way seizes the opportunity to make a powerful statement. It also values and loves the antagonist, not just the abused person. Historically, this behavior has also proven to be an effective and non-violent way of addressing forms of systematic oppression. It is difficult and takes a lot of self-control. It's merciful. It's peaceful. It's meek.

> *"You have heard that it was said, 'Love your neighbor and hate your enemy.' But I tell you, love your enemies and pray for those who persecute you, that you may be children of your Father in heaven. He causes his sun to rise on the evil and the good, and sends rain on the righteous and the unrighteous. If you love those who love you, what reward will you get? Are not even the tax collectors doing that? And if you greet only your own people, what are you doing more than others? Do not even pagans do that?*

Maybe I was wrong. *This* might be the most difficult and controversial passage of the sermon. The first part, "Love your neighbor," is again from scripture (and includes a command against seeking revenge).[1] The second part, "Hate your enemy," is not. The phrase must have been common in Jesus' listeners' society, though. Here, Jesus obliterates it. Loving a neighbor, who is likely friendly, even kin, and probably shares one's ethnicity, isn't that hard. It's easy to love people who you know well or are nice, and anyone can hate an enemy. But what does it mean to love or pray for an enemy? What does this look like in response to a rival, political opponent, bully, cruel boss, or someone like a terrorist? This is incredibly uncomfortable. Jesus points to God as the example. God is generous to all, even those that are evil. God should be our example.

Jesus mentions reward in heaven, but these situations don't seem otherwise rewarding. And these good actions don't outweigh our wrongdoing, as if our sins and good deeds could be balanced on a scale. Forgiveness for our sins can only come from God. But walking in obedience like this builds something like a credit with God, a reward that is yet to come.

This is meekness. This is peacemaking. This is mercy, and enduring persecution. This is living in the kingdom of God in a way that we "might be called Sons of God." If we are going to look like God, we are going to defy expectations. We are going to resemble something that is not of this world (born of the Spirit, not just flesh). This need not be a surprise. We are going to be different, and not simply for the sake of being different. It's because we are reflecting something heavenly working in the world.

Finally, Jesus closes this section of the body with a comment.

"Be perfect, therefore, as your heavenly Father is perfect.

This is also a passage from their scripture.[2] Perfect is a synonym for holy, a quality of goodness, purity, and wholeness. Perfection, holiness, is what distinguishes God from us (due to our imperfection). It, in contrast to our sin, is related to the separation that was experienced when Adam and Eve were exiled from Eden. Jesus is inviting us down a path to resemble God again. This was the whole purpose of their laws to begin with, that the people of Israel might resemble God to the world. We were created for this. It's good.

---

[1] Leviticus 19:18   [2] Leviticus 19:2

In the midst of all sorts of confusion and distortion of God's intentions within these laws, Jesus is bringing clarity and sight.

This finishes Jesus' teaching on the things people have been saying. In the second half of the body of the sermon, he will break down the things people are doing with some colorful commentary. As he does, he will continue to provide examples of true goodness that exemplify the qualities introduced in the Beatitudes.

SEVEN
A Voice on the Mountain (Part 2)

TO BEGIN THE SECOND portion of the body of his teaching, Jesus dives deeper into the motivations behind different actions. Where the previous six sections of the body were guided by the things people often say, this portion will be shaped by observations of things people commonly do. He has already addressed the various ways that different behaviors are often over-emphasized to the neglect of the heart or motive (interior) behind them. He is going to continue this now using examples that are generally praised as good or "righteous" deeds.

Bad Examples
Matthew 6:1-7:6

> *"Be careful not to practice your righteousness in front of others to be seen by them. If you do, you will have no reward from your Father in heaven.*

Who is the audience for our good deeds? This is of utmost importance. We can do what would appear to be good, but if done with the wrong motive then our actions lose their value to God. Who is being worshiped by these actions, God, others, or ourselves? Are we simply trying to look good? Like gathering fig leaves for garments, are we trying to cover our nakedness and make a new identity for ourselves? Doing this accomplishes nothing.

"So when you give to the needy, do not announce it with trumpets, as the hypocrites do in the synagogues and on the streets, to be honored by others. Truly I tell you, they have received their reward in full. But when you give to the needy, do not let your left hand know what your right hand is doing, so that your giving may be in secret. Then your Father, who sees what is done in secret, will reward you.

Jesus assumes that we are in fact giving to the needy but doesn't say much about who exactly, how, or when. Regardless, this isn't to be done as by the "hypocrites." This is a strong word. To be a hypocrite means to be two-faced. It's deception, posturing, insincerity, and duplicity. Everyone makes mistakes, but hypocrisy isn't simply erring. It is willful. It is hiding behind a false self.

It's the opposite of who God is.

Did people really announce gifts with trumpets? Not exactly, but there were several large coffers at the temple known as "trumpets" due to their shape (like a big horn). There, people would publicly make their gifts in a manner that could be pretty noisy (imagine metal coins jingling across metal). The setup drew attention to the action. Still today, generosity is often trumpeted with all sorts of plaques, memorials, and special privileges. Is this outward acclaim the motive to one's giving? If it is, then Jesus says the giving is of no value to God. The only reward for this kind of generosity is the praise received from people.

Instead, we are to give as though our own body is unaware what is happening. It's subtle. It's for the purpose of meeting a need, helping, being generous as God has been generous with us. It's about honoring God, not ourselves. This is true giving. This is where there is true reward.

"And when you pray, do not be like the hypocrites, for they love to pray standing in the synagogues and on the street corners to be seen by others. Truly I tell you, they have received their reward in full. But when you pray, go into your room, close the door and pray to your Father, who is unseen. Then your Father, who sees what is done in secret, will reward you. And when you pray, do not keep on babbling

like pagans, for they think they will be heard because of their
many words. Do not be like them, for your Father knows
what you need before you ask him.

Jesus uses the same structure again but to talk about prayer. As
with giving, he assumes that we are actually praying. And again, it is
not about appearances. Who is this for, and what is it all about? Being
seen by people or being heard by God? The motive matters. This is
beautiful. Ever felt like you weren't good enough to pray or didn't
know the special words? It doesn't matter how it sounds. Praying
isn't about words but your heart. You don't need to ramble or sound
fancy, just be humble, open, and honest. God already knows.

"This, then, is how you should pray:

'Our Father in heaven, hallowed be your name, your
kingdom come, your will be done, on earth as it is in heaven.
Give us today our daily bread. And forgive us our debts, as
we also have forgiven our debtors. And lead us not into
temptation, but deliver us from the evil one.'

Jesus even gives us an example known as The Lord's Prayer,
something that has been recited by Christians throughout the ages.
While it may be good to repeat, it was intended as a model for things
that we can pray about as we speak to God. I'll just touch on a few
things.

It addresses God intimately as Father. It's personal, not some
formal speech. Then, it moves into adoration. "Hallowed" means
holy. It's like bowing before the king. It's humble (poor in spirit) and
recognizes things in their right place. God is God, not us. This means
that in prayer we are to be both intimate and respectful. God doesn't
demand that we cease to be human when we pray.

Next, Jesus invites (hungers for) God's kingdom to come, that it
would exist on earth. This is our purpose in the world, to reflect the
affairs of this heavenly society in the present darkness and distortion
as beacons of hope for what lies ahead. It also implies that God's
kingdom has not yet arrived. God may be present and active, but
there is still plenty of unfinished business. Jesus also makes a request
for provision. "Daily bread" just means having enough for the day,

nothing more. It's simple and it is limited. It highlights simplicity through daily dependence on God, not lavish demands for prosperity. The prayer makes another request for forgiveness. Like a daily provision of bread, we require God's continual forgiveness because we will still make mistakes. We need to remember that we are still imperfect. We just need to remain humble and bring that imperfection before God our great doctor. Jesus connects this to forgiving others. We are to forgive just as we would ask for forgiveness. It's not just a request, it's an action. It is being merciful as we ask for mercy. It is making peace with others as we seek peace from God.

And finally, the prayer asks for direction. Lead us. Not toward temptation (the serpent and the fruit), but to deliverance and freedom (restoration, victory). It's proactive, not just reactive. This is hungering for righteousness. This prayer exemplifies the Beatitudes in its embodiment of humility, mercy, and pure motives.

"For if you forgive other people when they sin against you, your heavenly Father will also forgive you. But if you do not forgive others their sins, your Father will not forgive your sins.

Jesus continues to point to this theme of forgiveness and there is an interesting reciprocity. It's as though forgiveness lies at the center of things—necessary for our peace with God. If we truly desire peace and forgiveness, then we are to live it. Prayer isn't simply a matter of words muttered quietly before God, it is a message communicated with our lives. There is a connection between our treatment of others and our relationship with God. Only the forgiving are able to receive God's forgiveness.

After finishing with his discussion of prayer, Jesus returns again to the "hypocrite" pattern.

"When you fast, do not look somber as the hypocrites do, for they disfigure their faces to show others they are fasting. Truly I tell you, they have received their reward in full. But when you fast, put oil on your head and wash your face, so that it will not be obvious to others that you are fasting, but

only to your Father, who is unseen; and your Father, who sees what is done in secret, will reward you.

We've touched on fasting a little bit before. As with giving to others and praying, Jesus assumes that this is something that people are doing. For the most part, the Jewish people participated in fasts collectively as a part of their practice of various holidays. From the way Jesus talks about it, it sounds as if fasting had become quite a show which included some dramatic displays of behavior. Who is this behavior for, and what is it about? Is it of any real value to God? Our motive matters.

Jesus has just broken down three of the predominant religious practices of their day: giving, praying, and fasting. He's identified the way they are mishandled. These acts were about appearing good, not genuine worship of God. The heart is of utmost importance to God. Recalling his conversation with the woman at the well, Jesus is addressing what it means to worship God in "Spirit and in truth," the kind of worship that God desires.

Up next, Jesus addresses some broader practices and continues his critique of things that people often do. Instead of focusing on the "as the hypocrites" theme and general religious behavior, he'll now advise against some of the behaviors common to all people. He'll use the basic instruction "Do not."

"Do not store up for yourselves treasures on earth, where moths and vermin destroy, and where thieves break in and steal. But store up for yourselves treasures in heaven, where moths and vermin do not destroy, and where thieves do not break in and steal. For where your treasure is, there your heart will be also.

Have you ever seen someone store up treasure before? Money has a way of causing its own trouble. Having nice things comes with a cost. Things wear out, get stolen, have to be insured, protected, and fixed. They are temporary. Despite our efforts, they will not pass through the grave. Instead, why not focus on what can endure, that which extends beyond death? There are treasures that do not rot and cannot be taken. By now, Jesus has spoken several times about real reward from God through forgiveness, generosity, and mercy. It comes from pursuing what is good with a pure heart. Sadly, material possessions can become attached to our hearts, and we don't want our hearts to decay and rot.

What we desire matters. What we desire shapes us.

"The eye is the lamp of the body. If your eyes are healthy, your whole body will be full of light. But if your eyes are unhealthy, your whole body will be full of darkness. If then the light within you is darkness, how great is that darkness!

Here we go about lights again. Jesus compares our eyes to lights. To have a "good eye" was a phrase that meant to be generous. If someone is generous, they will be full of things like joy and compassion. Being greedy and worrisome has the opposite effect; it drains life away from a person. What do we see? What do we search for and look to? What is the source of our light? What happens if we look to the wrong things, like money, to make us happy?

"No one can serve two masters. Either he will hate the one and love the other, or he will be devoted to the one and despise the other. You cannot serve both God and money.

Money is essentially a tool, but I think we are all familiar with greed and the basic ways money can take control. It's scary to think about what this means, to be a servant of money. Is this our treasure? Is this our lamp and our light? Is this what we are looking to as our God? We have to choose, it's one or the other. Money and God can't share a throne.

"Therefore I tell you, do not worry about your life, what you will eat or drink; or about your body, what you will wear. Is not life more than food, and the body more than clothes? Look at the birds of the air; they do not sow or reap or store away in barns, and yet your heavenly Father feeds them. Are you not much more valuable than they? Can any one of you by worrying add a single hour to your life?

Where will I go? What will I do? Which restaurant? Which job? On, and on, and on. Worry and stress are basic to our lives. But why?

It's one thing to consider the future, but something different to worry. What do we gain by it? Why are we so afraid? It's so easy for all these decisions and concerns to rob us of the basic joys of life. We lose sight of the real priorities. What if we actually viewed things in their right places? What if we could accurately prioritize and embrace each moment rather than fear it? Would we not be more fully alive?

Living simply day-to-day is incredibly foreign to how we think. Here, Jesus gives an example. If God can supply for so many animals, is there not enough for us? Are we not more valuable to him? Worrying will accomplish nothing. It overwhelms and cripples. It expresses a lack of trust. It is a thief and a liar.

> *"And why do you worry about clothes? See how the flowers of the field grow. They do not labor or spin. Yet I tell you that not even Solomon in all his splendor was dressed like one of these. If that is how God clothes the grass of the field, which is here today and tomorrow is thrown into the fire, will he not much more clothe you – you of little faith?*

Now, another example. People obsess over fine clothes. It's basically a way to cover ourselves with money, the work of our hands. We try to make ourselves beautiful. Here Jesus points to the wealthiest and most successful figure in Jewish history, Solomon, and says that flowers are better dressed.

That's right, flowers.

We think we can provide for ourselves. We think we can make ourselves beautiful and more valuable. We think we can prove ourselves good and make an adequate covering for our nakedness. We think we can clothe ourselves better than God. We are wrong. Who are we trusting? What if we could just trust God, the value and beauty he has given us and the "clothing" he provides? Can we seek our identity from him instead of everyone else? Or will we go on making our own way?

> *"So do not worry, saying, 'What shall we eat?' or 'What shall we drink?' or 'What shall we wear?' For the pagans run after all these things, and your heavenly Father knows*

that you need them. But seek first his kingdom and his righteousness, and all these things will be given to you as well. Therefore do not worry about tomorrow, for tomorrow will worry about itself. Each day has enough trouble of its own.

God knows what he is doing. God knows what you need and is better able to provide for that than anyone. Instead of all this toil, prioritize the goodness of God's kingdom. Trust what he says and be clothed in his righteousness. Do what is good, and trust that God can take care of the rest.

"Do not judge, or you too will be judged. For in the same way you judge others, you will be judged, and with the measure you use, it will be measured to you.

"Why do you look at the speck of sawdust in your brother's eye and pay no attention to the plank in your own eye? How can you say to your brother, 'Let me take the speck out of your eye,' when all the time there is a plank in your own eye? You hypocrite, first take the plank out of your own eye, and then you will see clearly to remove the speck from your brother's eye.

In his next command, Jesus again highlights a kind of reciprocity as he did when he talked about forgiveness. As we forgive, he said, we will be forgiven. This time, he's talking about judgment. As we judge, he says, we will be judged. This is scary. It draws attention to the way that we confuse our place and role. We aren't the appointed judges. When we judge others, we take on a role that belongs to God.

But are we to confront people? Is this the same as judgment? Jesus uses a ridiculous example. I can imagine someone walking around with a 2x4 sticking out of his face. Of course, if this person was going to help a friend clear out some sawdust from their eye, they need to look in the mirror first. Take out the plank, then maybe the person can lend a hand. If not, things could get messy and everybody could get hurt. This is sound advice. The point is to help someone, not destroy them. Jesus is emphasizing our motive, our manner, and our relationship (brother). A brother is someone who is part of the clan and bears the same name (maybe that of Christian), not some stranger on the street. Jesus explains this further.

> *"Do not give dogs what is sacred; do not throw your pearls to pigs. If you do, they may trample them under their feet, and then turn and tear you to pieces.*

We need to pay attention to who we are confronting.[1] 'Pigs are seen as "unclean" in this culture. They are quite dirty, living in mud and dung to stay cool, and they have a well-known appetite, eating almost anything. To some extent, the same is true of dogs. If you've ever seen a wild or stray dog, it isn't pretty. They can be diseased and ferocious, and will also eat disgusting stuff including their own feces. What do these animals know of the value of a pearl? Similarly, there are people who have no interest whatsoever in holiness. Do they care what reflects God's character? If you throw them a pearl, they may only trample it, then turn to attack you.

Why, how, and who all matter. So we aren't to judge (pass a verdict upon someone), but there is still value to confrontation. It is for our good and that of those around us. It is basic to the pursuit of seeking God's kingdom and the attempt to accurately reflect him in our lives to the world. Yet it is also important to carefully consider who we confront.

CLOSING REMARKS
Matthew 7:7-27

Having finished with this section on the things you see people do, Jesus has finished the body of his teaching and starts to bring things to a close. Doing so, he repeatedly reconnects to the beginning of his teaching.

> *"Ask and it will be given to you; seek and you will find; knock and the door will be opened to you. For everyone who asks receives; the one who seeks finds; and to the one who knocks, the door will be opened.*

---

[1] Proverbs 9:8-9

"Which of you, if your son asks for bread, will give him a stone? Or if he asks for a fish, will give him a snake? If you, then, though you are evil, know how to give good gifts to your children, how much more will your Father in heaven give good gifts to those who ask him!

Has he covered everything? No. There is much left to learn, but fortunately we can ask God for wisdom. God listens, and if we will ask, he will guide us. If we are looking for what is good, God will show us the way. If even we understand the idea of a good gift, how much more does a God who is actually good! Can we just trust this? And did Jesus just call us evil? Ouch! This may come as a surprise. Jesus doesn't view people as the amount of good they've done weighed against the bad. It's much simpler. Anyone who has done evil has been corrupted by it and is therefore evil. In this way, no one is good. This will come up elsewhere and is actually part of the purpose of this whole sermon. Everyone is bankrupt before God and in need of forgiveness.

"So in everything, do to others what you would have them do to you, for this sums up the Law and the Prophets.

Jesus brings things back full circle to the Law and Prophets. Remember, Jesus hasn't come to abolish the scriptures but to fulfill them. Still struggling to understand what is good? Treat others as you would want them to treat you. Again, reciprocity. Justice. Fairness. This is a valuable rule that has become known throughout history as the "Golden Rule." This axiom is behind everything. It is good. It is just. God is just.

"Enter through the narrow gate. For wide is the gate and broad is the road that leads to destruction, and many enter through it. But small is the gate and narrow the road that leads to life, and only a few find it.

We are all headed somewhere. But where are we going? Jesus' teaching here is different than what the listeners have commonly seen or heard. If people will trust him and do the things he's been talking about, they will be taking a distinct path that is uncommon in their world. There aren't a lot of people on it, but it leads to life (maybe back to the tree of life). The other route? The one that looks really good and is really popular? It's deception. It leads to destruction. It is the way of the serpent and will only destroy us in the end. Remember, the bad salt, the muted lights, they just get thrown out.

"Watch out for false prophets. They come to you in sheep's clothing, but inwardly they are ferocious wolves. By their fruit you will recognize them. Do people pick grapes from thornbushes, or figs from thistles? Likewise, every good tree bears good fruit, but a bad tree bears bad fruit. A good tree cannot bear bad fruit, and a bad tree cannot bear good fruit. Every tree that does not bear good fruit is cut down and thrown into the fire. Thus, by their fruit you will recognize them.

He warns us, there will be fakers. Hypocrites. Expect it. They will look good on the outside, but inside are malicious and destructive. Pay attention to their fruit. Thorns and thistles don't give us fruit, they bring us pain and hard work. They waste valuable time and effort and leave us exhausted and disillusioned. Be careful. Consider, does the person trying to be a guide reflect what Jesus is teaching? If not, you may not want to ask this person for directions along the way. They are not salt or light.

"Not everyone who says to me, 'Lord, Lord,' will enter the kingdom of heaven, but only the one who does the will of my Father who is in heaven. Many will say to me on that day, 'Lord, Lord, did we not prophesy in your name and in your name drive out demons and in your name perform many miracles?' Then I will tell them plainly, 'I never knew you. Away from me, you evildoers!'

These roads lead somewhere, and something is coming. In the Beatitudes, the focus was the reward of the coming kingdom to its people. Apparently, when that kingdom arrives, not everyone who thinks they are included are indeed included. These are the hypocrites. All along they were fooled and didn't actually even know God. They may have even done spectacular things in his God's name, but he will turn them away. Our motives matter. It's not just about what you've done or how good we think we are. It's not about the spectacle. It's not about all the hype, or the crowds, or all the fancy things people do. Not everything that *looks* good *is* good. It's the simple and hard stuff done for the right reasons that is actually good. It's all about what God thinks, and God doesn't wear neon lights. God isn't trying to impress anyone.

> *"Therefore everyone who hears these words of mine and puts them into practice is like a wise man who built his house on the rock. The rain came down, the streams rose, and the winds blew and beat against that house; yet it did not fall, because it had its foundation on the rock. But everyone who hears these words of mine and does not put them into practice is like a foolish man who built his house on sand. The rain came down, the streams rose, and the winds blew and beat against that house, and it fell with a great crash."*

This resembles Jesus' opening comments about those who obey his commands becoming great. He's come full circle again. Want to endure? Want to survive the storm? Do what Jesus teaches. The kingdom is coming, and this is the road to life. Storms will come. Trouble will come. Be the wise man. Build on the rock (Jesus). Let him be the foundation. It will not fail you, and you will endure. Ignore him, and be without a foundation. Get washed away in the flood.

With this, Jesus finishes the sermon. We've made it through the end. It's dynamic, and a mammoth teaching that is to be a foundation for those following Jesus. This is what a life of following Jesus is to look like. This is the real path of righteousness. Our purpose is to be mirrors of God's heart and design as beacons of hope in a corrupted world. In the remainder of Jesus' ministry, we will see these principles continually on display in his own life. He's not just going to talk about these things, he's going to do them because he is God's living word.

A BRIEF RECAP
Matthew 7:28-29

He's now handed over his training manual, and it's different than what the disciples or their world expected. It's even different than many of their religious leaders have taught. This way of life will be in stark contrast to the values and behaviors of the serpent's kingdoms. It flips who the world sees as great. It highlights the overlooked and underprivileged. Instead of the wealthy, healthy, intelligent, popular, etc. who we usually think of as blessed, God is interested in those who need, hurt, hunger, and struggle. Remember that you need God, follow him, and you are the real lights in the world. Appearances can be deceiving. Motives matter to God. And all that Jesus is teaching and doing is actually the culmination of what has happened previously, not God jumping ship to start over again.

Jesus reprioritized numerous things. Using some common phrases, Jesus called out what was being overlooked and corrected the way God's instructions were getting misused. He called out the poison of slander, hatred, and contempt. God is interested in mending relationships. Jesus rebuked the harm of lust (covetousness) and sexual fantasy. This is a form of adultery, and sin is to be taken seriously and addressed severely. He corrected the abuses of divorce and pointed out that even when abiding by the law one can still do wrong and harm others. Marriage shouldn't be taken lightly. He called attention to a culture of dishonesty and deception stemming from the way that oaths were handled. We are to be honest, faithful to our promises and speak truth plainly, not twist and distort things to avoid commitments. He challenged the application of the legal standard used for justice. Instead of justifying revenge, we should be generous and kind. Instead of hatred, we should love and pray for our adversaries because that is what God does. We are to be merciful as God is merciful. He is to be our example and the guide we follow, not the serpent. God's intention all along was that we might reflect his goodness in the world. God is to be our standard and guide.

Jesus also zeroed in on our obsession with external behaviors and the common neglect of internal motives. He talked about several common religious behaviors. Who is the audience? Are we just trying to look good in front of people? If so, it's worthless to God. Is it unnoticed? God notices. Jesus said we need to pay attention to what we are treasuring and serving. Is it money? God won't stand for any rivals on the throne. We need to make our priority be that which truly matters beyond the grave, God and his kingdom. We shouldn't let the trivial concerns of each day overwhelm us. Such stresses rob us of life and joy. And we need to remember that our role here is as servants, not judges. Who, how, and why we confront people requires careful consideration or the results will be costly.

If all this isn't enough, Jesus closes with some final advice. God invites an ongoing relationship with us. We can continue to ask him as a Father for guidance. Generally, if we will treat each other fairly, we are on target with God's intent behind all of the laws. Still, we shouldn't expect this way of life to be popular or common. Instead, it's a "narrow" road. There will be fakers trying to lead us astray. And not everyone who thinks they are serving God really even knows him. But if we can trust Jesus and obey him, he is a firm foundation that will not fail us.

Having ironed out these expectations with his newly appointed apostles, Jesus sets out with them to continue his mission.

When Jesus had finished saying these things, the crowds were amazed at his teaching, because he taught as one who had authority, and not as their teachers of the law.

No one had ever heard anything like this before.

The Sermon on the Mount presents what many consider an impossible standard to live by, but this may actually be part of the point. In a climate where certain groups see themselves as good people, or "good enough" to be accepted by God, others are written off as hopeless. This is still true today. Surprisingly, Jesus has been challenging this view left and right. He's actually making the point that no one is good enough. He's addressed many ways that people have misunderstood what is good, or, who is good. It's not about how much good or bad someone does. He's repeatedly pointed to people's need for forgiveness. This entire teaching highlights the fact that everyone has made mistakes. Remember, "Blessed are the poor in spirit." Humility, repentance, honesty, motives... the difficult teachings of this sermon serve as a reminder that no one is perfect.

To think that we are "good enough" is to miss the point. Everyone is dependent upon God's kindness and forgiveness. This is the foundation of his teaching. It's why faith is so important. While people want to depend on their own power or their good deeds to save them, such efforts are actually in vain. Salvation can only come from God as a gift. But this is precisely what makes salvation so accessible.

At the same time, this isn't an argument against doing good! People were designed to resemble God as lights created to reflect the image of God. Doing so is to taste the flourishing of life God intended. Even imperfect people can still do this. And from what Jesus says, somehow our actions here echo into eternity. There's still much more to come, but what happens here in this world matters.

We are about to begin what many call the "Year of Popularity" in Jesus ministry. As you can guess, we will see Jesus' popularity soar to new heights, but with it will arrive even greater tension and turmoil. We will also continue to see many of these familiar themes developed further and further. So if you find yourself a little confused now, it's ok. Even the disciples were confused, and that will continue throughout the stories to come. As we are about to see, even one of Jesus' greatest proponents is suddenly caught in the midst of some intense confusion and doubt.

Part III

The Height of Popularity

EIGHT
Changing Times

JOHN THE BAPTIST HAS had a pretty rough turn of events. Just as things start to get interesting, he's put in prison and misses the opportunity to witness the culmination of all that he's been working toward. A victim of giving "pearls to swine" as he criticized Herod's marriage, he's still locked away in a dungeon.

FROM THE DUNGEONS
Matthew 11:2-5, 7-9, 12-15

> *When John, who was in prison, heard about the deeds of the Messiah, he sent his disciples to ask him, "Are you the one who is to come, or should we expect someone else?"*

Lonely and staring his likely death in the face, he could use some encouragement. He's surely been looking back on his life, questioning and apparently even doubting what he has accomplished. He had been so sure and gave everything to follow God. He thought that surely Jesus was the Messiah, and devoted his ministry to pointing people toward Jesus. Was he mistaken? Is this what's supposed to happen when someone serves God? Was this all really worth it?

Jesus doesn't ignore John.

> *Jesus replied, "Go back and report to John what you hear and see: The blind receive sight, the lame walk, those who*

have leprosy are cleansed, the deaf hear, the dead are raised, and the good news is proclaimed to the poor."

This sounds a lot like the scroll Jesus read in Nazareth. He refers to descriptions of the Messiah. It's a discreet way of saying, "Yes John, I am the one. Your work wasn't in vain." He's doing the things prophesied[1] about the Messiah and is exactly who John the Baptist had believed. Trapped in a cold and dark place, John must have felt incredibly relieved to hear these words. It wasn't all a waste. His work continues on, and God's kingdom is indeed advancing even if John the Baptist won't survive to see it.

As John's disciples were leaving, Jesus began to speak to the crowd about John: "What did you go out into the wilderness to see? A man dressed in fine clothes? No, those who wear fine clothes are in kings' palaces. Then what did you go out to see? A prophet? Yes, I tell you, and more than a prophet.

These people are familiar with John the Baptist. They know what has happened and that he could die any day. Is John the Baptist a fool? No. He is the specific desert prophet that had been foretold[2] who would prepare things for the Messiah. Jesus goes on to tell them that John the Baptist is a greater man than the world has ever known. Where many longed for a king to lead their revolt, John the Baptist was something else, and so is Jesus. The crowd's expectations are off. The kingdom of God isn't like what they expected. There will be no fine robes or palaces. There will be no castles or great cities. That's the temptation of the serpent, not the way of the Lord.

"From the days of John the Baptist until now, the kingdom of heaven has been subjected to violence, and violent people have been raiding it. For all the Prophets and the Law prophesied until John…Whoever has ears, let him hear."

Jesus counts John the Baptist among the great prophets and connects their work. They have all been pointing to and awaiting the coming of the Messiah, and that mission is still advancing. John the

---

[1] Isaiah 29:18-19, 35:5-6, 42:7, 61:1-2; Ezekiel 37:12-14; Micah 4:6-7; Zephaniah 3:19
[2] Isaiah 40:3-11; Malachi 3:1

Baptist was right, and they are about to witness the fulfillment of these promises from long ago. They need to pay close attention, because it's happening. Things are taking shape whether the listeners realize it or not. The climax is coming, and things are going as planned. The mission hasn't been derailed.

The revolution is coming.

AN UNINVITED GUEST
Luke 7:36-50

When one of the Pharisees invited Jesus to have dinner with him, he went to the Pharisee's house and reclined at the table.

In this period, it was common for people to host dinners in their homes. Jesus is an intriguing public figure, and so as he travels around we often find him as a guest at dinners like this. Getting invited to a dinner like this acknowledges Jesus' significance. There were also risks involved. A dinner invitation quickly connected the hosts and the guests socially and could bear serious ramifications for the host if someone behaved poorly. But although the invitation seems to communicate respect for this intriguing guest, it might have been a trap for the purpose of testing to see whether Jesus was in line with the beliefs of the Pharisees' movement.

A woman in that town who lived a sinful life learned that Jesus was eating at the Pharisee's house, so she came there with an alabaster jar of perfume. As she stood behind him at his feet weeping, she began to wet his feet with her tears. Then she wiped them with her hair, kissed them and poured perfume on them.

Well this is awkward. You don't just show up at a dinner party where you weren't invited. The detail that she'd lived a "sinful life" is referring to prostitution. In a small town, everyone would know who she is. Of all places, the house of a Pharisee may be the *worst* place for her to show up. This is the specific group of people that view her as the problem with their society. In their eyes, it's because of the sinful lives of people like her that they remain an oppressed people waiting for God's favor to return. Their typical response would have been to shame and expel people like this woman from their presence, something she had probably encountered numerous times.

This woman lives in an extremely male-dominated world where women are generally handled as property, and their culture places a very high value upon virginity. Men could also divorce a woman for any reason. After a divorce, a woman was viewed as less valuable (no longer a virgin) and it was unlikely she would remarry. In a culture where jobs were dominated by men, this left divorced women with very few options to support themselves if they weren't otherwise taken back into their families. Sadly, for some women the simple solution was prostitution, and this culture conveniently overlooked the basics of supply and demand involved and shamed such women with little accountability for the men.

Yet she comes to the dinner anyway.

This had to be terrifying. She's not there for dinner or a good discussion. She's there *only* to honor Jesus. He is the audience, and she's willing to endure whatever else may happen in order to see him. This is a desperate attempt, and she's walking into a dangerous social situation. She brings some perfume, which may be her most valuable possession, and falls at his feet weeping. She's just walked into a fire and she knows it. Was this a good idea? What will Jesus say to her? What will Jesus do? Is he like every other man at the table, or will he care about her? Will she even get the chance to see him, or will she be humiliated and thrown out?

> *When the Pharisee who had invited him saw this, he said to himself, "If this man were a prophet, he would know who is touching him and what kind of woman she is—that she is a sinner."*

It's no surprise that she is in tears. This man is shocked that Jesus would even let her *touch* his gross, grimy, and filthy feet. Keep in mind, people wore sandals and walked everywhere. Touching Jesus' feet would be a disgusting task. Because Jesus allows it, the host's view of him takes a turn for the worse. Test failed. He's thinking, "People say this guy is a prophet? Please. If he was a prophet, he'd make an example of this whore. She's the epitome of what's wrong with our nation and is keeping us from God."

Jesus answered him, "Simon, I have something to tell you."

"Tell me, teacher," he said.

"Two people owed money to a certain moneylender. One owed him five hundred denarii, and the other fifty. Neither of them had the money to pay him back, so he forgave the debts of both. Now which of them will love him more?"

Jesus knows what's going on in this guy's heart. It's full of contempt. He asks Simon (a very common name; this is not Simon Peter the disciple) a question and tells a little story. Simon pretends to respect him and addresses him as teacher. Would there have been a condescending tone to his voice? The story involves forgiving debts—one great and one small. A denarius is roughly a day's wage, so the amounts are something like a couple months' pay and a couple years' pay. Both debts are forgiven. The question, though, is about love—which person will love the lender more?
Where is Jesus going with this?

Simon replied, "I suppose the one who had the bigger debt forgiven."

An obvious answer, Simon is thinking, "What do you want with this silly story?"

"You have judged correctly," Jesus said.

Then he turned toward the woman and said to Simon, "Do you see this woman? I came into your house. You did not give me any water for my feet, but she wet my feet with her tears and wiped them with her hair. You did not give me a kiss, but this woman, from the time I entered, has not stopped kissing my feet. You did not put oil on my head, but she has poured perfume on my feet.

I love it. *Looking at her,* Jesus addresses the host. She is the one that he sees. She is the one that matters most to him. In the middle of her humiliation, Jesus contrasts the two of them, pointing out all that the host hasn't done while praising what the woman has done. He sees her. He receives her. He speaks on her behalf and in her defense. Then, he praises her. All the while, he slams Simon.

Hospitality is an important virtue in this culture, and Jesus calls out a number of ways that this "important" host has failed. He should have at least provided for his guests that they might wash their feet. Or, if he really wanted to honor them, he would have made arrangements for a servant to wash their feet as they entered. He did not greet Jesus with a kiss, a common greeting that welcomed someone as if they were family or a close friend. He did not provide the customary provision of oil (moisturizer and salve in a dry climate). Was Jesus really a valued guest? Yet she has gone above and beyond, personally washing his feet with her own hair and tears, providing fine perfumes to freshen up. Which one of them has loved him?

> *"Therefore, I tell you, her many sins have been forgiven—as her great love has shown. But whoever has been forgiven little loves little."*

What?!

It's absurd that Jesus let her approach him to begin with. Then, he confronts the very host that invited him. Now, praising a prostitute for her *love*, Jesus says her sins are forgiven and that Simon has been forgiven little! A religious person, Simon has constantly been offering numerous sacrifices and prayers as a plea for forgiveness, and Jesus here is saying God is happier with her, the whore, than the zealous and religious Pharisee.

This is a punch in the gut.

> *Then Jesus said to her, "Your sins are forgiven."*

> *The other guests began to say among themselves, "Who is this who even forgives sins?"*

In case it wasn't clear, Jesus says it directly to her. Everyone realizes what he's saying. Who does this guy think that he is? One's sins aren't for an individual to forgive like that. No one can forgive sins but God!

Once again, this is blasphemy.

Jesus said to the woman, "Your faith has saved you; go in peace."

Faith. She has been saved from her sins through her faith in Jesus. He is the savior.

In all the things people pay attention to, Jesus cuts right to the point. This isn't about what you've done. This isn't about how good you are, or how good you think you are. Peace with God isn't something someone *deserves*, it's a gift. When we will ask, when we will approach with faith as this woman did, we will be saved. Our sins are forgiven. And this forgiveness is like a rocket fuel for love. When someone understands what it means to be freed from their sin, it propels them to love in a similar way. It's a gift worth sharing and inspires radical generosity, compassion, patience, mercy, and more.

Can you imagine the scene? Can you imagine how liberating this had to be for the woman? She came simply to honor him, and he forgave her and even commended her faith! She came carrying loads of guilt, trapped in shame over her lifestyle and who she had become, and Jesus removed the weight. She entered the home vulnerable as if naked before them all—her accusers—and was showered with praise. This special man who appears to speak on God's behalf says that everything is all right. She can live in peace again with God. The most important person she knows actually values her. He knows her, sees her, cares for her, and has restored her identity. Jesus invites her to new life and out of the condition of the curse within which she was trapped.

This story displays much of what Jesus has just described in the Sermon on the Mount. We have the significant contrast between motives in the woman's authenticity and Simon's hypocrisy. She came humbly to honor Jesus and beg for forgiveness, while he was proud, selfish and judgmental. Once again, Jesus is the life of the party—there's never a dull moment around him. He's making friends and enemies as he goes, and not with the people who would be most advantageous. And this certainly isn't the last time that we will see Jesus in controversy.

THE STORYTELLER
Matthew 13:1-9, 18-30, 37-43, 31-33, 44-51

It's likely that Jesus had a basic set of teachings that he would share everywhere he went. As he's performing miracles, telling parables, giving lectures, and being confronted with questions, he uses different teaching methods to get his foundational message across. This means that the disciples likely saw and heard some of these teachings and miracles, or variations of them, quite often. Repetition is a valuable teacher.

One of the ways that Jesus often taught people was through the use of a kind of story called a parable (like the story he told about debts at the dinner party). These short stories were basic illustrations that used things from everyday life to communicate an idea. It's quite possible he was even using examples readily at hand and pointing to something nearby as he spoke. Jesus recognized pictures of truth all around him and was a master at making these connections with his audience.

Speaking in parables functioned as a natural filter. It required that the listener pay attention and actually *want* to know what Jesus is saying. If the listener didn't, they'd probably just hear some things about seeds or farmers and not really catch what is being said. Later on, speaking in parables will conveniently help to conceal some of the controversial things he'll say and ensure that things don't get too out of hand. But sometimes, the stories can just be confusing, and even his disciples were occasionally left scratching their heads. Fortunately, he explains a few of these parables here for us.

> *...Jesus went out of the house and sat by the lake. Such large crowds gathered around him that he got into a boat and sat in it, while all the people stood on the shore. Then he told them many things in parables, saying: "A farmer went out to sow his seed. As he was scattering the seed, some fell along the path, and the birds came and ate it up. Some fell on rocky places, where it did not have much soil. It sprang up quickly,*

149

because the soil was shallow. But when the sun came up, the plants were scorched, and they withered because they had no root. Other seed fell among thorns, which grew up and choked the plants. Still other seed fell on good soil, where it produced a crop—a hundred, sixty or thirty times what was sown. Whoever has ears, let them hear."

This parable paints a basic picture. A farmer is planting his crop. The seed lands in four different places. It lands on the path where it can't take root, and birds quickly eat it. It lands on the rocks where it can't establish its roots in needed soil, and it gets scorched in the heat. It lands among thorns (think weeds) which hog its needed resources (water and sunlight) so it dies. And finally, some lands on good soil and multiplies exponentially. That's one in four that actually produce fruit. This is hard work and seems like some rough odds except that the lone healthy plant goes on to produce 30, 60, and even 100 times more. It's not a failed venture after all.

So what exactly is Jesus talking about?

"Listen then to what the parable of the sower means: When anyone hears the message about the kingdom and does not understand it, the evil one comes and snatches away what was sown in their heart. This is the seed sown along the path. The seed falling on rocky ground refers to someone who hears the word and at once receives it with joy. But since they have no root, they last only a short time. When trouble or persecution comes because of the word, they quickly fall away. The seed falling among the thorns refers to someone who hears the word, but the worries of this life and the deceitfulness of wealth choke the word, making it unfruitful. But the seed falling on good soil refers to someone who hears the word and understands it. This is the one who produces a crop, yielding a hundred, sixty, or thirty times what was sown."

Jesus is the sower, and his message is the seed. People are the different soils. As he teaches, there are a variety of results. It's interesting that he mentions the "evil one." That antagonist is still at work. Sometimes, the task is over before it starts because of misunderstanding. Other times, the message sounds great but never really gets any further than that because of hard times. Truth gets lost in the struggle. Still other times, stress, greed, and other concerns take over and the truth can't develop and produce. "Thorns and thistles" get involved. This phrase highlights the effects of the curse still at work upon our world. But finally, in the right soil, this truth is of incredible power and potential. The multitude of the crop produced, up to a hundred times what was sown, outweighs the wasted potential of the other scenarios. There is great power to Jesus' message, it just has to find the right soil so as not to be wasted.

Jesus goes on to share more parables that complement this one.

"...The kingdom of heaven is like a man who sowed good seed in his field. But while everyone was sleeping, his enemy came and sowed weeds among the wheat, and went away. When the wheat sprouted and formed heads, then the weeds also appeared.

"The owner's servants came to him and said, 'Sir, didn't you sow good seed in your field? Where then did the weeds come from?'

'An enemy did this,' he replied.

"The servants asked him, 'Do you want us to go and pull them up?'

"'No,' he answered, 'because while you are pulling the weeds, you may uproot the wheat with them. Let both grow together until the harvest. At that time I will tell the harvesters: First collect the weeds and tie them in bundles to be burned; then gather the wheat and bring it into my barn."

Here is another parable about a farmer, but it takes things in a different direction. Now we aren't just talking about soils, we are talking about different kinds of plants, weeds growing among a good crop. Still having some trouble following things, the disciples later ask him to explain this one as well.

*He answered, "The one who sowed the good seed is the Son
of Man. The field is the world, and the good seed stands for
the people of the kingdom. The weeds are the people of the
evil one, and the enemy who sows them is the devil. The
harvest is the end of the age, and the harvesters are angels.*

*"As the weeds are pulled up and burned in the fire, so it will
be at the end of the age. The Son of Man will send out his
angels, and they will weed out of his kingdom everything that
causes sin and all who do evil. They will throw them into the
blazing furnace, where there will be weeping and gnashing
of teeth. Then the righteous will shine like the sun in the
kingdom of their Father. Whoever has ears, let them hear."*

His explanation is surprisingly straightforward. Piece by piece
he breaks things down. Here, the "Son of Man" sows good seed.
Unlike the previous parable, though, the different seeds are actually
people. There are two kinds, good and bad. They are both called
"sons." The wheat are the children of the kingdom, and the weeds
are sons of the evil one. Not everyone in this story is a "child of God."
Once again, the evil one, the devil, is a character in the story, and
what a jerk! Good is sown, but the evil one interferes. When the
servants notice that weeds are growing with the wheat, they are
understandably concerned. What should be done? How could this
happen? Should the weeds all be pulled? These kinds of questions
are often asked about God. Why is there so much bad in the world?
Why does God let it continue? The owner, God, warns that removing
the weeds (all the bad) would risk losing some of the wheat harvest
(all the good to come). For now, they will continue together until the
appropriate time. In the end, when it is time for the harvest, all will
be gathered and separated accordingly.

This parable speaks of judgment. It's not a popular topic today,
but this story actually casts it in a positive light. There is a time
coming when all that is evil will be removed from the world. Things
will be thrown out and destroyed. Afterward, there will finally be a
new kingdom free from evil.[1] In the meantime, there is still much

---

[1] This is consistent with one of the description of future events in Daniel 12:1-3.

good fruit developing, and God doesn't want to stop things prematurely. It isn't the right time yet for the harvest. Instead, the tension between good and evil will continue in the world. On one level, it sounds like a retelling of what happened in Eden. God and Adam were once gardeners, and an enemy, the serpent, snuck up and planted weeds (the temptation). God allowed the good and evil to grow together by not immediately punishing Adam and Eve with death as he could have, and so we still await the finale.

As Jesus proceeds, he tells a few shorter parables that compliment these.

> "...The kingdom of heaven is like a mustard seed, which a man took and planted in his field. Though it is the smallest of all seeds, yet when it grows, it is the largest of garden plants and becomes a tree, so that the birds come and perch in its branches."

> He told them still another parable: "The kingdom of heaven is like yeast that a woman took and mixed into about sixty pounds of flour until it worked all through the dough."

These both pick up the theme of potential from the parable of the sower. In each of these, something small (yeast, a mustard seed) grows exponentially. Something simple grows unexpectedly. Yeast expands through the dough which then rises while the tiny seed becomes an enormous tree. That tree is then a benefit to others (the birds).[1] Again, there is power and potential to the truth of God's kingdom. It grows, it multiplies, reproduces, expands, and spreads. Also, it can come from unexpected places (like prostitutes and tax collectors).

Still, Jesus continues.

> "The kingdom of heaven is like treasure hidden in a field. When a man found it, he hid it again, and then in his joy went and sold all he had and bought that field.

---

[1] Ezekiel 17:22-24

"Again, the kingdom of heaven is like a merchant looking for fine pearls. When he found one of great value, he went away and sold everything he had and bought it."

With such great potential to this kingdom, these two parables emphasize its value. It is a treasure to be cherished and of greater worth than all else. In fact, it's worth giving up or leaving all else behind to have it (as the disciples have done to follow him). As odd as this might sound, this kind of thing actually happened (treasures hidden in fields). With no banks, one of the best ways to "preserve" wealth was to store it away somewhere and, for example, bury it.

Finally, Jesus tells one last parable that is similar to the one about the weeds.

"Once again, the kingdom of heaven is like a net that was let down into the lake and caught all kinds of fish. When it was full, the fishermen pulled it up on the shore. Then they sat down and collected the good fish in baskets, but threw the bad away. This is how it will be at the end of the age. The angels will come and separate the wicked from the righteous and throw them into the blazing furnace, where there will be weeping and gnashing of teeth."

He finishes them all with a reminder of the costs of joining this kingdom. There is something at stake. This truth of the kingdom is of incredible worth, and those that reject it will have to pay a price. There will be consequences. Things will be thrown out. The good news of a time when all evil will be removed from the world also serves as a warning.

We now have a handful of themes from these parables. Jesus is a gardener spreading his message. This message is of incredible value. It's a treasure (the field, the pearl) worth more than all else and has incredible growth potential (the yeast, mustard seed), multiplying as a fruitful crop and benefiting others in the strangest and most unexpected places. This potential has to be handled appropriately so as not to be wasted (the soils), and there are other forces (the evil one) at work simultaneously (the weeds). Eventually, the time will come for the harvest when all will be gathered. At this time, all that is evil will be removed (the weeds, the net) and destroyed in the fire, and something new will be established on earth free from evil.

"Have you understood all these things?" Jesus asked. "Yes," they replied.

It's important that they understand—that they are to be like the good soil. If Jesus is a sower, then by default as his apprentices they will be sowers too one day. Their purpose is wrapped up in all that he is saying and doing. One day, these stories will be their own. But it isn't quite time for that yet. And before the excitement continues, we find Jesus in another surprising confrontation, this time with his own family.

FAMILY FEUD
Mark 3:20-26, 30-35

Then Jesus entered a house, and again a crowd gathered, so that he and his disciples were not even able to eat. When his family heard about this, they went to take charge of him, for they said, "He is out of his mind."

Despite the early attempts to bring his mission to a halt in Nazareth, the madness has indeed continued. Jesus continues to draw crowds and cause a stir. Apparently, he still sees himself as the Messiah bringing about God's kingdom, and his family is increasingly worried. Enough is enough. They have an idea as to how they can intervene and put an end to things.

They claim that he is "out of his mind." It's an attempt to take control of him by proclaiming him incapable of his responsibilities as the head of the house. It would also prevent the potential that Romans might punish him for claiming to be the Messiah, a revolutionary figure. At the same time, if people see Jesus as insane and not treasonous, it would conveniently spare the family some serious humiliation.

And the teachers of the law who came down from Jerusalem said, "He is possessed by Beelzebub! By the prince of demons he is driving out demons."

155

Jesus' family isn't the only group worried about his ministry, and their worries for his safety are well founded. Even some of the teachers from the capital have come to dissuade his following. Interestingly, they don't deny that he has performed miracles. Rather, they say that it is by the powers of evil that he is able to accomplish these things. This is a serious accusation. Unable to stop him thus far in debates, they are now accusing him of sorcery, an offence traditionally punished with death. Already, the attempts to have Jesus killed have begun. Jesus doesn't let it slip by unnoticed.

So Jesus called them over to him and began to speak to them in parables: "How can Satan drive out Satan? If a kingdom is divided against itself, that kingdom cannot stand. If a house is divided against itself, that house cannot stand. And if Satan opposes himself and is divided, he cannot stand; his end has come..."

He said this because they were saying, "He has an impure spirit."

Confronting the rumors, he calls out his opponents. He tries to reason with them and argues quite well for someone "out of his mind." Speaking words quoted later by Abraham Lincoln, Jesus argues that a kingdom fighting against itself can't last. Do they really think he could defeat evil forces if a part of them himself? To some, his words may have called to mind the way that the Jewish people once fought among themselves during their brief independence several hundred years before, a period that ended when both factions tried to cut a deal with Rome. This would imply that those involved were a house divided (the Pharisees and Sadducees) whose time of authority had come to an end.

It isn't long before his own family arrives at the scene to try to talk some sense into him.

Then Jesus' mother and brothers arrived. Standing outside, they sent someone in to call him. A crowd was sitting around him, and they told him, "Your mother and brothers are outside looking for you."

156

"Who are my mother and my brothers?" he asked.

Then he looked at those seated in a circle around him and said, "Here are my mother and my brothers! Whoever does God's will is my brother and sister and mother."

As his family arrives to put their plans in action, Jesus refuses to see them. Does Mary really think he has lost it? Or did Jesus' brothers persuade her to participate because she's afraid for his life? Either way, it doesn't work, and Jesus uses their arrival as a lesson for his students. While they might have heard someone speak about fellow Jewish religious adherents as though family, Jesus takes this even further in giving priority to this group above his own biological family and replacing them. Having been rejected by his family when he was run out of Nazareth, he has now found a new family of brothers, sisters, and mothers among his followers. They share God as their father and will remain loyal to his work. Christians would one day echo this application of family identity to include people across all sorts of ethnicities and social boundaries in ways unprecedented in the ancient world.

Left outside waiting, his family can either join them in doing the work of God or get on with their lives without him. The decision is theirs.

Once again, Jesus is on the move. After reinforcing the significance of the intimate relationship he shares with his disciples, he is about to take things to a new level and leave them wondering who, or what, he is.

NINE
Fireworks

ATTRACTING PEOPLE FROM FAR and wide as well as dealing with family tensions, Jesus begins to travel around the region more to spread his message elsewhere. At this time, the simplest ways to get around are by foot or by boat. Beginning to journey longer distances, one evening the disciples find themselves on a boat trip across some rugged waters. It's a night that will leave them with memories they won't soon forget.

STORM CHASER
Mark 4:35-41

> *That day when evening came, he said to his disciples, "Let us go over to the other side." Leaving the crowd behind, they took him along, just as he was, in the boat. There were also other boats with him. A furious squall came up, and the waves broke over the boat, so that it was nearly swamped. Jesus was in the stern, sleeping on a cushion. The disciples woke him and said to him, "Teacher, don't you care if we drown?"*

Did Jesus know the forecast? Surely this is poor planning. I haven't spent much time on boats, but this sounds pretty severe. What I imagine is probably a blend of some different movies and television shows that I've seen. Considering that some of the guys are fisherman, they are well aware of the risks that come with navigating the waters. If the boat capsizes, they could die.

I can picture them frantically moving about and shouting as they try to communicate over the sounds of the storm. I can hear the lightning and thunder. I can see water getting smashed across the deck as the men desperately try to keep things afloat in the crushing waves. This is chaos. Their rugged little boat will be fortunate to survive the dark depths of these waters. It makes sense that they are panicked as the boat is thrown back and forth. Then they notice something odd.

Where is Jesus?

He's comfortably asleep, on a pillow. It's a sharp contrast to the scene that surrounds him. They are shocked, even angry. How can someone rest in the middle of such a struggle? What kind of leader is this? Isn't he concerned that they could die?

Flabbergasted, they wake him.

He got up, rebuked the wind and said to the waves, "Quiet! Be still!" Then the wind died down and it was completely calm.

Umm…

He said to his disciples, "Why are you so afraid? Do you still have no faith?"

Umm…

What just happened? A second ago there were waves. No, a second ago there were *huge* waves. Men were tumbling about as they struggled to keep their footing. There was a lot of noise, a hammering wind, water falling like bullets, people yelling, crashes of lightning and thunder.

And then there was silence.

Jesus stands up and talks to the storm as if it's a person, as if nature is his servant and he its master.[1] It responds immediately. No more wind. No more waves. No more rain, or noise, or yelling, or rocking. With a couple of words, Jesus puts the waters in their place and brings order to the chaos as if he's seen this before.

It's an incredible scene.

---

[1] Psalm 107:28-30

Then he questions them. Why were they afraid? Really? Of course they were afraid. Have no faith? Faith in what? How were they supposed to know he'd pull this out of his back pocket as if it were no big deal? They were clearly afraid of dying. Is that a mistake?

We are all afraid of dying, but why?

They follow Jesus because they think he's something special. They think he's been sent by God and the one that's going to finally set them free, but from what?

Free from death.

Free from the curse.

They know this, or at least they thought they did. Maybe they do sometimes, even most of the time. But still, it's kind of hard to believe. It's hard to ignore the immediate struggles of the world and trust that magically God has got it all taken care of. Can they actually trust Jesus? Do they really think he can accomplish such a grand salvation?

It's because of the curse that deadly storms like this even exist. The natural world is indifferent to us. It can harm us. This is "thorns and thistles" from the curse.[1] But that's not all. Death is also a part of the curse. The disciples will die some day, and they don't know when or how. Will it be this storm? Like Adam and Eve, they are powerless. Death hangs overhead as a legitimate possibility. Then there's Jesus, a man who sleeps comfortably on a pillow in the midst of a great storm, a man coasting peacefully over the upheaval of the seas.

I don't think Jesus is actually angry, I think he's just making a point. He's inviting them out of something—the world as they have known it. They don't have to be afraid anymore. They don't need to fear the storm. They don't have to be enslaved by death any longer. Jesus has come to deal with it, like he dealt with the storm. He will bring peace to the chaos. By God's word, God brought life to the emptiness of the waters in Genesis. Through Jesus, God is bringing life to the void and disarray of death. He will restore the long-absent peace and save the disciples from what looms overhead. He's

---

[1] Genesis 3:18

inviting them into something new, liberation from the fear that holds them captive. He's inviting them to be something new because he has power over the curse.

> *They were terrified and asked each other, "Who is this? Even the wind and the waves obey him!"*

Who can control nature but...[1]

Sometimes you think you know and understand someone, what they are capable of, and then you discover that you were wrong. This isn't what they expected. Jesus isn't who they expected. Jesus routinely isn't who people expect. These guys are in for the ride of their lives. He's going to take them places that don't make sense, and they're going to be shocked at what happens.

A DEAD MAN WALKING

Mark 5:1-2; Luke 8:27; Mark 5:3-8; Luke 8:30-31; Mark 5:11-20

Still probably in shock at what they've just seen, the disciples find that it's not long before Jesus is back in the middle of the action.

> *They went across the lake to the region of the Gerasenes. When Jesus got out of the boat, a man with an impure spirit came from the tombs to meet him. For a long time this man had not worn clothes or lived in a house...This man lived in the tombs, and no one could bind him anymore, not even with a chain. For he had often been chained hand and foot, but he tore the chains apart and broke the irons on his feet. No one was strong enough to subdue him. Night and day among the tombs and in the hills he would cry out and cut himself with stones."*

As soon as he's off the boat, we encounter a bleak and eerie scene. It sounds like something you'd see in a horror film, not the Bible. This guy is beyond creepy. He lives among the dead. These tombs are basically little caves where you would place dead bodies to decay, where the flesh would rot until only bones remained. The

---

[1] Job 38:8-11; Psalm 104:1-7; Ecclesiastes 8:8

bones would then be collected, and the tombs would be reused. This man is surrounded by decay and has made his home among it.

This man would have reeked of death.

Why is he there? He has gone wild and is out of control. Exhibiting superhuman strength, he is too strong for anyone to handle. People are scared of him. This naked, crazed man now spends his time cutting himself and screaming. Driven from the city, his only refuge is among the dead. He's a lost cause and a hopeless outcast. It's chilling to think about. What is there to do?

I'm guessing that most people avoided this area around these tombs and the wild man. You know, the kind of place where the kids aren't allowed to go. It's interesting that once off the boat, this is exactly where Jesus ends up.

When he saw Jesus from a distance, he ran and fell on his knees in front of him. He shouted at the top of his voice, "What do you want with me, Jesus, Son of the Most High God? In God's name don't torture me!" For Jesus had said to him, "Come out of this man, you impure spirit!"

It's an abrasive introduction. The man and Jesus are both yelling. Exclamation points are all over the place. Did Jesus speak to him initially from afar? We aren't told the exact order other than that at some point Jesus told the spirit to leave. So the man approaches Jesus. I wonder what the disciples are thinking at this point. "Oh great, what has Jesus gotten us into now?"

The wild man yells as he pleads. Oddly, he already knows who Jesus is. Have they met before? Maybe the wild man sees something that nobody else does. It's as if by coming from some other realm of existence, the spirits understand who Jesus is—the Son of the Most High God. It's a hefty title that speaks of great authority. In most encounters this crazy man is the powerful one, but here, he is powerless before Jesus. In most encounters he strikes fear into others, but here, he is the one that's terrified.

The tables have turned.

Exorcisms are something that were more familiar to people in the ancient world than to the average person today. Such encounters probably didn't carry the same fright that they do with us thanks to their portrayal in movies. We actually have record of some ancient exorcisms from this time, and there is a noticeable pattern to them. The exorcist, often carrying various charms or devices of believed power, would approach the possessed person and invoke the power of their worshiped deity to send the spirit away. They'd say something like, "In the name of _____, I command you to leave." It was all about authority. Who was greater, the invoked deity or the spirit at hand? The outcome depended on this dynamic of power.

Jesus doesn't follow the protocol.

There are no special devices. As he performs exorcisms here and elsewhere, he doesn't speak "in the name of" some deity. He instructs the evil spirit as if *he is the deity*. This probably would have stood out to the ancient observer, and it's probably one reason he's been accused elsewhere of being the "prince of demons." Here though, Jesus is addressed by the man as "Son of the Most High God." It leaves little question as to who is the real authority. In the world of spirits, God Most High (and by default his son) is the boss.

Then Jesus asked him, "What is your name?"

"Legion," he replied, because many demons had gone into him. And they begged Jesus repeatedly not to order them to go into the Abyss.

Jesus speaks with Legion briefly. In the Roman army, a legion was a collection of troops between 3,000-6,000 in size. This is pretty serious. No wonder the man has been such trouble. This man is a person inhabited by many personas. Yet from the sound of things, Jesus could have sent them away into some dungeon-like chasm referred to as "the Abyss" here. It's like he has the authority to throw them away. It's curious that he doesn't, though they expect it's where they'll eventually end up.

The man has lost his identity. What remains is a shell of his former self, consumed by the spirits that battle within him. Jesus knows, though, that there is still more to this man beneath the surface.

A large herd of pigs was feeding on the nearby hillside. The demons begged Jesus, "Send us among the pigs; allow us to go into them." He gave them permission, and the impure spirits came out and went into the pigs. The herd, about two thousand in number, rushed down the steep bank into the lake and were drowned.

The story just gets weirder and weirder. Remember, pigs are viewed poorly by the Jews. An enormous herd of them outside of town means this area is predominantly gentile (non-Jewish).

Quickly, we see the destructive nature of these spirits at work. Jesus drives out what is evil, and that which is "unclean" gets destroyed as the enormous herd (about 2,000 pigs) runs off the cliff. It's no wonder the man was in such bad shape. Apparently the feared abyss is worse to a spirit than embodying a dead pig in the sea. Can you imagine the shock and fright of the herdsmen? Can you imagine how much this would have cost? I wonder if the herder had been watching Jesus and his crew the whole time they were with the wild man.

Those tending the pigs ran off and reported this in the town and countryside, and the people went out to see what had happened. When they came to Jesus, they saw the man who had been possessed by the legion of demons, sitting there, dressed and in his right mind; and they were afraid.

They don't know what to make of this.

They knew of the crazy guy and were already afraid of him. Everyone is afraid. The possessed man is afraid of Jesus. The people are afraid of the possessed man. Now, the people are afraid of Jesus. This man had been naked, screaming, living in tombs, incredibly powerful, and here he is sitting peacefully at Jesus' feet. What in the world is going on? A lot of money just jumped off a cliff. Aware of how much trouble the man once was, what are they to make of this visitor? What does he want? Why has he come, and what kind of damage could he do to a city full of people?

Those who had seen it told the people what had happened to the demon-possessed man—and told about the pigs as well. Then the people began to plead with Jesus to leave their region.

All they know is that he must be incredibly powerful, more so than they've ever encountered, and it scares them. They don't want to take any chances. They'd like to maintain their illusion of order and control. Unsure what to think, they ask him to leave before he even gets to town. Like the wild man that was previously too much to handle, now Jesus too is driven away.

Once again, Jesus gets kicked out of town.

It's a story of an outcast, nakedness, oppression, suffering, destruction, evil, and possibly some trickery. How did the formerly wild man end up like this? We don't know the backstory. Such stories today are pretty uncommon and confusing. Does this still happen? Is this just a way of describing mental illness? We do know that in that day (and today in other parts of the world) people sought to interact with the spiritual realm to gain special powers for healing or harming others. Commonly known as spiritists, shaman, witchdoctors, or medicine men, these individuals crafted and consumed various substances, some of which may have been pretty harmful, walking a fine line as they tried to understand and navigate the realm of spirits while avoiding harm.

This could be the case with this particular man. If so, it would mean this man might have incidentally brought this condition upon himself. Deceived by the allure of power, he may have gotten more than he bargained for—and quite the opposite of the control he expected. As with Adam and Eve, the search for power only left him controlled by a new master.

As Jesus was getting into the boat, the man who had been demon-possessed begged to go with him. Jesus did not let him, but said, "Go home to your own people and tell them how much the Lord has done for you, and how he has had mercy on you." So the man went away and began to tell in the Decapolis how much Jesus had done for him. And all the people were amazed.

It's interesting that Jesus turns the man away. This region, the Decapolis, was made up of ten gentile cities. There's an important story to be told that now only this man can share, and people may need to see it to believe it. He's been brought out of his destructive state, clothed, and restored to the community. Jesus has given him his life back. He's been freed from the bondage and suffering that trapped him, and now he has a new purpose. This man will now speak to people in a region where Jesus can't be present because he was asked to leave. This man will be the means through which many will encounter Jesus.

Because of the serpent, Adam and Eve were cast out of the garden. Because of Jesus, the serpent will be cast out of the earth. The serpent knows this, and the spirits in the possessed man understand this (the Abyss). Jesus is the one with power over the curse. He has come to cover people's nakedness and restore them again to God. He is the one who has come to crush Satan and remove all that is evil from the world. I love this story. If Jesus can save this man, then he can save anyone. No one is beyond hope.

There are no lost causes.

THE DOUBLE PLAY
Mark 5:21-43

> *When Jesus had again crossed over by boat to the other side of the lake, a large crowd gathered around him while he was by the lake. Then one of the synagogue leaders, named Jairus, came, and when he saw Jesus, he fell at his feet. He pleaded earnestly with him, "My little daughter is dying. Please come and put your hands on her so that she will be healed and live." So Jesus went with him.*

His reputation has spread quickly. Once again, as soon as he arrives, people are ready to ask for his help. In contrast to the previous story where he was greeted immediately by the wild man, someone of very low stature, here he is approached by someone who would have been held in high regard. As a synagogue ruler, Jairus would have been a recognized and respected public figure. It's significant that even someone as important as this is coming to Jesus and begging on his knees for help. He's confident that if Jesus will just touch his daughter she will be healed.

A large crowd followed and pressed around him. And a woman was there who had been subject to bleeding for twelve years. She had suffered a great deal under the care of many doctors and had spent all she had, yet instead of getting better she grew worse.

Consider, a local celebrity is asking for a miracle and has everyone's attention. At the same time, lost in the crowd is someone on the opposite end of the spectrum of significance. This unnamed woman doesn't matter to anyone. She isn't important. There's nobody gathering to see if Jesus will help her, but there she is just the same.

She's been bleeding for twelve years. She's tried everything at her disposal, and nothing has worked. She's trapped, defeated, and now in poverty. Her suffering has broken her. On top of it all, blood makes a person unclean to touch according to the law. This surely helped prevent the spread of disease, but here it also effectively isolates this woman from the community. It would have excluded her from social gatherings including religious activities.

For twelve years.

Can you imagine being excluded from the community for that long? Can you imagine being untouchable for more than a decade?

While we don't know exactly what the bleeding is from, there's a chance that it's a condition known as fistula. Throughout history, in a number of cultures such as this one, it was common practice for women to be given in marriage at a young age (as soon as they had begun their period). This still happens today. Unfortunately, for many of these young women, their bodies are not physically ready to give birth yet. This leads to a high-risk birth, endangering both the mother and child. The child is often lost. As a result of the trauma to the woman's body, the womb can't properly heal. This can cause perpetual bleeding, incontinence, and numerous other issues.

After this trauma, things often just get worse for the injured young lady. In many cultures, giving birth to a stillborn child carries the stigma of a curse. A woman may be divorced and abandoned as a result, left in poverty to provide for herself in a society where this would have been extremely difficult. Suddenly, the social structures that pressed her into these circumstances have left her without many options.

When you consider this possibility and the type of bleeding she would have been experiencing, it's not hard to imagine the alienation she would have encountered. Could she sit down in public? Would someone recognize her or notice her bleeding? Would anyone notice her smell? Would she risk being mocked and cursed again? Twelve years of being filthy to people, a walking liability. Unclean, ashamed, afraid, this woman suffers even more than most women from Eve's curse of an increased pain in child-bearing.

Yet there she is, quietly lost in the crowd and unnoticed as Jesus arrives on the shore.

When she heard about Jesus, she came up behind him in the crowd and touched his cloak, because she thought, "If I just touch his clothes, I will be healed."

Her courage is incredible. She has simply heard of this remarkable man but shows up despite all of the risks. Like Jairus, and nothing like Jairus, she has arrived trusting that if she can even just touch his cloak…

So she does.

Immediately her bleeding stopped and she felt in her body that she was freed from her suffering.

At once Jesus realized that power had gone out from him. He turned around in the crowd and asked, "Who touched my clothes?"

"You see the people crowding against you," his disciples answered, "and yet you can ask, 'Who touched me?'"

But Jesus kept looking around to see who had done it.

She can feel it immediately. Oh what relief and joy! Jesus can feel it in his body too. He knows someone has been healed. Does he really not know who? His disciples don't get it. Of course people touched him, he's in a crowd. As for the woman, attention is probably the last thing she wanted. She just wanted to leave as she came, unnoticed.

But someone has noticed.

Jesus has noticed and is asking the crowd. Now the crowd will know that she was there in their midst and that people were brushing up against her all along. The crowd will know that she deliberately touched a holy man. This is a disaster. What will they do to her now when they find out?

Then the woman, knowing what had happened to her, came and fell at his feet and, trembling with fear, told him the whole truth.

Her courage, again, brings her forward. She steps out of hiding. Trembling at his feet, she tells her story in front of everyone while waiting for the axe to drop. Will she be ridiculed? Will she be shamed for her filthiness in front of the crowd as has probably happened before?

He said to her, "Daughter, your faith has healed you. Go in peace and be freed from your suffering."

Daughter?! Against all expectations, he doesn't crush and humiliate her. He *praises her faith*! She is addressed as a child of God, even as *his* child. Who does he think that he is? Instead of belittling her as has probably been done by several people present, he commends her courage and sincere faith.

She is free.

She is free from her physical pain. She is free from the shame and the dirtiness that have plagued her for twelve years. She's free from the anxiety of what will happen around other people. She can be with people again—in their homes, in public, and in worship. This woman of little importance in society has been recognized, valued, honored, and restored again. She's been given a new life and identity.

But the story isn't over yet.

While Jesus was still speaking, some men came from the house of Jairus, the synagogue leader. "Your daughter is dead," they said. "Why bother the teacher anymore?"

It's too late. This situation with the woman has interrupted Jesus, and now the young girl has died. A "nobody" has gotten in the way of the saving of a "somebody." What does this say about Jesus' priorities? What does it say of their expectations? They thought he could heal, but surely death is too much to overcome. Who could possibly have power over death? After all, he is only human, right?

Overhearing what they said, Jesus told him, "Don't be afraid; just believe."

He did not let anyone follow him except Peter, James and John the brother of James. When they came to the home of the synagogue leader, Jesus saw a commotion, with people crying and wailing loudly. He went in and said to them, "Why all this commotion and wailing? The child is not dead but asleep." But they laughed at him.

Jesus isn't phased. He's still compassionate and wants to help even though they don't expect that he can. He continues on as planned to see the now-deceased little girl. He only takes a few people with him, but why? He does this with a few of his miracles and only an inner circle (Peter, James, and John) get to witness what happens. Later the distraction provided by the first healing will be quite useful because it distracted the crowd, allowing the events that follow to be kept private.

As he arrives, people are wailing. It's over. Yet Jesus asks why as if she is only asleep. Is he serious? He must be ridiculous to speak of death like this. Just asleep? They mock him.

They don't understand with whom they are dealing.

After he put them all out, he took the child's father and mother and the disciples who were with him, and went in where the child was. He took her by the hand and said to her,

"Talitha koum!" (which means, "Little girl, I say to you, get up!"). Immediately the girl stood up and began to walk around (she was twelve years old). At this they were completely astonished. He gave strict orders not to let anyone know about this, and told them to give her something to eat.

He clears the house, and now they are alone. It's an intimate group. Not everyone will get to see the incredible thing that is about to happen. Without any fancy procedure or fanfare, Jesus simply commands the girl to rise. He speaks, and she is alive. Again, he uses no special charms or "in the name of" qualifiers. At his word, there is life. The girl, twelve years old, was born around the time that the bleeding woman first became ill. As this girl was born, the other woman died socially as a victim of the curse. Today, twelve years later, both have been brought back to life.

Next, Jesus does something strange. He tells them to keep quiet. In the previous story we saw him send someone to spread the news, yet here he's commanding silence. This dynamic is referred to as the "Messianic Secret." Remember, these are tense times. People are hungry for a revolution and rumors abound. There are expectations and word is spreading quickly about Jesus. He arrived to a crowd begging him to heal. What would happen if the crowd found out about this? They already bring their sick to him, would they bring out their dead as well? Jesus understands that there is still much to do. It's probably for this reason, cautiously navigating numerous tensions, that he hushes people at times.

Once again, Jesus leaves people stunned. He is beyond their expectations. He is opening their eyes, showing them things they'd never imagined. People are stunned and asking, "Who is this man?" Once again, Jesus has entered into our dirt. He engages our shame, guilt, and fear. Instead of being made unclean, he is reversing the effects of the curse, bringing healing and restoration to those who trust him. He is the one. He is relief to suffering, freedom from oppression, victory and purpose amid toil, and resurrection from the grave. He removes alienation and restores communities. He finds us in our nakedness and clothes us. He turns our fear into confidence, and our guilt into liberation. He takes us from our exile and brings us back to God.

We've now seen a sort of trifecta of miracles. Jesus has displayed his power over creation (the catch of fish, calming the storm) as if it belonged to him, over the spiritual realm (the demon-possessed man) as though he's the supreme spiritual authority, and over all that ails us in sickness and death (the bleeding woman, the dead girl, the paralytic, the leper) as though these things were just bumps in the road. All are invited. The professional and laborer, the rich and the poor, male and female, Jew and gentile, healthy and sick, young and old. Faith is all that is required.

This is good news.

In fact, this is good news for everybody.

TEN
Tensions Build

AFTER A MEMORABLE FEW days around Galilee, Jesus begins to send out the twelve on missions of their own. As their mentor, he decides it is time that they begin to do these things themselves. As they go, he gives them some advice...

THE LOSS OF A FRIEND
Mark 6:7-11; Matthew 10:7-8, 16-18, 26-28, 40; Mark 6:21-28; Matthew 14:12

Calling the Twelve to him, he began to send them out two by two and gave them authority over impure spirits. These were his instructions: "Take nothing for the journey except a staff—no bread, no bag, no money in your belts. Wear sandals but not an extra shirt. Whenever you enter a house, stay there until you leave that town. And if any place will not welcome you or listen to you, leave that place and shake the dust off your feet as a testimony against them."

"As you go, proclaim this message: 'The kingdom of heaven has come near.' Heal the sick, raise the dead, cleanse those who have leprosy, drive out demons. Freely you have received; freely give.

"I am sending you out like sheep among wolves. Therefore be as shrewd as snakes and as innocent as doves. Be on your guard; you will be handed over to the local councils and be

flogged in the synagogues. On my account you will be brought before governors and kings...

"So do not be afraid of them, for there is nothing concealed that will not be disclosed, or hidden that will not be made known. What I tell you in the dark, speak in the daylight; what is whispered in your ear, proclaim from the roofs. Do not be afraid of those who kill the body but cannot kill the soul. Rather, be afraid of the One who can destroy both soul and body in hell.

"Anyone who welcomes you welcomes me, and anyone who welcomes me welcomes the one who sent me."

It is some heavy advice with stern warnings. He's preparing them now for what he knows will come down the road as they travel. Nomads, vagabonds, pilgrims, they will have no home and must get used to living simply and packing light. While they've enjoyed a streak of popularity, they won't always be met with such cheers. It would be foolish to expect such things. Opposition shouldn't be a deterrent, it's to be expected. They don't realize it, but they are just beginning a mission that has been in the works for centuries. It is going to be difficult. They are just getting their feet wet on what is likely their first journey apart from Jesus.

After some stunning experiences, Jesus and his disciples crash back into reality and the harsh conditions of their world as they receive some bad news. While his following grows, John the Baptist's struggles have only increased. A report arrives of a terrible turn of events...

...On his birthday Herod gave a banquet for his high officials and military commanders and the leading men of Galilee. When the daughter of Herodias came in and danced, she pleased Herod and his dinner guests.

The king said to the girl, "Ask me for anything you want, and I'll give it to you." And he promised her with an oath, "Whatever you ask I will give you, up to half my kingdom."

She went out and said to her mother, "What shall I ask for?"

"The head of John the Baptist," she answered

At once the girl hurried in to the king with the request: "I want you to give me right now the head of John the Baptist on a platter."

The king was greatly distressed, but because of his oaths and his dinner guests, he did not want to refuse her. So he immediately sent an executioner with orders to bring John's head. The man went, beheaded John in the prison, and brought back his head on a platter. He presented it to the girl, and she gave it to her mother.

It's an uncomfortable scene. Herodias had a beef with John the Baptist for speaking against her marriage to Herod (her former husband's brother). Criticism of the Herod family carried political significance and could even be painted as treasonous. But what is Herod really offering this young woman (now his daughter)? Is he drunk? He offers her half of the kingdom, is he suggesting marriage? An inheritance? Instead she asks for the execution of an innocent man. Is she drunk? Some people want money, others want revenge. He's stuck. Will he risk the humiliation of going back on his promise? It appears that his momentary boasts of power and authority have come back to bite him. While he's always been capable of executing John the Baptist, doing so would make him even less popular among the people he rules. Unfortunately, he follows through with his promise, and an innocent man dies. It's a vivid example of the absurd injustices and abuses of authority common among rulers in the ancient world.

John's disciples came and took his body and buried it. Then they went and told Jesus.

These are tense times.

After all the excitement, this sad event is a sobering reminder to the disciples of all that is at stake. This isn't just a game. They walk a fine line as they travel from place to place. A simple misstep could be the end of a life. Things are well underway, though, and there's no turning back now.

A MASSIVE MEAL
Mark 6:30-33; Matthew 14:14-17; John 6:7; Matthew 14:18-21

As his disciples begin returning to Jesus with some stories of their own, other people learn of their location and interrupt the reunion. It seems Jesus' fame won't allow him much time alone with his disciples anymore, or even a little privacy to mourn the loss of his dear friend.

The apostles gathered around Jesus and reported to him all they had done and taught. Then, because so many people were coming and going that they did not even have a chance to eat, he said to them, "Come with me by yourselves to a quiet place and get some rest."

So they went away by themselves in a boat to a solitary place. But many who saw them leaving recognized them and ran on foot from all the towns and got there ahead of them.

When Jesus landed and saw a large crowd, he had compassion on them and healed their sick.

As evening approached, the disciples came to him and said, "This is a remote place, and it's already getting late. Send the crowds away, so they can go to the villages and buy themselves some food."

The disciples have to be a little irritated. A lot has happened. There's much to discuss. They've been away and have a lot of catching up to do. They need some quality time with their teacher to talk things through. But here is another mass of needy people. Does it ever stop? By now it's getting late into the evening, and Jesus still hasn't dismissed people. Can't Jesus just send them away for dinner? That's a good excuse to call it quits for the day so that the disciples and Jesus can finally have some peace and quiet. Except Jesus has something else in mind.

Jesus replied, "They do not need to go away. You give them something to eat."

This is not what they had in mind. They are complaining to him to do something, and he throws it back at them. They wanted Jesus' attention, not the task of feeding a multitude. Besides, what are they supposed to feed them?

Apparently he isn't understanding them.

"We have here only five loaves of bread and two fish," they answered.

Philip answered him, "It would take more than half a year's wages to buy enough bread for each one to have a bite!"

As if highlighting the absurdity of his instruction, they go so far as to count what meager supplies they have. They're not cooperating, they're highlighting how ridiculous Jesus' instructions are. Remember, he just sent them on a journey where they didn't take anything extra (including bread) and had to rely on God through the generosity of others. It's not like they've got a bunch of food handy.

Apparently they aren't understanding him.

Things are changing quickly, whether the disciples realize it or not. Life is about to get much more difficult for everyone involved. Jesus knows this, and he's trying to prepare them. Right now, the crowds come for him. Soon, as his disciples, the crowds will come for them. This is why he's begun sending them out on their own. The disciples are entering a new stage of responsibility. It's time for another step of maturation where they begin to transition from students and into teachers.

It's time to grow up.

They will be in poverty, pilgrims constantly on the move and without any privacy or space. People will travel great distances to see and hear *them,* and they need to be ready. Jesus won't always be around to take care of things like this. They will have to step out in faith and embrace their dependence upon God against absurd odds and in extreme circumstances. It will be impossible.

Jesus has just given them authority to begin doing the very things that he has been doing all along. He's prepared them to do impossible things, even miraculous things—the very content of the stories they are probably anxious to share with him. He's begun to pass the torch. Of course there isn't enough bread. That's the point. Suddenly, they are right in the middle of another object lesson. But the disciples miss their chance. They're still not understanding that they can do this.

"Bring them here to me," he said. And he directed the people to sit down on the grass. Taking the five loaves and the two fish and looking up to heaven, he gave thanks and broke the loaves. Then he gave them to the disciples, and the disciples gave them to the people.

It will be impossible, like feeding a multitude with a few loaves and some fish.

A mass of people arrived longing for something, as if they've been fasting in a desert for some time. They are hungry, and Jesus feeds them. He teaches them and heals them until supper time. Then, as if it's no big deal, Jesus supplies everyone's food using a few scraps. Instead of turning stones to bread, he uses their meager leftovers. He can do something with what they've got, even if it doesn't appear to be enough. He can do something with *them,* even if they don't seem to be enough. He can turn even scraps into a divine feast. He can make something incredible out of nothing because *he* is the one behind all of creation. He is the one who has come to satisfy our greatest hunger. Just as he now hands them the bread to pass out, so they will pass along all that he has been teaching to them.

This is no accident.

They all ate and were satisfied, and the disciples picked up twelve basketfuls of broken pieces that were left over. The number of those who ate was about five thousand men, besides women and children.

When they finished, there was enough left for each of them to have a basket. They came empty-handed, and they left with more than they could carry. Their nets are bursting. God is their supply, and they don't need to worry. He is their provision, and they will have what they need for the journey. It will be enough. In fact, it will be more than enough. It will satisfy in ways as unimaginable as feeding five thousand people at the drop of a hat in the middle of a desert. It won't just be enough for them, it will be enough to share with everyone.

This supply will never run out.

HOVERING OVER THE WATERS
Matthew 14:22-33; Mark 6:51-52

> *Immediately Jesus made the disciples get into the boat and go on ahead of him to the other side, while he dismissed the crowd. After he had dismissed them, he went up on a mountainside by himself to pray. Later that night, he was there alone, and the boat was already a considerable distance from land, buffeted by the waves because the wind was against it.*

It's been a hectic few days. They've been constantly on the move and still haven't had time alone together. People are tired. Tempers have flared. The disciples are still nursing some frustrations of their own, and Jesus sends them ahead of him. He finally has a moment to be alone with himself. Close confines mixed with exhaustion can be challenging for even the strongest relationships. Some time apart might do everyone some good. After an evening alone in the mountains, he's ready to get moving. By this time, the disciples are well ahead on their way but being slowed by the winds and the waves. The trip has turned out to be quite difficult. They aren't making much headway without him and still have miles to go before they reach the shore.

> *Shortly before dawn Jesus went out to them, walking on the lake. When the disciples saw him walking on the lake, they were terrified. "It's a ghost," they said, and cried out in fear.*

With their action-packed schedule, they've got to be running on fumes by this point. As he has several times before, Jesus catches them off guard. Is this real? There are tales about spirits in the waters, is this just another one of those? Jewish people didn't believe in

179

ghosts like their gentile neighbors did, yet in a moment of fear the disciples quickly grasp for any apparent explanation. They try to make sense of what they are seeing. But it doesn't make any sense, and they are terrified.

But Jesus immediately said to them: "Take courage! It is I. Don't be afraid."

"Lord, if it's you," Peter replied, "tell me to come to you on the water."

Why does Jesus move like a spirit over the waters?

They still aren't sure what's going on, and it is pitch black out. But Peter is catching on. He recognizes this voice, and he sees an opportunity. He's ready for something special. If Jesus can do it, then so can his disciples. They just need his permission. At Jesus' word, it will be so.

This is a bold move.

"Come," he said.

Then Peter got down out of the boat, walked on the water and came toward Jesus. But when he saw the wind, he was afraid and, beginning to sink, cried out, "Lord, save me!"

Immediately Jesus reached out his hand and caught him. "You of little faith," he said, "why did you doubt?"

Jesus actually grants his request. It's pretty awesome. It means that Peter can actually walk on water as Jesus does, and he even does so for a moment. But what is happening, and why?

Probably in shock, Peter steps onto something where there is otherwise nothing to stand upon—until he sees the winds. He glances around, and it shakes his confidence. He panics. Did he really think this would work? Why isn't it working? Why am I drowning?

People are often a strange blend of faith and doubt.

Jesus hasn't abandoned him. Jesus is still with him by his side. Peter has grown afraid, but there is nothing to fear. Jesus is the one that commands storms and hovers over waters. The problem here is Peter's perspective. In this crucial moment, Jesus highlights the

180

power of *faith in him.* It's a matter of who Peter believes Jesus to be, not how powerful Jesus is. In the winds, Peter became distracted. He had trusted in Jesus' power, but as he looked around his faith grew dim, and he sank. This is how fear works. Like a trauma, it's a consciousness of evil that hangs over us. It's the great wound, an experience that has fooled us into thinking that even God prowls like an enemy waiting to destroy us. It distracts and overwhelms what we otherwise knew and trusted.

In this moment of terror, Jesus graciously catches him and points out the problem. But there is still a wound, a fear that remains hidden beneath the surface. Why are they still afraid? Why are we still afraid?

These are familiar waters.

The disciples don't know it now, but they will all soon be confronted by this fear. Peter specifically will be humiliated as this wound cripples him at a crucial moment. There is still much that they don't understand. There is still much that they *won't* understand. There are still lessons to be learned, and some won't be completed until after this story has ended.

> *And when they climbed into the boat, the wind died down. Then those who were in the boat worshiped him, saying, "Truly you are the Son of God."*

> *...They were completely amazed, for they had not understood about the loaves; their hearts were hardened.*

It's such a peculiar miracle.

As soon as they are getting used to him healing people, he begins another category of supernatural behavior and blows them away. The miraculous feeding and now this. What in the world is going on? God is a wonderful mystery, speaking in terms that are understandable yet continually shattering expectations. This is a God that glides through the unknown like walking through a park. This is a God who is comfortable among turbulent waters,[1] at peace amid confusion, and free of the compulsion to explain everything. This God is knowable

---

[1] Job 9:8

and still a beautiful secret. This God is a treasure and a journey of endless discovery.

After the confusion and frustrations, the disciples are together once again. After some stubbornness and argumentative behavior about the fish and loaves, their hardened hearts have softened again. He has their attention again, and they are listening. They are starting to understand that he's preparing them to follow his footsteps, as Peter has just done on the water. There's a lot that doesn't make sense, but they are as confident as ever in Jesus' identity. In fact, in response to what has happened we are told that they *worship* him. This goes beyond admiration. If Jesus isn't God, this is an incredible offense. *Surely* this is the one they've been waiting for even if they didn't know who or what exactly that would look like. Jesus is everything they've been waiting for. This must be it.

DIVISION IN THE RANKS
Matthew 14:34-36; John 6:24-29, 33-35, 40-42, 50-55, 60-63, 66-68, 7:1-6

> *When they had crossed over, they landed at Gennesaret. And when the men of that place recognized Jesus, they sent word to all the surrounding country. People brought all their sick to him and begged him to let the sick just touch the edge of his cloak, and all who touched it were healed.*

Stories have spread, and it sounds like they've even heard the story of the bleeding woman as they now seek to similarly touch his cloak. While Jesus is busy at Gennesaret, the multitude he fed in Bethsaida has returned for more. But he's not there.

> *Once the crowd realized that neither Jesus nor his disciples were there, they got into the boats and went to Capernaum in search of Jesus. When they found him on the other side of the lake, they asked him, "Rabbi, when did you get here?"*

> *Jesus answered, "Very truly I tell you, you are looking for me, not because you saw the signs I performed but because you ate the loaves and had your fill. Do not work for food that spoils, but for food that endures to eternal life, which*

the Son of Man will give you. For on him God the Father has placed his seal of approval."

Then they asked him, "What must we do to do the works God requires?"

Jesus answered, "The work of God is this: to believe in the one he has sent."

They aren't seeing the bigger picture yet. They are thrilled by the miracles that he performs for them, but they don't understand *why* he is doing them. They want another show and free food. They want to be healed. They are stuck with their immediate needs and missing the big picture. Jesus isn't just providing a quick fix for someone in a bind, he's come to realign creation, bringing it back into a right relationship with God. But all they want is more food.

When he speaks of eternal life, he has their attention again. They want that. Who doesn't? "What must we do?" they ask. They think it's a matter of work to be done. They are still trying to be good enough to please God as though eternal life were a wage to be earned. He replies on their terms. What deed must be done? Faith. Faith is the action. Faith is the "work" of salvation. There is no earning or an enough that comes from good deeds. They must depend on God. They are asking his advice, and his answer is "trust that I'm what you need." They are looking for food, and he is the bread.

"For the bread of God is the bread that comes down from heaven and gives life to the world."

"Sir," they said, "always give us this bread."

Then Jesus declared, "I am the bread of life. Whoever comes to me will never go hungry, and whoever believes in me will never be thirsty...For my Father's will is that everyone who looks to the Son and believes in him shall have eternal life, and I will raise them up at the last day."

At this the Jews began to grumble about him because he said, "I am the bread that came down from heaven." They said, "Is this not Jesus, the son of Joseph, whose father and mother we know? How can he now say, 'I came down from heaven'?"

It's understandable that people were often confused by what Jesus was saying. He's not giving the answer they expected. He's using examples, like food and water, to explain things. We are hungry and thirsty. Without food or water, we perish. He is the food and drink we need to not perish. He even goes so far as to make the shocking claim that he will raise people from the dead, though somehow this isn't what bothers them. Except this isn't "die and go to a spiritual paradise" talk. His listeners would have understood his words as flesh-and-blood, bodies-coming-out-of-their-graves talk.

What?

The idea of resurrection was a contested topic in their day. The Pharisees believed in a bodily resurrection at a coming day of judgment and the Sadducees rejected the idea. Jesus' words may have slipped by unnoticed, as if he was simply stating a shared view. Still, it's significant that Jesus claims he is behind it, and that it will happen.

They aren't catching on, though, and still want what sounds like an endless supply of food. What they do hear clearly is his claim to have come from heaven, and it bothers them. Wasn't Jesus born like everyone else? What does he mean he's from heaven? He's only human, right?

"But here is the bread that comes down from heaven, which anyone may eat and not die. I am the living bread that came down from heaven. Whoever eats this bread will live forever. This bread is my flesh, which I will give for the life of the world."

Then the Jews began to argue sharply among themselves, "How can this man give us his flesh to eat?"

Jesus said to them, "Very truly I tell you, unless you eat the flesh of the Son of Man and drink his blood, you have no life in you. Whoever eats my flesh and drinks my blood has eternal life, and I will raise them up at the last day. For my flesh is real food and my blood is real drink."

Jesus gets brutally specific as he tries to be clear, but things just start to get uncomfortable. He equates himself to a miracle in their scriptures where God provided the people miraculous bread from heaven called "manna" while they journeyed through the desert.[1] Here, Jesus is to be their bread for the journey. Basically, he's saying the miracle was pointing to him, that *he is a miracle*. While Jesus has been confusing on several occasions, for many this goes too far.

Is he saying that they will have to eat him?

On hearing it, many of his disciples said, "This is a hard teaching. Who can accept it?"

Aware that his disciples were grumbling about this, Jesus said to them, "Does this offend you? Then what if you see the Son of Man ascend to where he was before! The Spirit gives life; the flesh counts for nothing. The words I have spoken to you – they are full of the Spirit and life."

From this time many of his disciples turned back and no longer followed him.

After some rushes of excitement, suddenly Jesus isn't winning any popularity contests. Frustrated by the endless demands (and the selfishness) of the crowds, he's drawn a line in the sand and isn't backing down. It sounds like Jesus is angry, even exasperated at their response. Moments ago they bowed down to worship him *as God,* but now this is too much for them? Have they already forgotten?

At this point, people simply won't accept what he's saying. He's speaking of things on a scale that is beyond what they can imagine. Return to heaven? Who can do that? You're saying that you came from heaven? We have to eat you? To top it all off, he slams the "flesh" once again. It (flesh) counts for nothing. Their family line and ethnicity won't save them. They must listen to what he's saying. It's like Jesus' conversation with Nicodemus in the middle of the night.[2] It doesn't matter where you come from or what you've done. It's not about your race, gender, job, social status, or religiosity. Before God everyone is bankrupt. Something has to change, and it

---

[1] Exodus 16   [2] See the end of chapter 5.

has to come from God. Without God, the story ends with death. It's only through God's generosity that things can change. Everyone needs rebirth. Through faith, this happens, and something gets planted that will endure through even death.

For some, it's just too much to handle. Who does this guy think he is? The crowd has turned on him. Will this start to become more common? It's interesting that Jesus doesn't even seem to flinch when people walk away from him. Instead of trying to change their minds, he turns instead to the Twelve.

"You do not want to leave too, do you?" Jesus asked the Twelve.

Simon Peter answered him, "Lord, to whom shall we go? You have the words of eternal life."

Peter's response makes me chuckle. In what had to be an incredibly tense moment of provocation, he makes a comical observation. "Where else would we go?" By now, they're in pretty deep. They've left everything to follow him, and their association with him could very well ruin any hopes they have at another job (or avoiding punishment) if things turn sour. Jesus has gotten pretty controversial. At the same time, Peter highlights the very point Jesus is trying to make. Peter gets it. Well, sort of. While Jesus is talking nonsense (that whole cannibalism thing), and they don't understand that yet, they've been with him enough to know that he's the answer. He's the one they've been waiting for. His words bring them to life. If nothing else, they know that God can just be confusing.

To top things off, it isn't long before we see his own brothers back in the picture again. This time instead of arguing that he's insane, they mock him and seem to have joined with others who are plotting to kill him.

After this, Jesus went around in Galilee. He did not want to go to Judea because the Jewish leaders there were looking for a way to kill him. But when the Jewish Festival of Tabernacles was near, Jesus' brothers said to him, "Leave Galilee and go to Judea, so that your disciples there may see works you do. No one who wants to become a public figure acts in secret. Since you are doing these things, show yourself to the world." For even his own brothers did not believe in him.

Bickering with him as siblings often do, they question his legitimacy. They egg him on much like Satan did in the garden. While they've no doubt heard the stories, apparently they aren't buying it. Is this jealousy? They question his motives, thinking that it's all just about the attention. Like a dare, they challenge him to try what he's been doing where it really matters, in the capital. During the festival, people from across the region would be in town. If he's *really* who he says, why not put on a show for them? Doesn't he want to be famous? *Prove yourself!* His life would be at risk if he did, and they know it. These are the same kind of provocations Jesus heard during his temptation in the desert.

But maybe they've got a point. Why hasn't he done these kinds of things in Jerusalem? As an observant Jew he would have visited at least a few times each year, but so far his ministry efforts have pretty well excluded the capital. Is he shy? Is he trying to avoid the limelight? What's he waiting for? What else has to be accomplished?

Therefore Jesus told them, "My time is not yet here…"

The time for what? To die? Is there a "right time" for such a thing? Their attempts to be rid of him have failed once again, but how long will this continue?

Jesus' popularity has taken a serious turn for the worse. He's bothered particular groups all along with his practices and opinions, but now it's getting severe and scattering people that once followed him. People aren't taking his words so well, and even his siblings have joined his enemies' plots against him. But even while many desert the movement, the Twelve aren't jumping ship. They are sticking around. They are in this until the end no matter what the cost.

Or so they think.

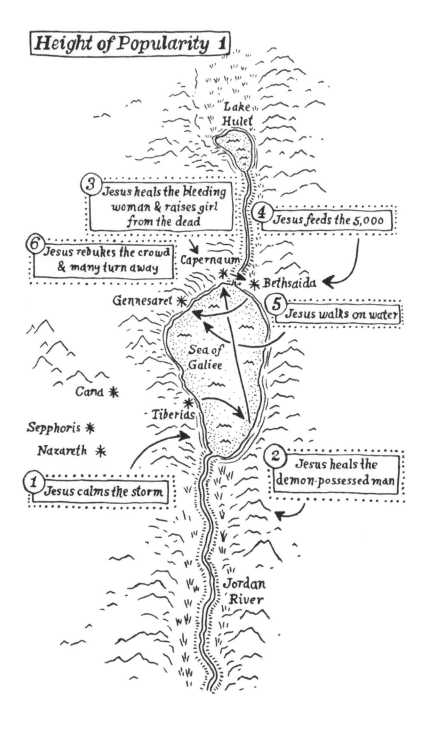

Height of Popularity 1

Lake Hulet

③ Jesus heals the bleeding woman & raises girl from the dead

④ Jesus feeds the 5,000

⑥ Jesus rebukes the crowd & many turn away

Capernaum

✳ Bethsaida

Gennesaret ✳

⑤ Jesus walks on water

Sea of Galiee

Cana ✳

Tiberias ✳

Sepphoris ✳

Nazareth ✳

① Jesus calms the storm

② Jesus heals the demon-possessed man

Jordan River

ELEVEN
New Horizons

A S WORD ABOUT JESUS continues to spread throughout the region, the authorities take notice. Even Herod Antipas has come to learn of what Jesus is doing and notices some striking similarities between Jesus and John the Baptist.

BAD MANNERS
Mark 6:14-16, 7:1-4; Matthew 15:2-14; Mark 7:17-23

King Herod heard about this, for Jesus' name had become well known. Some were saying, "John the Baptist has been raised from the dead, and that is why miraculous powers are at work in him."

Others said, "He is Elijah."

And still others claimed, "He is a prophet like one of the prophets of long ago."

But when Herod heard this, he said, "John, whom I beheaded, has been raised from the dead!"

No one knows quite what to make of what they're hearing. Intrigued previously by John the Baptist, Herod seems to be paranoid that his righteous entertainer has returned to continue stirring trouble in his domain. But Herod isn't the only one taking notice of these strange tales…

The Pharisees and some of the teachers of the law who had come from Jerusalem gathered around Jesus and saw some of his disciples eating food with hands that were defiled, that is, unwashed. (The Pharisees and all the Jews do not eat unless they give their hands a ceremonial washing, holding to the tradition of the elders. When they come from the marketplace they do not eat unless they wash. And they observe many other traditions, such as the washing of cups, pitchers and kettles.)

We've seen Jesus' popularity grow exponentially to this point so that hardly a person in the region of Galilee *doesn't* know who he is. While Jesus hasn't spent much time in Jerusalem, his reputation has spread enough that Jerusalem is now coming to him. Some bigwigs have made their way to Galilee, and it isn't long before they notice something out-of-line.

"Why do your disciples break the tradition of the elders? They don't wash their hands before they eat!"

It sounds funny to us that the issue here is washing hands before a meal. Today you might hear a parent rebuke a child for such a thing, but it's hardly a matter of politics or religion. As we've dug into before, this practice was of far more significance in their culture and was thought to influence an individual's standing before God (and possibly the standing of those the person was with). You might think of someone's caution with food today, carefully reading labels and considering ingredients if they deal with specific food allergies or dietary restrictions (peanuts, shellfish, meat or animal products). The Pharisees wanted to be careful. These practices were based on laws in scripture regarding particular things that shouldn't be touched or eaten.[1] These traditions often prevented people from fellowshipping with other cultures because how could someone be sure that the host prepared everything correctly? How could someone know how the host spent their day or whether they were "clean" or not if they didn't live by the same standards? These traditions were a cautious application of various dietary laws and included the meticulous

---

[1] Leviticus 11; Deuteronomy 14

190

washing of hands (among other things). They were also a way of embracing the unique identity and culture of their people. Yet the disciples weren't doing these things.

The gurus are angry.

How can they take Jesus seriously if his pupils have such a blatant disregard for the basic traditions of their people?

> *Jesus replied, "And why do you break the command of God for the sake of your tradition? For God said, 'Honor your father and mother' and 'Anyone who curses their father or mother is to be put to death.' But you say that if anyone declares that what might have been used to help their father or mother is 'devoted to God,' they are not to 'honor their father or mother' with it. Thus you nullify the word of God for the sake of your tradition."*

This is not the response that they anticipated. Jesus stands up for himself and his disciples as he confronts his opponents who treat their traditions as if on par with the scriptures. Do they really value the scriptures? If so, then why do some of their traditions set aside God's commands? Which is more important, what people think (traditions) or what God thinks (the scriptures)? He points out that something else they teach is an abuse of one of their most basic laws, one of the Ten Commandments.[1]

"Honoring" parents would have included caring and providing for them in their old age. It's basically their society's approach to retirement. But the Pharisees' traditions provided a loophole where a sort of donation or pledge to God freed someone of this responsibility. As you can imagine, this was bad news for the elderly. You might as well have cursed them for the rest of their lives as they would have had to endure the unnecessary hardships of neglect. Jesus equates this loophole to cursing parents, which was once previously so serious an offense that it was punishable by death.[2]

In other words, their tradition leads them into a serious crime. The bigwigs have trouble with some of their table manners, but he

---

[1] Exodus 20:12   [2] Leviticus 20:9

has trouble with their disregard of people and God's most basic commands.

But Jesus doesn't stop there…

"You hypocrites! Isaiah was right when he prophesied about you: 'These people honor me with their lips, but their hearts are far from me. They worship me in vain; their teachings are merely human rules.'

This is pretty direct.

He's spoken about hypocrisy before as a general practice. Now he's pointing it out in person. He uses a passage from one of the prophets[1] about God's judgment upon his people, and here he applies it to his opponents as people putting on a show with their insincere worship. Instead of following God and guiding people in wisdom, they offer only silly rules that are of no value.

Jesus called the crowd to him and said, "Listen and understand. What goes into someone's mouth does not defile them, but what comes out of their mouth, that is what defiles them."

Now, he's back to the topic of washing hands again. This had to be confusing for those present. There were dietary laws in their scriptures that specifically described foods that could make a person unclean.[2] Is Jesus disregarding these laws? What does he mean, "but what comes out of their mouth?" Does he know better than they do, or than the law, about how to remain in a healthy relationship with God?

Then the disciples came to him and asked, "Do you know that the Pharisees were offended when they heard this?"

He replied, "Every plant that my heavenly Father has not planted will be pulled up by the roots. Leave them; they are blind guides. If the blind lead the blind, both will fall into a pit."

---

[1] Isaiah 29:13   [2] Leviticus 11, 17; Deuteronomy 14

The disciples are worried. These were important people, and Jesus has just blown a great opportunity. This was his chance to take that next step to stardom in Jerusalem, and he's let it slip away! Instead, it now seems like things are heading the wrong direction. He's been losing followers, and now he's even provoking opposition among the big city politicians.

This is a trainwreck.

But Jesus isn't concerned. He compares people to plants, and those that aren't from God will be uprooted, he says. We've heard something like this before. He's told parables about farmers, and seeds, and weeds, and to everyone's surprise here he is now comparing these teachers to weeds planted by the enemy.[1]

This is really serious.

These offended teachers are incredibly devoted to their religion and calling for revival. But, as Jesus has already told them, they pay only lip service to God. In the spirit of Adam, they present a false self to God and others in an attempt to hide their nakedness. Their religious fervor is actually just an attempt to cover themselves with the appearance of goodness. They've gone astray, and as teachers they now lead others to do the same. They are blind guides.

After he had left the crowd and entered the house, his disciples asked him about this parable. "Are you so dull?" he asked. "Don't you see that nothing that enters a person from the outside can defile them? For it doesn't go into their heart but into their stomach, and then out of the body." (In saying this, Jesus declared all foods clean.)

The poor disciples must be struggling to keep up with everything. Jesus surely appears to be getting a shorter fuse. Is all the pressure getting to him? But Jesus has already sent the disciples out to teach some of these very ideas, so it is understandable that he's annoyed. They should get this.

In fact, they do.

Jesus isn't saying they're stupid. It's more like he's saying, "Are you too stubborn to accept this? Why do you refuse to understand?"

---

[1] See chapter 8 or Matthew 13:24-30

Intelligence isn't the issue. Sometimes people don't understand because they don't want to. Jesus has become controversial, and it's making them uncomfortable. The disciples have been flattered, sucked in by the significance of the Pharisees and other elders from the big city, Jerusalem. These men represent a new status, a different level of power, wealth, influence, and success. Their special attention was an opportunity, and Jesus' offending comments are interrupting the disciples' daydream. Surely he doesn't mean it, they hope. The teachers of the law guide an enormous movement, a massive following. If they are blind, what does that say for their people? The country? The temple?

The disciples don't want to understand. Jesus ignores their question about the parable (plants and blind guides) and returns to the topic of cleanliness.

He went on: "What comes out of a person is what defiles them. For it is from within, out of a person's heart, that evil thoughts come—sexual immorality, theft, murder, adultery, greed, malice, deceit, lewdness, envy, slander, arrogance and folly. All these evils come from inside and defile a person."

This is one heck of a list. It includes intentions, attitudes, and even behaviors as though they are tied to a person's core. These things have the power to shape and even destroy someone. The focus is internal. Something external like food can't make a person bad, he says. Dirt, spit, feces, food, none of these things enter the heart. It's the motivations, intentions, the internal foundations behind what a person does that can transform a person. It's these things that make someone "dirty," not someone's hands or food.

In saying this, Jesus has just shattered some perspectives. He has brought up an issue that will eventually come up in debate among the earliest Christians (and still some today): what are his followers to do with the laws from scripture? At the very least, Jesus is saying that people have misunderstood these purity laws.

Speaking again as one who understands the very mind of God, he explains how things have gone astray. In a general way, the law was understood to be the path for people to resemble God's goodness which would, as a result, set them apart from the world around them.[1] God was also clear that it was his intent to then use his people to reveal himself as the one true God and to bring salvation to all nations.[2] This was always the master plan. But along the way, following these commands actually became an obstacle to this mission. The meticulous application of these dietary laws was preventing them from interacting with people from other cultures.

Yet, this doesn't mean that God's dietary laws were a mistake. The context has changed significantly. For example, when God gave these laws Israel was an independent nation where everyone was expected to abide by these commands. At the time of Jesus, they are an occupied nation unnecessarily separating themselves socially from others. And while it's possible that these dietary laws were in part aimed at health, such a consideration was apparently never intended to supersede the basic opportunity to interact kindly with other people.

They've missed the point.

Jesus is now tearing down these common walls of separation between Jews and gentiles. The time has finally come for God's people to join this mission of carrying God's salvation to the nations as long intended, and the disciples are getting to witness the transition. In what follows, we will see the scope of Jesus' mission begin to extend beyond the familiar people and lands of his nation as he ventures further and further into gentile territories.

NEW DESTINATIONS
Mark 7:24-30

Following his dinner encounter, Jesus sets out for some distant northern lands inhabited more heavily by gentile populations. Yet even in these places he is unable to find much rest....

Jesus left that place and went to the vicinity of Tyre. He entered a house and did not want anyone to know it; yet he could not keep his presence secret. In fact, as soon as she heard about him, a woman whose little daughter was possessed by an impure spirit came and fell at his feet. The

---

[1] Exodus 19:5-6   [2] Isaiah 66:19-21

woman was a Greek, born in Syrian Phoenicia. She begged Jesus to drive the demon out of her daughter.

This is one of only a few encounters we see where Jesus is interacting specifically with a gentile. Here we are told specifically of her ethnicity, something that may play into the strange conversation that follows....

"First let the children eat all they want," he told her, "for it is not right to take the children's bread and toss it to their dogs."

This has to sting.

With a strange comment, Jesus is describing the Jewish people as his children, and gentiles as dogs. Obviously, a parent is concerned first with feeding their children. His obligation was first to the Jewish people, his "children." It isn't right for him to neglect this responsibility. Given the strong tensions between different ethnic and religious groups, this kind of response may have been expected from him. Would he, a Jew, help a gentile, or would he focus instead on the suffering of his own nation? This priority also fits his ministry. He has worked primarily among Jewish people up to this point. But why then would he come to such a gentile region if this were the case? Doesn't prioritizing his people contradict other statements he's made? Maybe this apparent shift in his ministry is by design and a part of his plan, a plan that he revealed at the beginning when he was run out of Nazareth. Begin with one group before moving on to the next. Also, as he said back in Nazareth, if his people won't accept him, he will gladly head elsewhere. It just so happens that Elijah, whom he had referred to in that encounter, was once active performing miracles in this very northern gentile region[1] that Jesus has now visited. Now that Jesus is facing resistance among his own people, the time has finally come for his ministry to extend beyond the bounds of the Jewish people, and now he has moved elsewhere.

At the same time, his response is also a test.

Let's step back to the detail of her ethnicity. The Jewish people were once ruled by a Syrian kingdom which no doubt had left some

---

[1] 1 Kings 17:7-24

lingering resentments. Could it be that Jesus is testing her by voicing the prejudiced sentiments often used against him (possibly in his work as a carpenter) to see if she holds these views as well? Will she be defiant and betray her own prejudice by saying something like, "Ha, it is you Jews who are dogs!" Or, is her humble request authentic?

> *"Lord," she replied, "even the dogs under the table eat the children's crumbs."*

> *Then he told her, "For such a reply, you may go; the demon has left your daughter."*

> *She went home and found her child lying on the bed, and the demon gone.*

She responds wisely to the test. Instead of fighting him, she remains humble and honors him. She's not about to demand his attention as if she is more important than anyone else, she is simply asking for his kindness without any pretense of ethnic superiority. She passes the test, and sure enough Jesus is now revealing God's goodness to even gentile people. It's worth noting that in healing this woman's son, Jesus has just served an "enemy" of his people.

A SURPRISING RETURN
Mark 7:31-37

> *Then Jesus left the vicinity of Tyre and went through Sidon, down to the Sea of Galilee and into the region of the Decapolis. There some people brought to him a man who was deaf and could hardly talk, and they begged Jesus to place his hand on him.*

After a brief stay in one Gentile area, Jesus heads straight for another. This happens to be a region we've encountered before, when Jesus healed the man called Legion possessed by demons. It appears that the exorcised man's testimony has influenced Jesus' reception. Instead of being rejected as he was in that story, Jesus is a recognized and welcomed figure, unable to find any solace from the crowds.

After he took him aside, away from the crowd, Jesus put his fingers into the man's ears. Then he spit and touched the man's tongue. He looked up to heaven and with a deep sigh said to him, "Ephphatha!" (which means "Be opened!"). At this, the man's ears were opened, his tongue was loosened and he began to speak plainly.

Is Jesus trying to avoid attention when he pulls the man aside? Performing what would have seemed like a strange inspection, Jesus touches his ears and tongue before letting out a sigh.

Is he growing tired of this?

And why does he spit?

Where healers often used different rituals and invoked the power of a deity, Jesus makes a strange display, almost mocking such practices. Once again, he heals as if *he is the deity.* Spitting is usually a gesture of rejection. Is he remembering the rejection of his own people as he heals a gentile? It is, in part, because of his rejection by his own people that he is now venturing to other lands. And ultimately, it is his rejection that will bring about the salvation he has long predicted.

Jesus commanded them not to tell anyone. But the more he did so, the more they kept talking about it. People were overwhelmed with amazement. "He has done everything well," they said. "He even makes the deaf hear and the mute speak."

"Overwhelmed with amazement," these are powerful words.

He's given this man ears to hear and a mouth to speak. Now, after years of silence, this man and the crowd can't shut up, and people are amazed at the diversity of miracles. He seems to be able to do *anything.* Unlike other healers they have seen who focus on one thing or another, Jesus does it all. This seems like a good thing, so why should they be silent?

Jesus seems to be traveling from town to town trying to keep a low profile. But as he attempts to evade the crowds, healing people seems to be doing more to inhibit his plans than help them. There's already a storm brewing for him in Jerusalem where leaders from all sorts of groups oppose him. But of these miracles, he is unable to stay or find any refuge around Galilee. The demands of the crowds are overwhelming. We've even seen them follow him from town to town (like when he fed the 5,000). Between all the popularity and controversy, it's difficult to find any rest. But the time isn't right yet for the great showdown. As we will see, Jesus is waiting for the Passover. Sure enough, as word continues to spread, Jesus must leave town once again.

RUMORS
Matthew 16:13-20; Luke 9:22-27

After a string of miracles in different locations, Jesus is finally able to evade the crowds. He comes to Caesarea Philippi, the home of Philip the Tetrarch (son of Herod), who is known for his tolerance of different peoples and for generally maintaining a peaceful society. At an elevation of about 1,100 feet, the city was actually carved into the side of a mountain. Caesarea Philippi was known for its pagan worship. It probably had the kind of stigma among Jewish people that Vegas does today among many religious folk as a "Sin City." But surrounded by altars to pagan gods, Jesus is finally able to get a little more intimate and direct with his disciples. He takes a moment to clarify what's happening and what lies ahead.

> *When Jesus came to the region of Caesarea Philippi, he asked his disciples, "Who do people say the Son of Man is?"*

> *They replied, "Some say John the Baptist; other say Elijah; and still others, Jeremiah or one of the prophets."*

Jesus asks what's being said to get the conversation started. He begins with one of the titles we've encountered before, the "Son of Man," the figure expected to rule to the ends of the earth.[1] It's the strange title Jesus has used on multiple occasions to speak vaguely of himself. It's a much less alarming title than say, "Son of God" which is far more obvious. As will become clear, he is referring to

---

[1] Daniel 7:13-14

himself here. What exactly are people saying about all that's happening? Who do they think he is?

They respond with some common associations. There are numerous opinions (as there are still today). Some think he is John the Baptist, a well-respected figure of their time, back from the dead. Others think of Elijah, the great desert prophet who is said to have ascended to heaven[1] and is one day to return as a messenger[2] just before the kingdom of God. Still others believe that another great prophet like Jeremiah, known for rebuking the nation of Israel, has returned. While there's plenty of debate, one thing is consistent.

Jesus is significant.

"But what about you?" he asked. "Who do you say I am?"

We've come to the point.

This isn't all fancy theological talk about parsing scriptural passages, this is about the identity of one person, Jesus. With all these ideas and expectations flying around, do they realize who he is? Identity has been the struggle all along since the days of Eden. Who is God? Jesus has been with them for multiple years at this point. He has surprised, confused and astonished them. But what do they actually believe about him? Do they get it yet, or are they just along for the ride?

It's a tense moment of serious depth.

Who do you think I am?

Simon Peter answered, "You are the Messiah, the son of the living God."

With words that have echoed through history, Peter boldly speaks on behalf of the group. *You are the one we've all been waiting for. You are the anointed one, the true son of God.*

God is not gone. God hasn't forgotten us but is still at work in the world. Peter's confession of faith, as it is called, becomes a foundation for all that follows as countless Christians through the ages have repeated these very words at their baptism. The disciples will stand on this claim. This is the foundation.

---

[1] 2 Kings 2:1-18   [2] Malachi 3:1, 4:5

These words can spark a revolution.

These are words to die for.

Jesus replied, "Blessed are you, Simon…I tell you that you are Peter, and on this rock I will build my church, and the gates of Hades will not overcome it. I will give you the keys of the kingdom of heaven; whatever you bind on earth will be bound in heaven, and whatever you loose on earth will be loosed in heaven." Then he ordered his disciples not to tell anyone that he was the Messiah.

Jesus gives Simon a new identity. Through faith, Simon becomes *Petros* or "the rock," a transliteration of his name. This is what faith does; it transforms. It makes something of nothing. It takes a common and sinful fisherman and makes him the foundation of a movement that will endure unto eternity. This is who God is. He is simple yet beyond understanding. He is magnificent yet as ordinary as a Judean man, and he can make something wonderful out of nothing, as was done in the beginning. God is still at work, and Peter's faith will be the foundation of an everlasting kingdom. Worlds are colliding. The heavens and earth are on a crash course, and this revolutionary movement is at its center. What happens here will resound for all eternity.

But that's not all. Teaching his disciples at a city carved into the side of a mountain, Jesus talks about building upon "this rock." He then speaks as though the coming revolution will overwhelm even the gates, or entrance, to hell. It so happens that there is a large cave with a natural spring just outside of the city. This cave was a sacred site for pagan worship and was believed to be the entrance to the underworld, a.k.a. hell. Perhaps Jesus was teaching them at this particular religious site. A city at the center of pagan worship, lush with gentile immorality, a city symbolic of the broader gentile world—it is places like this that before long will serve as hotbeds for the growing Christian movement. The so called "pits of hell" or "sin cities" will one day be transformed, just like Peter, into the historic foundations of God's kingdom spreading throughout the Roman empire. Instead of being repelled by these regions, the disciples are instead to be propelled *to* these places.

But *hush hush*, these are not things that can be spoken of out in the open yet. Jesus already had to step away from the realm of Herod Antipas in order to even speak freely about such things. There is still more to happen. The story is not yet finished...

And he said, "The Son of Man must suffer many things and be rejected by the elders, chief priests and the teachers of the law, and he must be killed and on the third day be raised to life."

This is a rather surprising turn. *I am going to suffer and be rejected by the leaders of our community—politicians, teachers, priests even...and I must be killed and raised to life.*

This is as about as bad a prediction as someone can make. As a reader, chances are that you've probably heard the ending to this story before. But consider the shock it would have been to his disciples. This is the man who can do *anything*. Jesus is supposed to be the Messiah, the one to free them from the oppression and rule of Rome. What on earth is he talking about? Here, Jesus is mixing passages in the Hebrew scriptures that describe a righteous "Suffering Servant" who dies on behalf of the people[1] with those about the "Son of Man" (the messianic figure of power).[2] But which is he? Is Jesus the man of pain or power? How could he be both?

They know that he's the Messiah. Unfortunately, they don't know what the Messiah is. They know Jesus, yet they hardly know him at all. God isn't who they expect. This is not going to lead where they believe. This is not what they have in mind.

Then he said to them all: "Whoever wants to be my disciple must deny themselves and take up their cross daily and follow me. For whoever wants to save their life will lose it, but whoever loses their life for me will save it. What good is it for someone to gain the whole world, and yet lose or forfeit their very self? Whoever is ashamed of me and my words, the Son of Man will be ashamed of them when he comes in

---

[1] Isaiah 50:4-11, 52:13-53:12 [2] Daniel 7:13-14

his glory and in the glory of the Father and of the holy angels.

Truly I tell you, some who are standing here will not taste death before they see the kingdom of God."

True self and false self, life and death, is this double speak? Jesus speaks of a cross, the reviled symbol of capital punishment used to torture and humiliate enemies of the Roman Empire. Crosses were what rebels died upon *if they failed.* Crucifixion sent a message— don't mess with Rome. How does one take this up daily? Is he saying that their mission will require the self-sacrifice of possible death?

Jesus has affirmed that he is the Messiah. But the rest of what he said is pretty confusing to the disciples. Is he about to lead a rebellion or not? Is the revolution going to fail or succeed? Wasn't all of this peace and enemy-love talk simply to mislead the authorities about the violent overthrow he was planning? When he talks about rising from the dead, is he being literal or metaphorical?

The kingdom isn't what they had anticipated. It isn't going to arrive all at once. Through death, Jesus is about to begin something in their lifetime, a new stage of existence in our world where people can become a part of this kingdom, but this kingdom will not yet be fully realized on earth. That is still to come. While it isn't clear to his disciples yet, we will see him continue to describe this strange kingdom that can be tasted but that still awaits a future completion.

In the meantime, this is about to go public. Jesus is about to accept the long-awaited faceoff with the authorities. The disciples must endure. He speaks of *coming in glory*, language used in common descriptions of the "Son of Man" who would rule in the power of God to the ends of the earth. This language also evokes someone getting crowned king and even echoes scriptural descriptions of God entering his dwelling place. In other words, God is about to return in a fantastic way, and Jesus will be revealed as the true king of this everlasting kingdom.

The revolution is coming.

BACK TO THE MOUNTAINTOP
Matthew 17:1-4; Mark 9:6; Matthew 17:5-8; Mark 9:9-10;
Matthew 17:10-13

After some intimate conversations, Jesus gathers just a handful of his disciples for an especially memorable experience. This group, nicknamed the "inner circle," were elsewhere the only disciples present when Jesus raised Jairus' daughter from the dead. He appears to have a unique relationship with this group, revealing himself to them in ways others haven't seen.

> *After six days Jesus took with him Peter, James and John the brother of James, and led them up a high mountain by themselves. There he was transfigured before them. His face shone like the sun, and his clothes became as white as the light. Just then there appeared before them Moses and Elijah, talking with Jesus.*

Here, God reveals his presence in a way that has otherwise been hidden beneath the surface. Could this be the Jesus that the evil spirits recognized previously when they cried out in terror before him? The disciples are catching a glimpse of God's fullness dwelling within skin and bones, the perfect marriage of the two realms of existence residing in human form. Suddenly, in their presence, he changes.

Jesus is transfigured.

It's a weird word, and one not common to our language. In Greek, this is the word for metamorphosis. But that's not all. There are others present. Moses and Elijah, two of the most significant figures of the scriptures, whose lives and ministries resembled Jesus' own ministry, are standing present with him discussing things as if they have all been laboring together... as if Jesus is the completion of their work. Is this a dream? Is this the glory that Jesus spoke of at Peter's confession?

Confused and terrified, Peter has an idea.

> *Peter said to Jesus, "Lord, it is good for us to be here. If you wish, I will put up three shelters—one for you, one for Moses and one for Elijah."*

(He did not know what to say, they were so frightened.)

Peter is thrilled and suggests that they build shelters to stay for a while. Why not remain in this place and dwell on this majestic experience? Has their journey finally ended here on this mountain? Could this be the rest they've all been waiting for?

While he was still speaking, a bright cloud covered them, and a voice from the cloud said, "This is my Son, whom I love; with him I am well pleased. Listen to him!"

When the disciples heard this, they fell facedown to the ground, terrified. But Jesus came and touched them. "Get up," he said. "Don't be afraid." When they looked up, they saw no one except Jesus.

Apparently not.

Their journey isn't complete. The suffering Jesus predicted has yet to happen. Repeating the words God spoke at Jesus's baptism, Jesus is again identified as God's beloved son. It's the same description that was once used to describe Abraham's son Isaac,[1] who was nearly sacrificed. But in that story God provided a lamb instead so that Isaac could be set free. Here, it is as though Jesus is that very sacrificial lamb, a beloved son linked to God's promises to Abraham, about to bring the reckoning once promised to come through Isaac's line.[2]

As they were coming down the mountain, Jesus gave them orders not to tell anyone what they had seen until the Son of Man had risen from the dead. They kept the matter to themselves, discussing what "rising from the dead" meant.

As he did at Peter's confession, Jesus has repeated something about rising from the dead. This probably sounds pretty plain and obvious to us—someone's coming back from the dead. But in the disciples' day, people understood resurrection to mean something much broader. One of the heated debates in their time was about whether or not God would return and resurrect *everyone* from the

---

[1] Genesis 22   [2] See chapter 2 or Genesis 21:12

dead for final judgment. Some disciples probably thought Jesus was saying that he, the Son of Man, was about to begin a war (Armageddon) to destroy their enemies (like Rome). Afterward, at the final judgment, all would be raised from the dead (necessary after a great battle where almost everyone dies), and God's kingdom would finally be installed upon the earth for all of eternity, with some to be transformed "in glory" and others punished.

So is this war about to happen?

The disciples asked him, "Why then do the teachers of the law say that Elijah must come first?"

Jesus replied, "To be sure, Elijah comes and will restore all things. But I tell you, Elijah has already come, and they did not recognize him, but have done to him everything they wished. In the same way the Son of Man is going to suffer at their hands." Then the disciples understood that he was talking to them about John the Baptist.

Thinking they've got part of things figured out, they instead bring up Elijah. If they are right about all this that is about to take place, has Elijah already come as the forerunner of God's kingdom? Or was this majestic mountain appearance actually the prophesied coming of Elijah?

Jesus affirms again that Elijah "will restore all things," and then he says that Elijah has already suffered and been rejected as Jesus will too. As he speaks, they realize that Jesus was referring to John the Baptist. The physical descriptions of the two men are actually quite similar. Rugged desert prophets, both men wore garments made of camel's hair with a leather belt.[1] Their ministries were also similar in that they repeatedly rebuked the nation's leaders. Surely, they probably think, this is all making sense. John the Baptist was the forerunner (one like Elijah) who suffered and was rejected. This will happen to Jesus too. And this, in turn, will bring the great revolution when God's kingdom will be installed upon the earth. Many will die and all will be raised for eternal judgment. It's all coming together.

---

[1] 2 Kings 1:8; Mark 1:6

It's all about to happen. This meeting was to discuss some final arrangements.

Except they are still wrong.

The revolution won't come in the form of a great war as they anticipate, and God's kingdom won't arrive all at once. As always, the disciples are catching glimpses but still missing what he is saying. As things unfold, it will become clear to them. While they've had a memorable time on this mountain, it's time to descend back to the countryside. Their journey must continue for one final stretch. A showdown in Jerusalem awaits them.

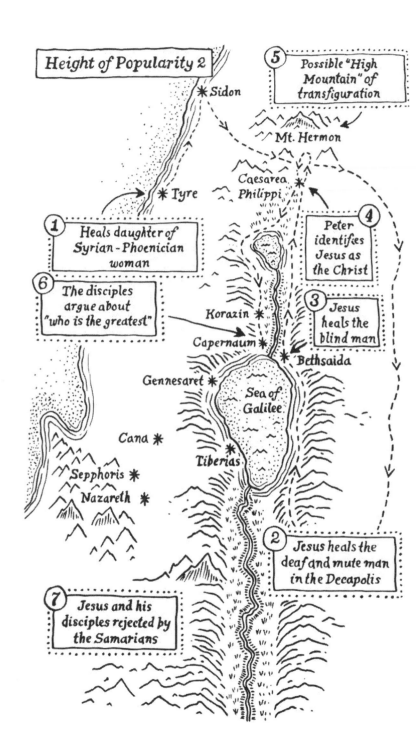

Height of Popularity 2

⑤ Possible "High Mountain" of transfiguration

Sidon

Mt. Hermon

Caesarea Philippi

Tyre

① Heals daughter of Syrian-Phoenician woman

④ Peter identifies Jesus as the Christ

⑥ The disciples argue about "who is the greatest"

③ Jesus heals the blind man

Korazin

Capernaum

Bethsaida

Gennesaret

Sea of Galilee

Cana

Tiberias

Sepphoris

Nazareth

② Jesus heals the deaf and mute man in the Decapolis

⑦ Jesus and his disciples rejected by the Samarians

Part IV

The Final Stretch

TWELVE

A Few Surprises

I
T APPEARS THAT JESUS' special relationship with the inner circle may be raising some eyebrows. Do these three think they are better than everyone else? A revolution is on the verge, yet they are stuck questioning which of them is greatest. Is it Peter, the rock that Jesus spoke of? Or, maybe one of the other members of the inner circle that has had some special invitations to be with Jesus.

GROWING RIVALRY
Mark 9:30, 33-37; Luke 9:49-50

> *They left that place and passed through Galilee. Jesus did not want anyone to know where they were...*

> *They came to Capernaum. When he was in the house, he asked them, "What were you arguing about on the road?" But they kept quiet because on the way they had argued about who was the greatest.*

Apparently the discussion had become an argument. This must have been awkward. Ever perceptive, Jesus inquires. He is met with silence. The craving to be great, or pride, once destroyed the harmony of Eden. Has it now infected his own fellowship as well?

> *Sitting down, Jesus called the Twelve and said, "Anyone who wants to be first must be the very last, and the servant of all."*

He took a little child whom he placed among them. Taking him in his arms, he said to them, "Whoever welcomes one of these little children in my name welcomes me; and whoever welcomes me does not welcome me but the one who sent me."

Jesus flips it. Greatness is not what they think. It isn't a matter of power, luxury, and prestige, but something quite the opposite. In the garden, Adam and Eve were actually invited to greatness through their service of God. But instead of trusting God, they attempted to seize greatness through their own power. Ever since, humanity has been similarly deceived. True greatness comes through love, sacrifice, kindness, and generosity—reflecting God's character. Greatness to God is being "last," a servant to all regardless of stature.

He calls their attention to a child, someone probably unimportant to them. Surely the greatest of a household would have been the figure of authority, right? Instead, Jesus highlights the role of caring for another, of child-rearing. This seemingly unimportant task (to them) generally relegated to women (of a low position in their society) is praised as a form of greatness. This unwarranted love honors God and uniquely reflects his character. It is likely because of Jesus' words here that the early Christian community eventually became known for taking in abandoned children. According to Jesus, even some of the most rudimentary acts of kindness can be profound acts of worship.

This is not the greatness the disciples had in mind.

But this isn't the only story we have about jealousy among the disciples. We are also told a story of a competitive spirit among them towards others.

"Master," said John, "we saw someone driving out demons in your name and we tried to stop him, because he is not one of us."

"Do not stop him," Jesus said, "for whoever is not against you is for you."

Addressing Jesus as *master* here, John has taken the previous lesson seriously. He implies that he is Christ's servant. But there's a problem, he thinks. Others are beginning to mimic their ministry. Who are these copy cats?

As we've discussed, Jesus performs miracles without calling on the power of God (which implies his own authority and divinity). Here, this copycat is actually performing miracles *in the name of Jesus*, a display of his faith in Christ.

Have the disciples gotten a little self-important? John, one of the inner circle, is concerned because this man isn't "one of us." Human beings can be shockingly tribal. For one reason or another, John sees this man as a threat, even an enemy. Jesus has previously given them authority and sent them out to do miracles. Are they becoming less necessary to his ministry? Shouldn't they be supervising these other do-gooders?

Apparently not.

Echoing his previous teaching about the way divided houses can't stand, Jesus isn't concerned. This movement is meant to spread. As seeds grow (faith), they will produce fruit, spreading his work elsewhere. This is part of the plan. It's a good thing. Once again, Jesus challenges the disciples' understanding authority.

We've now seen him address rivalries between the disciples themselves and with others. Next, we will see how he responds when the entire group is insulted and rejected.

A Detour Along the Way
Luke 9:51-56

> *...Jesus resolutely set out for Jerusalem. And he sent messengers on ahead, who went into a Samaritan village to get things ready for him; but the people there did not welcome him, because he was heading for Jerusalem.*
>
> *When the disciples James and John saw this, they asked, "Lord, do you want us to call fire down from heaven to destroy them?" But Jesus turned and rebuked them. Then he and his disciples went to another village.*

His plans are clear, and it's obvious to them. They are headed for Jerusalem. There's no stopping him now. He's making stops along the way and is now incorporating more messengers to spread word of his arrival. But he is prevented from entering a Samaritan village because the residents know he is headed to Jerusalem—the historic rival city and region of people who previously destroyed the temple in Samaria. We've seen these tensions on display before when Jesus encountered the woman at the well. The villagers don't want anything to do with "his kind."

Who wouldn't be offended by this?

Indignant, and possibly emboldened by their experience on the mountain, James and John ask Jesus to let them destroy the city. This was the plan, right? Begin the battle and call upon the heavenly forces to destroy their enemies? After all, in the scriptures,[1] God once destroyed a city by fire from heaven. But Jesus doesn't agree to their plan. Instead, he rebukes *them*, and they move on. Their righteous indignation is no excuse for seeking revenge.

Once again Jesus plays the role of an exile in search of a place to stay. We've seen him run out of his hometown of Nazareth and one of the cities of the Decapolis, and we've seen him chased relentlessly throughout Galilee by crowds with never-ending demands. Homeless along the road, Jesus and the disciples continue wandering in search of a place to rest. His path isn't a life of comfort, and popularity isn't all that it's cut out to be.

SOME NEW RECRUITS
Luke 10:1-3, 8-20, 23-24

Yet despite the steep challenges of following Jesus, the number of followers has grown. We've already seen Jesus send out the 12 on their own missions and others ahead of him to prepare the way in Samaria, and we are about to see even more. As his following continues to grow, his mission is building momentum that will be difficult to stop.

---

[1] Genesis 19

After this the Lord appointed seventy-two others and sent them two by two ahead of him to every town and place where he was about to go. He told them, "The harvest is plentiful, but the workers are few. Ask the Lord of the harvest, therefore, to send out workers into his harvest field. Go! I am sending you out like lambs among wolves."

Sharing much of the same advice given to the Twelve when he first sent them, Jesus has expanded the mission significantly. There is much work to be done. It's time to begin training more workers. They will be going to new places, and he cautions them to be careful. They will not always be well received.

The Twelve were recently concerned about others performing miracles, and now Jesus has sent out an enormous group to do much the same. Could the disciples be wondering again if their role is diminishing? Where his choice of twelve apostles symbolizes his mission to the 12 tribes of Israel, his choice of 72 here likely symbolizes what was understood to be 72 gentile (non-Jewish) nations. In other words, the time has come to begin sending people to "the ends of the earth." It's no longer a matter of here or there, but everywhere. While we just saw Jesus beginning to do more in gentile areas, that focus is going to continue. His time in Galilee is may be coming to a close, but his gentile mission is expanding.

When you enter a town and are welcomed, eat what is set before you. Heal the sick who are there and tell them, 'The kingdom of God has come near to you.' But when you enter a town and are not welcomed, go into its streets and say, 'Even the dust of your town we wipe from our feet as a warning to you. Yet be sure of this: The kingdom of God has come near.' I tell you, it will be more bearable on that day for Sodom than for that town.

Woe to you, Chorazin! Woe to you, Bethsaida! For if the miracles that were performed in you had been performed in Tyre and Sidon, they would have repented long ago, sitting in sackcloth and ashes. But it will be more bearable for Tyre and Sidon at the judgment than for you. And you,

Capernaum, will you be lifted up to the heavens? No, you will go down to Hades.

Whoever listens to you listens to me; whoever rejects you rejects me; but whoever rejects me rejects him who sent me.

As he's warned before, they won't be welcomed everywhere. As God's agents, rejecting them is akin to rejecting God. But where they are rejected, they are to brush it off and move on. There is too much work to be done. They can trust God to settle things at judgment one day. Surprisingly, it will be worse for these places that have rejected them than even a place destroyed by fire from the skies in a story from their scriptures.[1]

Chorazin and Bethsaida are both in the region of Galilee. Why this sudden change of tune about them? Weren't crowds there flocking to him? While plenty have joined the movement, plenty have turned their backs. Some have done so outright, others have in their shallow use of him for entertainment and free food, interested simply in what they can get out of Jesus rather than a genuine concern for God's will. So, here he praises the gentile territories of Tyre and Sidon as though they are better off in God's eyes than the places (including his hometown) where he has spent most of his ministry. These gentile territories embraced him and so embraced God.

His ministry is taking a new shape, and, as we will see, he will even begin working "beyond the Jordan," the historic border to the land of his people.

The seventy-two returned with joy and said, "Lord, even the demons submit to us in your name."

He replied, "I saw Satan fall like lightning from heaven. I have given you authority to trample on snakes and scorpions and to overcome all the power of the enemy; nothing will harm you. However, do not rejoice that the spirits submit to you, but rejoice that your names are written in heaven."

---

[1] Genesis 19

215

Much like the Twelve's own excitement when they returned initially from their trips, this group is amazed at what has been done. Jesus warns them not to let it go to their heads (as described about Satan's downfall). This isn't about their power or ability but rather God's work of salvation in the world. Instead, they should delight at their participation in God's kingdom. They are its citizens.

He also makes a shocking statement. Even today there is much discussion about who or what Satan is. As many today still believe, people thought that Satan was a great angel who rebelled against God and was cast to the earth from the heavens before the creation of the world.[1] Here, Jesus is claiming that he was present at this event *before* the world began.

Jesus also emphasizes his passing of authority. He says they will "trample snakes" as was foreshadowed in Eden.[2] This is his work and so now it is theirs also. Their true enemy isn't Rome, it's the work of the serpent. This revolution or holy war is one between worlds or realms of existence, not between the nations of people on earth.

Then he turned to his disciples and said privately, "Blessed are the eyes that see what you see. For I tell you that many prophets and kings wanted to see what you see but did not see it, and to hear what you hear but did not hear it."

This message is different than anything they've heard. God is restoring the world in ways that prophets and kings have longed for. The scriptures are being fulfilled in their midst. But this restoration isn't going to come through a typical war or the powers associated with wealth and strength. Instead, it is something being revealed to the humble, the sincere trust of people that come to God as "little children."

A SURPRISING HERO
Luke 10:25-37

So far, we've seen examples of Jesus teaching in several ways. He's lectured, taught through miracles, spoken in response to

---

[1] People have long interpreted Isaiah 14:12-15 to be a description of Satan's fall from heaven before the creation of the world. Jesus may be echoing this language here. [2] Genesis 3:15

situations, and even answered specific questions asked of him. One way to challenge a well-known figure would have been to question him in public debate. In fact, he was probably asked some of the same questions about the most controversial issues a number of times. Typically, these sorts of questions weren't for the purpose of gathering information but rather for gaining honor by displaying one's wisdom while shaming one's opponent. Questions asked to gain knowledge and clarification were usually communicated in private (as we often see with the disciples) to maintain respect.

Among the common debates of the day were questions about which laws were the most important. How does one truly please God? Is it through proper temple worship as the Sadducees said, or strict adherence to the law and traditions of the elders as the Pharisees said? He has proven to be an interesting teacher. With whom will he align? Sure enough, someone comes to test him on this very subject.

On one occasion an expert in the law stood up to test Jesus. "Teacher," he asked, "what must I do to inherit eternal life?"

This expert in religious law would be very well versed in the scriptures. This man was probably seen as an authority. He's not asking the question out of honest interest in learning something. It's a test, possibly even a trap. At the heart of the question is the topic of salvation. What must be done to receive the reward of life in the world to come?

This is a big question.

"What is written in the Law?" he replied. "How do you read it?"

He answered: "'Love the Lord your God with all your heart and with all your soul and with all your strength and with all your mind'; and, 'Love your neighbor as yourself.'"

Jesus enters the volley by returning a question. By pointing to the law, Jesus affirms a basic answer that most everyone knew. It's like saying, "Do what God says."

The man responds by quoting a passage from a common prayer called the Shema.[1] One of the best known teachers of their time, a Pharisee named Hillel taught that this was a summary of the law.

"You have answered correctly," Jesus replied. "Do this and you will live."

But he wanted to justify himself, so he asked Jesus, "And who is my neighbor?"

Jesus agrees with his answer. Our behavior is to be fueled by a motive, that of love for God. Is the volley now over?

Not quite.

The man clearly had other intentions and is embarrassed. Instead of sparking an intriguing debate, he has simply quoted a well-known idea as an answer to his own question. Why ask a question if you know the answer? His attempt to challenge a respected teacher has failed. He must recover to save face and will try again to prove himself. The discussion takes a significant turn.

Who exactly am I supposed to love?

This is an understandable question. We typically think of a neighbor as someone living next door or at least in close proximity. In their time people debated the precisely what this "proximity" meant, exactly. Within what distance was someone obligated by the law to offer assistance? Within a mile of home? The next village? Were other factors like religion, ethnicity, or political affiliation to be considered? Some went so far as to take "neighbor" to refer only to ethnic and religious kindred within a designated proximity (excluding the foreign, sinful and irreligious). What does Jesus think?

In response, Jesus tells one of his best-known parables.

In reply Jesus said: "A man was going down from Jerusalem to Jericho, when he was attacked by robbers. They stripped him of his clothes, beat him and went away, leaving him half dead. A priest happened to be going down the same road, and when he saw the man, he passed by on the other side. So

---

[1] Deuteronomy 6:4-9, 11:13-21

too, a Levite, when he came to the place and saw him, passed by on the other side."

A man coming from Jerusalem (meaning he's probably a religious pilgrim), gets jumped while travelling. This was actually a common occurrence in their time, as roads were popular locations for bandits. It was dangerous to travel alone. The religious routinely travelled to the city in groups for different festivals. Was this man travelling alone because he was the only faithful religious adherent in his village? Such a thought would endear him even more to anyone listening. Next, Jesus goes on to describe three other travelers.

The first two, a priest and Levite, are the servants of the temple who are commonly associated with the aristocracy. They are probably Sadducees, who emphasize temple worship. Listeners may have nodded their heads in disgust at the reviled wealthy failing to assist a fellow Judean. Has this priest rejected a religious pilgrim as his "neighbor?" This would be upsetting, though it was actually justifiable by their law. If a priest was travelling to Jerusalem, it might be in order to perform necessary duties at the temple. Providing assistance to this bloodied man (who might have appeared to be dead) would leave him "unclean" for a period of multiple days and so unable to perform such duties. But in this case, the Levite should still have stopped. Levites provided assistance in the temple but were a sort of buffer between the priests and other people.[1] Their purpose was in part to help prevent the priests from being made "unclean" during their duties. But that isn't what happens either.

So now where will the story go?

A Pharisee would have hoped that another faithful religious Jew making a similar pilgrimage, a "true Israelite," would embrace the poor traveler as a neighbor. This would reinforce the common resentment for the priesthood while expanding the scope of a neighbor to encompass any faithful religious adherent from other villages.

To a zealot, the answer would be ethnic: a neighbor is any fellow Jew, religious or not. The enemy is other nations. A zealot may have wanted the story to end as a rallying cry to stoke their revolutionary

---

[1] Numbers 18

interests. Find the bandits and punish them. Or, better yet, use this opportunity to inflame the people against Rome's gross injustices as the unlawful and indifferent oppressor of their nation. Except Jesus doesn't go either direction, shocking his listeners instead with someone from a much different fold.

> *"But a Samaritan, as he traveled, came where the man was; and when he saw him, he took pity on him. He went to him and bandaged his wounds, pouring on oil and wine. Then he put the man on his own donkey, brought him to an inn and took care of him. The next day he took out two denarii and gave them to the innkeeper. 'Look after him,' he said, 'and when I return, I will reimburse you for any extra expense you may have.'*

This would have been pretty uncomfortable to hear. To anyone listening to this conversation, Samaritans were enemies. In fact, they were the very group of people who just turned Jesus away *because he was travelling to Jerusalem*. We've already talked about the serious prejudices existing between the regions. We also know historically that, later, circumstances similar to this story brought an end to Pilate's rule. Some Judeans travelling to Jerusalem were murdered along the road around Samaria. Pilate did nothing, and some Samaritans were then killed in retaliation. As a result, an envoy from Samaria travelled to Rome to describe the conflict and the looming risk of war, and Pilate was deposed.

Here, with Jesus it is a Samaritan that goes above and beyond to help this man, his obvious enemy. He personally cares for the wounded man, covers all the expenses, and even pays in advance for future costs by promising to return with money. This is excessive. But the story isn't really about Samaritans, it's about the crowd's own prejudices.

> *Which of these three do you think was a neighbor to the man who fell into the hands of robbers?"*

> *The expert in the law replied, "The one who had mercy on him."*

Jesus told him, "Go and do likewise."

Jesus makes the expert of the law answer, and the man can't even utter the words "the Samaritan." "*The one who had mercy on him,*" he says. Who is the hero of the story? Whoever loves God as this man has, caring for even an "enemy." What does this say about who we are to love? What does this say about who can inherit eternal life? Apparently, they've had it all wrong.

Where the people were concerned about things like proximity, ideology, and ethnicity, Jesus blows the conversation open. If the love of God, and so also one's neighbor (which includes one's enemy) is what is required to inherit eternal life, then everyone has been missing the mark. We are to love anyone and everyone we encounter, even those that reject us. Why? Because, that's who God is. It is God's love, mercy, and generosity that make eternal life even possible. Despite being rejected by Adam and Eve, God has still been gracious and has now come to rescue humanity from the curse. Like the good Samaritan of the story, God has stopped along the road to care for all humanity in its wounded state.

We aren't told any more about what happens after this parable. We don't know if the debater has a change of heart and follows Jesus or not (though it seems unlikely). Instead, we are left with a stunning conclusion and shocked listeners.

But regardless of whether or not anyone new joined his following, it isn't long before we learn of another interesting individual who becomes a significant part of his followers.

A SURPRISING NEW DISCIPLE
Luke 10:38-42

As Jesus and the disciples continue their journey, they come to a village called Bethany, not too far from Jerusalem. Here Jesus stays with a family that will become some of his closest friends. One evening, as dinner approaches, Jesus stuns one of his hosts.

As Jesus and his disciples were on their way, he came to a village where a woman named Martha opened her home to him. She had a sister called Mary, who sat at the Lord's feet listening to what he said. But Martha was distracted by all

*the preparations that had to be made. She came to him and
asked, "Lord, don't you care that my sister has left me to do
the work by myself? Tell her to help me!"*

This has been his common practice as they have travelled, find a
welcoming place and stay until it is time to move on. He instructed
his disciples to do this as well. His hosts would have to prepare for
the possibility of large crowds and make sleeping arrangements for
him and the disciples. There would be much work to do, of which
Martha is well aware. She is stressed and working hard. As a woman,
she was expected (possibly with the help of others) to prepare the
meal for her guests and likely stay somewhat behind the scenes while
Jesus would teach his disciples and other men in her home. These
women were expected to be the servants, not students. Working
diligently, Martha suddenly notices that her sister Mary isn't helping.

This is outrageous.

If Mary cares about Jesus, she is expected to show it through her
service in hospitality, not busying the teacher with questions. He is
an important man, and Mary has forgotten her place! Confounded,
Martha brings this to Jesus' attention, frustrated and confused by his
lack of rebuke. She expects Jesus to side with her, reinforcing the
traditions of her society.

Except he doesn't.

*"Martha, Martha," the Lord answered, "you are worried
and upset about many things, but few things are needed—or
indeed only one. Mary has chosen what is better, and it will
not be taken away from her."*

He knows that she means well, but Martha is missing out on
something beautiful. In all the preparations for the meal, she's
overlooked the true bread standing in the midst of her home. Her
sister Mary, however, has recognized the weight of this moment and
cherished this opportunity to listen at his feet. Loving Jesus, she has
embraced something that will not fade.

Instead of "putting her in her place," though, Jesus teaches Mary
as he would anyone else. Unlike his broader culture, he doesn't
assume women to be intellectually inferior. In a world where men

rule over women, Jesus is leveling the playing field. He is bringing harmony and equality, restoring the peace that once existed in the garden between men and women.

Mary has chosen wisely, treasuring the right thing, and it will not be taken from her. Or maybe Jesus has chosen wisely as he made the most of an opportunity to encourage a follower. As we will see, Mary's devotion will be on display again one day as she plays an important role in what's to come.

A SURPRISING REBUKE
Luke 14:1-14

Around this time, Jesus is invited to another dinner banquet where he keeps the surprises rolling.

One Sabbath, when Jesus went to eat in the house of a prominent Pharisee, he was being carefully watched. There in front of him was a man suffering from abnormal swelling of his body. Jesus asked the Pharisees and experts in the law, "Is it lawful to heal on the Sabbath or not?"

It is the Sabbath, and Jesus has been invited to this meal so that people can test him once again. How will he respond to these prominent men and their thoughts on the world? Having heard stories of miracles, it appears they have brought a suffering man out like a toy to test Jesus.

This man's condition is known today as edema. It is swelling caused from the buildup of fluid beneath the skin, and is often related to problems that can be life-threatening. It is an outwardly visible condition that causes a lot of pain.

Seeing an opportunity, Jesus poses a question pinpointing this very situation. The Pharisees are meticulous in their adherence to the Sabbath laws, which clearly forbid work on that day. But is healing considered work?

But they remained silent. So taking hold of the man, he healed him and sent him on his way.

Then he asked them, "If one of you has a child or an ox that falls into a well on the Sabbath day, will you not immediately pull him out?" And they had nothing to say.

This would have caused a scene.

Jesus steps up to the plate. They want to know who he really is, so he is going to show them. They want to test him, but he is going to test them. So he draws a simple comparison to something that would have been obvious to them. If it's common sense to help a wounded animal, even on the Sabbath, how could "concern" for God's commands allow people to blatantly ignore an ailing person? Once again, Jesus seems to peek behind the curtain of the Sabbath laws to highlight their intent. These restrictions were not designed to excuse one's duty to help others (as loving neighbors) but rather to bring about restoration and wholeness.

So is it ok to help someone on the Sabbath? Don't be ridiculous.

Still, the dinner has just begun. The table is now set, and there is still much more to happen.

When he noticed how the guests picked the places of honor at the table, he told them this parable: "When someone invites you to a wedding feast, do not take the place of honor, for a person more distinguished than you may have been invited. If so, the host who invited both of you will come and say to you, 'Give this person your seat.' Then, humiliated, you will have to take the least important place. But when you are invited, take the lowest place, so that when your host comes, he will say to you, 'Friend, move up to a better place.' Then you will be honored in the presence of all the other guests. For all those who exalt themselves will be humbled, and those who humble themselves will be exalted."

Jesus has already called out these people's blatant disregard for the well-being of others, and now he takes it even further. These people are self-important. They desire honor and recognition, and it ruffles Jesus' feathers. He uses a wedding feast to make his point. Even today, we often have seating charts arranged to highlight the significance of particular guests. At a meal with obvious seats of honor, Jesus is bold enough to rebuke numerous guests. Jesus calls for humility, not self-importance. Better to be praised publicly than rebuked, he says. Why not let the host make the decision about where one sits?[1]

Except this isn't just about dinner, this is about everything. Whether these Pharisees have realized it or not, they have already attended a wedding feast and overlooked the groom, Jesus. God has come to be reunited with his people in a special covenant relationship, yet many have grabbed seats they're not worthy of taking. As a result, many will be humbled, while others will be exalted.

> *Then Jesus said to his host, "When you give a luncheon or dinner, do not invite your friends, your brothers or sisters, your relatives, or your rich neighbors; if you do, they may invite you back and so you will be repaid. But when you give a banquet, invite the poor, the crippled, the lame, the blind, and you will be blessed. Although they cannot repay you, you will be repaid at the resurrection of the righteous."*

This is backwards. Daily, we encounter situations where particular categories of people are routinely overlooked and devalued. Instead of serving oneself, why not serve others? Instead of looking for honor in the presence of guests, why not seek honor before God? Who is the real audience? We want it to be about us, not others. We want to receive, yet Jesus seems to think it is better to give. Giving to those in need, he says, is as if doing God a favor. What treasure or honor do we seek? Is it something fleeting like prestige among prominent people, or an everlasting honor from the God of all creation? Which is more valuable?

Jesus came to reveal what is truly good, and it doesn't fit very well with the ways of our world. We misunderstand opportunity and overlook genuine greatness. It's startling to think that some of the greatest deeds in history may not even be known to us.

At least, not yet.

---

[1] Proverbs 25:6-7

THIRTEEN
A Good Shepherd

JESUS OFTEN USES PUNCH lines to his stories, reversals where he flips ideas around like being humbled and exalted, ideas that may get repeated in multiple stories. For example, at Peter's confession he said, "Whoever wants to save his life must lose it, but whoever loses his life for my sake will find it." Such repetition and catchy phrases helped his disciples learn. It made ideas memorable for them. He does this here with the punch line of being humbled and exalted.

SOME NEEDED REPETITION
Luke 18:9-14

> To some who were confident of their own righteousness and looked down on everybody else, Jesus told this parable: "Two men went up to the temple to pray, one a Pharisee and the other a tax collector. The Pharisee stood by himself and prayed: 'God, I thank you that I am not like other people—robbers, evildoers, adulterers—or even like this tax collector. I fast twice a week and give a tenth of all I get.'
>
> "But the tax collector stood at a distance. He would not even look up to heaven, but beat his breast and said, 'God, have mercy on me, a sinner.'
>
> "I tell you that this man, rather than the other, went home justified before God. For all those who exalt themselves will

be humbled, and those who humble themselves will be exalted."

With this story we are told Jesus is addressing people who think very highly of themselves (maybe like those he just confronted at dinner). To do so, he tells a story of two people who appear to be on opposite ends of the moral spectrum. One is very religious and viewed as a good person, while the other is a tax collector, someone the listeners would perceive as very sinful. One comes forward confidently and prays about himself, while the other stands at a distance.

But Jesus doesn't address the men's everyday deeds. Instead, he focuses on the way these two men approach God. One would probably think that the Pharisee, who has obeyed the religious laws, is in good standing with the creator. One might even agree with the Pharisee's implication that he is happy to be better off than others. But there's a problem. This man's pride stands between him and God. As he rattles off all the good he's done, he never mentions his sins. If he only wants to boast and not ask for forgiveness, why has he come to pray? Is this what God wants?

No.

Shockingly, Jesus praises the sinner! Not because of the man's wrongdoing, but because the tax collector has come humbly before God and begged for mercy. As a result, the sinner has been made right before God while the "good" person hasn't. This may describe Jesus' initial encounter with Matthew, the tax collector, who left his booth to follow Jesus.[1]

Jesus is saying that no amount of doing good or being better than someone can solve the problem of sin. We are all imperfect and make mistakes, and our goodness doesn't undo any wrong that has been done. Only forgiveness can address sin. People would be foolish to approach God as if they had reason to boast. Instead, people are to approach God in humility, recognizing their dependence upon his mercy. They are to be "poor in spirit." Better to be restored than rebuked.

---

[1] See chapter 5 or Luke 5:27-32

But it's so easy to mix this up. It's so easy to get caught in comparisons and appearances to the point that this can stand in the way of someone's peace with God. Surprisingly, good deeds can actually get in the way of restoration as people attempt to fix things for themselves. This isn't because God doesn't want people to do good but because doing good doesn't erase a wrong that's been done and can distract someone from the real solution. We can't earn forgiveness (which would imply that it is deserved), it is a gift. That peace can only come through the work of God.

Interestingly, this story depicts the very heart of the problem in Eden. Instead of approaching God in humility as servants relying upon God for life, Adam and Eve became self-important. Then, when God called their wrongdoing into account, Adam was too busy talking about others' mistakes to take responsibility for his own. What if Adam had instead confessed and asked for mercy, like the tax collector here?

According to Jesus, everyone needs God, no matter how good they think they are. And on the flip side, this is some fantastic news. No matter how *bad* someone thinks they are, they need God's forgiveness *and can have it.*

This forgiving love is at the center of another group of parables Jesus teaches when he finds himself speaking to more tax collectors and some teachers of the law.

LOOKING FOR WHAT'S LOST
Luke 15

> *Now the tax collectors and sinners were all gathering around to hear Jesus. But the Pharisees and the teachers of the law muttered, "This man welcomes sinners and eats with them."*

We just saw an example in the last parable of people valuing themselves above others. Here we see it again. The Pharisees decide that the fact that Jesus welcomes sinners is a mark against his character. Unlike the last story where the sinner stood "far off" as he prayed, this time the "sinners" are gathering close to Jesus while the "good people" stand back as part of the peanut gallery. Jesus switches who is close and who is distant. This is the banquet parable in action. He just told people to invite the unwanted to dinner. Now he's doing that very thing.

He responds to their criticism with a few stories.

Then Jesus told them this parable: "Suppose one of you has a hundred sheep and loses one of them. Doesn't he leave the ninety-nine in the open country and go after the lost sheep until he finds it? And when he finds it, he joyfully puts it on his shoulders and goes home. Then he calls his friends and neighbors together and says, 'Rejoice with me; I have found my lost sheep.' I tell you that in the same way there will be more rejoicing in heaven over one sinner who repents than over ninety-nine righteous persons who do not need to repent.

Using a common-sense example, Jesus compares himself to a shepherd looking for sheep. The shepherd leaves the 99 to find the one that's gone. When he finds it, he returns to celebrate with everyone, throwing a party with his friends. Jesus compares the lost sheep to these "sinful" people whom God celebrates when they return home. They are more of a priority than the many who never left the pasture.

Next, he continues with another example of the same thing.

Or suppose a woman has ten silver coins and loses one. Doesn't she light a lamp, sweep the house and search carefully until she finds it? And when she finds it, she calls her friends and neighbors together and says, 'Rejoice with me; I have found my lost coin.' In the same way, I tell you, there is rejoicing in the presence of the angels of God over one sinner who repents."

It's possible that Jesus is referring to the coin of a dowry (the bride price), coins worn by a woman on her headdress at a wedding. If so, losing it would be more like a woman losing her wedding ring than some spare change. It's priceless. You can imagine, a person would probably call all sorts of people in the search—work, stores, restaurants, homes… anywhere they might have been. Then, when they found it, they would be ecstatic, maybe have everyone that helped the search over to celebrate. In the same way, God and the angels rejoice when someone returns to God. But if this weren't enough, Jesus tells one more story to really get his point across. This time though, he adds an additional character.

> *Jesus continued: "There was a man who had two sons. The younger one said to his father, 'Father, give me my share of the estate.' So he divided his property between them.*

> *"Not long after that, the younger son got together all he had, set off for a distant country and there squandered his wealth in wild living. After he had spent everything, there was a severe famine in that whole country, and he began to be in need. So he went and hired himself out to a citizen of that country who sent him to his fields to feed pigs. He longed to fill his stomach with the pods that the pigs were eating, but no one gave him anything.*

The young son has asked his father for his inheritance *while his dad was still living.* This is an enormous request and essentially says, "You are dead to me." It is surprising that the father actually complies with the request. Instead of shaming or disowning his son, he cooperates and relinquishes what was likely a fortune to the young man, who quickly blows it on "wild living." It isn't long though before the money runs out and hard times come. In poverty in a foreign place, the young man is forced to become a servant and ends up jealous of the animals he tends to, fed better than he. And Jesus adds that he was tending to pigs, an animal generally reviled by the Jewish people (maybe like the disgust we feel toward rats). He has fallen far indeed.

> *"When he came to his senses, he said, 'How many of my father's hired servants have food to spare, and here I am starving to death! I will set out and go back to my father and say to him: Father, I have sinned against heaven and against you. I am no longer worthy to be called your son; make me like one of your hired servants.' So he got up and went to his father.*

In desperate need, he remembers how well his father used to treat their servants. Hoping for his father's kindness, he decides to confess his mistake and beg for a job as a servant, nothing more. He will humble himself. He probably knows that there is much at stake. His irresponsibility has probably smeared the family's name and reputation. In returning, he risks the public humiliation of his father's rejection. The son decides it worth the risk and heads home.

"But while he was still a long way off, his father saw him and was filled with compassion for him; he ran to his son, threw his arms around him and kissed him.

"The son said to him, 'Father, I have sinned against heaven and against you. I am no longer worthy to be called your son.'

"But the father said to his servants, 'Quick! Bring the best robe and put it on him. Put a ring on his finger and sandals on his feet. Bring the fattened calf and kill it. Let's have a feast and celebrate. For this son of mine was dead and is alive again; he was lost and is found.' So they began to celebrate.

He has not been forgotten. As if waiting for the son to return, the father sees him at a distance and is overjoyed, running out to meet him as though he were an anticipated guest. The son admits his wrongdoing and doesn't even get the chance to make his request before the father quickly cleans him up, restores him to his position in the family (the significance of the ring), and makes arrangements for an enormous party. It is time to celebrate.

So far, this story is basically a more elaborate version of the previous two, except it isn't over yet. Instead of the typical refrain about rejoicing in heaven, this story continues.

"Meanwhile, the older son was in the field. When he came near the house, he heard music and dancing. So he called one of the servants and asked him what was going on. 'Your brother has come,' he replied, 'and your father has killed the fattened calf because he has him back safe and sound.'

"The older brother became angry and refused to go in. So his father went out and pleaded with him. But he answered his father, 'Look! All these years I've been slaving for you and never disobeyed your orders. Yet you never gave me even a young goat so I could celebrate with my friends. But when this son of yours who has squandered your property with prostitutes comes home, you kill the fattened calf for him!'

There was another son, remember? The older son stayed and faithfully worked the fields while his brother was away. Perhaps he's even endured some scorn because of his younger brother's foolish behavior. Returning from a hard day's work, he is confused by the commotion and gets updated on the situation. He is angry and jealous. How can his father quickly move past the wrongs that have been done? This son has been "good" and labored continually, yet hasn't received such favor. Isn't his father rewarding the wrong person and the wrong behavior?

"'My son,' the father said, 'you are always with me, and everything I have is yours. But we had to celebrate and be glad, because this brother of yours was dead and is alive again; he was lost and is found.'"

The father is rejoicing over the restoration of a relationship. It's not about money or good deeds. The older son has been with him all along and could celebrate at any time. He has even witnessed the father's generosity before (giving an early inheritance). So why is he jealous? He already has his father's love and enjoys the fruits of their shared home. But he's jealous because he's been working in vain all along. Like the "good person" at the beginning of the chapter, he thought that love was something to be earned and so has missed out on the joys of a relationship with his father.

He was wrong.

But this is how the story ends, and we aren't told how the older son responds. Does he join the party? Or will he continue to sulk outside? This parable leaves us hanging. The Pharisees, Jesus implies, are just like the older brother. They stand outside, jealous of the celebration that's taking place as the countless "sinners" gather around Jesus. Will they embrace their repentant peers? Yet again, Jesus has brilliantly taught to his circumstances and opened a door for those that would otherwise seem to be his enemies.

At one point or another we've probably resembled both sons. At times, we miss God's love in our arrogance and pursuit of moral perfection. Instead, we've been invited to something different. It's time to celebrate restoration. It's time to come home. It is time to delight in the presence of God in our world, communion with the father in a relationship that cultivates abundant life. But will we join the party?

A GOOD SHEPHERD
John 10:7-11, 16, 19-21, 7:31, 40-44

While we've seen Jesus speak frequently about farming, this is the first time we've seen him speak of shepherds, and it is significant. The great king David was known for his work as a shepherd both of sheep[1] and of the people of Israel.[2] As a songwriter, David spoke of God as a great shepherd[3] guiding his people. Later, the prophets used similar language to describe the nation's leaders,[4] and even refer to the people of Israel as lost sheep.[5] In fact, some even describe a particular time when God would search for his sheep, rescue them, and appoint a great servant like David to shepherd them again.[6] God is doing just what this prophet described. The time has come, and through Jesus God is gathering his flock once again.

Jesus keeps using sheep and shepherd language elsewhere. In another altercation around this time with some Pharisees, Jesus says the following …

> *"Very truly I tell you, I am the gate for the sheep. All who have come before me are thieves and robbers, but the sheep have not listened to them. I am the gate; whoever enters through me will be saved. They will come in and go out, and find pasture. The thief comes only to steal and kill and*

---

[1] 1 Samuel 16:1-13   [2] 2 Samuel 5:1-2; Psalm 78:70-72   [3] Psalm 23   [4] Isaiah 56:9-11; Jeremiah 3:15, 23:1-4; Zechariah 10:3   [5] Jeremiah 50:6   [6] Ezekiel 34, 37:24; Micah 2:12-13

destroy; I have come that they may have life, and have it to the full.

"I am the good shepherd. The good shepherd lays down his life for the sheep.

"I have other sheep that are not of this sheep pen. I must bring them also. They too will listen to my voice, and there shall be one flock and one shepherd."

Jesus describes himself as the awaited entry to life.[1] His enemy, the thief (the weed planter, serpent, etc.) is intent only on harm. He steals and kills as has happened ever since the beginning. But Jesus isn't just the gate. He is the good shepherd who gathers the sheep from among the nations, and the time has come for God to restore more than just the Israelites.[2]

This restoration isn't specific to a particular ethnicity or heritage. Just as he taught in Nazareth when he was driven out of town, this salvation is for more than just the Jewish people. Instead of destroying the nation's enemies, Jesus has come to invite them to join the party. This shepherd has "other pens," and it is time to bring them all together.

The Jews who heard these words were again divided. Many of them said, "He is demon-possessed and raving mad. Why listen to him?"

But others said, "These are not the sayings of a man possessed by a demon. Can a demon open the eyes of the blind?"

Still, many in the crowd believed in him. They said, "When the Messiah comes, will he perform more signs than this man?"

...Some of the people said, "Surely this man is the Prophet."

Others said, "He is the Messiah."

---

[1] Psalm 118:19-21 [2] Isaiah 49:6

Still others asked, "How can the Messiah come from Galilee? Does not Scripture say that the Messiah will come from David's descendants and from Bethlehem, the town where David lived?" Thus the people were divided because of Jesus. Some wanted to seize him, but no one laid a hand on him.

His teaching continues to divide people. Here we see him accused again of serving the devil, possessed, and insane. Others think he is a peculiar miracle worker that they just aren't sure what exactly to make of. Is he the prophet like Moses that they have longed for?[1] Is he the Christ? But the messiah is to be from Bethlehem.[2] They wonder, "Isn't Jesus from Galilee?"

Elsewhere we see Jesus speak harshly to some of his criticisms and critics as he debates with a crowd.

CHILDREN OF THE DEVIL
John 8:31-46, 49-53, 56-58

... "If you hold to my teaching, you are really my disciples. Then you will know the truth, and the truth will set you free."

They answered him, "We are Abraham's descendants and have never been slaves of anyone. How can you say that we shall be set free?"

Jesus replied, "Very truly I tell you, everyone who sins is a slave to sin. Now a slave has no permanent place in the family, but a son belongs to it forever. So if the Son sets you free, you will be free indeed. I know that you are Abraham's descendants. Yet you are looking for a way to kill me, because you have no room for my word. I am telling you what I have seen in the Father's presence, and you are doing what you have heard from your father."

Jesus again makes some bold claims about his teachings as the very way of life intended by God. Again, he is the path, and is even so bold to emphasize obedience to *his* teaching where prophets were

---

[1] Deuteronomy 18:14-22   [2] Micah 5:2

careful to instruct obedience to *God's* teachings. Jesus understands himself to be God.

We also see Jesus use the language of slavery to describe the general public. While it's true that the Jewish people often perceived Roman taxation as akin to slavery, they are shocked by the boldness of his statement. They also feel that he's belittling their status as the favored descendants of God's people. Jesus attempts to explain that before God all bear the status of slaves, not heirs. This leaves them dumbfounded.

He then describes himself as the Son who has come to set them free. How could he claim such a favored status before God after pronouncing all others negligent? What makes him so different? Is he claiming to be sinless, unlike them? He even claims that he is sharing what he has seen *in the presence of God.* But who could ever stand in the presence of God? Even the great prophet Moses had to hide his face from God's radiance![1] And he says that their loyalty is to a different father.

"Abraham is our father," they answered.

"If you were Abraham's children," said Jesus, "then you would do what Abraham did. As it is, you are looking for a way to kill me, a man who has told you the truth that I heard from God. Abraham did not do such things. You are doing the works of your own father."

"We are not illegitimate children," they protested. "The only Father we have is God himself."

Jesus said to them, "If God were your Father, you would love me, for I have come here from God. I have not come on my own; God sent me. Why is my language not clear to you? Because you are unable to hear what I say. You belong to your father the devil, and you want to carry out your father's desires. He was a murderer from the beginning, not holding to the truth, for there is no truth in him. When he lies, he speaks his native language, for he is a liar and the father of

---

[1] Exodus 33:19-23

lies. Yet because I tell the truth, you do not believe me! Can any of you prove me guilty of sin? If I am telling the truth, why don't you believe me?

In line with popular belief, they cite their lineage (Abraham's) as evidence that they are free of the slavery to sin that Jesus has just described. Still thinking of God's favor in terms of blood lines, they explain that they aren't "illegitimate." He must be mistaken.

But they misunderstand their own purity. If they are Abraham's children, then they should behave as he did, Jesus says. Abraham never conspired to kill anyone, so what are they doing? When they respond with a much broader claim to be the children of God (avoiding his point), Jesus spells out his argument more plainly. If they were God's children, then they would receive him (God's son, their brother). But they don't. They have a different father, the devil.

This is an enormous accusation. He points again to their plots to have him killed. These resemble the devil, a murderer and liar, a stark contrast to God's behavior as well as his own as a bringer of truth. He then implies that he is sinless! But how could anyone claim to be perfect? Only God is perfect!

"I am not possessed by a demon," said Jesus, "but I honor my Father and you dishonor me. I am not seeking glory for myself; but there is one who seeks it, and he is the judge. Very truly I tell you, whoever obeys my word will never see death."

At this they exclaimed, "Now we know that you are demon-possessed! Abraham died and so did the prophets, yet you say that whoever obeys your word will never taste death. Are you greater than our father Abraham? He died, and so did the prophets. Who do you think you are?"

Jesus replied..."Your father Abraham rejoiced at the thought of seeing my day; he saw it and was glad."

"You are not yet fifty years old," the Jews said to him, "and you have seen Abraham!"

As the debate proceeds, Jesus continues to clarify some of what he has said. Now he speaks of himself as God's son, not a "slave" to sin like them. Surprisingly, he also now speaks of them as children of Abraham, suddenly acknowledging their biological lineage (something he didn't actually disagree with before). He is here to do his father's work, which will spare them on the day of judgment if they'd listen to him. Their lineage won't save them. His words are the path to eternal life, just as God's were in the beginning. Obey Jesus and never "taste death." And with this comment, they think they've got him.

Abraham, the one at the center of God's promises historically, died. So did the prophets. If Jesus is speaking the words of God just as these men did, then does this mean Abraham (a true follower of God) and other prophets shouldn't have died? How can Jesus know better than the prophets? Does he think himself greater?

Yes, he does.

Jesus speaks as though having intimate knowledge of Abraham, someone who lived about two thousand years prior to their conversation. They point out the absurdity of his statement with the observation that Jesus isn't even fifty yet. How could this be? On top of this, he says that Abraham longed to see his "day" (the time of the Messiah) and now has actually seen it (as though Abraham still lives). How could this be?

> *"Very truly I tell you," Jesus answered, "before Abraham was born, I am!"*

Jewish beliefs don't involve individuals existing as spirits prior to birth. Yet Jesus, in his mid-30s at the time, claims an eternal existence as one preceding Abraham, something believed to be true of only God. In doing so, he also cleverly uses the sacred name of God (who identified himself to Moses as "I am") of himself. It's like saying, "I've always been, and I always will be." If this isn't the truth then it is certainly blasphemy, a crime punishable by death.

Jesus has now hinted at a few things that don't mesh well with their understanding of eternal life and the things to come. In their discussions about resurrection and eternal life, the debate was about how God's kingdom would one day come to reside again *on earth*, not whether people would be removed from the world to exist forever in some spiritual realm. Here, Jesus has hinted at another possibility as he has spoken of Abraham as though living presently somewhere else. It's as though there is some in-between stage, a bridge between someone's death and the arrival of God's restored kingdom on earth (when people will be resurrected physically from the dead). While we've only begun to see these ideas come up, Jesus will echo this framework elsewhere along the way.

Understandably, it isn't long before Jesus is on the move again. Passing through Judea, he heads across the Jordan River and into the desert.

SEARCHING FOR SATISFACTION
Mark 10:1; John 10:40-42; Mark 10:17-27; Matthew 19:27-30

Jesus then left that place and went into the region of Judea and across the Jordan…

…the place where John had been baptizing in the early days. There he stayed, and many people came to him. They said, "Though John never performed a sign, all that John said about his man was true." And in that place many believed in Jesus.

The Jordan River, the place where it all began. His ultimate destination is Jerusalem, and his disciples know this, yet he has been somewhat flexible with his planning. The authorities know of his arrival in Judea and something is brewing. But before everything unfolds, he will make a brief trip to the area where it all started, the place where he was baptized, the stomping grounds of his dear and departed friend John the Baptist. He will walk the depths of the desert valley (the Dead Sea is the lowest place on earth) before returning for his final visit to the mountaintop and the capital city which towers overhead.

Along the way, Jesus is approached by a wealthy young man with a burning question. Despite his success and moral living, something still seems to be missing.

As Jesus started on his way, a man ran up to him and fell on his knees before him. "Good teacher," he asked, "what must I do to inherit eternal life?"

We've heard his question before. It's the same question that was asked by the lawyer in the conversation that eventually led to loving neighbors and the story of the Good Samaritan. So how will Jesus answer this time?

"Why do you call me good?" Jesus answered. "No one is good—except God alone. You know the commandments: 'You shall not murder, you shall not commit adultery, you shall not steal, you shall not give false testimony, you shall not defraud, honor your father and mother.'"

No one is good?

Seizing an opportunity, Jesus makes a quick point. Only God is good. Cleverly, Jesus is testing if this man is suggesting Jesus is God. Jesus may also be setting up the conversation which is about to follow. Does this man think people are good? As we will discover, this man thinks highly of himself as a "good" man. Even today, we would like to think of people as good. Jesus seems to see things differently. This is a jarring and uncomfortable response to the man's question.

Next, Jesus points to the standard of the law as if to say, "If you want to earn eternal life, be perfect and obey everything God says."

"Teacher," he declared, "all these I have kept since I was a boy."

Jesus looked at him and loved him. "One thing you lack," he said. "Go, sell everything you have and give to the poor, and you will have treasure in heaven. Then come, follow me."

This guy thinks he's made the cut. But if so, why is he still searching? Besides, does he really believe he's never violated these basic commands in any way? Like the righteous man boasting of his deeds before God, or like the older brother, the man is overlooking his own imperfection, as though salvation is something that can be achieved by his actions alone.

But Jesus isn't angry. He sees the man with love and responds.

Speaking to a wealthy person, Jesus says, "You want life beyond death? Get rid of everything." The man's wealth provides him false hope and security. It stands between him and God. It cannot lead him to life. He needs to give it up and follow Jesus. Jesus is the way to eternal life.

At this the man's face fell. He went away sad, because he had great wealth.

Jesus looked around and said to his disciples, "How hard it is for the rich to enter the kingdom of God!"

The disciples were amazed at his words. But Jesus said again, "Children, how hard it is to enter the kingdom of God! It is easier for a camel to go through the eye of a needle than for someone who is rich to enter the kingdom of God."

The disciples were even more amazed, and said to each other, "Who then can be saved?"

Jesus looked at them and said, "With man this is impossible, but not with God; all things are possible with God."

Jesus was right on. This man's wealth stands in the way. He isn't willing to give this up and rely upon God, so he walks away sad.

Addressing the disciples as "children," an example of dependence that he has praised elsewhere, Jesus warns of the deceit of wealth. Instead of a mark of favor, it is often an obstacle between someone and entry into the kingdom of God. But the problem isn't simply money, it's that the rich man is full of himself rather than humble as Jesus has commended elsewhere. He sees himself as "wealthy" in regards to his good behavior, not as someone who is poor and in need. Good deeds are often viewed as a sort of currency that purchases a place in the afterlife. Many people think that if they can do enough good then they are "secure." But here, clearly that's not the case. Instead of arguing the finer points of the law, Jesus points to the heart of the matter. Neither this man's wealth or his believed perfection are enough. In fact, both are a problem. The first of the ten commandments[1] is actually about worship of God, and this young man has overlooked his own idolatry. He's been worshiping himself and money, not God.

The disciples can't see past their commonly held values. They wonder aloud how anyone can enter the kingdom of God if not this righteous wealthy man. But that's exactly the point. Neither money or good deeds can guarantee entry into God's kingdom. It is only because of God's kindness that salvation is possible. Because of God's generosity, anyone can access this kingdom, even poor and sinful people, if they will just let go of their fake solutions.

Excited by the implications of what's been said, one of the disciples chimes in.

Peter answered him, "We have left everything to follow you! What then will there be for us?"

Jesus said to them, "Truly I tell you, at the renewal of all things, when the Son of Man sits on his glorious throne, you who have followed me will also sit on twelve thrones, judging the twelve tribes of Israel. And everyone who has left houses or brothers or sisters or father or mother or wife or children or fields for my sake will receive a hundred times as much and will inherit eternal life. But many who are first will be last, and many who are last will be first."

Speaking directly to the 12, Jesus goes on to say quite a lot. Yes, they have dropped everything to follow him, and it will be well worth it. He is the treasure in the field worth everything, the pearl of great price.[2] Any sacrifice will pale in comparison to what is to come at "the renewal of all things," the time when God will finally restore all of creation. At the time of judgment, Jesus will be enthroned, and the disciples will be appointed as his justices.

To finish things off, Jesus uses another of his common reversals, highlighting the inverse relationship between life on earth and life in eternity. For those willing to give here, much more will be gained

---

[1] Exodus 20:3   [2] See chapter 8 or Matthew 13:44-45

and it will all be worth it in the end. But those who put themselves above others will find themselves lacking and last.

EMPTY THREATS
Luke 13:31-33

Once again, Jesus doesn't go unnoticed and it isn't long before he hears again from an irritated antagonist.

> *At that time some Pharisees came to Jesus and said to him, "Leave this place and go somewhere else. Herod wants to kill you."*

Instead of a welcome, he gets a warning. He's back in Herod's territory (this is Herod Antipas), and he is being watched. In what may be some empty threats, these men try to hurry him on his way out of town.

> *He replied, "Go tell that fox, 'I will keep on driving out demons and healing people today and tomorrow, and on the third day I will reach my goal.' In any case, I must press on today and tomorrow and the next day—for surely no prophet can die outside Jerusalem!"*

Speaking boldly, he says that he will continue his work as planned and be on his way shortly. It won't be long. Referring to himself as a prophet, he reveals that he's headed for Jerusalem. If Herod really intends to kill him, surely it would happen there, he says, as it has happened to so many other prophets before him!

FOURTEEN
A Dead Man Walking

NOT LONG AGO, the disciples were scratching their heads about whether they mattered any more to Jesus. After their first mission, they could hardly find a moment alone with their teacher. Jesus even said things that scared many away, but the dust has settled since the days of the overwhelming crowds around Galilee. They have travelled to new, distant lands, and along the way their conviction and purpose has only been strengthened. Here, their confidence has grown enough that they are willing to make a significant request.

A BOLD REQUEST
Mark 10:35-45

Then James and John, the sons of Zebedee, came to him. "Teacher," they said, "we want you to do for us whatever we ask."

"What do you want me to do for you?" he asked.

They replied, "Let one of us sit at your right and the other at your left in your glory."

These are two of the disciples who witnessed the dead girl raised to life and were present at the transfiguration. They've also seen people humbled for claiming the seats of honor, yet they are brave enough to approach their master with this request. Will Jesus oblige?

"You don't know what you are asking," Jesus said. "Can you drink the cup I drink or be baptized with the baptism I am baptized with?"

"We can," they answered.

Jesus said to them, "You will drink the cup I drink and be baptized with the baptism I am baptized with, but to sit at my right or left is not for me to grant. These places belong to those for whom they have been prepared."

Like a kind parent, Jesus explains that they are in over their heads. While they've seen a side of him yet to be revealed to everyone else, they still don't comprehend what is to come, and Jesus knows it's more than they expect.

Jesus isn't saying they are about to have some wine and get baptized together in the Jordan. Instead, he's speaking of the coming events as a baptism and cup that they will experience with him. His looming death is a baptism, and the cup is the bittersweet redemption to come through his suffering. Though they don't know how, he tells them that one day they will indeed follow in his footsteps of death and suffering, but the seats of honor they are requesting are not his to award. These seats are already destined for two others. In fact, these seats may already belong to the other two people that appeared at the transfiguration.

When the ten heard about this, they became indignant with James and John. Jesus called them together and said, "You know that those who are regarded as rulers of the Gentiles lord it over them, and their high officials exercise authority over them. Not so with you. Instead, whoever wants to become great among you must be your servant, and whoever wants to be first must be slave of all. For even the Son of Man did not come to be served, but to serve, and to give his life as a ransom for many."

The others are miffed by James and John's private conversation. It's as if the two disciples were trying to get a promotion behind everyone's back. Tensions clearly remain, so Jesus addresses the group as a whole. He tells them they are still thinking in the familiar terms of their world when it comes to leadership, pointing to the way rulers of various regions oppress people with their power. This is not the disciples' path. They are to be servants, not power-hungry tyrants. Greatness comes through service of others and sacrifice, and Jesus has come to be a great servant. He has come not to take life, but to give of his life on behalf of all. The road ahead is paved with suffering, and their coming baptism is death. Are they ready for this?

ON TO JERICHO
Mark 10:32-34, 46; John 11:1-6; Luke 19:1-10

> *They were on their way up to Jerusalem, with Jesus leading the way, and the disciples were astonished, while those who followed were afraid. Again he took the Twelve aside and told them what was going to happen to him. "We are going up to Jerusalem," he said, "and the Son of Man will be delivered over to the chief priests and teachers of the law. They will condemn him to death and will hand him over to the Gentiles, who will mock him and spit on him, flog him and kill him. Three days later he will rise."*

After some time beyond the Jordan, the group is headed southwest again to Jerusalem. "Up" here refers to Jerusalem's location on the top of a mountain. The disciples have an uphill journey ahead of them. They will pass through Jericho, a welcomed break along the way. But, before they reach the city, Jesus takes a moment to remind them of what is about to happen. Betrayal, rejection, condemnation, slander, abuse, death... and after three days he will rise. This language of rising has confused them before and probably does again here.

This time, they don't ask.

> *Then they came to Jericho... Now a man named Lazarus was sick. He was from Bethany, the village of Mary and her sister Martha. This Mary, whose brother Lazarus now lay sick, was the same one who poured perfume on the Lord and wiped his feet with her hair. So the sisters sent word to Jesus, "Lord, the one you love is sick."*

*When he heard this, Jesus said, "This sickness will not end
in death. No, it is for God's glory so that God's Son may be
glorified through it." Now Jesus loved Martha and her sister
and Lazarus. So when he heard that Lazarus was sick, he
stayed where he was two more days.*

It doesn't take long for their travel plans to be interrupted again.
Just as soon as Jesus arrives in Jericho, he is requested in another
place, Bethany. But Jesus isn't going to leave right away. There is
some work to be done here first, and he will see it through.

*Jesus entered Jericho and was passing through. A man was
there by the name of Zacchaeus; he was a chief tax collector
and was wealthy. He wanted to see who Jesus was, but
because he was short he could not see over the crowd. So he
ran ahead and climbed a sycamore-fig tree to see him, since
Jesus was coming that way.*

I can remember an old song in church about Zacchaeus the "wee-
little man." It's a fun story. Lowly in height and religious stature,
Zacchaeus is curious. He has climbed the economic rungs of his city
through dishonest gain (as we will later see) in order to find the
wealth and advancement he was looking for. But, like the young rich
man, it has left him wanting. Now reviled, he climbs the branches of
a tree in search of something else, a simple glimpse of the man named
Jesus.

*When Jesus reached the spot, he looked up and said to him,
"Zacchaeus, come down immediately. I must stay at your
house today." So he came down at once and welcomed him
gladly.*

*All the people saw this and began to mutter, "He has gone
to be the guest of a sinner."*

Instead of an enemy to be despised, Jesus sees something else, a
small man with a redeeming faith. In a direct manner, Jesus calls
upon Zacchaeus, of all people, and suddenly the disciples have a
place to stay. The crowd is frustrated. As discussed before,
associating with someone of such ill repute would have been

scandalous behavior, especially to Pharisees. Zacchaeus would have been an outcast among his people for his association with Roman authority.

But Zacchaeus stood up and said to the Lord, "Look, Lord! Here and now I give half of my possessions to the poor, and if I have cheated anybody out of anything, I will pay back four times the amount."

Jesus said to him, "Today salvation has come to this house, because this man, too, is a son of Abraham. For the Son of Man came to seek and to save the lost."

Once back at his house, we see Zacchaeus undergo a beautiful transformation. Previously someone who helped make people poor, he is suddenly bursting with generosity. Debts are being forgiven and money (and possibly property) is being restored to its rightful owners. As Jesus has said before, those who are forgiven much love much. Like Matthew once before, Jesus has found a lost sheep. Like the lost son in the parable, the genuine and repentant Zacchaeus has been restored to the family of God. He is now "a son of Abraham."

The story contrasts with Jesus' recent encounter with the rich young man. That man also sought salvation, but where that wealthy and "good" person refused to part with his precious money, here this wealthy and immoral man is more than happy to give up what he has for the chance of a life with God. Like the "sinful woman" once before who washed Jesus' feet, Zacchaeus has been forgiven much and is now bursting with love. But this story isn't over. Following what has happened, we find Jesus again teaching in parables.

GREAT EXPECTATIONS
Luke 19:11-27

While they were listening to this, he went on to tell them a parable, because he was near Jerusalem and the people thought that the kingdom of God was going to appear at once. He said: "A man of noble birth went to a distant country to have himself appointed king and then to return.

So he called ten of his servants and gave them ten minas. 'Put this money to work,' he said, 'until I come back.'

"But his subjects hated him and sent a delegation after him to say, 'We don't want this man to be our king.'

"He was made king, however, and returned home. Then he sent for the servants to whom he had given the money, in order to find out what they had gained with it.

"The first one came and said, 'Sir, your mina has earned ten more.'

"'Well done, my good servant!' his master replied. 'Because you have been trustworthy in a very small matter, take charge of ten cities.'

"The second came and said, 'Sir, your mina has earned five more.'

"His master answered, 'You take charge of five cities.'

"Then another servant came and said, 'Sir, here is your mina; I have kept it laid away in a piece of cloth. I was afraid of you, because you are a hard man. You take out what you did not put in and reap what you did not sow.'

"His master replied, 'I will judge you by your own words, you wicked servant! You knew, did you, that I am a hard man, taking out what I did not put in, and reaping what I did not sow! Why then didn't you put my money on deposit, so that when I came back, I could have collected it with interest?'

"Then he said to those standing by, 'Take his mina away from him and give it to the one who has ten minas.'

"'Sir,' they said, 'he already has ten!'

"He replied, 'I tell you that to everyone who has, more will be given, but as for the one who has nothing, even what he has will be taken away. But those enemies of mine who did *not want me to be king over them—bring them here and kill them in front of me.'"*

Jesus tells another long parable. He teaches it in part because of their location and the common views of the coming kingdom of God. People expected it to arrive all at once, likely in the form of a revolution overthrowing their oppressors (the Roman Empire). Jesus, however, goes on to describe a kingdom arriving in different stages which will extend beyond the coming revolutionary events to soon follow in Jerusalem.

The parable involves a man, his servants, and his enemies. As the man departs "to a distant country" to be appointed king, his servants are left with the task of putting his generous gift to work until he returns. A mina, the amount mentioned here, is the hefty sum of a few months' wages. These elements represent Jesus (the man to be king) preparing to depart (suffer and die), generously providing salvation (the minas) and giving his followers (servants, a repetitive theme in his teachings) the task of continuing his message and work (as we saw in the parable of the sower) while he is gone.

In the parable, the noble man is then rejected by the populace, though this doesn't prevent his appointment as king. Once king, the man returns home and calls everyone to account for their work. The first two servants are rewarded generously for their wise use of the king's kind gift. The last servant is rebuked both for his failure to do anything with what he was given and his lack of faith in the king's goodness (portrayed as he insults the king's character). As a result, he is left empty-handed as the mina is taken away and awarded instead to a faithful servant.

Finally, the enemies that rejected the king are brought for punishment (here depicted as death) and we are left with another catchy refrain. Those that have will be given more. Those that don't will forfeit everything. This isn't about having money while here on earth but rather the treasure that Jesus has spoken of elsewhere, storing up treasure that awaits in eternity. Those who have been faithful with their appointed tasks will be given far more in the coming kingdom. Instead of treasuring things that will not last (fame, fortune, etc.), people are to invest in that which endures for eternity.

Jesus is preparing to depart and will one day return as king. When he leaves, his followers will be left with much work to do. Their faithfulness won't earn them a place in the kingdom. Salvation, entry into the kingdom, is a gift (like the mina) and cannot be earned. It is independent of the reward, just as the servants didn't earn the initial money their master gave them. However, obedience is expected and will influence the reward within the kingdom that comes. Jesus' followers are to be wise managers of this gift of salvation, faithfully serving the king and doing good until his return. When he returns, there will be a time of judgment. At judgment, there will be reward for the way that the gift was invested. Having been forgiven by God, did his followers extend this love and kindness to others (like Zacchaeus)? Or, did they hide it away and prevent it from growing and spreading, restricting its transformational power?

To be clear, there is a difference between salvation (the gift of the mina) and reward (the master's response to the use of the gift). Forgiveness is essential for entry into the kingdom of God, and, like the mina, it is an unearned gift that fuels work. Judgment will ultimately bring about the "renewal of all things" that Jesus has mentioned previously, and in God's kingdom there will be reward based upon the work of God's servants in the world. The story won't end in Jerusalem, and Jesus is preparing his followers to be faithful investors of God's generous gift of salvation.

THE HOME STRETCH
John 11:7, 11-16; Mark 10:46-52

>...*and then he said to his disciples, "Let us go back to Judea."*

>...*"Our friend Lazarus has fallen asleep; but I am going there to wake him up."*

>*His disciples replied, "Lord, if he sleeps, he will get better." Jesus had been speaking of his death, but his disciples thought he meant natural sleep.*

So then he told them plainly, "Lazarus is dead, and for your sake I am glad I was not there, so that you may believe. But let us go to him."

Then Thomas (also known as Didymus) said to the rest of the disciples, "Let us also go, that we may die with him."

They're about to embark on the very road described at the center of his story about the Good Samaritan. But Jesus isn't travelling alone. He has done enough in the area to have a crowd behind him for the last leg of his trip. He is on his way to Jerusalem, or at least Bethany (near Jerusalem), to visit Mary, Martha and Lazarus.

But the disciples know that this is risky for other reasons. Tensions have grown between Jesus and other religious leaders, and even Herod has sent threats. It's gotten so bad that Thomas here fully expects that going to Jerusalem will bring about Jesus' death and the coming revolution, something they wouldn't dare to miss. Excited by the possibilities, they don't want to miss the action and will gladly join him for this dangerous trip to the capital.

...As Jesus and his disciples, together with a large crowd, were leaving the city, a blind man, Bartimaeus (which means "son of Timaeus"), was sitting by the roadside begging. When he heard that it was Jesus of Nazareth, he began to shout, "Jesus, Son of David, have mercy on me!"

Many rebuked him and told him to be quiet, but he shouted all the more, "Son of David, have mercy on me!"

Just as they are leaving Jericho, they come across a noisy bystander named Bartimaeus. Including the man's name like this is a sort of ancient citation. For the first generation of readers, it was a way of including the source so that the story could be verified. If someone wanted to double-check things, they'd just ask for Bartimaeus from Jericho.

The blind man now begs on the busy road into his city, a location where numerous religious travelers heading to the capital would pass by him. As far as most people in his town are concerned, he's dead to them (maybe like the wounded man in the parable of the Good

252

Samaritan). Will he find a kind "neighbor" to help him or a busy priest eager to pass him by? Bartimaeus catches wind of the man at the center of the crowd.

It is Jesus of Nazareth.

This is a name that he recognizes, and like Zacchaeus, he knows that this might be the opportunity of a lifetime. He calls out to the "Son of David," a unique title that highlights his faith in Jesus as the Messiah and coming king (a descendent of King David). It is a significant title, especially spoken publicly in broad daylight so close to the capital. These are risky claims to be shouting in a crowd. What if the wrong person hears him? He is quickly hushed by onlookers.

But he doesn't give up.

His desperation stirs a fresh boldness as he begs for the Messiah's kindness. Will Jesus notice him? This could be his only chance…

Jesus stopped and said, "Call him."

So they called to the blind man, "Cheer up! On your feet! He's calling you." Throwing his cloak aside, he jumped to his feet and came to Jesus.

"What do you want me to do for you?" Jesus asked him.

Ever observant, Jesus takes notice. He stops the caravan before it gets started, and the overjoyed blind man tosses his cloak aside as he runs to Jesus. There, he is met by a strange question.

What does he want?

It would seem obvious, but it's an interesting question. The blind man has been begging by the road. Does he want money? Food? What does he mean as he asks for mercy? Also, he has proclaimed belief in Jesus as the Messiah. If this is so, there is much more that he could request. A few stories ago we saw Jesus ask a couple of his own disciples this same question, and they asked to be seated by his side when he becomes King. Then again, maybe Jesus just wants the man to be clear to himself. It's easy to blindly ask for all our problems to be solved. Does this man know what he is about to ask for? James and John didn't.

The blind man said, "Rabbi, I want to see."

"Go," said Jesus, "your faith has healed you." Immediately he received his sight and followed Jesus along the road.

There it is, plain and simple. Bartimaeus may be blind, but he has full sight of the truth. He knows that Jesus has the power to heal him because he already sees plainly who Jesus is. As has happened several times before, the man is healed *immediately* with Jesus' words. No fancy methods or ceremony. Bartimaeus believed that Jesus was the Messiah, and he was willing to risk ridicule in response to his faith. Now, that very faith is the doorway through which he will see the world anew.

Jesus has himself a new follower.

It's interesting to think about the number of wonderful stories behind Jesus. He has touched lives everywhere he's been, and the strange diversity of people now devoted to him is incredible. Prostitutes, nationalists, religious leaders, blind beggars, wealthy tax collectors, Judeans and foreigners, men and women, adults and children... the celebration feast has become quite the party as people continue to return to God. And now, it's time for the difficult ascent up the mountain to Jerusalem. Much will happen, and there is still some time for more wonder and laughter before we will see the crowd's tune change.

ANOTHER DEAD MAN WALKING
John 11:17-50, 53-54

Jesus finally makes it to Bethany, a village just outside of Jerusalem where he will likely stay during the coming festival. As he arrives, he finds what he anticipated: Lazarus has passed away. As has happened once before, Jesus comes upon a family mourning the loss of a loved one.

On his arrival, Jesus found that Lazarus had already been in the tomb for four days. Now Bethany was less than two miles from Jerusalem, and many Jews had come to Martha and Mary to comfort them in the loss of their brother. When

Martha heard that Jesus was coming, she went out to meet him, but Mary stayed at home.

"Lord," Martha said to Jesus, "if you had been here, my brother would not have died. But I know that even now God will give you whatever you ask."

Four days.

Martha has come out to greet him, but Mary has stayed behind. Could she be upset that Jesus didn't come sooner? I also can't help but wonder about Martha's tone as she speaks. Does she believe that Jesus can bring him back from the dead? Or is she angry over the preventable loss of her brother, viewing Jesus as a celebrity who gets everything he wants while others suffer?

Jesus said to her, "Your brother will rise again."

Martha answered, "I know he will rise again in the resurrection at the last day."

Jesus said to her, "I am the resurrection and the life. The one who believes in me will live, even though they die; and whoever lives by believing in me will never die. Do you believe this?"

Jesus' statement that Martha's brother will rise again could be taken as simple condolences. They both agree that Lazarus will rise again, but disagree about when. Martha interprets these words to refer generally to the future judgment day when all are raised from the dead. That doesn't help them or her brother now. Then Jesus speaks of himself as this resurrection in the present, the one who will one day raise everyone. If she believes he is the Messiah, then this means he has the power to raise Lazarus from the dead. Does she believe this?

The comforting conversation just got incredibly theological.

"Yes, Lord," she replied, "I believe that you are the Messiah, the Son of God, who is to come into the world."

And after she had said this, she went back and called her sister Mary aside. "The Teacher is here," she said, "and is asking for you."

She may not understand the point he has just made, that he presently has the power to raise Lazarus from the dead. She may instead be wondering whether Jesus came intending to heal Lazarus or to lecture her on her beliefs about future events. Using very similar language to Peter's confession previously, she answers with a yes, she believes Jesus is the Messiah, the Son of God. Then, either comforted and convinced or otherwise tired of the banter, she scurries off to tell Mary that the "teacher" has arrived.

When Mary heard this, she got up quickly and went to him. Now Jesus had not yet entered the village, but was still at the place where Martha had met him. When the Jews who had been with Mary in the house, comforting her, noticed how quickly she got up and went out, they followed her, supposing she was going to the tomb to mourn there.

When Mary reached the place where Jesus was and saw him, she fell at his feet and said, "Lord, if you had been here, my brother would not have died."

Mary's first words are the same as those of her sister. If Jesus had been present, this wouldn't have happened. Why didn't he show up? While they believe he could have prevented Lazarus' death, they don't expect Jesus to be able to bring him back from the dead.

When Jesus saw her weeping, and the Jews who had come along with her also weeping, he was deeply moved in spirit and troubled. "Where have you laid him?" he asked.

"Come and see, Lord," they replied.

Jesus wept.

Then the Jews said, "See how he loved him!"

But some of them said, "Could not he who opened the eyes of the blind man have kept this man from dying?"

We've seen Jesus express a variety of feelings by now. Anger, joy, compassion, but this is the first time we've seen him cry. This isn't just a little sadness either. At the sight of everyone mourning, we are told that Jesus is deeply moved and *wept*. I guess it's a little different when something happens to someone you know and love dearly. But isn't Jesus going to make everything better? It's easy to just think in terms of outcomes and miss the experience at hand. Jesus has entered into a situation with several people whom he loves dearly and one of them has died. Sure, it's nice that one day God will set things straight, but there is still a sting to death, and even Jesus mourns over the hurting state of our world which is constantly jarred by harsh reminders of our separation from God.

> *Jesus, once more deeply moved, came to the tomb. It was a cave with stone laid across the entrance. "Take away the stone," he said.*

> *"But, Lord," said Martha, the sister of the dead man, "by this time there is a bad odor, for he has been there four days."*

Martha's not just stating the obvious, that the body would stink. This body has been wrapped and prepared for decay, as was the custom, and interactions with a dead body were forbidden by law and left one unclean.[1] As before, when Martha spoke up about her sister not helping in the kitchen, her gut reaction is to speak up about social decency. Jesus should know better than to do something as indecent as this. Life after death is about the last thing on anyone's mind. So Jesus gives a little reminder...

> *Then Jesus said, "Did I not tell you that if you believe, you will see the glory of God?"*

> *So they took away the stone. Then Jesus looked up and said, "Father, I thank you that you have heard me. I knew that you always hear me, but I said this for the benefit of the people standing here, that they may believe that you sent me."*

---

[1] Numbers 19:11-16

When he had said this, Jesus called in a loud voice, "Lazarus, come out!" The dead man came out, his hands and feet wrapped with strips of linen, and a cloth around his face.

Jesus said to them, "Take off the grave clothes and let him go."

Once again, no fancy rituals. Jesus speaks with authority, and it is so. To the amazement of everyone, that which was lifeless and rotting is suddenly restored. The body prepared for the grave must be re-clothed. A new covering has arrived, and it's Jesus. Just as God provided a new garment when Adam and Eve tried to cover themselves, Jesus is providing freedom from the grave and the burdens of our dirtiness, a fresh skin for our rotting bones.

But not everyone is pleased...

Therefore many of the Jews who had come to visit Mary, and had seen what Jesus did, believed in him. But some of them went to the Pharisees and told them what Jesus had done. Then the chief priests and the Pharisees called a meeting of the Sanhedrin.

"What are we accomplishing?" they asked. "Here is this man performing many signs. If we let him go on like this, everyone will believe in him, and then the Romans will come and take away both our temple and our nation."

Then one of them, named Caiaphas, who was high priest that year, spoke up, "You know nothing at all! You do not realize that it is better for you that one man die for the people than that the whole nation perish."

...So from that day on they plotted to take his life.

Therefore Jesus no longer moved about publicly among the people of Judea. Instead he withdrew to a region near the wilderness, to a village called Ephraim, where he stayed with his disciples.

Where some see reason for celebration, others see an immense threat. It's taken a lot of time and effort for the Jewish people to get relations with the Romans where they are. While Romans occupy the region and collect taxes, the Jewish people still maintain numerous freedoms to function according to their own laws, religious customs, and courts. An uprising of any kind risks further Roman intervention and the possible loss of more freedom and power. For this reason, Jesus' popularity poses an enormous risk to anyone in a position of power. Caiaphas, the high priest (and leader of the Jewish court) even says that it'd be better for an innocent man (i.e. Jesus) to die than for there to be another violent uprising. Both the Sadducees and Pharisees agree on this. Despite their turbulent past (they fought a civil war against each other), both factions see Jesus as a rival and threat to their power. As the old saying goes, "the enemy of my enemy is my friend." While they might not agree on much, they can agree on this. Jesus must die.

Aware of the growing schemes, Jesus sneaks away to a village nearby in order to avoid confrontation until the time is right. The plot has advanced and tensions have reached a boiling point which ensures that a grand finale is about to take place. Just as Jesus has predicted, the imminent showdown will indeed involve rejection, suffering, and death. Expectations will be confronted, but the war that many expect won't begin. Jesus is indeed about to overthrow their great enemy, just not precisely *who* nor *how* they anticipate, and their faith will be tested in ways unlike anything they've ever experienced before.

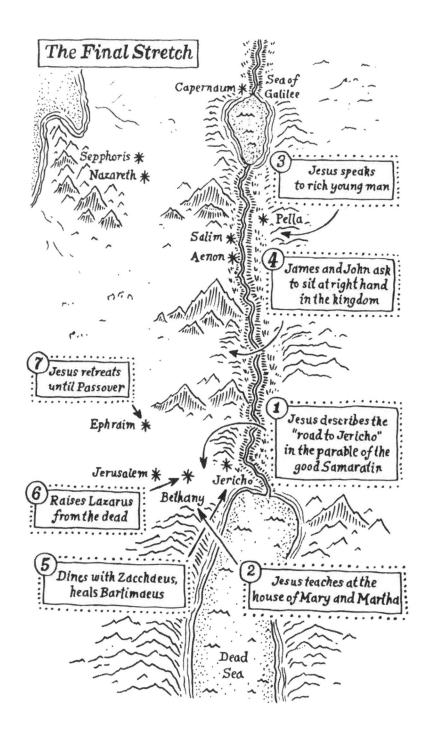

The Final Stretch

Capernaum ✳   Sea of Galilee

Sepphoris ✳
Nazareth ✳

③ Jesus speaks to rich young man

✳ Pella

Salim ✳
Aenon ✳

④ James and John ask to sit at right hand in the kingdom

⑦ Jesus retreats until Passover

Ephraim ✳

① Jesus describes the "road to Jericho" in the parable of the good Samaritin

Jerusalem ✳   ✳
Bethany   ✳ Jericho

⑥ Raises Lazarus from the dead

⑤ Dines with Zacchaeus, heals Bartimaeus

② Jesus teaches at the house of Mary and Martha

Dead Sea

Part V

A Showdown in Jerusalem

FIFTEEN

Let the Games Begin

WITH ALL THAT HAS happened in Bethany, Jesus has made his presence known to the region and his opponents are on edge. Word of Lazarus's return from the dead quickly spreads through the area and people begin to gather as Jesus makes his way to Jerusalem. He seems to be heading into a storm...

THE PROCESSIONAL
John 11:55-57; Mark 11:1-3; Luke 19:32; Mark 11:7-8; Luke 19:37; Mark 11:9-10; Luke 19:39- 40; John 12:19; Luke 19:41-44; Matthew 21:10-11; Mark 11:11

> *When it was almost time for the Jewish Passover, many went up from the country to Jerusalem for their ceremonial cleansing before the Passover. They kept looking for Jesus, and as they stood in the temple courts they asked one another, "What do you think? Isn't he coming to the festival at all?" But the chief priests and Pharisees had given orders that anyone who found out where Jesus was should report it so that they might arrest him.*

The authorities are on the lookout for his impending arrival. He will arrive along with well over a million other Jews from across the empire to celebrate the Passover, one of their most significant festivals. But how and when will he finally make his appearance?

As they approached Jerusalem and came to Bethphage and Bethany at the Mount of Olives, Jesus sent two of his disciples, saying to them, "Go to the village ahead of you, and just as you enter it, you will find a colt tied there, which no one has ever ridden. Untie it and bring it here. If anyone asks you, 'Why are you doing this?' say, 'The Lord needs it and will send it back here shortly.'"

Those who were sent ahead went and found it just as he had told them. When they brought the colt to Jesus and threw their cloaks over it, he sat on it. Many people spread their cloaks on the road, while others spread branches they had cut in the fields.

When he came near the place where the road goes down the Mount of Olives, the whole crowd of disciples began joyfully to praise God in loud voices for all the miracles they had seen:

"Hosanna!"

"Blessed is he who comes in the name of the Lord!"

"Blessed is the coming kingdom of our father David!"

"Hosanna in the highest heaven!"

The Pharisees are not the only people watching for Jesus. As he arrives riding upon a colt, an enormous parade hails him as the Messiah. One of the Hebrew prophets had described the Messiah, carrying salvation, riding into Jerusalem on "a colt, the foal of a donkey."[1] Not long ago around Jericho, we saw the disciples ask about the coming of God's kingdom. They may think this parade marks the inauguration of this kingdom.

It also happens that Jesus has entered in a fashion resembling that of another historic King, Solomon, the son of David, who was anointed King by his father amid the false claims to the throne by another.[2] God had promised that the "son of David" would build the

---

[1] Zechariah 9:9   [2] 1 Kings 1:28-53

263

temple and install an everlasting kingdom on earth.[1] During his coronation, Solomon entered the capital riding upon a mule. While he did go on to build a temple in Jerusalem,[2] Solomon didn't turn out to be the "Son of David" who would install the everlasting kingdom. Ultimately, his disobedience to God (worshipping other gods) tore the nation apart[3] before it was later conquered by foreign enemies.[4]

Here Jesus arrives to praises as *the* "Son of David," which links him to the unfulfilled promises. The exclamation *hosanna* means "save." They are proclaiming that Jesus is the rightful heir, the fulfillment of the long-promised kingdom of God that would restore peace and justice to the world. This also places him in comparison to Solomon as a builder of the temple, God's dwelling place on earth. This is no small claim. While we've discussed the way that Jesus is a temple, we have yet to discuss how he will build a new temple.

The crowd confirms all these things by singing some of the words of a song from scripture.[5] Other words in this song describe the Lord God, their rejected foundation (specifically called the "stone the builders rejected"), saving the people in a marvelous manner as he returns to his house (the temple). It also describes the people praising with branches in hand as he approaches the altar (the ultimate place of sacrifice). Whether they realize it or not, their songs proclaim the very things finding fulfillment in their midst.

> *Some of the Pharisees in the crowd said to Jesus, "Teacher, rebuke your disciples!"*
>
> *"I tell you," he replied, "if they keep quiet, the stones will cry out."*
>
> *So the Pharisees said to one another, "See, this is getting us nowhere. Look how the whole world has gone after him!"*

It's not surprising that the Pharisees are greatly offended. How can Jesus allow his followers to speak such blasphemy? But Jesus will not stop the procession because "even the stones will cry out."[6] What's about to happen cannot be stopped.

---

[1] 2 Samuel 7:12-16 [2] 1 Kings 6 [3] 1 Kings 11-12 [4] 2 Kings 17, 25 [5] Psalm 118:22-27
[6] Isaiah 55:12-13; Habakkuk 2:11

It's becoming clear to his opponents that something must be done. He's not changing his tune, and the crowds grow daily around him. How can they remove him without inciting a revolt from his crowd? It would be a catastrophe if the Roman soldiers had to step in and would mean further reductions to his opponents' power. They have a difficult task before them which will require incredible craftiness and secrecy.

As Jesus finally arrives at the city, one would expect to see satisfaction or pleasure as he completes his long journey. Yet that's not what Jesus expresses in the slightest...

As he approached Jerusalem and saw the city, he wept over it and said, "If you, even you, had only known on this day what would bring you peace—but now it is hidden from your eyes. The days will come upon you when your enemies will build an embankment against you and encircle you and hem you in on every side. They will dash you to the ground, you and the children within your walls. They will not leave one stone on another, because you did not recognize the time of God's coming to you."

Just moments after being showered with praises, Jesus is suddenly weeping at the sight of Jerusalem. It is the second time in a short period that we have seen such an outburst of tears. He is weeping because something terrible is about to happen, and peace will come at a great cost. There is a coming ransacking that will leave no stone unturned. To be clear, Jesus is saying that he is God, and God's long-awaited arrival is finally taking place. Yet because people will reject him, their precious temple will be destroyed.

When Jesus entered Jerusalem, the whole city was stirred and asked, "Who is this?"

The crowds answered, "This is Jesus, the prophet from Nazareth in Galilee."

Jesus entered Jerusalem and went into the temple courts. He looked around at everything, but since it was already late, he went out to Bethany with the Twelve.

Likely exhausted from an emotional day of travel, Jesus gets a brief glimpse of the empty spaces that he will soon occupy. This will serve as the stage for the last days of his life. As darkness falls, he returns with the disciples to Bethany, just beyond the city, where he will stay with Mary, Martha and Lazarus.

While we don't know the precise days of these events, Jesus' arrival at the temple is traditionally placed on Sunday (now known as "Palm Sunday").

THE HOLY CITY

The name Jerusalem means something like "house" or "foundation of peace." Thousands of years old at the time of Jesus, the city was about four miles in circumference and occupied the top of four hills. It was surrounded on three sides by steep valleys forming a natural fortress. Three of these hills lined up in a row running north to south. The temple was on the middle summit, which was called Moriah. Just to the southwest was the fourth and tallest hill (by a couple hundred feet) called Zion, the location of the "upper city." Winding between these hills was a valley that dropped a couple of hundred feet and separated the different sections of the city.

Approaching Jerusalem from the east, one would ascend from the Jordan River valley up a steep incline passing through Jericho and Bethany along the way. As one approached, the city would actually be hidden from sight by the Mount of Olives, which rose slightly above the peaks of the city, its shaded slopes covered in greenery and the gnarly olive trees which gave the mountain its name. From the summit, one would have a majestic overlook of the city, with the gates to the temple about 1,000 yards away through an arched path that wandered across the Kidron Valley. The eastern wall of the temple overlooked this valley, which dropped over 600 feet at its deepest point. Scattered in and around the city were numerous pools used for the necessary bathing upon arrival.

Easily the architectural jewel of the region, the temple was built with enormous stones ranging between 20-40 feet long and weighing up to 100 tons. The temple platform was about 1,000 feet across and was made of multiple courts and terraces. The temple courts were designated for specific groups. The outer court was surrounded by a

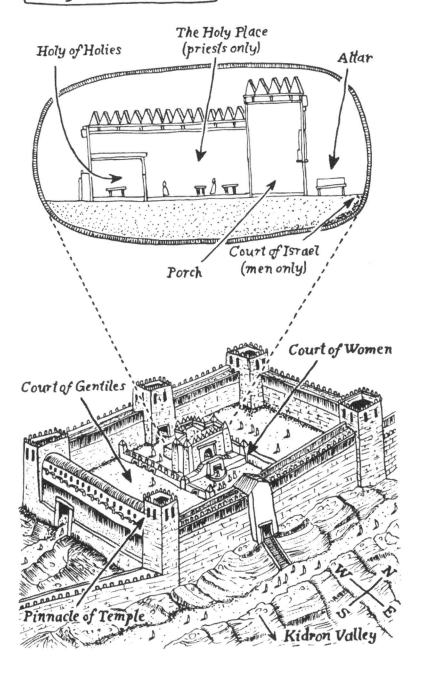

Temple in Jerusalem

Holy of Holies

The Holy Place
(priests only)

Altar

Porch

Court of Israel
(men only)

Court of Gentiles

Court of Women

Pinnacle of Temple

Kidron Valley

W N S E

large wall about 40 feet high that wrapped around the entire courtyard. Called the "Court of the Gentiles," this court was for people who were not descendants of Israel, provided they followed the appropriate guidelines of reverence and decorum. The next area was the "Court of Women," which included several depositories spread about as receptacles for different offerings. From there, only men could enter the "Court of Israel," which included an enormous altar where sacrifices and offerings were made. Within this court was a T-shaped structure called the Holy Place. This enclosed space had several sacred artifacts and was intended only for priests. Within this enclosed space was a specific chamber called the "Most Holy Place" or the "Holy of Holies." This was the special dwelling place of God, separated from the rest by an enormous curtain and only entered once a year by the high priest.

Just outside of the temple on its northwest corner was the "Antonia Fortress," with a tower that rose about 100 feet above the outer wall to the temple so that the Romans could keep an eye on things. This space may have functioned as the Praetorium (courthouse) and Pontius Pilate's residence in the city. To the west of the temple were a couple of main roads leading out of the city. One of these, heading straight west, was a large bridge that made its way across the valley toward the outer wall of the city. There along the outer wall was Herod's palace. Another road headed northwest and beyond the city to what was the flattest boundary of the city.

CLEANING HOUSE
Mark 11:12-17; Matthew 21:14-15; John 2:18-20; Mark 11:18; Matthew 21:17; Luke 19:47-48; Mark 11:20-25

> *The next day as they were leaving Bethany, Jesus was hungry. Seeing in the distance a fig tree in leaf, he went to find out if it had any fruit. When he reached it, he found nothing but leaves, because it was not the season for figs. Then he said to the tree, "May no one ever eat fruit from you again."*

This is a strange story to include in what otherwise seems to be the building climax. It isn't the last we will hear of the fig tree. We actually first heard of fig leaves in the Eden story. Immediately after realizing they were naked, Adam and Eve use fig leaves to cover themselves. This covering lasted only until God made a more suitable covering from skins. For this reason, fig leaves are a natural symbol of humanity's covering from nakedness (and sin) before God. But there's plenty more…

Descriptions of fruitful figs throughout the scriptures symbolized God's blessings of peace and prosperity resulting from Israel's obedience to their covenant relationship (their covering before God).[1] In the books of the prophets, the destruction or withering of figs is often accompanied with calls for God's judgment upon a wicked people.[2] Here, Jesus curses this tree as though it is no longer useful. With the prophets in mind, this would signify a call for God's judgment, much like Jesus has predicted about the temple's destruction. The temple, and the relationship with God provided by the laws, have served their purpose and are coming to completion. Now a new covering has come. Just as God once provided skins in Eden to replace Adam and Eve's fig coverings, Jesus is about to set the new parameters of a covenant relationship with God, new skins to cover as the laws were previously intended to do.

> *On reaching Jerusalem, Jesus entered the temple courts and began driving out those who were buying and selling there. He overturned the tables of the money changers and the benches of those selling doves, and would not allow anyone to carry merchandise through the temple courts. And as he taught them, he said, "Is it not written: "'My house will be called a house of prayer for all nations'? But you have made it 'a den of robbers.'"*

The outer court of the temple, which was intended as a place of worship for foreigners, had been transformed into a sort of market where money could be exchanged and goods purchased. Roman coinage (considered unacceptable since it bore the image of Caesar), had to be exchanged for an acceptable currency to be used at the temple for offerings. With the Passover less than a week away, it was

---

[1] Deuteronomy 8:6-9; 1 Kings 4:25   [2] Jeremiah 8:13; Hosea 2:9-13; Amos 4:9

a time of much business in the temple courts and likely the sort of profiteering that left many with a bad taste in their mouths toward the temple authorities who were busy lining their pockets. These transactions desecrated the temple.

As Jesus turns over the tables, he is not "losing control" in a fit of rage. His action is premeditated. The day before, Jesus had walked around the vacant temple and examined everything, including these tables and booths which littered the outer court. Yet he did nothing. Instead he called it a night and probably thought long and hard about the lines that he would recite during his actions the next day. Speaking the words of multiple prophets as he "teaches," he calls out the wrongdoing of those present.

The first phrase about "a house of prayer" comes from a prophet describing a time when people from all nations (not just Israel) would gather to worship God at the temple.[1] The second phrase, "den of robbers," comes from another prophet who, standing at the temple gates, railed against the fake religion of Israel and warned of the coming destruction of the city and temple.[2]

Christ's actions also echo those of several other scriptural reformers confronting the wrongdoing of religious leaders who disregarded God's purposes for the temple.[3] Instead of a place for all to worship (rich and poor, Israelite and foreigner), the space had become an example of exclusion. The temple had been transformed from a worship space into a marketplace and an opportunity for the wealthy religious establishment to exploit people while creating obstacles for true worship. In dramatic fashion, Jesus cleans house, restoring the space to its original purpose as a place for all nations to gather in fellowship with others and God.

The blind and the lame came to him at the temple, and he healed them. But when the chief priests and the teachers of the law saw the wonderful things he did and the children shouting in the temple courts, "Hosanna to the Son of David," they were indignant.

---

[1] Isaiah 56:3-8   [2] Jeremiah 7:1-20   [3] Ezekiel 8, 11, 34:1-10; Nehemiah 13:4-9; Zephaniah 1:10-12; Zechariah 5:3-4, 14:20-21; Malachi 2:1-9, 3:1-5

"What sign can you show us to prove your authority to do all this?"

Jesus answered them, "Destroy this temple, and I will raise it again in three days."

They replied, "It has taken forty-six years to build this temple, and you are going to raise it in three days?"

The temple was to be a place of communion with God, teaching, healing, and the forgiving of sins—the instrument of restoration for the world. Now the sick and lame come to Jesus, and he restores them. The true temple has come. God has returned to his dwelling. Just as people all over Jerusalem would traditionally begin to remove all the leaven, symbolic of sin, from their homes in preparation for Passover, Jesus has started to do some house cleaning of his own in the temple.

When people resume their praises of him, the authorities take notice. How can he do this? Surely he must prove himself (the very challenge of Satan during the temptation). What will he do? Destroy the temple, he says, and he will rebuild it. His response leaves his opponents aghast. Thinking he's describing the stone building, they point out how long it has taken to rebuild it. How on earth could he accomplish such a thing? He is referring not to the stone building around him (as they misunderstand) but instead to himself. They will kill him, but he will return from the dead. The new temple is about to arrive.

Since arriving in town, Jesus' behavior has been confrontational yet discreet enough to float under the radar of the Roman authorities. Riding into town on a young donkey wouldn't stand out in the way it might if he'd been riding upon a magnificent steed, like a conqueror. The songs the crowd sang as Jesus rode among them were the hymns they sang every year at this time. To their oppressors, phrases like "Son of David" didn't stick out as obvious calls for a rightful heir to the throne. Making a mess in the temple may have just appeared to be a brief tussle when some cranky and jealous elders were pushed aside by the crowd at the sight of a young celebrity—hardly anything for soldiers to get upset about. Following his own advice, Jesus has acted "as shrewd as a serpent and innocent as a dove,"[1] surely salt in the wounds of his opposition, and they aren't going to stand for it.

The chief priests and the teachers of the law heard this and began looking for a way to kill him, for they feared him, because the whole crowd was amazed at his teaching.

And he left them and went out of the city to Bethany, where he spent the night.

Every day he was teaching at the temple. But the chief priests, the teachers of the law and the leaders among the people were trying to kill him. Yet they could not find any way to do it, because all the people hung on his words.

Another day passes, and Jesus returns to his lodging in Bethany for the night. But he will be back for more in the coming days. This is not over yet. Battle lines have been drawn.

As a new day begins, Jesus makes his way back to the temple to pick up right where he left off. But along the way, one of the disciples makes a surprising discovery.

In the morning, as they went along, they saw the fig tree withered from the roots. Peter remembered and said to Jesus, "Rabbi, look! The fig tree you cursed has withered!"

"Have faith in God," Jesus answered. "Truly I tell you, if anyone says to this mountain, 'Go, throw yourself into the sea,' and does not doubt in their heart but believes that what they say will happen, it will be done for them."

What Jesus had said has come to pass. The fig tree has withered. God's judgment has arrived. God's presence has returned, and by the power of his Spirit nothing is impossible. Things are about to change drastically in ways that will shock everyone.

Jesus' mention of mountains here is significant. John the Baptist's ministry was in the valley, the low place overshadowed by

---

[1] See chapter 10, Matthew 10:16

the magnificence of Jerusalem. As foretold, John cautioned people to prepare because in the words of a prophet,[1] "every mountain will be made low." In stark contrast to the temple's ministry, he and Jesus baptized, healed, and taught as part of the beginning of something new. As Jesus told the Samaritan woman,[2] in this new day, people will worship God in truth, and not just in Jerusalem on a mountaintop. There will be a new space for forgiveness and healing. God is leveling the playing field (here symbolized by the landscape). Mountains have stood in the way for too long. Geography, ethnicity, and architecture have been too much of an obstacle. It's time to throw them into the sea. There will be a new relationship, a new temple established, and a new covering that is not made of fig leaves. The exalted will be humbled, and the humbled will be exalted.

Jesus' words echo yet another prophet who spoke of a time when one would come by the Spirit of God and level the ground of the temple with his own hands, building the foundation and finishing it as proof of his authority.[3] God has come near. And now the disciples can walk in this same authority.

> *"Therefore I tell you, whatever you ask for in prayer, believe that you have received it, and it will be yours. And when you stand praying, if you hold anything against anyone, forgive them, so that your Father in heaven may forgive you your sins.*

Through faith, even the impossible will happen. It's time to be humbled before God. It's time to set down burdens and let go of anger. It's time to forgive and be forgiven. A restored relationship with God has finally arrived.

UNCERTAIN ALLEGIANCES
Mark 11:27-33

> *They arrived again in Jerusalem, and while Jesus was walking in the temple courts, the chief priests, the teachers of the law and the elders came to him. "By what authority*

---

[1] Isaiah 40:4   [2] See chapter 4, John 4:21-24   [3] Zechariah 4:6-10

273

are you doing these things?" they asked. "And who gave you authority to do this?"

The priestly aristocracy (Sadducee) was the standing authority and functioned as the temple guardians. Yet while they were the dominant temple authority (as approved by the Romans), they weren't the dominant social movement. That status belonged to the Pharisees. So the Sadducees had to be careful not to upset the masses at the risk of losing their place. So far, we have primarily seen Jesus' exchanges with Pharisees, but now he is on Sadducee turf—the temple. Here, his actions have stood in clear defiance of the role the Sadducees believe God gave them. Who does he represent, and what gives him the right to do such things?

Jesus replied, "I will ask you one question. Answer me, and I will tell you by what authority I am doing these things. John's baptism—was it from heaven, or of human origin? Tell me!"

Responding as was culturally common in debates, Jesus gives them a question. How did they view John the Baptist, who had also defied their authority? Are they willing to express their own faith (or lack thereof) in John the Baptist's work? Or are they merely attempting to preserve their power? Interestingly, the answer to their question is actually veiled within Jesus' question. By what authority is Jesus doing these things? By the same authority behind the ministry of John the Baptist.

They discussed it among themselves and said, "If we say, 'From heaven,' he will ask, 'Then why didn't you believe him?' But if we say, 'Of human origin'..." (They feared the people, for everyone held that John really was a prophet.)

So they answered Jesus, "We don't know."

Jesus said, "Neither will I tell you by what authority I am doing these things."

Like a game of chess, they consider the possible outcomes. They are too concerned with popularity and the power at stake to answer this question seriously. If they acknowledge John the Baptist's authority to minister in defiance of the temple, they would be confirming that John the Baptist was in fact the forerunner preparing the nation for God's coming.[1] And this would have led them to Jesus. If they speak up in denial of John the Baptist's ministry (their preference), there could be an uprising among the crowds now filling the temple courts daily.

They decide to take the safe route and disengage from the debate in order to save face (at least for the moment), but Jesus isn't finished yet.

PARABLE OF THE TENANTS
Mark 12:1; Matthew 21:28-46

Jesus then began to speak to them in parables...

"What do you think? There was a man who had two sons. He went to the first and said, 'Son, go and work today in the vineyard.'

"'I will not,' he answered, but later he changed his mind and went.

"Then the Father went to the other son and said the same thing. He answered, 'I will, sir,' but he did not go.

"Which of the two did what his father wanted?"

This resembles another story we've heard about two sons. In that story, one "obeyed" while the other ran off and embarrassed the family. After the wayward son repented, the Father celebrated with him (as Jesus celebrates with "sinners") while the other son stood outside (like the angry Pharisees). In this story, one son does something that was considered wrong by defying his father's orders, but he later realizes his mistake and obeys. The other son pays only lip service—the thing Jesus has accused so many religious people of doing. Which son has done wrong? Well, both. But which son did what was asked? The answer is obvious.

---

[1] Isaiah 40:3-5; Malachi 3:1, 4:5

"The first," they answered.

Jesus said to them, "Truly I tell you, the tax collectors and the prostitutes are entering the kingdom of God ahead of you. For John came to you to show you the way of righteousness, and you did not believe him, but the tax collectors and the prostitutes did. And even after you saw this, you did not repent and believe him.

They are getting roasted publicly. Now, the "sinners" Jesus has been spending so much time with are being praised for doing the right thing despite their initial rebellion. The authorities, despite their lip service to God, have gone astray. As John the Baptist once said, they are "serpents!"[1]

As if it wasn't clear enough yet...

"Listen to another parable: There was a landowner who planted a vineyard. He put a wall around it, dug a winepress in it and built a watchtower. Then he rented the vineyard to some farmers and moved to another place. When the harvest time approached, he sent his servants to the tenants to collect his fruit.

Jesus uses what would have been a common situation in their time. The wealthy (which included some of the priesthood) controlled lands far and wide, and tenant farming was quite common. It's possible some of the high priests listening to the parable were regional landowners.

The story could also be seen as a rendering of the story of the Eden and the scriptures as a whole. God planted a vineyard (the garden, Israel), handed it over to tenants (Adam and Eve, Israel's leadership), and sent servants to collect (walked through Garden, sent the prophets). Some hearers may have even associated the vineyard symbolism with the temple itself.

"The tenants seized his servants; they beat one, killed another, and stoned a third. Then he sent other servants to

---

[1] See chapter 3, Matthew 3:7

them, more than the first time, and the tenants treated them the same way. Last of all, he sent his son to them. 'They will respect my son,' he said.

We see a rebellion brewing. Where the previous story touched on familial devotion, this parable highlights labor and legal responsibility. There's no indication here of injustice on the part of the landowner. But the workers attempt to keep more than their lawful wage of the fruits, killing the servants who would have collected the landlord's portion. The crowd would have likely scoffed at the tenants' evil and stupidity and been surprised by the owner's patience. As things progress, the owner finally sends in one with greater authority than the rest: his own son.

"But when the tenants saw the son, they said to each other, 'This is the heir. Come, let's kill him and take his inheritance.' So they took him and threw him out of the vineyard and killed him.

"Therefore, when the owner of the vineyard comes, what will he do to those tenants?"

"He will bring those wretches to a wretched end," they replied, "and he will rent the vineyard to other tenants, who will give him his share of the crop at harvest time."

Again, the answer is obvious, and Jesus is even able to get the crowd to answer with some passion. But where is Jesus taking this? The tenants' rebellion could resemble some of the revolts of the day, which risked the well-being of the entire nation at the hands of angered Romans. So is this parable describing zealots as foolish? Or do the murderous tenants instead represent the Romans, who have abused their role as overseers of the nation?

Jesus said to them, "Have you never read in the Scriptures: 'The stone the builders rejected has become the cornerstone; the Lord has done this, and it is marvelous in our eyes'?

"Therefore I tell you that the kingdom of God will be taken away from you and given to a people who will produce its

fruit. Anyone who falls on this stone will be broken to pieces; anyone on whom it falls will be crushed."

This must have been a nasty surprise. Jesus is describing *them* as the rebellious tenants rejecting him, the son, God's foundation for a restored relationship. *They* have been given a responsibility and have refused to turn the fruits over to God. *They*, the authorities working alongside the Herods and Rome, have rejected God's messengers (like John the Baptist), so God finally sent one of greater authority than those previously—Jesus, God's son. *They* are the cursed fig tree.

According to Jesus, a storm is brewing. He's predicting his own death as the foundation of a reformation as well as a coming "wretched end" for the establishment, including the temple's destruction. Jesus is the rejected stone for building the new temple that will ultimately become the final "capstone."[1] He is a threat to them as the foundation stone[2] of a new temple. The privilege and authority they have enjoyed will disappear, and God's kingdom will be handed over to other obedient servants. This stone will be a stumbling block[3] for those in rebellion and will crush[4] "anyone on whom it falls." This language echoes God's promise in Genesis that the serpent will strike and be crushed. Jesus is bringing about the fulfillment of this promise.

> *When the chief priests and the Pharisees heard Jesus' parables, they knew he was talking about them. They looked for a way to arrest him, but they were afraid of the crowd because the people held that he was a prophet.*

The growing crowds continue to present an enormous problem. There is an increasing need to remove Jesus if they wish to maintain their power, yet such action could provoke their overthrow. They will have to be very careful.

Without losing a beat, Jesus continues with another parable.

---

[1] Psalm 118:22-23; Zechariah 4:7   [2] Isaiah 28:16; Zechariah 10:4   [3] Isaiah 8:13-15
[4] Genesis 3:15; Psalm 2:7-9, 72:1-4, 89:19-29; Daniel 2:44-45

PARABLE OF THE WEDDING BANQUET
Matthew 22:1-14

> *Jesus spoke to them again in parables, saying: "The kingdom of heaven is like a king who prepared a wedding banquet for his son. He sent his servants to those who had been invited to the banquet to tell them to come, but they refused to come.*

> *"Then he sent some more servants and said, 'Tell those who have been invited that I have prepared my dinner: My oxen and fattened cattle have been butchered, and everything is ready. Come to the wedding banquet.'*

> *"But they paid no attention and went off—one to his field, another to his business. The rest seized his servants, mistreated them and killed them. The king was enraged. He sent his army and destroyed those murderers and burned their city.*

Using a wedding banquet scene, this parable combines elements from multiple other teachings. Like the jealous, self-righteous older brother in the parable of the Lost Son, these invited guests refuse a party invitation. Also, we just heard about tenants killing the landowner's servants at the harvest time.

In Jesus' time, a preliminary invitation (more of an engagement announcement by our standards) was sent once a couple was betrothed. As the date approached and the couple's new home was prepared, another announcement was sent to notify people that the time had finally arrived for a grand banquet. For a king's son, the wedding festival would probably have lasted for a week. An invitation to such an affair from a king would have been a great honor, and blatantly disregarding it would risk the king's displeasure. To make matters worse, harming a king's representative was akin to treason, a crime punishable by death. Here, the angry king punishes the rebellious criminal people, just as happened in the parable of the tenants. No one listening would have batted an eye at the king's response to his rebellious people. But the story isn't over...

"Then he said to his servants, 'The wedding banquet is ready, but those I invited did not deserve to come. Go to the street corners and invite to the banquet anyone you find.' So the servants went out into the streets and gathered all the people they could find, the bad as well as the good, and the wedding hall was filled with guests.

"But when the king came in to see the guests, he noticed a man there who was not wearing wedding clothes. He asked, 'How did you get in here without wedding clothes, friend?' The man was speechless.

"Then the king told the attendants, 'Tie him hand and foot, and throw him outside, into the darkness, where there will be weeping and gnashing of teeth.'

"For many are invited, but few are chosen."

Ignored by the first group, the king describes them as "undeserving" and opens the invitation to anyone and everyone the servants can find. And finally, the banquet hall is filled. Even a commoner would have known to dress appropriately out of respect for the occasion. But some slouch makes it inside, is thrown out for dishonoring the host, and we are left with a contrast between the celebration inside and the brutal darkness outside.

Not all who are invited will be included.

Similar to the previous parables, this continues the story of a people rejecting their king (God) and his servants (the prophets). It mentions both the king's wrath and his kindness towards even a commoner (as Jesus has exemplified in his ministry). But after multiple rebukes aimed at the temple authorities, this parable seems to shift focus back toward the crowd. God has planned a grand banquet for his son Jesus to celebrate the beginning of a new covenant relationship with his people (like a marriage). Some reject the invitation, rebel against the king, and are punished (something we've seen before). But this time, Jesus warns those that *do* respond to the invitation, a rebuke that may be aimed at even his own disciples. Not all who respond will remain guests. The question that remains is, what does it mean to be appropriately clothed for the banquet? How is one to be appropriately reverent toward the king?

A lack of clothing signified Adam and Eve's alienation and sin in Eden. Through a death, the sacrifice of an animal, God responded kindly by providing a covering to replace their hastily-grabbed fig leaves. Jesus has already cursed the fig tree, the symbol of the law as a covering over people's sin. And we've seen Jesus consistently welcome "unclean" or "sinful" people into his presence, people viewed as "cursed" under the law, simply because of their faith in him. It's as though a new and better covering has finally arrived, the new parameters to a relationship with God.

We've seen another wedding story before with Jesus' first miracle. There as a guest, he was thrust into the limelight but said that his time had not yet come. Here, this parable refers to a wedding and a time that has come. Jesus is describing the long-awaited fulfillment of his messianic role. Jesus is finally going to perform a grand finale to cement his identity as the Messiah. In Jesus, a new covering has arrived. As we will see, a new sacrifice will address people's nakedness before God and has come to complete all others. God is finally going to address sin once and for all. And the covering he provides is essential for anyone attending the great wedding banquet, life within God's presence.

After a round of teachings rebuking both the temple authorities and insincere followers, Jesus is about to face off in a series of debates. Just as might happen today to any sort of rising star, he is quickly challenged with a number of the hot topics of their day. How he responds will be a matter of life and death.

SIXTEEN

The Great Debater

A S THEY ARE STILL today, taxes were a matter of serious debate. Unlike today though, Judeans viewed these taxes (and Caesar's image on coins) as sacrilegious—something demanding and forcing loyalty toward a foreign oppressor in a manner appropriate only as an offering to God. In fact, anti-tax sentiment had even caused violent revolts during Jesus' youth. In 6 A.D., shortly after Herod's son Archelaus was deposed, Rome finally stepped in and made Judea a province. For the first time, people were required to pay taxes (also known as a "tribute"), and they were even required to use Roman coinage to pay this tribute. They revolted, only to experience a bitter defeat and the threat of heavier taxes. Taxes continued to be a sore spot, and coinage stamped with the image of Caesar was reviled. The money changers Jesus condemned at the temple, in fact, were there in part to ensure that nobody offered coins defiled with the image of a false God.

NOBODY LIKES TAXES
Matthew 22:15-22

> *Then the Pharisees went out and laid plans to trap him in his words. They sent their disciples to him along with the Herodians. "Teacher," they said, "we know you are a man of integrity and that you teach the way of God in accordance with the truth. You aren't swayed by others, because you pay*

no attention to who they are. Tell us then, what is your
opinion? Is it right to pay the imperial tax to Caesar or not?"

Curious about Jesus' allegiances, his opponents have formed a peculiar partnership. The Pharisees were well known nationalists. While great in number, they didn't hold many positions of power. They would benefit greatly if Jesus upset his following (their potential adherents). The Herodians, on the other hand, were holdovers from the previous regime who desired to see power over Judea restored to the Herod family once again. Reviled as potential foreign overlords, they sought cooperation with Rome and could benefit if this messianic claimant were removed. At the same time, they needed to be careful not to incite further conflict which might result in more Roman involvement in Judea, an obstacle to their desire for more control. Typically enemies, these two factions have found a common ground—the desire to get rid of Jesus. Can they get him to speak treasonously by defying Roman taxation? Or can they get him to speak favorably of Caesar, and so alienate the frustrated, perhaps revolutionary populace forming some of his following?

To set up the question, they try to trap him in some of his behaviors. He doesn't seem to care about a person's class (something we've seen countless times). Surely this means he doesn't care for Caesar's stature either, right? They are trying to call Jesus a hypocrite, an accusation that he has directed toward them numerous times.

But Jesus, knowing their evil intent, said, "You hypocrites,
why are you trying to trap me? Show me the coin used for
paying the tax." They brought him a denarius, and he asked
them, "Whose image is this? And whose inscription?"

"Caesar's," they replied.

Jesus immediately takes issue with their hypocrisy and turns their attempt against them. They question his loyalties even though everyone knows that they too hate paying taxes to Rome, yet they pay them anyway. They even pretend curiosity in a blatant attempt to get him killed. So he returns the volley with his own question.

Jesus calls direct attention to the images and description on the coin. On one side, along with a picture of Tiberius, the coins read "Augustus Tiberius Caesar, son of the divine Augustus." On the other side, the inscription reads, "high priest of Rome." The inscriptions signify that Caesar has honored himself as God. To most everyone, these claims reeked of idolatry. This inscription would have been uncomfortable to look at or acknowledge, let alone at the temple while discussing allegiances.

Then he said to them, "So give back to Caesar what is Caesar's, and to God what is God's."

When they heard this, they were amazed. So they left him and went away.

Here is the response that has left people arguing for centuries. The ambiguity of his answer is part of its brilliance. He effectively sidesteps their trap and stuns everyone, enough that his opponents leave with their heads hanging, for now. But what exactly does he mean? What *truly* belongs to Caesar, and what *truly* belongs to God?

They aren't about to try to answer this and risk the punishment of Rome or dishonoring God. But is this really about honoring God? Their motive could be their own desire for more money and power through paying less in taxes, or it could be their general disgust with Roman authority and occupation. What he says could be taken to mean that the people are to pay the required taxes (what is Caesar's) *and* tithes (what is God's) as if these things aren't in conflict. If Rome is forcing someone to pay the tribute, then do so. There's no problem so long as everyone is getting their necessary share. At the same time, his comment could just as easily be taken as an expression of indifference, as if to say, "Just give people what you owe them and quit arguing." Could it be that he sees money simply as a man-made toy and worthless to God? If Caesar wants to worship himself as a God, let him.

Jesus confronts Caesar's idolatry as well as the misunderstanding about what is actually of value. We've heard mention of "image" or "likeness" before in Genesis. In the creation story, God didn't mint coins in his image but *people*. What God

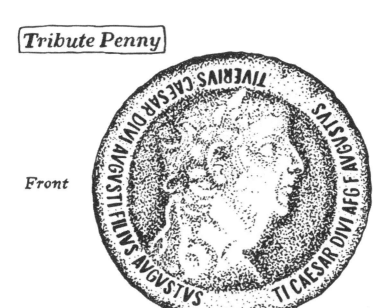

Front

"*Augustus Tiberius Caesar,
son of the divine Augustus*"

Back

"*High Priest*"

wants isn't our money through required sums but *us*. What belongs to God is a person's worship. What interests God most isn't one's money but the motives of one's heart, the offering of one's person to God. This was explained before in the Sermon on the Mount when Jesus discussed the essential role of motives in our actions—that if for the wrong motive (honoring self), even giving (tithes or charity) could be worthless to God. "They have received their reward in full," he said of such people.

Just as the young rich man had done before, his opponents walk away. Stunned, confused, unable to foil their perceived enemy, they leave disappointed and defeated.

ARGUMENTS ABOUT THE AFTERLIFE
Matthew 22:23-33; Luke 20:39

As one group of challengers exits, another regroups to question him once again. This time it's the Sadducees. They bring up an example about the afterlife. Will people be resurrected from the dead? The issue was hotly debated in their time. Pharisees and Jesus alike affirm the resurrection, but Sadducees thought it was ridiculous. Whose side will Jesus take? Does he have any wisdom to impart?

That same day the Sadducees, who say there is no resurrection, came to him with a question. "Teacher," they said, "Moses told us that if a man dies without having children, his brother must marry the widow and raise up offspring for him. Now there were seven brothers among us. The first one married and died, and since he had no children, he left his wife to his brother. The same thing happened to the second and third brother, right on down to the seventh. Finally, the woman died. Now then, at the resurrection, whose wife will she be of the seven, since all of them were married to her?"

They use an example from the law that protected women and families (in order to ensure the continuation of family lines). If one's husband died, it was the responsibility of his family to care for his wife (marry her) so that his line would continue. They may be aware that Jesus has already taken a strict and unpopular view of divorce.

286

In the Sermon on the Mount, he taught that in God's eyes the marriage covenant was still in place even after a divorce. Here, they combine an example both challenging this strict view of the marriage covenant and the belief that one day all will be resurrected. Wouldn't this mean that all of the marriages from their example were still intact? By this time, polygamy had long been done away with as a distortion of God's design for marriage, in favor of the example of monogamy between Adam and Eve in the Garden of Eden. One way or another, they think they've got him trapped.

> *Jesus replied, "You are in error because you do not know the Scriptures or the power of God. At the resurrection people will neither marry nor be given in marriage; they will be like the angels in heaven. But about the resurrection of the dead—have you not read what God said to you, 'I am the God of Abraham, the God of Isaac, and the God of Jacob'? He is not the God of the dead but of the living."*

> *When the crowd heard this, they were astonished at his teaching.*

> *Some of the teachers of the law responded, "Well said, teacher!"*

In a surprising turn, Jesus begins by arguing that they don't understand scripture and they doubt the power of God (a rebuke Pharisees would likely have cheered). It so happens that the Sadducees also reject the belief in spirits or any form of eternal life, another view that Jesus addresses in his answer. What will happen after death? Jesus says that at the resurrection of the dead, there will be no marriages between people (question answered) because they will be like angels (which affirms the existence of angels). It was believed that angels didn't reproduce but were a fixed number created by God (which Jesus seems to confirm). If that weren't enough, he quotes a passage[1] from the Torah, the only group of books that the Sadducees acknowledge as scripture. Taking the passage as literally as possible, Jesus highlights the way God speaks of dead

---

[1] Exodus 3:6

people (Abraham, Isaac, and Jacob) in the present tense as though they are still alive. This means that eternal life isn't simply a matter of the resurrection to begin at the final judgment but a present reality.

His answer is problematic for the Sadducees. Jesus has now affirmed belief in a future resurrection, supported his prior claims about the bond of marriage, verified the existence of angels, and explained that eternal life begins before the resurrection as though there is some form of an intermediate stage for life after death, a realm where Abraham, Isaac, and Jacob are present awaiting the final judgment. The scribes are amazed by his attention to such detail, while the crowds are probably shocked by how simply he dealt with a topic that people argued endlessly about. It's also interesting that while he may share an opinion from time to time with one movement or another, he clearly doesn't fit their ideologies well at all.

But the debates aren't over yet.

SEEING THE BIG PICTURE
Matthew 22:34-40

After a question built around a crazy hypothetical situation, Jesus is asked about a much more basic concern. As in our society, they had laws for all areas of life. The average person may have had some general impressions of how legal matters would be handled but would have relied upon legal experts to interpret and apply the law to their lives. The different movements were known to emphasize different things. The Pharisees were known particularly for the extra traditions they taught as essential for the arrival of God's kingdom. They gave excruciating attention to the purity laws and careful restrictions around the Sabbath, issues we've already seen Jesus challenge. Did Jesus share these views?

> *Hearing that Jesus had silenced the Sadducees, the Pharisees got together. One of them, an expert in the law, tested him with this question: "Teacher, which is the greatest commandment in the Law?"*

Last time he was asked this, Jesus returned the question before sharing the parable of the Good Samaritan. This time, Jesus keeps things brief.

Jesus replied: "'Love the Lord your God with all your heart and with all your soul and with all your mind.' This is the first and greatest commandment. And the second is like it: 'Love your neighbor as yourself.' All of the Law and the Prophets hang on these two commandments."

Jesus cites a passage at the center of one of their most common prayers called the Shema.[1] It is of utmost importance to them. This daily prayer begins by describing the oneness of God. "Hear O Israel, the Lord is our God, the Lord is one." Then it continues with what Jesus refers to as the greatest commandment. People are to love God with the entirety of our being. This isn't simply a matter of specific rituals, specific behaviors, or occasional words. Love is to be at the central motive of everything. Without love for God, one's actions are empty and worthless.

But Jesus doesn't stop there. He goes on to add a second (and less obvious) command from scriptures[2] as though the two are connected. We are to love or value others as we do ourselves. Loving God is directly related to how we value others. By connecting these passages, Jesus is saying that the common reflection on God's unity (love) is to be expressed in relationship toward God *and* others.

This is a huge claim.

It means that God is greatly concerned with our behavior towards others. Worship stands at the center of everything. Wrong worship leads to distorted relationships. It also means that all laws in the Hebrew scripture can be understood as applications of these two commands to various circumstances. God is interested in the way that we honor him in our lives and in our treatment of others.

And with this question answered, Jesus moves on quickly to ask his own question. It's time for him to test the very people attacking him. In doing so he will call into question their common misconceptions of the Messiah.

---

[1] Deuteronomy 6:4-9, 11:13-21; Numbers 15:37-41 [2] Leviticus 19:18

WHO IS GREATER?
Matthew 22:41-46

While the Pharisees were gathered together, Jesus asked them, "What do you think about the Messiah? Whose son is he?"

"The son of David," they replied.

By this point, it seems the Sadducees are all but out of the picture. They reject the coming of the Messiah, so by default this question isn't for them. He addresses his faithful opposition, the Pharisees. This is a pretty easy question to answer at first. The scriptures clearly describe the Messiah as the "Son of David," an apparently clear reference to both the Messiah's genealogy and his stature. It was believed that a descendent of David (thus, his "son") would rule one day in his likeness as a righteous warrior and king. No one anticipated that the Messiah would be divine. But Jesus is about to highlight something from this passage that rocks their understanding of the Messiah.

He said to them, "How is it then that David, speaking by the Spirit, calls him 'Lord'? For he says, 'The Lord said to my Lord: "Sit at my right hand until I put your enemies under your feet."' If then David calls him 'Lord,' how can he be his son?"

Jesus quotes from a psalm[1] that was written by David. In the song, it's as though David is witnessing a conversation taking place in heaven. David describes two different "Lords." One figure, "my Lord," is generally recognized as the Messiah, sitting at the right hand of "the Lord," God. But this presents a problem. If David is witnessing a conversation taking place, how can David's son (the Messiah), who hasn't even been born yet, be present? Also, it calls into question which person is greater—David or "my Lord" the Messiah. Jesus isn't questioning if the Messiah is of David's line (his "son"), but rather of greater honor. The questioners would have

---

[1] Psalm 110

believed that a father is greater than his son. It wouldn't make sense to them that someone would call his son "Lord." If the Messiah is of David's lineage, as they understand, then clearly David should be "greater." This passage would only make sense to them if the Messiah ("my Lord") is more than human, something they didn't anticipate.

> *No one could say a word in reply, and from that day on no one dared to ask him any more questions.*

Jesus has shaken their understanding of the Messiah's humanity. They, like most everyone, can still only think of a leader in typical human terms as someone of great power and prestige, themes that Jesus has challenged again and again. Greatness is not what they think, and Jesus is more than they understand. He is the Messiah, the divine man, and one greater than even David. His question puts an end to the debates. Jesus finishes as the clear victor, while his challengers are left embarrassed by their best attempts to foil him. As a teacher addressing a variety of debate categories, he has proven himself a proficient rabbi. At the same time, questions surely remain about his allegiances. He doesn't seem to support the Herods or Rome, nor does he line up with the basic beliefs of the Pharisees, Sadducees, or zealots. So who is this guy? But their interactions aren't quite over yet. Jesus still has much more teaching to do.

TRUE OFFERING
Luke 20:45-21:4

> *While all the people were listening, Jesus said to his disciples, "Beware of the teachers of the law. They like to walk around in flowing robes and love to be greeted with respect in the marketplaces and have the most important seats in the synagogues and the places of honor at the banquets. They devour widows' houses and for a show make lengthy prayers. Such men will be punished most severely."*

Jesus points to the way particular teachers wear fine clothing to distinguish themselves by highlighting their stature and possibly their wealth. There may be people like this right in front of the disciples as Jesus speaks. This showboating behavior is the opposite of the authenticity and love that Jesus has just described in the discussion of the greatest commandment.

Jesus also talks about "widows' houses." In this society, widows were generally a defenseless and vulnerable group. While the synagogues allotted provisions for them, they were socially powerless and tended to have little or no means of income. "Devouring houses" was the kind of accusation usually directed towards tax collectors as they made ruthless demands of even the poor. But Jesus now uses this language towards religious authorities, saying they exploit even the poor among their own people by demanding offerings from them. Starting from when he expelled the money changers, Jesus has been confronting the way those controlling the temple treasury took advantage of the poor while enjoying lavish foods, fine clothing, and other luxuries.

Just as he says these things, he sees an example nearby....

As Jesus looked up, he saw the rich putting their gifts into the temple treasury. He also saw a poor widow put in two very small copper coins. "Truly I tell you," he said, "this poor widow has put in more than all the others. All these people gave their gifts out of their wealth; but she out of her poverty put in all she had to live on."

Motives matter. As a poor widow, this woman just offered "all she had." The two small coins mentioned are *lepta*, coins that amounted to about fifty cents. This is money that was probably given to her by the temple as a form of assistance. When it comes to value, her offering was basically worthless, paling in comparison to the lavish amounts given by others. Yet, instead of giving God a portion of her wealth, she gave everything. Despite the fact that she had (by our standards) nothing to give, in God's eyes her genuine and faithful offering was actually worth the most.

Angered by the temple leadership's exploitation and mismanagement, Jesus now begins another of his lengthier discourses. In a pattern common to the prophets as they confronted and condemned various behaviors and even entire nations,[1] Jesus pronounce a number of woes upon his religious opponents in a similar fashion, a sharp contrast to his blessings in the Sermon on the Mount. After days of rigorous debates, this discourse serves as a sort of grand finale to Jesus' interactions at the temple.

PRONOUNCING THE VERDICT
Matthew 23

> *Then Jesus said to the crowds and to his disciples: "The teachers of the law and the Pharisees sit in Moses' seat. So you must be careful to do everything they tell you. But do not do what they do, for they do not practice what they preach. They tie up heavy, cumbersome loads and put them on other people's shoulders, but they themselves are not willing to lift a finger to move them.*

It's interesting that Jesus acknowledges the authority of the Pharisees here as the teachers of the scriptures, and not the Sadducees who presided over the temple. "Teachers of the law" may very well include some from both groups, though. Regardless, Pharisees functioned as the gatekeepers of the scriptures that were expected to guide people along the path of righteousness.

Jesus acknowledges that they have some authority due to their role, like Moses, as teachers of the scriptures. Elsewhere in scriptures, even King David continued to honor a sinful king named Saul rather than overthrow him by force.[2] However, Jesus goes on to accuse these leaders of hypocrisy. They tell people to follow extensive rules and rituals, but they don't practice what they preach and actually make it harder for people trying to follow God.

> *"Everything they do is done for people to see: They make their phylacteries wide and the tassels on their garments long; they love...to be called 'Rabbi' by others.*

Building upon the first paragraph, Jesus rebukes their motives just as he did in the Sermon on the Mount. They do things to be seen

---

[1] Isaiah 5:8-30, 10:1-2, 28-31; Jeremiah 23:1; Ezekiel 34:2; Habakkuk 2:6-20
[2] 1 Samuel 24, 26

by people rather than to honor God. *Phylacteries* were boxes containing scripture that were worn on people's arms and heads. In an odd application of commands to "wear" God's instructions,[1] the Pharisees applied this to mean ornaments and clothing rather than thoughts and behavior that made such teachings apparent in action. Jesus also reiterates a previous point we've seen about stature and prestige, challenging the ways these individuals sought to distinguish themselves through titles rather than through right conduct.

> *"But you are not to be called 'Rabbi,' for you have only one Teacher and you are all brothers. And do not call anyone on earth 'father,' for you have one Father, and he is in heaven. Nor are you to be called instructors, for you have one Instructor, the Messiah. The greatest among you will be your servant. For those who exalt themselves will be humbled, and those who humble themselves will be exalted.*

Jesus continues by challenging the different titles they use to honor themselves. When he speaks of calling someone "father," he refers to the way Jewish people identified with their great "father" Abraham to distinguish themselves as favored. Next, Jesus isn't putting down teachers. He has been preparing his disciples to be teachers, after all. He's addressing stature, not function. The title "teacher" doesn't make someone any more important than someone else. This can also be said of "father." He isn't saying that people should disrespect their parents or teachers. No one person is more important than another. Instead, he is saying that God is to be the one most revered even above earthly kinship. The Messiah is to be "Rabbi," the revered and authoritative teacher.

This alters the common approach of Pharisees. Somewhat like judges, scientists, and scholars today, Pharisaic rabbis would cite and build upon the work of other rabbis. Casting aside this approach, Jesus announces that he is the only true rabbi and interpreter of scripture. Others are to pass on his teachings, not add to them. And because of the way Jesus has been teaching them all along as one

---

[1] Deuteronomy 6:8-9

with unique authority and insight in the scriptures, he has also just implied that he is the Messiah.

Instead of seeking honor or reward, people are to serve, to value and honor others. In doing so, they can look forward to a time when God will remove wrongful leaders, strip away false honor, and recognize those who have been humble and served him.

> *"Woe to you, teachers of the law and Pharisees, you hypocrites! You shut the door of the kingdom of heaven in people's faces. You yourselves do not enter, nor will you let those enter who are trying to."*

> *"Woe to you, teachers of the law and Pharisees, you hypocrites! You travel over land and sea to win a single convert, and when you have succeeded, you make them twice as much a child of hell as you are.*

Not only have these authorities made following God more difficult, they've flat out denied others who seek truth, barring them because of their social position or religion. As a result, they will have no place in God's kingdom! This statement echoes a statement from the Sermon on the Mount that to enter the kingdom, a person would need to be more righteous than a Pharisee. Here he makes the point again, but in a direct rebuke of their behavior. Instead of serving God, they have opposed him and will not enter God's kingdom.

This is probably the strongest rebuke we've ever heard from Jesus. While the Pharisees are interested in multiplying (their source of power is scriptural knowledge and popularity), it is in service of the wrong "father." Instead of being "sons of God" or "sons of heaven" (like the peacemakers in the Sermon on the Mount), they stoke rebellion, greed, and self-righteousness. Instead of displaying comfort, kindness, or humility (as Jesus advocated in the Beatitudes), they embody a proud cruelty, making things more difficult. Jesus pronounces them condemned. Instead of God, they serve hell.

Wow!

They are the false teachers Jesus has warned of, wolves in sheep's clothing. They take advantage of those in need. They bear bad fruit and stifle the work of God.

"Woe to you, blind guides! You say, 'If anyone swears by the temple, it means nothing; but anyone who swears by the gold of the temple is bound by that oath.' You blind fools! Which is greater: the gold, or the temple that makes the gold sacred? You also say, 'If anyone swears by the altar, it means nothing; but anyone who swears by the gift on it is bound by that oath.' You blind men! Which is greater: the gift, or the altar that makes the gift sacred? Therefore, anyone who swears by the altar swears by it and by everything on it. And anyone who swears by the temple swears by it and by the one who dwells in it. And anyone who swears by heaven swears by God's throne and by the one who sits on it.

We've seen oaths come up before in the Sermon on the Mount. Here we see Jesus highlighting the absurd exceptions that the Pharisees made to allow various kinds of dishonesty. To the Pharisees, an oath would be more or less important depending on what it was sworn upon. In allowing these different kinds of oaths, instead of encouraging faithfulness, they have been permitting people to break promises. They have actually caused people to sin through their wrongful teachings. To Jesus, all oaths are made before God, and violating an oath is a serious offense that these teachers are now complicit in. Unlike the pure in heart who will see God (like blind Bartimaeus), these Pharisees are blind.

"Woe to you, teachers of the law and Pharisees, you hypocrites! You give a tenth of your spices—mint, dill and cumin. But you have neglected the more important matters of the law—justice, mercy, and faithfulness. You should have practiced the latter, without neglecting the former. You blind guides! You strain out a gnat but swallow a camel.

Behind their problems is the inability to rightly prioritize things. Pharisees emphasized tithing (giving a tenth of their income), even advocating tithing from different traded goods such as spices. In a society that didn't use banks, these goods often represented one's savings and wealth. Yet while tithing from these goods, they overlooked other good things that were actually more important, such as justice (think fairness, impartiality), mercy (think kindness or charity), and faithfulness (devotion, loyalty, and trustworthiness). Jesus' teachings and actions demonstrate these good things. His "Golden Rule" is the epitome of justice. His never-ending compassion exemplifies mercy. His teachings on marriage and oaths and his perseverance in the face of rejection exhibit his faithfulness. Instead of focusing on these virtues, however, the Pharisees and teachers of the law obsess over gnats (tiny things) while swallowing camels (enormous and absurd things to overlook).

Humorously, the example actually highlights one of their strict views. These men were so concerned with purity that they argued that a dead gnat could make a glass of wine unclean and would meticulously fish it out. All the while, camels were about the largest (and dirtiest) animal they knew. They obsess over the smallest things while ignoring the important stuff.

> *"Woe to you, teachers of the law and Pharisees, you hypocrites! You clean the outside of the cup and dish, but inside they are full of greed and self-indulgence. Blind Pharisee! First clean the inside of the cup and dish, and then the outside also will be clean.*

> *"Woe to you, teachers of the law and Pharisees, you hypocrites! You are like whitewashed tombs, which look beautiful on the outside but on the inside are full of bones of the dead and everything unclean. In the same way, on the outside you appear to people as righteous but on the inside you are full of hypocrisy and wickedness.*

These men have focused on appearances as though the external can change the internal. But it cannot. Their sparkling exteriors conceal inner darkness. Both examples Jesus gives were actual arguments and practices. Is it ok to use a bowl if it has only been cleaned outside? Or only cleaned inside? Pointing to the absurdity of this debate, Jesus states that *people* must be made clean on the inside (motives). Whitewashed[1] tombs were caves hosting decaying

---

[1] Ezekiel 13 describes false prophets as a flimsy "whitewashed" wall that will crumble.

bodies. The white paint warned people not to come near. Comparing his listeners to these tombs, he calls them dead, rotten sacks of bones with no understanding of true cleanness. Their external cleanliness stands as a warning for anyone that would approach.

Wow!

"Woe to you, teachers of the law and Pharisees, you hypocrites! You build tombs for the prophets and decorate the graves of the righteous. And you say, 'If we had lived in the days of our ancestors, we would not have taken part with them in shedding the blood of the prophets.' So you testify against yourselves that you are the descendants of those who murdered the prophets. Go ahead, then, and complete what your ancestors started!

It's easy to look back on history with a critical eye and proclaim that you would have acted differently. While Pharisees and teachers of the law often placed great emphasis on their lineage, they simultaneously tried to displace themselves from the wrongdoing of their ancestors. Here Jesus identifies their behavior with that of their forefathers who rejected the prophets. While they build tombs for their heroes who were rejected by their ancestors, they also, like their ancestors, reject and even kill people sent by God, such as John the Baptist and Jesus.

"You snakes! You brood of vipers! How will you escape being condemned to hell? Therefore I am sending you prophets and sages and teachers. Some of them you will kill and crucify; others you will flog in your synagogues and pursue from town to town. And so upon you will come all the righteous blood that has been shed on earth, from the blood of righteous Abel to the blood of Zechariah son of Berekiah, whom you murdered between the temple and the altar. Truly I tell you, all this will come on this generation.

As John the Baptist had previously, we see Jesus now refer to them as snakes. They are deceitful like the serpent in Eden, pretending to do good to others while leading them astray. Then Jesus speaks as if he is God—the one who sends prophets and teachers. He predicts a continued rejection of those speaking God's truth, as has been the case for centuries. Pointing to Abel's and Zechariah's murders (the first and last prophets murdered in their ordering of the scriptures), he warns that God's wrath over all of this history is about to be poured out in their day.

> *"Jerusalem, Jerusalem, you who kill the prophets and stone those sent to you, how often I have longed to gather your children together, as a hen gathers her chicks under her wings, and you were not willing. Look, your house is left to you desolate. For I tell you, you will not see me again until you say, 'Blessed is he who comes in the name of the Lord.'"*

The people said this last line before as Jesus was entering Jerusalem. It was a line from a song welcoming God's return to the temple. Now, Jesus mourns his reception by his people. He has longed to gather them as their parent (i.e. God),[1] yet they refused. Instead, he is about to leave, and things are desolate and in disarray. He refers to the temple as "your house," as though this is their dwelling and not God's. He says he won't return again until the people welcome him.

This polarizing speech serves as his final lecture in the temple grounds. It stays in the minds of his disciples as they depart. They are left with all sorts of questions about what is about to happen. Apparently they aren't the only ones. Witnessing what has happened, an interesting group approaches him to see if they can have a word.

GENTILE VISITORS
John 12:20-24, 31

> *Now there were some Greeks among those who went up to worship at the festival. They came to Philip, who was from Bethsaida in Galilee, with a request. "Sir," they said, "we would like to see Jesus." Philip went to tell Andrew; Andrew and Philip in turn told Jesus.*

---

[1] Isaiah 66:13

We've talked a lot about the different movements within Judaism. Here, we have some gentiles also at the temple to worship. They are the people who could gather in the outer court where Jesus turned the tables. These people are clearly excited and intrigued by his teachings. Will he explain things a little further for them? They've just seen the authorities knocked off their high horse, what's about to take place as a result? What changes are coming?

Jesus replied, "The hour has come for the Son of Man to be glorified. Very truly I tell you, unless a kernel of wheat falls to the ground and dies, it remains only a single seed. But if it dies, it produces many seeds...Now is the time for judgment on this world; now the prince of this world will be driven out."

Changes are indeed in the works, but Jesus is finished with his lectures for now. It is time to leave, and Jesus uses this departure to speak of something else. He is to be a seed, and it is through death that more will be planted. Judgment has come, and his real enemy, the serpent and "prince of this world," is about to meet his match.

SEVENTEEN
One Last Meal

T
O MOST ANY JEW, the thought of the temple's destruction
would have been horrible. It was easily the most magnificent
structure in the region. Despite frustrations about the actions
and politics of the temple authorities, the temple stood out as the
center of Jewish heritage and culture. As they leave, the disciples
draw attention to the temple's structure. There appear to be some
lingering concerns over Jesus' stiff closing remarks in the temple
courts. Without speaking against his predictions, they find a subtle
way to approach the topic and get some clarity. Does he really mean
this beautiful place is finished?

AN END IS COMING
Mark 13:1-3; Matthew 24:3-8; Mark 13:9-13; Luke 21:20-24;
Matthew 24:23-25, 27; Mark 13:24-33; Matthew 24:37-41

> *As Jesus was leaving the temple, one of his disciples said to
> him, "Look, Teacher! What massive stones! What
> magnificent buildings!"*

> *"Do you see all these great buildings?" replied Jesus. "Not
> one stone here will be left on another; every one will be
> thrown down."*

> *As Jesus was sitting on the Mount of Olives opposite the
> temple, Peter, James, John, and Andrew asked him privately,*

*"Tell us," they said, "when will this happen, and what will
be the sign of your coming and of the end of the age?"*

His reply to their praise of the temple quiets them. Yes, it's all
going to be destroyed. This isn't what they wanted to hear. They wait
until they cross the valley to the privacy of the Mount of Olives
before speaking again. There, with the temple in view, a small group
approaches him to ask for more information. Still expecting that
these things will happen all at once, they come to Jesus inquiring
about what could be separate events. When will the temple be
destroyed? What will signal the arrival of Jesus' new kingdom?
When will this age (or stage of existence) come to pass?

What follows is called the "Olivet Discourse." In it, Jesus speaks
to these themes within a broader framework of prophecies about
judgment and salvation. Using descriptions and phrases from several
prophets, Jesus locates his own predictions among these other
writings. Still, these passages were confusing and heavily debated as
people tried to understand when and how things would happen. Add
to it Jesus' symbolic language, and things get complicated pretty
quick. Much of what he describes is still heavily debated today and
contributes to Christians' expectations of future events. This
discourse is too significant to overlook, so I will try to help illuminate
Jesus' words without diving too deeply into these debates.

*Jesus answered: "Watch out that no one deceives you. For
many will come in my name, claiming, 'I am the Messiah,'
and will deceive many. You will hear of wars and rumors of
wars, but see to it that you are not alarmed. Such things must
happen, but the end is still to come. Nation will rise against
nation, and kingdom against kingdom. There will be famines
and earthquakes in various places. All these things are the
beginning of birth pains.*

*"You must be on your guard. You will be handed over to the
local councils and flogged in the synagogues. On account of
me you will stand before governors and kings as witnesses
to them. And the gospel must first be preached to all nations.
Whenever you are arrested and brought to trial, do not*

worry beforehand about what to say. Just say whatever is given you at the time, for it is not you speaking, but the Holy Spirit.

"Brother will betray brother to death, and a father his child. Children will rebel against their parents and have them put to death. Everyone will hate you because of me, but the one who stands firm to the end will be saved.

We've talked before about some of the conflicts and the messianic pretenders that led revolts during Jesus' life. Jesus seems to say that these kinds of things will continue. There will be conflicts, natural disasters, and more messianic claimants, but it's not the "end" (think goal or completion referring to the arrival of God's everlasting kingdom) that they await. They are to expect persecution. Arrests, abuse, betrayal, things will get really bad, but they are to carry their message to all nations. This element of their mission is unique among the different religious and cultural movements. Most people emphasized the way that the Messiah would come to save them from foreign oppression, not redeem foreign nations. The phrase "standing firm" to their ears would echo a call to martyrdom. Provided opportunities to renounce their faith in the face of execution, the disciples are to stay the course.

"When you see Jerusalem being surrounded by armies, you will know that its desolation is near. Then let those who are in Judea flee to the mountains, let those in the city get out, and let those in the country not enter the city. For this is the time of punishment in fulfillment of all that has been written. How dreadful it will be in those days for pregnant women and nursing mothers! There will be great distress in the land and wrath against this people. They will fall by the sword and will be taken as prisoners to all the nations. Jerusalem will be trampled on by the Gentiles until the time of the Gentiles are fulfilled.

"At that time if anyone says to you, 'Look, here is the Messiah!' or, 'There he is!' do not believe it. For false Messiahs and false prophets will appear and perform great

*signs and wonders to deceive, if possible, even the elect. See,
I have told you ahead of time.*

*For as lightning that comes from the east is visible even in
the west, so will be the coming of the Son of Man.*

Now Jesus describes the destruction of the temple. In other
accounts of this same speech,[1] he uses language that specifically
echoes descriptions by prophets[2] of a previous occasion when the
temple was destroyed. The temple will indeed be destroyed, yet this
is still not the "end" they await. The coming war is not the revolution
that will lead to their freedom and independence from Rome. As
these things develop, Jesus' followers are to flee immediately rather
than join the struggle. If they remain, they will be killed or sold into
slavery. There will be more messianic claimants, but they are not to
be fooled. This is still not the completion they seek. When the Son
of Man arrives with his kingdom, there will be no mistaking it. It will
be visible to all, stunning like a flash of lightning.[3]

*"But in those days, following that distress, 'the sun will be
darkened, and the moon will not give its light; the stars will
fall from the sky, and the heavenly bodies will be shaken.'*

*At that time people will see the Son of Man coming in clouds
with great power and glory. And he will send his angels and
gather his elect from the four winds, from the ends of the
earth to the ends of the heavens.*

*"Now learn this lesson from the fig tree: As soon as its twigs
get tender and its leaves come out, you know that summer is
near. Even so, when you see these things happen, you know
that it is near, right at the door. Truly I tell you, this
generation will certainly not pass away until all these things
have happened. Heaven and earth will pass away, but my
words will never pass away.*

---

[1] Matthew 24:15; Mark 13:14   [2] Jeremiah 6, 7:30-34, 15:1-10, 21:8-10; Ezekiel 7, 24:21;
Daniel 9:27, 11:31, 12:11; Micah 7:13   [3] Zechariah 9:14

"But about that day or hour no one knows, not even the angels in heaven, nor the Son, but only the Father. Be on guard! Be alert! You do not know when that time will come.

After the distress of the temple's destruction, there will be what sounds like cosmic disarray.[1] Reciting some lines from a prophet,[2] Jesus says that these things still precede the arrival of the Son of Man "coming in clouds with great power and glory."[3]

There's some disagreement about what he means by "this generation" which won't pass away until these things have happened. This may refer specifically to the temple's destruction as coming within a generation (40 or so years). Likewise, we have spoken previously of the fig tree's symbolism, and here it is again. The tree could be symbolic of the temple or Jewish people, or it could instead symbolize the idea that these events will progress over time.

Afterwards, he also speaks of the eternal nature of his words, that they too will remain as the very words of God. While *heaven and earth* will pass away,[4] his words will remain. Only God's words have this sort of timelessness. And about that "end" (heaven and earth passing away), nobody knows exactly when that will take place. He has given the disciples some warnings of the temple's destruction while clearly stating that no one will know the precise time of Jesus' return in glory, or when heaven and earth will pass away. They are separate events. There's no secret language or symbol interpretation that will reveal this detail. It remains a mystery even to him.

Interestingly, the language Jesus uses may resemble some wedding language of the time. During a betrothal, the groom would build a home for himself and his wife, but it was up to his father to declare precisely when the wedding would take place. The time may seem to be near, but nobody knows when except the father.

"As it was in the days of Noah, so it will be at the coming of the Son of Man. For in the days before the flood, people were eating and drinking, marrying and giving in marriage, up to the day Noah entered the ark; and they knew nothing about

---

[1] Ezekiel 32:7-8; Joel 2:10, 30-31, 3:15   [2] Isaiah 13:10, 34:4   [3] Daniel 7:13
[4] Psalm 102:25-28; Isaiah 51:6, 65:17, 66:22; Matthew 5:18

what would happen until the flood came and took them all away. That is how it will be at the coming of the Son of Man. Two men will be in the field; one will be taken and the other left. Two women will be grinding with a hand mill; one will be taken and the other left.

Before the Son of Man comes, life will seem normal, as was the case in the story of Noah and the flood from their scriptures.[1] People were going about their usual business when suddenly swept away (taken from the field or work in the hand mill).

SOME FINAL PARABLES
Mark 13:35-37; Matthew 25:1-13

"Therefore keep watch because you do not know when the owner of the house will come back—whether in the evening, or at midnight, or when the rooster crows, or at dawn. If he comes suddenly, do not let him find you sleeping. What I say to you, I say to everyone: 'Watch!'"

"At that time the kingdom of heaven will be like ten virgins who took their lamps and went out to meet the bridegroom. Five of them were foolish and five were wise. The foolish ones took their lamps but did not take any oil with them. The wise ones, however, took oil in jars along with their lamps. The bridegroom was a long time in coming, and they all became drowsy and fell asleep.

"At midnight the cry rang out: 'Here's the bridegroom! Come out to meet him!'

"Then all the virgins woke up and trimmed their lamps. The foolish ones said to the wise, 'Give us some of your oil; our lamps are going out.'

"'No,' they replied, 'there may not be enough for both us and you. Instead, go to those who sell oil and buy some for yourselves.'

---

[1] Genesis 6-8

"But while they were on their way to buy the oil, the bridegroom arrived. The virgins who were ready went in with him to the wedding banquet. And the door was shut.

"Later the others also came. 'Lord, Lord,' they said, 'open the door for us!'

"But he replied, 'Truly I tell you, I don't know you.'

"Therefore keep watch, because you do not know the day or the hour.

Jesus now exhorts them to be prepared because God, the owner of the house, is going to come back. The parable then describes this preparation. It isn't some strange tale of polygamy but a story built around the common elements of a wedding. There's still plenty of uncertainty about ancient Jewish weddings, but the occasion may have looked something like this. The bridesmaids would wait with the bride at her house for the arrival of the groom (think of our preparation times before a ceremony). Once it was the right time, an announcement would alert everyone, and the bridesmaids would go out (lamps lit if evening) to greet him. Everyone would then go to his father's house for the reception.

Here in the parable, after much waiting, the call sounds to find only half of the bridesmaids ready. This would be embarrassing for these women and an obvious reason for a rebuke. The foolish virgins are locked out of the party. They aren't allowed to enter and disturb things or embarrass the host. In fact, their behavior is such an insult to the host that they are disowned. "I don't know you," he says and excludes them from the celebration. Jesus instructs his followers to be like the faithful virgins, prepared and ready to accompany the Son of Man upon his return for the grand finale.

Where the previous parable encouraged their readiness for this unknown time, this next parable describes a little more about the event and what Jesus' followers are to do in the meantime.

SHEEP AND GOATS
Matthew 25:31-46

> *"When the Son of Man comes in his glory, and all the angels with him, he will sit on his glorious throne. All the nations will be gathered before him, and he will separate the people one from another as a shepherd separates the sheep from the goats. He will put the sheep on his right and the goats on his left.*

Jesus previously mentioned that the good news of salvation must first travel to all nations before his return would take place. Sometime afterward, all nations will be brought before him for judgment, a role elsewhere given to God,[1] and Jesus will sit on a throne as a king. Just as God once brought the animals before Adam to name them, so now all nations will be brought before Jesus and assigned their identity. This judgment will be like the separating of sheep from goats.[2] Though they often pastured together, these animals were known to have distinctly different characteristics. Sheep were known for their gentle dependence and obedience, while goats were typically stubborn and troublesome. Jesus draws upon these stereotypes as the sheep are gathered to his right (favorable) and goats to the left (disfavor).

> *"Then the King will say to those on his right, 'Come, you who are blessed by my father; take your inheritance, the kingdom prepared for you since the creation of the world. For I was hungry and you gave me something to eat, I was thirsty and you gave me something to drink, I was a stranger and you invited me in, I needed clothes and you clothed me, I was sick and you looked after me, I was in prison and you came to visit me.'*
>
> *"Then the righteous will answer him, 'Lord, when did we see you hungry and feed you, or thirsty and give you something to drink? When did we see you a stranger and invite you in,*

---

[1] Psalm 75:7; Isaiah 24:21, 33:22; Ezekiel 7:1-4   [2] Ezekiel 34:11-19

308

*or needing clothes and clothe you? When did we see you sick
or in prison and go to visit you?'*

*"The King will reply, 'Truly I tell you, whatever you did for
one of the least of these brothers and sisters of mine, you did
for me.'*

These sheep are the "blessed" and rewarded with the inheritance
of a kingdom, language we've heard elsewhere in the Beatitudes.
Jesus describes this kingdom as one prepared "since the creation of
the world." When God rested in the very beginning, he wasn't
finished with his work after all. There was always more in mind, a
goal destined from the beginning, the culmination of all creation.

Jesus highlights several different behaviors indicative of the
sheep. Referring to himself finally as a king at this awaited future
time, he commends generosity, hospitality, kindness (tending to the
sick), and devotion (loyalty to the oppressed and persecuted). He has
warned that those who showed these traits would be abused and
imprisoned pilgrims, depending on the hospitality of others as they
carried his message to foreign places. At the same time, some of
these behaviors were generally expected of Jewish people,
particularly toward the poor, and Jesus elsewhere commands such
kindness to even one's enemy (the parable of the Good Samaritan).

In their world, one's treatment of the king's agent was seen as
reflective of one's attitude toward the king. Jesus draws this parallel
here as the sheep inquire, "When did we see you?" Any such
treatment of the least of his servants (whom he calls "brothers")
would be considered actions directed toward him.[1]

*"Then he will say to those on his left, 'Depart from me, you
who are cursed, into the eternal fire prepared for the devil
and his angels. For I was hungry and you gave me nothing
to eat, I was thirsty and you gave me nothing to drink, I was
a stranger and you did not invite me in, I needed clothes and
you did not clothe me, I was sick and in prison and you did
not look after me.'*

---

[1] Proverbs 19:17

"They also will answer, 'Lord, when did we see you hungry or thirsty or a stranger or needing clothes or sick or in prison, and did not help you?'

"He will reply, 'Truly I tell you, whatever you did not do for one of the least of these, you did not do for me.'

"Then they will go away to eternal punishment, but the righteous to eternal life."

Using a lot of repetition, Jesus points out the contrasting behavior of the goats and how they will be judged as a result. They overlooked the way that God was interested in their treatment of others, and now they are on their own.[1] They are cast away to the same end as the devil and his assistants. Echoing the language of the prophets and his previous teachings like the broad and narrow road, Jesus places himself in the middle of this action as the groups face two different outcomes: eternal life and punishment.

This brings an end to his discourse on the coming events. As history plays out, we see many of these things described in the Olivet Discourse transpire. In the years that follow, Jesus' teachings continue to spread among both Jews and gentiles alike, and his followers face rejection and persecution from both groups of authorities. Beaten, imprisoned, and executed, his disciples walk a difficult road. Within about a year of these words comes the first Christian martyr named Stephen.[2] Within another decade, the first of the Twelve is executed (James, son of Zebedee, one of the "inner circle").[3] Beginning in 64 A.D. under Nero, somewhere between several hundred and a few thousand Christians (including Peter and Paul) are brutally executed. Fed to lions, beheaded, and burned alive as torches in gardens, Christians endure a time of distress unlike anything they'd yet encountered. More messianic claimants appear and more rebellions ensue. Finally, in 66 A.D., zealots (led by Judas the Galilean, grandson to a prior insurrectionist) slaughter several priests in the temple, desecrating it. Anyone who flees quickly enough to the hills survives the subsequent war, while all others are either butchered in the city during the Roman siege or carried off as

---

[1] Proverbs 21:13   [2] Acts 7:54-8:1   [3] Acts 12:1-2

slaves across the empire. Things get bad enough during the siege that women feed on their own children, and anyone caught fleeing is cut to pieces in search of jewels that they may have swallowed. In 70 A.D. (about 40 years after his teaching), Jerusalem falls to Rome and the temple is destroyed. Yet these things did not bring about the end of the heavens and earth as many probably feared was happening.

Most arguments over this discourse revolve around its chronology and symbolism. Was Jesus describing only the coming wars, or speaking of them as shadows of something else still to come? Regardless, these teachings distinguish separate stages and events that the disciples expected to happen all at once. Taking heed of Jesus' warnings, such as the exhortation to flee from Jerusalem when armies arrive, would have spared the early Christian community at a pivotal time in its infancy.

However, there is still much to happen. As another day comes to a close, we still have a grand festival to witness, one that will change history forever.

A BUDDING CONSPIRACY
Luke 22:1-2; Mark 14:2; Matthew 26:14-16

> *Now the Feast of Unleavened Bread, called the Passover, was approaching, and the chief priests and the teachers of the law were looking for some way to get rid of Jesus, for they were afraid of the people.*
>
> *"But not during the Feast," they said, "or the people may riot."*
>
> *Then one of the Twelve—the one called Judas Iscariot—went to the chief priests and asked "What are you willing to give me if I deliver him over to you?" So they counted out for him thirty pieces of silver. From then on Judas watched for an opportunity to hand him over.*

The concern over Jesus' popularity is significant. As seen by his actions at the temple, he clearly poses a threat to their authority, and the Passover was a time of some prior revolts and therefore reason for heightened security. Even the Herods often travelled to the area now controlled by Pilate, and extra troops remained ready to squash any uprising. For the religious authorities, removing such a popular leader risked the present peace which their power still relied upon.

But suddenly, an opportunity presents itself in the form of one of Jesus' trusted companions. It is impossible to locate Jesus in the city overflowing with religious pilgrims, but one of his disciples has now approached them with information about his private affairs. Where exactly does Jesus stay? When does he leave each evening? This is crucial information that will allow them to work swiftly and quietly without stirring much suspicion.

There's been much speculation about Judas the Iscariot's intentions. Given the unfamiliar and focused intensity of the temple confrontations (turning tables, debates, and woes), perhaps Judas saw a conflict that could easily end in the disciples' deaths (which Jesus speaks of repeatedly). Was betraying Jesus a way to save his own skin? Others suspect that he may have been a zealot who was tired of all the talk. Why not spark the fire? Or why not at least make some money on the side? His name, the "Iscariot," even resembles the word for a particular dagger popular later among the zealot assassins. Either way, it will become clear that he remains conflicted and uncertain of what he is doing and will soon regret his decision.

The payment of thirty coins was the cost to purchase a cheap slave.[1] During a celebration of their nation's freedom from slavery, Jesus has just been sold to the authorities as a slave.[2]

THE LAST SUPPER
Matthew 26:17; Luke 22:8, 10-14; John 13:2, 4-9, 12-17;
Matthew 26:21-25; John 13:27-30; Luke 22:19; Matthew 26:27-30

The Passover is imminent. This historic feast and festival mark the most significant holiday of Jewish society. One of the world's oldest religious traditions (still practiced today), this special feast dates back to almost 1500 B.C. during the time of the Pharaohs.

During this time, the people of Israel were slaves in Egypt. God performed numerous supernatural events inciting the Pharaoh to let them go before the great prophet Moses led them to freedom. The

---

[1] Exodus 21:32   [2] A couple of significant figures from the scriptures, Joseph (Genesis 37:12-36) and Samson (Judges 16), are sold and betrayed for silver.

final wonder was a plague upon firstborns, a response to Pharaoh's brutal murder of countless infants among the Hebrew people (for he feared their great numbers). God required a special sacrifice in order to be spared God's wrath. Israelites were to sacrifice a lamb of prime age and without defect, one for each household, and to put its blood over their doorways.

That evening, the firstborn son of any household that trusted and obeyed God was spared as death "passed over." The next morning, Egypt's wailing included even the Pharaoh's own household. As a result, the Egyptians showered the Jewish people with riches as they begged them to leave in order to remove the curses that had befallen Egypt. The Israelites were forced to leave so quickly that they didn't have time to add any leaven (yeast) to their bread for the journey. From that day forward, they were told to remember and celebrate this occasion through a special feast, the Passover, and a week-long festival of "Unleavened Bread."[1]

By the time of Jesus, the people had been celebrating these events for almost 1500 years. Everyone physically capable was expected to travel to Jerusalem to participate. The feast (the Passover) and the weeklong festival (Unleavened Bread) were closely connected and came to be celebrated in one pilgrimage, one of the three times each year that all Jewish men were expected to assemble in Jerusalem.

Upon arrival to Jerusalem, they were to participate in a ritual bath and were to remain "clean" until the time of the Passover meal. The week leading up to the feast, everyone would remove all the leaven (goods with yeast, symbolic of wrongdoing) from their homes to be burned just outside of the city. There was to be no yeast remaining in the city during the festival. They would also purchase a healthy lamb of prime age "without blemish" to be sacrificed later that week at the temple. None of its bones were to be broken. After this, the meat was then taken home for an intimate dinner celebration with family, full of symbolism and tradition, celebrating what God had done to free their people from slavery and death. Joining with 10-20

---

[1] The full story can be found in Exodus 1-14.

others for the meal, people were to consume the entire lamb (or any leftovers burned) so that nothing remained.

The following week was a festival to remember their pilgrimage from Egypt during which only flatbread (without yeast) was eaten. This festival commemorated their hurried departure from Egypt as they were showered with gifts. It is for this special occasion that Jesus has been waiting, and he is now present in Jerusalem with something planned. Except, instead of just following their typical traditions, Jesus is about to alter things in significant ways still remembered today.

On the first day of the Festival of Unleavened bread, the disciples came to Jesus and asked, "Where do you want us to make preparations for you to eat the Passover?"

Jesus sent Peter and John…

… "As you enter the city, a man carrying a jar of water will meet you. Follow him to the house that he enters, and say to the owner of the house, 'The Teacher asks: Where is the guest room, where I may eat the Passover with my disciples?' He will show you a large room upstairs, all furnished. Make preparations there."

They left and found things just as Jesus had told them. So they prepared the Passover.

It was uncommon to see a man carrying water (typically the task of women), so this would have been a noteworthy detail. Just as Jesus describes, the disciples find this certain person and are led to a spacious guest room in the upstairs of a home where they will have ample space for their meal. Typically only immediate family members were included in this feast. Here Jesus will eat with his disciples as though they are his own family, a sad reminder of the tensions that have divided his own household.

Beyond the instructions in scripture and small glimpses provided through some historical tidbits, we don't know exactly how the dinner was organized during Jesus' time. However, given the consistency and careful observance of other Jewish traditions, there's good reason to think that it might resemble the meal even today.

The purpose of the meal was to remember both what God did to free his people and his promises of a coming kingdom. Both themes have special relevance to Jesus' ministry. The meal, or *Seder,* consisted of multiple stages distinguished by 4 different cups of wine (also common to Roman feasts) which represented God's promises to his people while they were still in Egypt. In between these cups, there were numerous blessings and symbolic activities (singing songs and eating particular foods with unique actions). There were ritual hand washings, dipping and eating a bitter herb (such as horseradish), the "breaking of bread" (matzos), telling the Passover story, a meal centered around the roasted lamb, and discussions afterwards that could last all night. During the evening, there was also a distinct transition from sitting upright (the posture of a slave) to reclining (the posture of freedmen). What we see in the story of the last supper mirrors a number of these things in fascinating ways, but Jesus also appears to reinterpret the meal in surprising fashion.

Devoted disciples, Peter and John spend the day in preparation, and at twilight the Seder begins. As we will see, the meal has just started, and the disciples are reclining at the table while the food is being served, and Jesus already begins to stray from the script...

When the hour came, Jesus and his apostles reclined at the table.

The evening meal was in progress, and the devil had already prompted Judas, the son of Simon Iscariot, to betray Jesus... so he (Jesus) got up from the meal, took off his outer clothing, and wrapped a towel around his waist. After that, he poured water into a basin and began to wash his disciples' feet, drying them with the towel that was wrapped around him.

For a dinner like this, especially one where people would have travelled, it was basic hospitality to provide means for someone to wash their feet once they entered. We've discussed this custom previously when Jesus turned water to wine and when the sinful woman washed his feet with tears and perfume. Here, mixing this practice with the occasion, Jesus pulls off a stunning maneuver by humbling himself in ways shocking to anyone in his community. Where disciples were commonly expected to serve their rabbis, Jesus reverses things, focusing on his role as a servant *cleansing them* so that they can approach God.

> *He came to Simon Peter, who said to him, "Lord, are you going to wash my feet?"*
>
> *Jesus replied, "You do not realize now what I am doing, but later you will understand."*
>
> *"No," said Peter, "you shall never wash my feet."*
>
> *Jesus answered "Unless I wash you, you have no part with me."*
>
> *"Then, Lord," Simon Peter replied, "not just my feet but my hands and my head as well!"*

Peter, often the first to speak up, is stunned by Jesus' degrading action. In an attempt to honor his leader, he questions the strange behavior only to be rebuked. Jesus asserts not only that he is going to do this but that he *must,* or Peter can't have fellowship with him. While it may not make sense now, Jesus promises that it will later. He's teaching them something. His actions have everything to do with what is about to transpire. Though it is confusing, Peter quickly reaffirms his devotion to Jesus. He responds as if to say, "If I must be washed to be with you, then why stop with my feet!" He's happy to obey Jesus and expresses his desire for the fullness of their relationship.

The disciples understand that Jesus is claiming to be the one to make them clean before God, but they probably don't get how he expects to accomplish such forgiveness. Elsewhere, when James and John sought the seats of honor in his kingdom, Jesus spoke of baptism (washing) as though referring to death. Is this baptizing death to come through martyrdom as they fight in the revolution to establish a new kingdom on earth? In ways that may be misunderstood, Jesus ties these themes together, predicting that his coming death will be the source of their cleansing and future celebration.

> *When he had finished washing their feet, he put on his clothes and returned to his place. "Do you understand what I have done for you?" he asked them. "You call me 'Teacher' and 'Lord,' and rightly so, for that is what I am. Now that I, your Lord and Teacher, have washed your feet, you also should wash one another's feet. I have set you an example that you should do as I have done for you. Very truly I tell you, no servant is greater than his master, nor is a messenger greater than the one who sent him. Now that you know these things, you will be blessed if you do them."*

He's not just doing this for their personal good. He's setting an example. Just as he has humbled himself as their servant, they too are to humble themselves in service of others. This would be uncomfortable to hear for a group of men who have repeatedly argued over their positions and stature. But this is their great purpose and task.

Created in the garden as God's servants, we saw Adam and Eve reject this role as servants to become rulers. The consequences of their disobedience were a world full of oppression and brutal suffering. Now Jesus has come to restore this right role and relationship with God. He has come to them not as a ruler but as the servant intended from the beginning. But their dinner is not one of complete harmony. As in Eden, there is a deceiver among them.

> *And while they were eating, he said, "Truly I tell you, one of you will betray me."*
>
> *They were very sad and began to say to him one after the other, "Surely you don't mean me, Lord?"*
>
> *Jesus replied, "The one who has dipped his hand into the bowl with me will betray me. The Son of Man will go just as it is written about him. But woe to that man who betrays the Son of Man! It would be better for him if he had not been born."*

Then Judas, the one who would betray him, said, "Surely you don't mean me, Rabbi?"

As part of the Seder, people would dip and eat a bitter herb to remember the harsh sufferings of their people in slavery. This herb was often bitter enough to evoke tears. As they do this, Jesus predicts his own betrayal, a fitting parallel as he is about to be handed over as a prisoner, sold as a slave, to suffer at the hands of his nation's authorities. As you can imagine, Jesus' prediction causes quite the stir. What is he saying is about to happen? Who among them has changed allegiance?

As soon as Judas took the bread, Satan entered into him.

So Jesus told him, "What you are about to do, do quickly." But no one at the meal understood why Jesus said this to him. Since Judas had charge of the money, some thought Jesus was telling him to buy what was needed for the festival, or to give something to the poor. As soon as Judas had taken the bread, he went out. And it was night.

Jesus makes clear to Judas that he knows what will happen. This is undoubtedly a terrifying realization for Judas. Meanwhile, the others haven't yet figured out who he is describing. The tempter has finally returned for another bout with Jesus as the "opportune time"[1] has finally arrived. Twilight has passed and darkness has come. This is symbolically the hour of death's arrival as it passes over the homes marked with the blood of the lamb, and the streets of the city would have been empty. Probably shaken to the bone, Judas the Iscariot scrambles away[2] to do his work while Jesus continues the Seder with the remaining disciples.

And he took bread, gave thanks and broke it, and gave it to them, saying, "This is my body given for you; do this in remembrance of me."

---

[1] See chapter 3, Luke 4:13 [2] Psalm 41:7-9 seems to describe this scene

Then he took a cup, and when he had given thanks, he gave it to them, saying, "Drink from it, all of you. This is my blood of the covenant, which is poured out for many for the forgiveness of sins. I tell you, I will not drink from this fruit of the vine from now on until that day when I drink it new with you in my father's kingdom."

When they had sung a hymn, they went out to the Mount of Olives.

The broken matzo is also called the "bread of affliction" and represents the hardship of the people in Egypt. Jews eat this unleavened bread to remember their poverty and rushed departure as God delivered them from Egypt. Now, Jesus identifies this bread as *himself.* He is the bread of affliction necessary to accomplish redemption as a sacrifice "given" for the people (like the lamb). He is to be their sustenance as they endure the journey. He is God's provision for their poverty that will deliver them from slavery. He is the Messiah bringing about this awaited redemption.

In a scandalous move, Jesus alters this age old religious feast as if it was always pointing to him and this fulfillment. Now, they are to observe this tradition in remembrance of *him,* a fulfillment of the age-old story of the Exodus. He is accomplishing a new kind of exodus as he redeems them from slavery and death.[1]

This brings the disciples to the third cup of the evening, called the "Cup of Redemption." The red wine symbolized the blood of the sacrificed lamb central to the dinner. Here Jesus states that this is *his blood.* Again, Jesus alters the significance of their traditions as if the whole thing is finding fulfillment in him. Through his death, like the sacrifice of the Passover lamb, they will now have freedom from death and be delivered from their slavery to sin.[2] Just as God once brought the people of Israel out of Egypt to begin a new relationship with them, Jesus is establishing a new covenant relationship with them just as predicted by the prophets.[3] It is through Jesus that their shame will finally be covered and the power of death will be

---

[1] Hosea 2:14-15; Micah 7:15   [2] Isaiah 52:13-53:12; Zechariah 9:11, 12:10-13:1
[3] Isaiah 42:6, 55:3; Jeremiah 31:31-34; Ezekiel 37:26

removed.[1] He is providing the parameters for a newly restored relationship with God.

After Jesus gives thanks for this cup, he passes it to the disciples, stating that he won't be partaking again until the kingdom of God has finally arrived. The end of a Seder typically points to the coming kingdom of God. Some go so far as to set a place at the table for Elijah, the expected forerunner of the Messiah, and open a door to welcome him. But why welcome the coming redemption if you already believe the forerunner has come and the Messiah is present in your midst? Instead of opening the door for Elijah, the disciples depart with Jesus, likely expecting to initiate this very redemption and coming kingdom.

Next, they head outside the city walls and back to the familiar setting of the Mount of Olives, where Jesus has taught them privately each night. Singing the special songs of Passover, the disciples continue the celebration. It is common for men to stay up all night discussing things. Here, they too will be up all night, but for reasons they'd never expect.

---

[1] Isaiah 25:8, 28:18; Hosea 13:14

EIGHTEEN
Another Garden

A FTER SOME EXCITING VARIATIONS to their traditional dinner, Jesus continues his talk of the coming kingdom. We've seen Judas already identified as his betrayer (which the disciples don't realize yet), but Jesus is about to surprise them all by predicting their desertion as though it was long foretold in the scriptures.[1]

IN DENIAL
Mark 14:27-29; Luke 22:31-33; Mark 14:30-31; Luke 22:35-38

> *"You will all fall away," Jesus told them, "for it is written:*
> *'I will strike the shepherd, and the sheep will be scattered.'*
> *But after I have risen, I will go ahead of you into Galilee."*

To the disciples, this might sound like he's predicting that they will flee from battle. Numerous other insurrectionists led revolts only to later hide away in the mountains of Galilee to continue from there, and here they may think Jesus is describing the same plan. But the disciples are again confused and reject the prediction of disloyalty.

> *Peter declared, "Even if all fall away, I will not."*

---

[1] Psalm 31:11-12; Zechariah 13:7

"Simon, Simon, Satan has asked to sift you as wheat. But I have prayed for you, Simon, that your faith may not fail. And when you have turned back, strengthen your brothers."

But he replied, "Lord, I am ready to go with you to prison and to death."

"Truly I tell you," Jesus answered, "today—yes, tonight— before the rooster crows twice you yourself will disown me three times."

But Peter insisted emphatically, "Even if I have to die with you, I will never disown you." And all the other said the same.

In a display of overconfidence, Peter proclaims his faithfulness. He will not be deterred, but Jesus corrects him. Jesus already knows what is going to happen and has prayed for their recovery. The disciples will momentarily lose heart but not completely lose faith. They will be frightened into hiding when he suffers but will later regain confidence when he is resurrected and appears to them. Peter will then play a pivotal role and help to reorganize the group.

As for their disbelief of his prediction, Jesus gets even more specific. This will all happen *tonight!* The second crowing of the rooster indicated the wee hours of the morning—probably just a few hours after this conversation. Before then, Peter will deny his allegiance to Jesus three times. This is a heck of a prediction. How could something so unimaginable happen so soon?

Then Jesus asked them, "When I sent you without purse, bag, or sandals, did you lack anything?"

"Nothing," they answered.

He said to them, "But now if you have a purse, take it, and also a bag; and if you don't have a sword, sell your cloak and buy one. It is written: 'And he was numbered with the transgressors';[1] and I tell you that this must be fulfilled in me. Yes, what is written about me is reaching fulfillment."

The disciples said, "See, Lord, here are two swords."

"That's enough!" he replied.

When Jesus first sent them off in pairs, it was with specific instructions to take no extra provisions and to rely solely upon the hospitality of others. Here, his instructions take a significant turn. They will need extra provisions to last for the journey, and it will be dangerous (a sword was basic for self-defense). They aren't going to be greeted with singing crowds anymore. Thinking that they understand, they grab a couple of swords. Surprisingly, Jesus says two swords is enough, hardly the weaponry necessary for a rebellion.

As Jesus continues to encourage them, we are given a bit of new information. As we will see, they won't be alone. He may not be with them much longer, but someone else is going to accompany them along the way.

A NEW COMPANION
John 14:1-3, 6, 15-19, 25-27, 15:1-4, 9-15, 18, 20-21, 26-27, 16:1-3, 12-13

"Do not let your hearts be troubled. You believe in God; believe also in me. My Father's house has many rooms; if that were not so, would I have told you that I am going there to prepare a place for you? And if I go and prepare a place for you, I will come back and take you to be with me that you also may be where I am.

Jesus uses some metaphorical language to describe what is about to happen. As he speaks of going to his father's house, it may sound like he's speaking of the temple, and saying that he is about to disappear for a while as he sets up a shelter for them in it. While the disciples may have overlooked the similarity at the time, his language also resembles what a groom might say to his bride once they were betrothed. The groom would then go to his father's house to build an addition where they would make a new home together. Jesus has

---

[1] Isaiah 53:12

used wedding imagery before, and it sounds like the betrothal[1] is about to begin.

> ... "I am the way and the truth and the life. No one comes to the Father except through me.

> "If you love me, keep my commands. And I will ask the Father, and he will give you another advocate to help you and be with you forever—the Spirit of truth. The world cannot accept him, because it neither sees him nor knows him. But you know him, for he lives with you and will be in you. I will not leave you as orphans; I will come to you. Before long, the world will not see me anymore, but you will see me. Because I live in you, you also will live.

> "All this I have spoken while still with you. But the Advocate, the Holy Spirit, whom the Father will send in my name, will teach you all things and will remind you of everything I have said to you. Peace I leave with you; my peace I give you. I do not give to you as the world gives. Do not let your hearts be troubled and do not be afraid."

Jesus makes a number of significant claims here. The Jewish people understood themselves to be in a special covenant relationship handed down by God through Moses as "the way to the father."[2] Jesus now describes himself as the way to the Father[3] as if *he is the new law or covenant*, the new means to peace with God. Instead of stone tablets with written laws, this covenant has come in the form of a person,[4] a *helper*, who will write the laws on their hearts.[5] Elsewhere he spoke of the love of God as the greatest commandment, and now he implores their love and obedience to *him* as if he is God!

Jesus then goes on to describe this new companion, the Spirit, who as promised long ago,[6] will be a sort of compass, teaching,[7] counseling, and reminding them of everything. In the scriptures, prophets had long cried out to God for an advocate or special

---

[1] Hosea 2:19-20; Isaiah 61:10, 62:5; Jeremiah 3:14-15   [2] Psalm 25:4-12, 103:7
[3] Isaiah 2:3, 35:8; Micah 2:13   [4] Isaiah 42:6   [5] Jeremiah 24:7, 31:33; Ezekiel 11:19-20, 36:26-27   [6] Isaiah 32:15, 44:3, 59:21; Ezekiel 37:14, 39:29; Joel 2:28-29   [7] Job 32:8

mediator,[1] and that advocate has now come. Their helper has arrived. This Spirit of holiness (the one who hovered over the waters in the creation story) will now live in *them* as though they are temples, God's dwelling place on the earth. And all of these things will be done in the name of (or by the power of) Jesus. If Jesus isn't God, this is blasphemy.

"I am the true vine, and my Father is the gardener. He cuts off every branch in me that bears no fruit, while every branch that does bear fruit he prunes so that it will be even more fruitful. You are already clean because of the word I have spoken to you. Remain in me, as I also remain in you. No branch can bear fruit by itself; it must remain in the vine. Neither can you bear fruit unless you remain in me.

"As the Father has loved me, so have I loved you. Now remain in my love. If you keep my commands, you will remain in my love, just as I have kept my Father's commands and remain in his love. I have told you this so that my joy may be in you and that your joy may be complete. My command is this: Love each other as I have loved you. Greater love has no one than this, to lay down one's life for one's friends. You are my friends if you do what I command. I no longer call you servants, because a servant does not know his master's business. Instead, I have called you friends, for everything that I learned from my Father I have made known to you.

Jesus describes God as a gardener, something we've discussed elsewhere. Some prophets once described Israel as God's vine that came to ruin,[2] but here Jesus speaks of himself as the "true" vine,[3] one that hasn't strayed from God. Pruning is a basic practice in a vineyard, necessary for the health and fruitfulness of the vine. Jesus describes the way that God will continue to prune dead branches from the disciples as a part of this true vine just as a gardener would work in a vineyard. As his disciples remain "in him" (referring to

---

[1] Job 9:33-34, 16:18-21, 33:23-28; Isaiah 59:15-16; Ezekiel 22:30-31   [2] Isaiah 3:14, 5:1-8; Jeremiah 12:10; Ezekiel 15:1-6   [3] Hosea 14:4-7; Amos 9:11-15; Zechariah 8:12-13

love and obedience), he will continue to prune and transform them so that they can bear much good fruit.

Jesus is describing himself as a new tree of life. Remain in him and flourish, stray and wither lifelessly until death. Just as Adam and Eve were once presented with two ways in the two trees and they ate of the wrong fruit, Jesus has now described himself as bearing the fruits of a new tree of life. Just as he said when he fed the 5,000 and scared many away,[1] and as he told them at the Passover meal,[2] they are now to eat his body and blood to be sustained. He is the way to the Father. His love is to be their guide, and they are to go so far as to lay down their lives in love of each other. Now they aren't just his servants but his friends as they play an important role carrying out "the master's business."

This sounds more and more like a farewell address.

"If the world hates you, keep in mind that it hated me first... Remember what I told you: 'A servant is not greater than his master.' If they persecuted me, they will persecute you also. If they obeyed my teaching, they will obey yours also. They will treat you this way because of my name, for they do not know the one who sent me.

"When the Advocate comes, whom I will send to you from the Father—the Spirit of truth who goes out from the Father—he will testify about me. And you also must testify, for you have been with me from the beginning.

"All this I have told you so that you will not fall away. They will put you out of the synagogue; in fact, the time is coming when anyone who kills you will think they are offering a service to God. They will do such things because they have not known the Father or me.

"I have much more to say to you, more than you can now bear. But when he, the Spirit of truth, comes, he will guide you into all the truth. He will not speak on his own; he will

---

[1] John 6:53-66   [2] Matthew 26:26-28

speak only what he hears, and he will tell you what is yet to come.

Things are about to change, and it should be expected. They should take note of the way he is treated and expect the same. Their task remains, though. They are to testify (along with this Spirit) about Jesus because they have been with him from the beginning of his ministry. The things they've learned aren't just for them but for the whole world, and they have an important role to play as his appointed messengers. There is much more to say, but he has already given them more than they can handle. Their new companion, the Spirit, will pick up where he has left off to guide them on this great mission.

His time with them is coming to a close. While he has functioned as a temple in their presence, another important development is about to take place. The temple is about to become an entire people.

ANOTHER GARDEN
Mark 14:32-43; John 18:2-3; Matthew 26:49; Luke 22:48; Mark 14:46; John 18:10; Luke 22:51; Matthew 26:52-56; Mark 14:51-52

It seems everyone could use a little time to pray as the dust settles from their conversations. As the night continues, even Jesus has some things he needs to think about. Across the Kidron Valley from Jerusalem, on the Mount of Olives, there is a specific garden area and an olive grove named Gethsemane facing the temple from across the valley. In privacy, as the Passover celebrations continue all over the city, this garden provides the scenery for our next story.

They went to a place called Gethsemane, and Jesus said to his disciples, "Sit here while I pray." He took Peter, James and John along with him, and he began to be deeply distressed and troubled. "My soul is overwhelmed with sorrow to the point of death," he said to them. "Stay here and keep watch."

Going a little farther, he fell to the ground and prayed that if possible the hour might pass from him. "Abba, Father," he said, "everything is possible for you. Take this cup from me. Yet not what I will, but what you will."

We see Jesus separate from the group with only his inner circle, the same few that witnessed the transfiguration[1] and the raising of the dead girl.[2] They join him and proceed a little farther before receiving instructions. He is in the midst of serious struggle and his soul is "overwhelmed with sorrow to the point of death," he says. They have seen him mourn before, but what's going on? As someone who's fully human, even Jesus dreads the prospect of suffering and death. He's mentioned betrayal at dinner, and now he's predicted their desertion before the night is over. Without much explanation, he simply instructs them to keep watch, the same command he gave them the previous night in his "Olivet Discourse" when they asked about the coming Kingdom. They need to ready themselves for what's about to happen.

As Jesus prays, he uses a familiar and intimate title, *Abba*, for Father (not one typically used to address God). He asks God to "take this cup," an interesting phrase. Elsewhere, when James and John asked to be seated at his side in his kingdom, Jesus spoke of his coming death as a cup. Elsewhere in the scriptures, God's wrath is often described as a cup.[3] During the Passover Seder Jesus spoke of the cup as though it was his own blood and he was the sacrificial lamb. The time has come for him to submit to death as a sacrifice, the object of God's wrath, and he pleads with God, searching for some alternative.

Daunted by the weight of his circumstances, Jesus submits as God's servant[4] much like he did during his temptation in the desert. No, he will not resist this purpose and plan. He will stay the course. This is his path, and he will serve God's will.

Then he returned to his disciples and found them sleeping. "Simon," he said to Peter, "are you asleep? Couldn't you keep watch for one hour? Watch and pray so that you will not fall into temptation. The spirit is willing, but the flesh is weak."

---

[1] See chapter 11, Mark 9:2   [2] See chapter 9, Mark 5:37-42   [3] Job 21:20; Isaiah 51:17-22; Jeremiah 25:15-29; Habakkuk 2:16   [4] Psalm 40:7-13, 116:3-19

Once more he went away and prayed the same thing. When he came back, he again found them sleeping, because their eyes were heavy. They did not know what to say to him.

One hour has already passed as Jesus prayed. As he returns, his disciples have failed to keep watch. They are tired. It is late. If only they understood what was about to happen. He specifically calls out Peter, the one who boldly declared his allegiance just hours before. Now, even Peter is fading, and they are speechless. Before leaving and returning a second time to find the same thing has happened again, he exhorts them to pray that they don't "fall into temptation." Jesus has told them that they will all abandon him. Maybe they ought to be giving this some thought and praying so that they don't lose heart and jump ship as he has predicted. Another hour passes as Jesus leaves them once more.

Returning the third time, he said to them, "Are you still sleeping and resting? Enough! The hour has come. Look, the Son of Man is betrayed into the hands of sinners. Rise! Let us go! Here comes my betrayer!"

Just as he was speaking, Judas, one of the Twelve, appeared...

Three times, just as Jesus had said, but this isn't actually the denial Jesus predicted of Peter. "The hour has come," he proclaims. It is quite the comment to wake up to. Whatever is about to transpire is now underway. As they rub the sleep from their eyes, they see Judas, the *betrayer*, and he isn't alone.

Now Judas, who betrayed him, knew the place, because Jesus had often met there with his disciples. So Judas came to the garden, guiding a detachment of soldiers and some officials from the chief priests and Pharisees. They were carrying torches, lanterns and weapons.

Going at once to Jesus, Judas said, "Greetings, Rabbi!" and kissed him.

...Jesus asked him, "Judas, are you betraying the Son of Man with a kiss?"

The men seized Jesus and arrested him.

Then Simon Peter, who had a sword, drew it and struck the high priest's servant, cutting off his right ear. (The servant's name was Malchus.)

But Jesus answered, "No more of this!" And he touched the man's ear and healed him.

"Put your sword back in its place," Jesus said to him, "for all who draw the sword will die by the sword. Do you think I cannot call on my Father, and he will at once put at my disposal more than twelve legions of angels? But how then would the Scriptures be fulfilled that say it must happen in this way?"

In that hour Jesus said to the crowd, "Am I leading a rebellion, that you have come out with swords and clubs to capture me? Every day I sat in the temple courts teaching, and you did not arrest me. But this has all taken place that the writings of the prophets might be fulfilled." Then all the disciples deserted him and fled.

This is a rude awakening for the disciples. And where was the rest of the group? Were they asleep as well? Judas uses a common intimate greeting, a kiss, to identify Jesus as the mob's target, and Jesus rebukes him.

Peter quickly jumps into the fray. Surely this is the reason for their swords, right? As he hacks away someone loses an ear, which is very bad news for Peter. But just as the battle seems to begin, Jesus brings it to an end. Healing the wounded man, he rebukes his disciples. Jesus has no need for weapons. He is turning his cheek just as he taught them. There is no secrecy here, and Jesus hasn't been outsmarted. He then makes an enormous claim—that he could command 12 legions of angels (72,000) if he so desired. But this must happen. He must go with them. The time has finally come.

Next, Jesus rebukes those arresting him. He calls out their evil intent and unjust behavior. If he had committed a crime, they could have arrested him in broad daylight any of the days he was with them. But they didn't, because he hasn't done anything wrong. They are the ones in the wrong and arrest him in the cover of night because of their cowardice. And they have come with weapons, expecting a fight. Everyone expected a fight, including Jesus' own disciples. Instead, Jesus has healed one of the high priest's own soldiers (which may save Peter's life), a stunning response from this apprehended criminal. Afraid, surprised, confused, it's fight or flight for the disciples. Once Jesus tells them not to fight, his disciples vanish.

Just as Jesus said, "Strike the shepherd, the sheep will scatter."

A young man, wearing nothing but a linen garment, was following Jesus. When they seized him, he fled naked, leaving his garment behind.

And suddenly, we find ourselves right back in the story of Eden. Naked and afraid. Ashamed and in hiding. Betrayal, guilt, these experiences abound. It's no coincidence that Jesus brought the disciples here speaking of temptation. These are the very problems we saw in Eden that Jesus has now come to face. This is the reason he prays. It was in a garden that God warned his servants not to give in, but they did. But the enemy was unable to trick Jesus into killing himself in their earlier temptation encounter, so he's now convinced others to murder Jesus instead.

The opportune time has arrived.

Just as in the garden, the betrayer approaches pretending to be a friend, a deceiver aimed only at death and destruction. Adam and Eve were suddenly left naked like this young man now fleeing to hide without his garment. The disciples disperse to hide in the shadows, creeping away through the brush, afraid, just as their great forefather Adam once was. Death looms overhead as they too await what's coming—a trial, and ultimately, death.

THE INTERROGATION BEGINS
John 18:12-23; Matthew 26:59-68, 71-74; Luke 22:61-62

There are a few different groups of authorities in the region. Each has specific jurisdictions and limitations. It's somewhat like local, state, and federal authorities today. There are the Jewish religious authorities, who are allowed to handle most civil affairs. They aren't, however, permitted to carry out a death penalty. That requires the approval of the appointed Roman authority, Pontius Pilate. Beyond this, Pilate presides only over Judea. Philip the Tetrarch and Herod Antipas rule over the surrounding regions (like Galilee to the north). These territorial rights will come into play as Jesus goes to trial.

Then the detachment of soldiers with its commander and the Jewish officials arrested Jesus. They bound him and brought him first to Annas, who was the father-in-law of Caiaphas, the high priest that year. Caiaphas was the one who had advised the Jewish leaders that it would be good if one man died for the people.

Simon Peter and another disciple were following Jesus. Because this disciple was known to the high priest, he went with Jesus into the high priest's courtyard, but Peter had to wait outside at the door. The other disciple, who was known to the high priest, came back, spoke to the servant girl on duty there and brought Peter in.

"You aren't one of this man's disciples too, are you?" she asked Peter.

He replied, "I am not."

It was cold, and the servants and officials stood around a fire they had made to keep warm. Peter also was standing with them, warming himself.

First, Jesus appears in a secret gathering before the Sanhedrin (the Jewish court) and its presiding officials, the family of the High Priest. These are the officials who had Jesus arrested, and they will use this time to interrogate him as they sort through his potential charges. They will have to present a convincing case to Pilate if Jesus is to be executed. This might also provide them a chance to get him to say something to warrant the consequences they desire.

As the questioning begins, Jesus hasn't done anything to break free, and his disciples are surely wondering if he's got something up his sleeve. Will he perform a miracle? Will he finally be revealed? A couple of the disciples (Peter and John) are able to slip into the courtyard as things proceed, a risky and courageous maneuver. They could easily be apprehended and thrown into the interrogation.

Then, with much at stake, Peter is somehow recognized. Suddenly, Peter seems to regress back to the man on the fishing boat overwhelmed with his insecurities. Hiding among strangers, he denies his identity for what he believes will keep him safe and alive, hardly the boldness he has displayed in previous conversations among the disciples. Trembling in fear, Peter rejects any association with his teacher.

Meanwhile, the high priest questioned Jesus about his disciples and his teaching.

"I have spoken openly to the world," Jesus replied. "I always taught in synagogues or at the temple, where all the Jews come together. I said nothing in secret. Why question me? Ask those who heard me. Surely they know what I said."

When Jesus said this, one of the officials nearby struck him in the face. "Is this the way you answer the high priest?" he demanded.

"If I said something wrong," Jesus replied, "testify as to what is wrong. But if I spoke the truth, why did you strike me?"

Things seem to be going nowhere, and Jesus draws attention to the fact that they have no reason to arrest him, let alone punish him. Unlike most, he has nothing to hide, and he has taught and even confronted people openly in public. He is not the violent zealot they might expect. This is what it means to "turn the other cheek" as he taught his disciples. He confronts the wrong but refuses to do wrong.

The chief priests and the whole Sanhedrin were looking for false evidence against Jesus so that they could put him to death. But they did not find any, though many false witnesses came forward.

Finally two came forward and declared, "This fellow said, 'I am able to destroy the temple of God and rebuild it in three days.'"

Then the high priest stood up and said to Jesus, "Are you not going to answer? What is this testimony that these men are bringing against you?" But Jesus remained silent.

In this court, there are some basic legal standards required to bring a charge against someone. The Sanhedrin violates basic procedures by conducting such an investigation in secret in the middle of the night. There must also be eye-witnesses, and giving false testimony was a serious and punishable offense, particularly regarding crimes punishable by death. A number of people are brought forward but nothing sticks. Finally, misquoting something Jesus said (as though he was plotting to destroy the temple), they turn to him only to find silence. He makes no effort to prove his innocence to them. He's spoken to them all week long, and they've rejected him. They aren't really interested in the truth, simply a means to accomplish their goal.

The high priest said to him, "I charge you under oath by the living God: Tell us if you are the Messiah, the Son of God."

"You have said so," Jesus replied. "But I say to all of you: From now on you will see the Son of Man sitting at the right hand of the Mighty One and coming on the clouds of heaven."

Then the high priest tore his clothes and said, "He has spoken blasphemy! Why do we need any more witnesses? Look, now you have heard the blasphemy. What do you think?

"He is worthy of death," they answered.

Then they spit in his face and struck him with their fists. Others slapped him and said, "Prophesy to us, Messiah. Who hit you?"

Finally, they ask Jesus a straightforward question invoking the authority of God about his identity. In response, Jesus gives them an answer. As they have said, he is the Messiah and the Son of God. In contrast to Peter's denial of his identity as a disciple, Jesus states his identity plainly. As if this weren't enough, he follows it up with the prediction that he, the Son of Man, will sit at the right hand of God and will come to rule to the ends of the earth, as described by the prophet Daniel.

At this, the High Priest loses it. Tearing his garment as though it were just destroyed by these words, he accuses Jesus of blasphemy. This clothing has been provided to the high priest as commanded by Jewish law for his special role as a mediator between people and God. Has his role just been ripped apart by Jesus' testimony? On top of claiming the titles of Messiah and "Son of God," Jesus has just claimed divine authority as the cosmic figure foretold in prophesy (which the Sadducees reject).[1] Whether it is because the High Priest believes these things to be obviously false (a lie under an oath sworn by the name of God), or that Jesus has claimed to be divine, the High Priest considers this enough to charge Jesus with blasphemy and will seek the death penalty, the traditional punishment for blasphemy. Others are in agreement. Next they will have to convince Pontius Pilate, who isn't interested in religious matters, that Jesus is indeed worthy of execution. This task could prove to be quite difficult.

All the while, Peter has continued to watch nervously...

Then he went out to the gateway, where another servant girl saw him and said to the people there, "This fellow was with Jesus of Nazareth."

He denied it again, with an oath: "I don't know the man!"

---

[1] Daniel 7:13-14

After a little while, those standing there went up to Peter and said, "Surely you are one of them; your accent gives you away."

Then he began to call down curses, and he swore to them, "I don't know the man!"

Immediately a rooster crowed.

The Lord turned and looked straight at Peter. Then Peter remembered the word the Lord had spoken to him…And he went outside and wept bitterly.

Things aren't looking good for Jesus or Peter, whose response to the others' growing suspicions gets even stronger. Peter swears an oath, something Jesus taught against. Such dishonesty was believed to call a curse upon the liar. Just as others bear false testimony against Jesus, so too does Peter about their relationship. We have seen Jesus speak in parables about people being disowned (the 10 virgins, the sheep and goats) with the statement, "I never knew you." Here, Jesus is being disowned by these very words. As the scene comes to a close, Peter has behaved just as predicted. Instead of offering his testimony, he's been kept silent by fear. He knows that if Jesus is indeed executed, his relationship with Jesus could make him susceptible to the same punishment. Saving his own life (or so he thinks), he denies Jesus a third time just as the rooster crows. Suddenly, he looks up to see Jesus and experiences a moment of realization and humiliation. He excuses himself in order to weep.

He is covered in shame.

The story has continued to parallel that of Eden as we get through the investigation. In the garden, there were false testimonies and accusations as Adam and Eve tried to save themselves, displacing guilt at the expense of others. Where Adam and Eve couldn't acknowledge their imperfection, Jesus is completely forward about his identity and innocence, a stark contrast to the deception and cruelty that surrounds him. Meanwhile, Peter is also caught up in Adam's struggle as he denies the truth of his identity as a servant of Christ, violating numerous pledges of allegiance to his Master. Like

Adam, he has broken his allegiance, is guilty, and shame abounds. Death is imminent.

Jesus is pronounced guilty and shamed all because they are afraid of him. He is a threat to their power and the stability of their nation. A humble servant,[1] he simply does not fit within their desire to rule. It is all *his* fault, the same accusation directed toward God in Eden, when Adam suggests God is responsible because he made Eve and put her in the garden. In a grand substitution, Jesus has now taken Adam and Eve's place as the one receiving the punishment appropriate for their own wrongdoing, treason. Their treason was trying to usurp God. Jesus receives the same punishment pronounced upon them in the very beginning, death. But this time the punishment isn't for treason against God but against…Rome? His people? The temple? The world?

This is hardly the revolution anyone anticipated.

THE TRIAL CONTINUES

Matthew 27:3-7; John 18:28-29; Luke 23:2; John 18:33-38; Luke 23:4; Matthew 27:12-14; Luke 23:5-15; Mark 15:6-11; John 19:12; Matthew 27:22-23; John 19:15; Matthew 27:24, 26

Meanwhile, we are given an update about Judas, who has discovered the verdict of the trial.

When Judas, who had betrayed him, saw that Jesus was condemned, he was seized with remorse and returned the thirty pieces of silver to the chief priests and the elders. "I have sinned," he said, "for I have betrayed innocent blood."

"What is that to us?" they replied. "That's your responsibility."

So Judas threw the money into the temple and left. Then he went away and hanged himself.

The chief priests picked up the coins and said, "It is against the law to put this into the treasury, since it is blood money."

---

[1] Isaiah 50:4-11 describes an obedient servant of God who endures abuse and condemnation late at night like the scenes we've just witnessed.

So they decided to use the money to buy the potter's field as a burial place for foreigners.

We see Judas's inner turmoil erupt. What was he expecting? Did he think Jesus would pull off some stunning miracles to prevent such a horrendous outcome? Whatever his intentions, he now expects that what he did will indeed end in Jesus' death and that this makes him guilty of innocent blood. Despite Jesus' talks of resurrection, Judas appears to have either misunderstood these comments or disbelieved them as he clearly doesn't expect Jesus to raise from the dead.

Full of regret, Judas attempts to undo what's been done. The money is worthless to him now. Unable to stop things, Judas seeks an escape by enacting his own punishment for the life he has just betrayed. He has committed a crime deserving of death, so he will kill himself. But in the end, his death doesn't change anything. It fails to prevent or rectify anything and instead robs him of experiencing the surprising finale to this story.

In response, his partners in crime don't argue with his assessment of Jesus' innocence. Instead, they displace the blame onto Judas. Surely this all falls on him, not them. Unable to accept the "blood money" (as if it wasn't wrong to previously make such a payment), the chief priests use the money to buy the "potter's field"[1] for burials. The payment for Jesus' life goes to provide a resting place for impoverished foreigners, a fitting investment for a Messiah who spoke of uniting the nations and welcomed the poor.

Meanwhile, Jesus is taken to the next stage of his interrogation.

Then the Jewish leaders took Jesus from Caiaphas to the palace of the Roman governor. By now it was early morning, and to avoid ceremonial uncleanness they did not enter the palace, because they wanted to be able to eat the Passover. So Pilate came out to them and asked, "What charges are you bringing against this man?"

---

[1] Zechariah 11:13

And they began to accuse him, saying, "We have found this man subverting our nation. He opposes payment of taxes to Caesar and claims to be Messiah, a king."

It is the day of the Passover (which began at sunset the previous evening), so the delegation of priests cannot do anything to make themselves unclean, such as entering a palace inhabited by gentiles. As Pilate gets up to begin his workday, he sees a crowd gathering and comes out to meet them, finding out that someone has been arrested. This is where things get tricky. The Sanhedrin agreed upon the charge of blasphemy, but they know that Pilate doesn't care about such religious issues. Instead, they will have to convince him that Jesus poses some other threat. On these grounds, they begin accusing him of behaviors typical of other violent revolutionaries, proper reasons for Pilate to have someone executed. He refuses taxes! He subverts the nation! He claims to be a king! All of these are accusations typical of insurgents and worthy of investigation. However, it isn't quite so simple. It would be strange for such a figure to have been apprehended so easily and handed over by the religious leaders. Usually, Roman forces had to pursue such brigands for a long time, so it's pretty obvious there are other motivations at play. Pilate decides to investigate whether these claims hold any ground.

Pilate then went back inside the palace, summoned Jesus and asked him, "Are you the king of the Jews?"

"Is that your own idea," Jesus asked, "or did others talk to you about me?"

"Am I a Jew?" Pilate replied. "Your own people and chief priests handed you over to me. What is it you have done?"

Jesus said, "My kingdom is not of this world. If it were, my servants would fight to prevent my arrest... my kingdom is from another place."

"You are a king, then!" said Pilate.

Jesus answered, "You say that I am a king. In fact, the reason I was born and came into the world is to testify to the truth. Everyone on the side of truth listens to me."

"What is truth?" retorted Pilate.

Then Pilate announced to the chief priests and the crowd, "I find no basis for a charge against this man."

Pilate is curious and starts with the obvious. Does Jesus really claim to be a king? In response, Jesus tactfully dialogues with Pilate while hinting that others see him as a king, which reveals his popularity. "Did you hear this claim from others?" he asks. Sidestepping the question, Pilate points out that Jesus must have done something wrong in order to be handed over by his own people. What's going on?

This would be an ideal spot for Jesus to make his case against his wrongful accusers. But instead, Jesus gives him a surprising answer. Yes, he is a king (a scandalous answer), but his kingdom is of another world (an insane answer). This is hardly the response expected of a zealot, who would have responded defiantly. Jesus doesn't sound like someone trying to avoid execution, or he would surely speak more carefully. Yet now Jesus has proclaimed himself a king, and Pilate thinks he may be onto something. Maybe Jesus is challenging Roman authority after all. But Jesus reiterates his answer as though he is *from somewhere else*, from another world. To Pilate, this sounds like delusional religious banter, the kind of beliefs common among gentiles who believed there were half-gods roaming around on earth, unlike the Jewish religion. Does Jesus believe he has come from the gods? If so, he's not an insurrectionist who would concern Pilate, he's just a lunatic who poses no threat to Pilate's power (or so he thinks). Truth? Pilate isn't interested. He's a pragmatist with a problem to solve during a typical day at work. He's heard enough, and there's no need to continue.

But the commotion is far from over. Back before the crowds, the allegations continue.

When he was accused by the chief priests and the elders, he gave no answer. Then Pilate asked him, "Don't you hear the testimony they are bringing against you?" But Jesus made no reply, not even to a single charge—to the great amazement of the governor.

But they insisted, "He stirs up the people all over Judea by his teaching. He started in Galilee and has come all the way here."

On hearing this, Pilate asked if the man was a Galilean. When he learned that Jesus was under Herod's jurisdiction, he sent him to Herod, who was also in Jerusalem at the time.

To the shock of Pilate, Jesus says nothing in response to the allegations. The crowd continues to accuse him of raising a ruckus throughout the region, which is alarming, but Pilate catches on to a small detail. Did they say he was from Galilee? If so, Herod may take interest in this man and so free Pilate of the hassle. This might be a simple solution to this mess, and it just so happens that Herod is in town for the Passover. Pilate feels relieved to be rid of this headache. So, Jesus is carted off to his next interrogation.

When Herod saw Jesus, he was greatly pleased, because for a long time he had been wanting to see him. From what he had heard about him, he hoped to see him perform a sign of some sort. He plied him with many questions, but Jesus gave him no answer. The chief priests and the teachers of the law were standing there, vehemently accusing him. Then Herod and his soldiers ridiculed and mocked him. Dressing him in an elegant robe, they sent him back to Pilate. That day Herod and Pilate became friends—before this they had been enemies.

Herod is delighted. Unlike Pilate, he has heard all about Jesus the miracle worker and has even sent messengers to him previously with threats. Herod was once intrigued by John the Baptist, the strange man he then beheaded. Now, Jesus too stands before him for his enjoyment. But this also presents a problem. As much as Herod would be happy to see Jesus dead, Jesus is known across the region, and harming him risks damaging Herod's already poor reputation.

As Jesus stands silent, it doesn't take long for Herod's interest to fade, and Jesus is sent back to Pilate. They are in Jerusalem after all, so this is Pilate's problem, not his.

This is hardly the resolution Pilate had hoped for.

Pilate called together the chief priests, the rulers and the people, and said to them, "You brought me this man as one who was inciting the people to rebellion. I have examined him in your presence and have found no basis for your charges against him. Neither has Herod, for he sent him back to us; as you can see, he has done nothing to deserve death."

Now it was the custom at the festival to release a prisoner whom the people requested. A man called Barabbas was in prison with the insurrectionists who had committed murder in the uprising. The crowd came up and asked Pilate to do for them what he usually did.

The basic story of the Passover includes slaves getting set free, so it's fitting that this had become a part of the Passover tradition. As a few people approach Pilate to remind him of this tradition, he sees a possible resolution to the mess. Pilate brings out another prisoner named Barabbas, someone actually guilty of the crimes which Jesus stands accused of. Barabbas was part of a rebellion and killed someone, a crime worthy of capital punishment. His name is quite interesting as well. *Bar* means "son of," and *Abba*, as we've seen used elsewhere, is an intimate word for father. It could mean "son of *a* father" which is pretty generic, "son of *the* father" (referring to God), which is more specific and carries messianic overtones, or "son of the teacher," which could mean a variety of things.

As the "son of a father," the name is fitting as a general description of all of humanity. In this way, Barabbas represents all people, trapped in the curse and rebellious against God. But as a revolutionary, he may also have taken this name as a title proclaiming himself the "Son of God," the prophesied messianic figure who would rule with an iron scepter as long foretold.[1] In this

---

[1] Psalm 2

342

way, he better fits people's expectations of the Messiah as a warrior-like ruler than Jesus. "Son of the teacher" is equally interesting, since the Jewish people saw themselves as a people formed under the covenant of Moses, the giver and "teacher" of their law. It is this law that they are, in a sense, held captive to. Violators of the law are punished, and since no one is perfect, all people are therefore dependent upon God's forgiveness as prescribed through the sacrificial system. It is the story of Adam and Eve and the rest of humanity in their likeness. Like Barabbas here, everyone is trapped under a death sentence because of the law.

This intriguing individual now stands side by side with Jesus, and one of them is going to be set free. Will it be the insurrectionist named Barabbas, or Jesus, the non-violent revolutionary and self-proclaimed servant, "Son of God," and "Son of Man"? Whom will the people choose?

"Do you want me to release to you the king of the Jews?" asked Pilate, knowing it was out of self-interest that the chief priests had handed Jesus over to him. But the chief priests stirred up the crowd to have Pilate release Barabbas instead.

"...If you let this man go, you are no friend of Caesar. Anyone who claims to be a king opposes Caesar."

"What shall I do, then, with Jesus who is called the Messiah?" Pilate asked.

They all answered, "Crucify him!"

"Why? What crime has he committed?" asked Pilate.

But they shouted all the louder, "Crucify him!"

"Shall I crucify your king?" Pilate asked.

"We have no king but Caesar," the chief priests answered.

When Pilate saw that he was getting nowhere, but that instead an uproar was starting, he took water and washed his hands in front of the crowd. "I am innocent of this man's blood," he said. "It is your responsibility!"

Then he released Barabbas to them. But he had Jesus flogged, and handed him over to be crucified.

Much to Pilate's surprise, the crowd is ready to see someone die. They have selected which man will be sacrificed. Provoked by the priests, the crowd calls for Barabbas to be set free. It is strange that the Sadducees, who are attempting to maintain peace and so preserve their power, are seeking the release of someone who has been involved in an uprising. Yet that's precisely what happens. By now, Pilate is pretty sure that he knows what is going on. This is a power struggle, a popularity contest. He knows that the Sadducees have long since lost their popularity, and now they seem dead set on eliminating one of their opponents. But is Pilate actually going to follow through? Even his allegiance to Caesar is now on trial, a dangerous turn for his career aspirations. Will he give into their demands? Attempting to redirect them, he calls their attention back to Jesus only to be met with demands for a crucifixion. Pilate questions this outcome, but they continue to call for the death, and Pilate is in hot water.

We know that after a brutal beginning to his time as a governor, Pilate now has a new boss who isn't so fond of him and might be looking for a reason to remove him from his post. His former boss, Sejanus, was executed by Tiberius Caesar for treason, which has left Pilate on shaky ground. Pilate is in his position in order to squash uprisings, not provoke them by arguing with a crowd over the punishment of one of their own people. If a revolt ensues because Pilate tried to free an accused insurgent, it could look very bad to Rome. It will already be hard enough to justify his accepting a Jewish tradition and releasing a violent prisoner like Barabbas. How would it look if there were another revolt at Passover? Attempting to save his own life (or so he thinks), Pilate symbolically washes his hands and leaves. Like Herod and the elders before him (along with Adam and Eve in the garden), he passes the buck as though it isn't his problem. Surely, he thinks, he's done nothing wrong.

Crucifixion was the most brutal form of Roman capital punishment and was reserved for the most extreme criminals. It was considered so shameful a death that the criminal's family wasn't even allowed to honor the dead by mourning publicly, and Roman citizens weren't crucified. The punishment was very public in nature. The individual was required, often naked, to carry their own cross as they were paraded through town toward a hill just outside of the city. There, they would be hung by nails through their wrists and ankles on a wooden crossbeam as a public statement against any that might try to defy the power of Rome. Once on the cross, as painful is it was, individuals typically died of asphyxiation after repeated attempts to pull themselves up in order to breathe. The process could last for days. Then the bodies were often left to be picked away by scavenging birds, a further disgrace which could begin even while someone was still alive and defenseless on the cross, a dishonorable end to a shameful death. If the process was taking too long, soldiers would break the criminal's legs to hurry things.

Crucifixion was a grotesque and reviled sign of shame that would have carried some of the associations we might have for a noose or guillotine. It was not until a few hundred years later that the cross ever became a cherished symbol. Here, this form of execution is quickly called upon for Jesus, who takes the punishment reserved for criminals like Barabbas. In a strange substitution, Jesus is taken away to be flogged and executed while Barabbas is set free.

THE DAY OF ATONEMENT

The events of the trial bear a striking resemblance to another sacred assembly held by the Jewish people at the temple, the Day of Atonement.[1] To atone, an uncommon word today, means to make peace or reconcile. In Hebrew, the word means "to cover over."[2] While the law and the temple provided the means and location for people to interact with God, no animal offering could ever really undo a person's wrongdoing. The Day of Atonement was a yearly reminder of this fact that pointed to the perpetual need for some great sacrifice to take place to ultimately bring forgiveness for people's

---

[1] Leviticus 16   [2] Job 14:17

sins.[1] In the meantime, this special occasion was a time of repentance for Jewish people, who remembered their sin, pleaded for God's covering again, and were forgiven.

When the day finally arrived, the high priest alone would enter the most holy place to make an offering on behalf of the priesthood, the temple, and the nation to "cover over" them until the following year. Two goats would be brought to the high priest before all the people. One would be sacrificed and the other spared. In front of the people, the sins of the nation would be confessed upon both goats, but one would be sacrificed while the other would be led out of the temple, over the Mount of Olives, and released into the wilderness.

Just as once happened with Adam and Eve as they were covered by the skins of a sacrificed animal and released into the wild, the same things appear to have happened again. One man has been condemned to die, offered by the high priest on behalf of the people, and another accused of the same crime has been released. This is yet one more strange scene, like the Passover, which has occurred to fulfill the most basic traditions of the Jewish religion.

---

[1] Some prophets described a future time when this would happen and bring an end to sacrifices (Isaiah 66:2-4; Ezekiel 16:63, 39:17; Daniel 9:24, 27; Micah 7:19; Zechariah 3:8-9).

NINETEEN
Another Tree

IN A GRUESOME WAY to begin his execution, Jesus is first flogged. Known as the "forty lashes," scourging was intended to beat people within an inch of their death. For this punishment, soldiers would use all sorts of nasty whips threaded with metal and bone to lash the person, stripping the skin and exposing muscle and vital organs. It wasn't uncommon for someone to die during this torture. Not all who were condemned to crucifixion were scourged. If nothing else, it would speed his execution on the cross as he hung dehydrated and losing blood from his abundant wounds.

THE FRUIT OF THE TREE
Mark 15:16-32; Luke 23:34, 39-43; John 19:25-27; Mark 15:33-35; John 19:28; Mark 15:36; John 19:30; Luke 23:46; John 19:30; Matthew 27:51; Mark 15:39-41; John 19:31-34; Mark 15:42-45; John 19:38-42

> *The soldiers led Jesus away into the palace (that is, the Praetorium) and called together the whole company of soldiers. They put a purple robe on him, then twisted together a crown of thorns and set it on him. And they began to call out to him, "Hail, king of the Jews!" Again and again they struck him on the head with a staff and spit on him. Falling on their knees, they paid homage to him. And when they had mocked him, they took off the purple robe and put his own clothes on him. Then they led him out to crucify him.*

A certain man from Cyrene, Simon, the father of Alexander and Rufus, was passing by on his way in from the country, and they forced him to carry the cross. They brought Jesus to the place called Golgotha (which means "the place of the skull). Then they offered him wine mixed with myrrh, but he did not take it. And they crucified him. Dividing up his clothes, they cast lots to see what each would get.

Adding insult to injury, Jesus is mocked during his torture. In a moment of serious dramatic irony, the very man once hailed the Messiah as he entered the city is crowned king. The crown, made of thorns, is significant in ways they couldn't have understood. In Eden, the ground was cursed to produce "thorns and thistles," the new fruit of working the ground. Thorns stand as a reminder of Adam's curse of toil. Now Jesus has come as a new Adam to carry this curse upon himself, wearing this toil as his crown, symbolic of the very work and purpose of his ministry. This is why he has come. This is what he's been waiting for. This is what must be done to overcome the curse.

Once they've finished with their beatings, Jesus is led away to be crucified. Along the way, since Jesus is staggering under the weight of the crossbeam he carries, the rushed soldiers force a bystander to step in and carry the fugitive's cross. Soldiers could legally force citizens to assist them with carrying loads for given distances (a harsh reminder of Roman oppression). Unable to refuse, the man named Simon (not one of The Twelve) cooperates and shares this burden for a short while. Suddenly, we have someone being shamed and carrying a cross just as Jesus once told his disciples that they must do if they wanted to follow him.[1] We are also told the names of this man's sons as though they might have been familiar to some reader in the Christian community long ago. Such mention of names functioned as an ancient citation, a way that ancient writers revealed sources and invited investigation and review. It appears that sometime after this encounter Simon came to follow Christ, and that his sons mentioned here later become well known witnesses to the early Christian community.

---

[1] Luke 9:23

As they get just outside of town, Jesus is nailed to the cross. Where death once arrived through the fruit of a tree, Jesus is now cursed to death upon a "tree." The drink mixture described, wine and myrrh, is thought to be something to dull the senses as death approaches. Wine is the drink being shared across the city as people celebrate the Passover, the very drink Jesus pledged to abstain from until the arrival of God's kingdom. Surprising those present, Jesus refuses.

It was nine in the morning when they crucified him. The written notice of the charge against him read: THE KING OF THE JEWS.

They crucified two rebels with him, one on his right and one on his left. Those who passed by hurled insults at him, shaking their heads and saying, "So! You who are going to destroy the temple and build it in three days, come down from the cross and save yourself!" In the same way the chief priests and the teachers of the law mocked him among themselves. "He saved others," they said, "but he can't save himself! Let the Messiah, this king of Israel, come down now from the cross that we may see and believe."

Jesus said, "Father, forgive them, for they do not know what they are doing."

It is just a few hours since Jesus first arrived before Pilate (just before dawn). By his sides are a couple of others condemned to die, possibly those who collaborated with Barabbas in a revolt. Pilate's labeling of Jesus as "King of the Jews" is a slight to the Jewish population as though their king were no match for Rome, and the mob would have disagreed with the claim that Jesus was their king. If Jesus is a king, is this his inauguration?

While on the cross, Jesus continues to be mocked and cursed. Similar to the challenges posed by Satan during Jesus' temptation, he is dared to prove himself again and again. It seems ridiculous to everyone that he would put up with such suffering if he had the power to change matters. Why would a God allow people to humiliate, beat up, and kill him? Why wouldn't he call upon an army of angels to end this? Didn't Jesus claim that he'd replace the temple? Wasn't he to begin an everlasting kingdom? Such ideas seem absurd now to all who watch.

All the while, their slander is met with love. It would have been common for someone facing execution to pray that their punishment would stand as payment for their sins as they pleaded to God for mercy. Instead of pleading for *his* forgiveness, Jesus prays for *theirs*—as if his death is actually intended to atone for *their* sins,[1] not his. As he is cursed and mocked, he prays for and blesses others, just as he taught his followers to do. Having been declared a King, his first kingly act is to intercede on behalf of others' sins like a priest. They don't understand, but he will indeed prove himself to them yet.

It is through these events that he will accomplish the forgiveness and restoration he proclaims. From now on, instead of coming to the temple for forgiveness, people will look to the cross where Jesus, God dwelling among people as a human being, was sacrificed as an offering on their behalf.[2] He is the temple, and the temple is being desecrated.

One of the criminals who hung there hurled insults at him: "Aren't you the Messiah? Save yourself and us!"

But the other criminal rebuked him. "Don't you fear God," he said, "since you are under the same sentence? We are punished justly, for we are getting what our deeds deserve. But this man has done nothing wrong."

Then he said, "Jesus, remember me when you come into your kingdom."

Jesus answered him, "Truly I tell you, today you will be with me in paradise."

As one of the men by his side joins the chorus, the other speaks up in his defense. On a day when no one spoke up on Jesus' behalf,

---

[1] Psalm 109:18-28   [2] Isaiah 52:13-53:12 describes in stunning detail as God's servant, a man of ordinary appearance, endures rejection and oppression, is disfigured, "pierced," and led away to slaughter like a silent lamb to die on behalf of others' sins as a guilt offering that brings healing. This figure is ultimately "raised" and exalted.

this dying criminal speaks the truth. Acknowledging his own guilt and just punishment, the criminal has come to see Jesus as the Messiah[1] and pleads for mercy. As though he understands that Jesus came to suffer and die, he begs Jesus to remember him when Jesus returns with his kingdom. This interesting profession of faith is met by a stunning response. Jesus declares that they will be together *today,* not in his kingdom, but in "paradise." Jesus offers this man hope and describes something in between death and God's future kingdom on earth. This paradise he describes may also be where Abraham also lives presently, as Jesus once declared to some stunned Pharisees.[2] This repentant criminal has just been promised a gift in what proves to be a significant few moments just before his death.

> *Near the cross of Jesus stood his mother, his mother's sister, Mary the wife of Clopas, and Mary Magdalene. When Jesus saw his mother there, and the disciple whom he loved standing nearby, he said to her, "Woman, here is your son," and to the disciple, "Here is your mother." From that time on, this disciple took her into his home.*

We are given a brief glimpse into the experience of those standing near to witness these events.[3] In a moment that seems to alienate Jesus from the rest of the world, we find some of those most loyal to him by his side—a group of bold women that includes his mother and a disciple (presumably John, the youngest of them).

Notably, Jesus' brothers are absent, a reminder that they have rejected him. In contrast to his brothers stands the faith and loyalty of those with him, his true family as he has long taught. In this moment, he hands over his responsibility as head of his house to this young disciple who will now be a member of the family responsible for caring for his aging mother Mary (who, by association with Jesus, appears to have been similarly disowned by her sons).

> *At noon, darkness came over the whole land until three in the afternoon. And at three in the afternoon Jesus cried out*

---

[1] Psalm 89:38-51 describes God's anointed one, as we see with Jesus on the cross.   [2] Matthew 22:32; John 8:56   [3] Zechariah 12:10

in a loud voice, "Eloi, Eloi, lama sabachthani?" (which means, "My God, my God, why have you forsaken me?").

When some of those standing near heard this, they said, "Listen, he's calling Elijah."

Later, knowing that everything had now been finished, and so that the Scripture would be fulfilled, Jesus said, "I am thirsty."

Someone ran, filled a sponge with wine vinegar, put it on a staff, and offered it to Jesus to drink. "Now leave him alone. Let's see if Elijah comes to take him down," he said.

When he had received the drink, Jesus said, "It is finished."

Jesus called out with a loud voice, "Father, into your hands I commit my spirit." When he had said this, he breathed his last.

With that, he bowed his head and gave up his spirit.

As the day passes, we are told of several strange events. First, around noon when the sun is usually highest in the sky, there is complete darkness for three hours. Waiting beneath this darkness, Jesus cries out to God with the words of a song from scripture. It's possible that this is quoted to us as he recites or even sings the song to himself. The song, Psalm 22, describes in great detail what sounds like the very events surrounding him on the cross. "All who see me mock me," it says, "and all my bones are out of joint... my tongue sticks to the roof of my mouth... they pierce my hands and my feet... they divide my clothes among them and cast lots for my garment." Jesus also speaks a translation of the last words of this same Psalm, "He has done it." Or, as we are told, "It is finished." The Psalm ends with a description of salvation coming to all peoples as the Lord is exalted and honored unto future generations. As Jesus identifies with the suffering of the song, he still awaits the conclusion it predicts.

At the same time, we also see the familiar cries of a human being in pain as he calls out to God in the face of what seems to be abandonment. Even the sun hides its face from him as he shudders in agony. Was this really the only way? Why did it have to come to this? This is a plea familiar to many who have uttered similar words in the midst of great suffering. But it is this significant plea that has also comforted many Christians throughout the ages. At moments when they felt furthest from God due to their suffering, they were instead reminded of Jesus on the cross. Instead of distance, there is a strange comfort that God is *intimately with them* during such times, not angry and cursing them from afar.

Mistaking one of Jesus' words for what sounded like the name Elijah, people go into a flurry of activity. There's all sorts of intrigue surrounding Elijah, who was expected to come as the forerunner of God's kingdom.[1] What's about to happen next? Someone rushes to get some wine vinegar, a stringent drink that would arouse and awaken Jesus from his state of suffering delirium. Interestingly, this too fits other Psalms that describe someone in suffering and with great thirst[2] given only vinegar[3] for comfort.

Then with his last words, Jesus, like a priest, recites a line from yet another song,[4] one frequently recited around this time with the evening sacrifice at the temple that might have been taking place during these very moments. This song also describes one abandoned, broken, and dying, with pleas for redemption and even resurrection from the grave. With these, his last words, Jesus surrenders his spirit and dies.

We've already seen Jesus submit to the common human experiences of oppression, toil, and suffering, and now death can be added to the list. He has embraced the basic human condition fully and endured being shamed, feared, and pronounced guilty, all while remaining innocent. He has been made an exile, kicked out of the world just as Adam and Eve were once banished from Eden. Jesus' crucifixion as he is cursed upon a tree is the fruit of the knowledge of good and evil. Now, as the Sabbath approaches with the setting of the sun, Jesus rests.

At that moment the curtain of the temple was torn in two from top to bottom. The earth shook, the rocks split...

---

[1] Malachi 4:5   [2] Psalms 69:1-4, 143:3-12   [3] Psalm 69:19-21   [4] Psalm 31:1-13

And when the centurion, who stood there in front of Jesus, saw how he died, he said, "Surely this man was the Son of God!"

When Jesus dies, there is an earthquake and suddenly the rocks are indeed crying out as Jesus had declared. One of the effects of this earthquake is also described—a curtain is torn. But, this is no ordinary curtain. It is a specific curtain, several inches thick, which stood as a barrier to the most sacred space in the temple, called the "Holy of Holies," where God dwelled. A priest was only allowed to enter this space once every year on the Day of Atonement to offer sacrifices on behalf of all the people. Like the High Priest's garment torn during Jesus' interrogation, the temple curtain's cloth is split as though some abomination or radical change has just occurred. Miraculously, the division between people and God's presence has just been removed. Jesus, a new high priest, has just entered this sacred space to offer a sacrifice on behalf of all people. Because of Jesus' sacrifice, people now have a special and new access to the healing and life-giving presence of God.

The sacrifice system has just found its completion.

These sacrifices had been in place in some fashion since the story of Eden when God used animal skins to cover the shame of Adam and Eve. Ever since, as outlined in the covenant laws entered into under Moses, the people offered sacrifices as a substitutionary payment for their wrongdoing. On the special Day of Atonement, the High Priest, as appointed by God, offered a sacrifice on behalf of the people. But this system had long been awaiting some fulfillment. As first foreshadowed in Eden, it was said that someone would come, the Messiah, and offer a pleasing sacrifice to God that would finally restore the relationship once and for all. Jesus, like a great priest, has just made his life that offering. Now, the old garments provided to Adam and Eve (from the sacrifices of animals to cover their shame), are no longer necessary. The sacrifice system of the temple, where death was required to bring harmony with God, has just found its fulfillment.

It is finished.

But this torn curtain isn't the only strange event of the afternoon. Even the centurion standing guard comes to a stunning realization. Seeing all that is happening around him as well as Jesus' peculiar behavior on the cross, he comes to the conclusion that these claims of Jesus' divinity were right. But why exactly? Fortunately, the cosmos works like clockwork, and we are able to corroborate the Jewish calendar with other historical events to narrow down the possible dates for the crucifixion to a couple of options. The most popular are April 7th, 30 A.D., and April 3rd, 33 A.D. It just so happens that during the afternoon of April 3rd, 33 A.D. there was a lunar eclipse. As the moon broke through the horizon, it would have been tinted red. Just as with Jesus' birth, it's as though the entire universe was scripted for these strange events on this particular day. All of creation was proclaiming this news.

In the ancient world, a lunar eclipse was seen as an omen that meant gods were angry, and earthquakes were associated with divine judgment. Combine these things with the darkness, the different accusations and rumors, Jesus' humble integrity and piety, and the soldier is confronted by his own understanding of celestial events and realizes that they have indeed just crucified God's son on the cross.[1] To the soldier, it suddenly makes perfect sense that God would be mad. Surprisingly, a violent criminal and a pagan soldier are the first to recognize what has just happened.

But they aren't the only ones witnessing these things.

Some women were watching from a distance. Among them were Mary Magdalene, Mary the mother of James the younger and of Joseph, and Salome. In Galilee these women had followed him and cared for his needs. Many other women who had come up with him to Jerusalem were also there.

Now it was the day of Preparation, and the next day was to be a special Sabbath. Because the Jewish leaders did not want the bodies left on the crosses during the Sabbath, they

---

[1] Several prophets mention strange occurrences like these as they describe the coming "day of the Lord" (Isaiah 13:9-13, 24:21-23; Joel 2:10, 30-32, 3:15-16; Amos 8:9-10).

asked Pilate to have the legs broken and the bodies taken down. The soldiers therefore came and broke the legs of the first man who had been crucified with Jesus, and then those of the other. But when they came to Jesus and found that he was already dead, they did not break his legs. Instead, one of the soldiers pierced Jesus' side with a spear, bringing a sudden flow of blood and water.

Once again, we are given several specific names, eyewitnesses to these events as they unfold. These women had been a part of a broader group of disciples following Jesus as his pupils. They had travelled with Jesus and the disciples far and wide. Their presence at the crucifixion wouldn't have been suspicious to the authorities in the same way that the disciples, a group of men, would have.

We are also reminded specifically that this was the day of preparation just before the Sabbath. This means it is Friday, the last chance for people to tie up loose ends before the day of no work. It was also the Passover. It was on this day long ago that a sacrifice was made in order to spare people from death and free them from slavery. A lamb of prime age was to be slaughtered without breaking any bones. Then, it was consumed in its entirety with nothing left to remain. As they now celebrate this occasion thousands of years later, God has done the same thing all over again. A man, of prime age, is sacrificed without any bones being broken. As we will see, there will soon be nothing left of his remains. And all of this is happening to free the people from their slavery to sin and death.

For the Jewish people, the day began and ended at sunset (not midnight) which means that as dusk approached the Sabbath was about to begin. Out of respect to the special holiday, we are told that the soldiers take action to hurry the deaths of those crucified by breaking their legs. This prevents the offensive possibility of naked and tortured bodies left rotting on crosses outside of the city during such a sacred holiday.[1] As the soldiers approach Jesus, they see that he already appears to be dead. Taking a spear, they pierce his side

---

[1] Deuteronomy 21:22-23

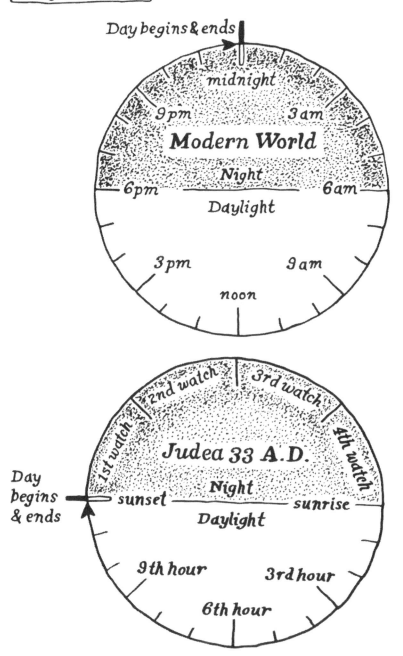

Day & Time

Day begins & ends

midnight

9 pm | 3 am

Modern World

Night

6 pm | 6 am

Daylight

3 pm | 9 am

noon

2nd watch | 3rd watch

1st watch | 4th watch

Judea 33 A.D.

Night

Day begins & ends — sunset | sunrise

Daylight

9th hour | 3rd hour

6th hour

(around his heart) to confirm that he is dead. As they do this, blood pours out like that of an offering in the temple, and there are much deeper parallels.

One of the prophets once spoke of a suffering servant who would be "poured out" unto death to bear the sins of the people.[1] Also, it was in the garden that Adam was put under a "deep sleep" so that God could create a suitable companion. During his slumber, God used a chunk of flesh from his side to craft a spouse.[2] Here, Jesus had come like a groom (a common character in his parables) searching for a bride but found no one suitable. All of the earth had been corrupted by sin. Like Adam, he has been put into a deep sleep (death), and through the piercing of his side, God is using his flesh (a sacrifice) to craft a bride, those who will trust in him. Through Jesus' death, God has made forgiveness available to people once and for all. In a stunning parallel, we have another strange wedding scene, a covenant being made as God is bringing about the fullness of relationship as first intended in the garden. Jesus, the new Adam, has just made a way for humanity to become his bride.[3]

But, we aren't there quite yet. As we step back into the story, Jesus is still in his slumber on the cross.

> ...As evening approached, Joseph of Arimathea, a prominent member of the Council, who was himself waiting for the Kingdom of God, went boldly to Pilate and asked for Jesus' body. Pilate was surprised to hear that he was already dead. Summoning the centurion, he asked him if Jesus had already died. When he learned from the centurion that it was so, he gave the body to Joseph.

> Now Joseph was a disciple of Jesus, but secretly because he feared the Jewish leaders. With Pilate's permission, he came and took the body away. He was accompanied by Nicodemus, the man who earlier had visited Jesus at night. Nicodemus brought a mixture of myrrh and aloes, about seventy-five pounds. Taking Jesus' body, the two of them wrapped it, with the spices, in strips of linen. This was in

---

[1] Isaiah 52:13-53:12   [2] Genesis 2:21-22   [3] Isaiah 62:4-5; Hosea 2:14-20

accordance with Jewish burial customs. At the place where Jesus was crucified, there was a garden, and in the garden a new tomb, in which no one had ever been laid. Because it was the Jewish day of Preparation and since the tomb was nearby, they laid Jesus there.

We are given the specific name of a man, a member of the Jewish council, who requests the body. As someone "waiting for the kingdom," Joseph of Arimathea is a follower of Jesus. Apparently troubled by all that had taken place, he uses his political clout to provide Jesus a respectable burial in a new tomb instead of a mass grave. The centurion confirms the report of Jesus' death, and with the help of Nicodemus,[1] Joseph takes his body to a garden nearby. Moving quickly due to the special holiday and Sabbath, they wrap Jesus' body and place it in the tomb. As the scene closes, the Sabbath begins just as Jesus rests in a tomb in the garden.

Suddenly we are back to where it all started. Genesis began with six days of work to build a home where humanity could fellowship with God, and on the seventh day God rested. That story described creation as "good," even "very good," but not as "finished." Is it possible that all that would follow, the serpent, betrayal, exile, and even Jesus were actually well within God's view from the very beginning? Is it possible that instead of simply returning creation to that original state, all that has happened since the garden was all part of God's ongoing creative work, a grand metamorphosis leading to something greater which was simply paused for that first Sabbath? Here with surprising parallels, Jesus has spent the week working in the temple courts to rebuild a place where humanity (people of all nations) could fellowship with God, and now he too rests on the Sabbath in a tomb in a garden. In Genesis, that garden home was corrupted by wrongdoing, an attempt to overthrow God for selfish gains, the result of which was exile and death for Adam and Eve. Here, this temple in Jerusalem has also been corrupted by selfish ambitions and a rebellion against God's purposes resulting in the

---

[1] Nicodemus is our late-night visitor from chapter 5 (John 3:1-21) whom Jesus talked to about being reborn.

death of Jesus. In Jesus' own words, that home (the temple), like his body, is now left "desolate."

THE FIRSTFRUITS

As the day of the Passover was coming to a close (Thursday evening to Friday evening), another special event was about to take place.[1] About the time that Jesus' body was being taken down from the cross, a throng of people would have made their way with some elders from the Sanhedrin across the Kidron Valley to the Mount of Olives. There, at a designated place, three men with sickles and baskets would harvest a given amount of grain to signify the beginning of the harvest. No barley was to be sold or used in the land until after this special ceremony had taken place. The grains were then taken into the temple where they were ground into flour which was to be used for loaves of unleavened bread (leaven was symbolic of sin) as part of a special offering called the "Firstfruits," the first offering of the harvest. This offering was made sometime on the 16th of their month Nissan, probably Sunday morning. In another surprising parallel, Jesus' life was just harvested at the same time as the grain for this special firstfruits offering to represent the beginning of the harvest. As he had taught the crowds, Jesus was that very bread, without leaven, now gathered to be offered to God.

ANOTHER GARDENER
Luke 24:1-12; John 20:11-16

As Passover has come and gone, the disciples remain in hiding. With a special Sabbath on Saturday, no one was to do any work. It was the day of rest, a time to reflect on God's presence and work as modeled in the beginning. Scared, confused, shocked, disappointed, ashamed, and mourning the death of their dear friend and mentor, they all know that they must tread carefully for the remainder of their time in Jerusalem and possibly thereafter. As his associates, if any attention is drawn to them, they could be next. Are they ready to die like this? Is this what Jesus had in mind? What went wrong? Jesus

---

[1] *The Temple* by Alfred Edersheim goes into great detail about Jewish feasts and festivals.

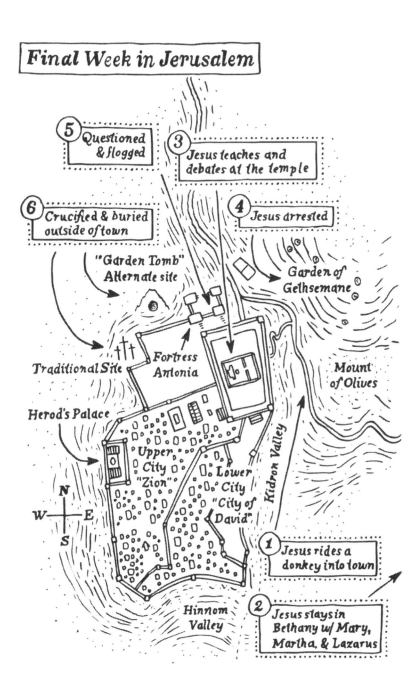

Final Week in Jerusalem

5 Questioned & flogged

3 Jesus teaches and debates at the temple

6 Crucified & buried outside of town

4 Jesus arrested

"Garden Tomb" Alternate site

Garden of Gethsemane

Traditional Site

Fortress Antonia

Mount of Olives

Herod's Palace

Upper City "Zion"

Lower City "City of David"

Kidron Valley

N
W — E
S

1 Jesus rides a donkey into town

2 Jesus stays in Bethany w/ Mary, Martha, & Lazarus

Hinnom Valley

always seemed so prepared; how did he not see this coming? And now, what are they to do? They left everything to follow him.

As we have discussed, the disciples were probably lost in the currents of many of their cultural expectations of the Messiah. While the scriptures describe numerous things about the Messiah, the people of their time predominantly anticipated a warrior-like king who would lead a revolution to overthrow Rome and establish the nation once again as God's kingdom on earth. While Jesus had spoken of a resurrection, they still probably understood this in one of two ways—that the miracle worker would ultimately lead people to victory through the war, or that they would all "rise" afterwards as they were rewarded by God at the resurrection on judgment day. The disciples have listened to Jesus' teachings and predictions through this lens, and now they realize that somehow or another they were wrong. They are struggling to understand what has just happened and how to proceed.

But Jesus isn't even properly buried yet. While Joseph and Nicodemus were able to tend to his body, it still remains in a tomb awaiting more honorable treatment. As the Sabbath passes, a new week begins. First thing Sunday morning, the time of the Firstfruits offering, a few of the women boldly break free to visit the tomb.

On the first day of the week, very early in the morning, the women took the spices they had prepared and went to the tomb. They found the stone rolled away from the tomb, but when they entered, they did not find the body of the Lord Jesus. While they were wondering about this, suddenly two men in clothes that gleamed like lightning stood beside them. In their fright the women bowed down with their faces to the ground, but the men said to them, "Why do you look for the living among the dead? He is not here; he has risen! Remember how he told you, while he was still with you in Galilee: 'The Son of Man must be delivered over to the hands of sinners, be crucified and on the third day be raised again.'" Then they remembered his words.

When they came back from the tomb, they told all these things to the Eleven and to all the others. It was Mary

Magdalene, Joanna, Mary the mother of James, and the others with them who told this to the apostles. But they did not believe the women, because their words seemed to them like nonsense. Peter, however, got up and ran to the tomb. Bending over, he saw the strips of linen lying by themselves, and he went away, wondering to himself what had happened.

As if the events of the previous few days weren't traumatic enough, this had to be a shocking experience. The women arrive to care for their deceased master only to find him missing. What?! Has someone stolen his body? Who could do such a thing? Then, they are stunned by angelic visitors who remind them of Jesus' words. He promised that these things would happen. There hasn't been some mistake or foul play. He has risen!

But what does *risen* mean?

The women seem confused, and we've seen this before. While Lazarus was dead in a tomb, Jesus spoke with Martha about resurrection.[1] He said that Lazarus would rise, and she seemed to think Jesus was referring to a time when all would be raised for judgment which wasn't very comforting. Except then Jesus spoke of himself as the source of this resurrection and life and brought Lazarus back from the dead. So what does it mean for Jesus to be risen? And why would his body be missing? It's starting to come together, but their timeline is all messed up. This must still have been a confusing and exciting mess. Quickly, the women rush away to tell the disciples what they've found.

You can imagine what this may have sounded like to the disciples. He's missing? You saw angels? He's risen? Where did he go? What are you saying? In surprise and disbelief, the group of fearful men seem to either dismiss the strange tale or ignore it in order to avoid investigating things at the risk of their own harm, but Peter wants to see for himself. He knows that something strange has happened.

As he arrives to the tomb (followed by John),[2] he finds it just as the women have described—empty. And oddly, the linens that were used to wrap a bloodied and dead body are lying there on the slab. It

---

[1] See chapter 14, John 11:17-27   [2] John 20:3-6

just doesn't make any sense. If someone had stolen the body, why on earth would they unwrap it first, especially in such a disfigured state? Who would ever want to drag around a bloody and naked corpse? And all of this on the Sabbath? Whoever was behind such a thing couldn't be Jewish!

Struck by the peculiarity, Peter knows that something is amiss and heads back to confirm the odd report of the women. Surely stunned by what he has seen, he's got to be running through different memories as he tries to put it all together.

Now Mary stood outside the tomb crying. As she wept, she bent over to look into the tomb and saw two angels in white, seated where Jesus' body had been, one at the head and the other at the foot.

They asked her, "Woman, why are you crying?"

"They have taken my Lord away," she said, "and I don't know where they have put him." At this, she turned around and saw Jesus standing there, but she did not realize that it was Jesus.

He asked her, "Woman, why are you crying? Who is it you are looking for?"

Thinking he was a gardener, she said, "Sir, if you have carried him away, tell me where you have put him, and I will get him."

Jesus said to her, "Mary."

She turned toward him and cried out in Aramaic, "Rabboni!"

Still thinking that surely someone has taken the body, Mary Magdalene is overwhelmed with sadness as she searches for answers. Why won't these angels tell her where his body has been taken? Then she turns around to find him, the *gardener,* but it isn't until he speaks her name that she recognizes him. Suddenly, it clicks.

He's alive!

Jesus wasn't predicting some sort of spiritual rising where he would join God in the heavens, freed from his body. All along, he was predicting the very events that they have just witnessed. He has suffered, was rejected by the elders and chief priests, was executed, and has now returned from the dead.[1]

He is resurrected.

When Jesus spoke with Martha about Lazarus, he wasn't just saying that one day all would be raised before God for judgment. Instead, he was proclaiming that he was the very source and power that would bring about the resurrection.[2] He is the resurrection and the life. Now, he has resurrected from the dead in his restored body to live eternally, just as he said he would.

It's significant that Mary first mistook Jesus for a gardener. We are once again reminded of Eden. There God, like a *gardener,* had crafted a home to share with humanity, and upon Adam and Eve's exile two angels came to guard the entrance, and no one could enter that way any longer. Here we find two angels again standing guard, but this time it is at a tomb where Jesus' body was placed.

We were also told in the Eden story that the struggle with evil would continue, but ultimately the serpent would strike Eve's offspring only to be crushed.[3] These things have just come to pass. Jesus, an offspring of Eve (fully human), has just been struck by the serpent at the "opportune time"[4] with a fatal blow, crucifixion. But as we've now seen, it was through these events that the serpent has been (or will be) brought to an end. It was the serpent's strike (death) that turned out to be his greatest vulnerability, and through the resurrection Jesus has just reclaimed his enemy's greatest weapon. The very tool the serpent used to keep people captive (death) has been turned into the means of transformation through resurrection in a way that the sacrifices of animals never could. There is a new path open to a restored relationship with God. There is a new way[5] back to the abundant life of Eden. The gateway is his empty tomb. Through his death and resurrection, Jesus has opened a new door to this restoration, a new creation.

---

[1] Mark 8:31, 9:31, 10:33-34 [2] John 11:25 [3] Genesis 3:15 [4] Luke 4:13 [5] Isaiah 2:3, 35:8; Micah 2:13; Matthew 7:13-14; John 14:6

Final Week in Jerusalem

Jewish Calendar		Activities of Jesus

Sunday

10th of Nissan ········· Sunset ········· Triumphal Entry

Monday

Sunrise ········· Clears the Temple

11th of Nissan ········· Sunset

Tuesday

12th of Nissan ········· Sunset

Wednesday

13th of Nissan ········· Sunset ····· Woes, Olivet Discourse

Thursday

14th of Nissan ········· Sunset ········· the "Last Supper"
Passover

Friday

Sunrise ············· before Pilate

9 am ················· crucifixion

3 pm ················· death

15th of Nissan ········· Sunset ················· burial

Sabbath **Saturday**

16th of Nissan ········· Sunset ················· in tomb

Sunday

Sunrise ············· resurrection

It's Sunday, and a new week has begun. There is hope beyond the grave, and Jesus has overcome the curse.

God is back to gardening once again.

Ministry Timeline

29 A.D.   Spring / Summer

"Early Ministry"

Baptism
Temptation
Water into Wine
Samaritan Woman

30 A.D.   April 7th - First Passover

"Growing Movement"

Catches Fish
Heals Leper
Heals Paralytic
Sermon on the Mount

31 A.D.   April 25th - Second Passover

"Height of Popularity"

Calms Storm
"Legion"
Dead Girl, Bleeding Woman
John the Baptist Beheaded
Feeds 5,000
Walks on Water
Peter's Confession
Transfiguration

32 A.D.   April 13th/14th - Third Passover

"Final Stretch"

Young Rich Man
Zacchaeus
Blind Bartimaeus
Raises Lazarus

33 A.D.   April 3rd - Fourth Passover

Crucifiction
Resurrection

TWENTY
A New Week Begins

A S WE WILL SEE, Jesus has been quite busy for a dead man. Mary isn't the only one that he has visited. It's Sunday evening now, and Jesus has already appeared to people (not shared here)[1] including Peter.[2] As Peter returns and tells the disciples of this, they are all met with a surprise of their own.

STRANGE TALES
John 20:19; Luke 24:36-43; Acts 1:3; Luke 24:44-50

On the evening of that first day of the week, when the disciples were together, with the doors locked for fear of the Jewish leaders...

While they were still talking about this, Jesus himself stood among them and said to them, "Peace be with you."

They were startled and frightened, thinking they saw a ghost. He said to them, "Why are you troubled, and why do doubts rise in your minds? Look at my hands and my feet. It is I myself! Touch me and see; a ghost does not have flesh and bones, as you see I have."

When he had said this, he showed them his hands and feet. And while they still did not believe it because of joy and amazement, he asked them, "Do you have anything here to

---

[1] Luke 24:13-32   [2] Luke 24:34

*eat?" They gave him a piece of broiled fish, and he took it
and ate it in their presence.*

It's no surprise that they are dumbfounded by what they see.
How could this be? Jesus has a body made of skin and bone, and he
invites them to touch him to verify that this is so. Did he manage to
survive somehow? But the Romans would never make such a
mistake. Scourging alone was difficult to withstand. No one could
survive three days in such a wounded state, especially after being
crucified. Is this a hallucination? But the disciples are all seeing him
at once. Is this a ghost? They asked this same question once before
as he walked across the waters to them. But he has a body that they
can touch, and he even *eats* with them. A ghost can't eat food. But
the doors were all locked. How did he get in?

Jesus isn't just alive again, he is *changed.*

We've seen Jesus bring people back from the dead before in the
stories of the dead young girl and of Lazarus, but this isn't just a
resuscitation. Jesus isn't just returning from the grave to continue his
life so that he can die again sometime later (as Lazarus will). This is
different. Jesus is transformed. He's appearing and disappearing,
even entering rooms with locked doors, miracles we haven't seen
from him before. Jesus still has a material body, but it is one with
newly enhanced qualities as though intended for life eternally in the
renewed creation. Still God in flesh and bones, Jesus has initiated a
new kind of humanness. This final miracle offers not just comfort but
a solution, not just a happy ending but a resolution to the problem, a
means of liberation from the brokenness of creation and an entry into
God's new creation, a new and restored physical world.

But where people today often associate such liberation with an
eternal spiritual reality, Jesus is shockingly physical. This isn't
someone moving on from life into a "better place" in order to remain
in some spiritual realm forever. Through the resurrection, Jesus has
begun God's transformative process upon the earth. God's goal or
"end" isn't to remove us from the material world but to remake it.
The goal is a "new heavens and new earth" where God will again
reside with his people in a special way. The resurrected Jesus is the
"firstfruits" of this restoration, the first to come of this transformed

creation. Now through him others will similarly pass through death and be remade.

In a conversation once with Nicodemus, Jesus described the need to be reborn. In that conversation, he described two births, one of the spirit and one of the flesh. At that time, he spoke of the necessary rebirth by the spirit of God. Now, through the resurrection, Jesus has displayed what is to come in the rebirth of human flesh as well, renewed bodies designed for everlasting life in the kingdom of God. God isn't abandoning his creation, he's remaking it. Now death is but a doorway, a transition, not necessarily the doomed ending people have feared throughout the ages. Jesus' resurrection stands out as a beacon highlighting the reality of the world still to come.

Jesus knows that this is going to take some explaining, so he spends some significant time with the disciples over the next few weeks to make sure that they understand what has happened.

> *...he presented himself to them and gave many convincing proofs that he was alive. He appeared to them over a period of forty days and spoke about the kingdom of God.*

The gospels tell us other stories[1] about his appearances to the disciples after his resurrection. With each visit, Jesus continues to verify that which seems utterly impossible to many people. One early Christian named Paul wrote that Jesus appeared to over 500 people during this period of 40 days after his resurrection, many of whom Paul says were still alive at the time that he wrote (around 60 A.D.).[2] Paul even mentions that James, Jesus' oldest brother, is one of the witnesses. This is especially interesting considering the way that Jesus' brothers rejected his ministry, but we know that they go on to be key figures in the early Christian community.[3] A couple of his brothers even go on to write books in the New Testament,[4] and James is later martyred because of these beliefs. Jesus' resurrection appearances are the best explanation for this radical change of heart.

---

[1] John 20:24-21:19   [2] 1 Corinthians 15:3-7   [3] Acts 1:12-14, 15:12-19; Galatians 2:9
[4] The books of James and Jude.

He said to them, "This is what I told you while I was still with you: Everything must be fulfilled that is written about me in the Law of Moses, the Prophets and the Psalms."

Then he opened their minds so they could understand the Scriptures. He told them, "This is what is written: The Messiah will suffer and rise from the dead on the third day, and repentance for the forgiveness of sins will be preached in his name to all nations, beginning at Jerusalem. You are witnesses of these things. I am going to send you what my Father has promised; but stay in the city until you have been clothed with power from on high."

Jesus wants to make sure that it's clear to everyone that what has taken place wasn't a mistake, so he walks through the scriptures with them to point out how everything has come together. God has been orchestrating things from the very beginning. This was always about the flourishing of life as intended in Eden, and Jesus has been working to restore that relationship and harmony once again. As he has taught them before, he didn't come to throw away the scriptures as though they were wrong or had failed, but to complete them. He has come to fulfill the story.

As we saw in Eden, all of creation was intended for goodness and abundant life, but rebellion against God destroyed the harmony that originally existed between God, humanity, and creation. Marred by the effects of shame, fear, and guilt, Adam and Eve were cast out of God's presence as exiles into a world distorted by the curse. Living in a world shaped by the deception of the serpent, they embarked on a journey constrained by the influences of suffering, oppression, toil, and death. But as was foreshadowed in the serpent's curse, God wouldn't abandon them completely to their own devices.

And so, God entered this corrupted world as a human being. Jesus didn't just stand from afar to call people out of something; he stepped into the flesh and blood of the struggle in order to lead people through it. Instead of someone who simply relayed the words of a message, Jesus was the living word who proclaimed the message with all of his being. Teaching and behaving with authority as one familiar with the mind of God, forgiving and healing as though the very finger of God, Jesus displayed his unique power and identity as both "Son of God" and "Son of Man." As a divine man, he repeatedly took the burden of our alienation and rejection upon himself as people were restored time and time again to their communities and God. Exiled in their place, he routinely invited people out of their condition and displayed his power over the curse, even when it meant getting kicked out of town or, ultimately, crucified. Whether it be forgiving sins, healing the sick, or making untouchable people clean, restoring harmony had been his task throughout his ministry.

We saw this all come together uniquely in the crucifixion, where Jesus was publicly shamed and condemned to die as people feared him. We also saw the surprising ways each element of the curse appeared throughout the story. There was the crown of thorns highlighting the curse of toil; his unjust trial and conviction which stand out as examples of oppression; his brutal suffering as he was flogged and crucified; and ultimately his death. Taking the punishment of one guilty of leading a rebellion (just as Adam and Eve once were), Jesus was sentenced to crucifixion. He was cursed to hang upon the wooden beams of a "tree." The king of a different kind of kingdom, he exemplified humanity's intended role as servants within creation and embraced the very punishment prescribed to Adam and Eve in the garden, death, in order to overcome it. In doing so, he completed the long-awaited fulfillment of the law, the sacrifice necessary to finally "cover over" or atone for human sin. Jesus became that covering, once and for all, that people might begin a new kind of covenant relationship with God. Inviting us to follow his footsteps, Jesus has changed death from an obstacle into the path to the coming restoration of all creation, a new kind of physical reality that awaits all who will trust in him.

We saw this forgiveness accomplished in the substitution that took place on the cross. An example of servanthood and self-sacrificing love, Jesus was willing to give of himself on behalf of others. This is also often described in terms of debts, that all of humanity was bankrupted before God by sin and unable to pay the debt for the destruction that has been done to the world. On the cross, Jesus has ultimately paid off that debt for anyone who will entrust him with it. As a result, people can finally be reconciled to God and no longer have to live in fear, ashamed of who we are or crushed by the weight of guilt. But this doesn't just restore us to God. We can make peace again with each other. In humility, we can take responsibility for our wrongs and ask for forgiveness. We can similarly be a part of setting others free by releasing them of their indebtedness for the ways that they have wronged us. In this way, Jesus has opened the floodgates of forgiveness and redemption to anyone who will place their faith in him.

But that's not all.

The story still isn't over. Although Jesus has invited people to be free from the effects of shame, fear and guilt, he didn't provide an immediate escape from the curse, as we might wish. Our world continues in disarray, strangled by the influence of suffering, oppression, toil, and death, which continue to shape the human experience. Creation has yet to be finally restored. But in his resurrection, Jesus has shown us the ultimate way through it. He has revealed the way that our lives can reflect the goodness of all that is to come while bringing a small taste of that restoration into the present. There is hope.

While we may continue to combat the curse as servants representing another world, we still live in the harsh circumstances of this one. This is why death is so necessary. The world in this present form must pass away. While God has assumed the costs of our evil, it's still necessary for everything to be remade. Jesus didn't come so that we could just avoid these conditions but to lead us through them. Now, we have a path and await the final chapter of the story where, as Jesus has promised, he will return to make all things new. No more death, no more suffering, no more oppression or toil but instead a *new creation* completely free from evil. But for now, we still await the final resurrection. Jesus is the first, and all must be changed in his likeness.

This is the revolution.

It may seem strange, but the plan didn't go awry. Jesus is the Messiah, and this was the design all along. He is the one who will rule to the ends of the earth. As we've discussed, there was a lot of confusion surrounding the Messiah. While the Sadducees had rejected the hope of a Messiah, Pharisees and others still held to these beliefs. We know that many thought Elijah was going to return to prepare things somehow. They also clearly expected the Messiah to be a descendant of David who would rule as king and overthrow their enemies (such as Rome). Beyond this, it appears some people expected the arrival of God's kingdom to happen all at once and to bring a resurrection of the dead for judgment.

As I've tried to point out along the way, Jesus often said things that people may have misunderstood because of these expectations. For example, when he predicted his crucifixion, I doubt anyone thought this meant submitting peacefully to death. They were too deeply entrenched in their association of a cross with insurrection, the cause of countless crucifixions in their time period. Still other times, Jesus confounded his listeners by the way he combined prophesies and defied their expectations. For example, Jesus incorporated several prophesies about the suffering servant figure (who would suffer, die, and be "raised")[1] into predictions about himself. All the while, he would describe himself as the "Son of Man"[2] and "Son of God,"[3] a person expected to rule to the ends of the earth. But no one expected that this "Son of Man" would suffer or that God would become a human being.[4] So as Jesus repeatedly did things as if he were God, people were outraged by what seemed to be blatant blasphemy.

Jesus also challenged the expected timeline of these prophesied events, describing them as developing over a long period of time in multiple stages rather than occurring all at once. He spoke of John the Baptist as the "Elijah" figure who would prepare the way for God's return,[5] whereas people expected Elijah to literally come back. He also repeatedly confirmed his identity as the "Son of Man" who would rule to the ends of the earth and the "Son of David" who would establish the everlasting kingdom. But this wouldn't all happen at once as they anticipated. Instead, Jesus came as a suffering servant to be rejected, crucified, and resurrected. This was all to bring about the forgiveness necessary[6] to establish a new covenant relationship with God[7] and ultimately the outpouring of God's healing Spirit

---

[1] Isaiah 42:1-9, 49:1-6, 50:4-11, 52:13-53:12   [2] Daniel 7:13-14   [3] Psalm 2   [4] Isaiah 9:6
[5] Isaiah 40:3-5; Malachi 3:1, 4:5   [6] Jeremiah 33:8; Micah 7:18-20; Zechariah 13:1
[7] Isaiah 55:3; Jeremiah 31:31-34; Ezekiel 37:26-28

among his people to make them his new temple.[1] Through this, God's salvation and mission has been extended to gentile people.[2] And instead of an epic apocalyptic battle when God would conquer their enemies, Jesus predicted that the temple would soon be destroyed in a war in which they were to flee![3] Afterwards, Jesus promised that he would return one day at an unknown time.[4] He confirmed that there would be a resurrection of the dead[5] and ultimately a new heavens and new earth where God's people would dwell in his kingdom forever.[6] In the meantime, God's people are to be servants even unto death, not warriors leading a violent rebellion. In fact, their belief that death isn't the end will be on display when they are threatened with death because of their belief in his resurrection.

This is the revolution, a truly strange revolution, NOT the war that they had expected. This is the path that leads to life. This is the way that God will ultimately reclaim his creation. Now God's servants are to continue his work, baptizing others into his death and resurrection, living and teaching his ways, and sowing the seeds of this good news[7] to all nations so that it can continue to multiply. This is the kingdom of heaven at work in our world right now as the revolution continues to grow. And, instead of everything happening all at once, it has only just begun.

SOME FINAL WORDS
Matthew 28:18-20

The disciples still have an important role to play, a crucial mission, so he wants to be sure that they understand. They are to be his witnesses, sharing their testimony about all that has happened. They are his messengers. This story *must* be told.

Before he leaves them, Jesus passes along some final marching orders. In what is known as the "Great Commission," Jesus reminds them of what this mission together looks like.

"All authority in heaven and on earth has been given to me. Therefore go and make disciples of all nations, baptizing

---

[1] Ezekiel 36:25-27; Zechariah 1:16, 6:12-13, 12:10 [2] Isaiah 25:6-9, 42:6, 49:6,22, 66:19-21; Hosea 2:23 [3] See chapter 17, Luke 21:20-22 [4] Matthew 24:36 [5] See chapter 16, Matthew 22:30 [6] Matthew 19:28, 24:35, 25:34-36 [7] Isaiah 52:7-10

them in the name of the Father and of the Son and of the Holy Spirit, and teaching them to obey everything I have commanded you. And surely I am with you always, to the very end of the age."

Jesus' crucifixion was effectively his coronation (as we saw with the crown of thorns). It's just a different kind of kingdom than anything they've known before. He is now in charge and has "all authority,"[1] which is being passed on to them. This is what he's been preparing them for all along. They've seen him doing these very things and have even been sent out on their own for a taste of this work. While they've focused their efforts so far primarily on the region of Palestine, the scope of their mission has just gotten much broader. Now they will go to *all nations*, making disciples just as they have experienced through being immersed in his way of living. They are to carry the kingdom to the ends of the earth, continuing to baptize people into this death and resurrection just as they have come to know it. This death and resurrection is the path to life. And this path isn't simply a teaching of Jesus that defies past revelations handed down by the scriptures. It is to be done *in the name of the Father, the Son, and the Holy Spirit.* As he has preached, Jesus has brought all of these things together. It's the same mission, one God, and the message of the ancients finally completed.

For those that enter this faith, the disciples are to then build upon this foundation through carefully instructing people about his ways. Jesus wants them to be transformed that they too might resemble the goodness of God for which they were created. This is the fruit of his kingdom, the seeds of a new tree of life as it spreads and multiplies. While this is happening, Jesus will still be with his followers, guiding them along the way until everything is completed.

God is beginning something that will spread throughout the world, and Jesus' death and resurrection stand at the center. In the past, a temple was seen as the building God dwelled in. Now, his followers have become a foundation or a temple that he will one day restore as a part of the still-awaited completion. A new community is spreading from the one that began among his first followers. There

---

[1] Daniel 7:13-14

is a new family growing across the globe as people are brought into the family of God.

Ultimately, Jesus' resurrection serves as a sort of capstone to his wonders, the culmination of his ministry as he finally overcame death. The cross coupled with the empty tomb offers verification of his teachings all along, that God was pleased to honor Christ's request on the cross to forgive everyone. We no longer have to be afraid. We don't have to try to cover ourselves or hide in our guilt (as Adam and Eve did). We can rest assured that peace has been made and forgiveness can be ours. But God has only just begun the process of re-creating our world, and Jesus is the first to undergo this transformation as a sign of what is to come. Just as Adam and Eve were provided new skins as a covering for their new lives outside of the garden, Jesus' resurrection provides a new flesh for eternal life within God's presence. It is the perfected creation, no longer marred by the imperfections waged upon it in Eden by sin. No more decay or illness. No more suffering or death.

As he once told Martha,[1] Jesus is the resurrection, a sign of the new creation still to come, the new source of life available to all who will come to him just as the Tree of Life was once available to nourish Adam and Eve in the garden. Now, as he taught the disciples at the Last Supper, people are to eat of his fruit, his body and blood, participating in his death and resurrection to be forever restored to God as a part of his renewed creation. The resurrection story isn't just a happy ending to an otherwise gloomy story, it's the story of God initiating the transformation of our world into something new. This is the good news to be proclaimed to the ends of the earth.

In the meantime, death has been defeated, and everyone needs to know. God has arrived as promised to crush the enemy and reverse the curse. Faith is the foundation that he will build upon, and it will begin in Jerusalem, where they must go next. He has promised someone else will join them there. Before it starts, they are still to receive another companion as he told them after the Last Supper, a new "clothing" from on high, just like Adam and Eve received as they set out on their journey after their exile from Eden.

---

[1] John 11:25

A NEW COVERING ARRIVES
Luke 24:50-52; Acts 1:13-14, 2:1-4

> *When he had led them out to the vicinity of Bethany, he lifted up his hands and blessed them. While he was blessing them, he left them and was taken up into heaven. Then they worshiped him and returned to Jerusalem with great joy.*

> *When they arrived, they went upstairs to the room where they were staying. Those present were Peter, John, James and Andrew; Philip and Thomas, Bartholomew and Matthew; James son of Alphaeus and Simon the Zealot, and Judas son of James. They all joined together constantly in prayer, along with the women and Mary the mother of Jesus, and with his brothers.*

And so, after he blesses them, Jesus ascends. This is not to say that Jesus has mysteriously dissolved into nothingness or transitioned from the physical back into the spiritual as if to undo his humanity. Jesus is still fully human, fully physical, and fully divine and now sits "at the right hand of the father," concealed from view. With his resurrected human body, he is now in the eternal presence of God. This same glorified body will one day return in a manner apparent to all, just as he once described to the disciples in the Olivet Discourse.[1]

Notice that the disciples' response is to *worship* him, behavior only appropriately directed towards God. In case there was any doubt, these events have made clear to them that Jesus is God in the flesh. Now, they must wait for God's promised companion as he has commanded, so they return to Jerusalem. There they gather together in prayer and worship: the remaining 11 disciples (no longer 12 because Judas the Iscariot is dead), the group of women, and Jesus' biological family.

As Jesus' followers wait in Jerusalem, it just so happens that another significant festival approaches, a holiday, like Passover, when all faithful believers were expected to travel to Jerusalem. Many of these people had likely heard the strange stories about Jesus. This festival, called Pentecost, occurred 50 days after the Passover.

---

[1] See chapter 17, Matthew 24:27

It celebrated the time when God gave the law through Moses on Mt. Sinai following the exodus, and it corresponded with the end of the harvest season (which began at Passover). We've already seen that the crucifixion and resurrection could be described as another Passover and a new exodus. Now God is finally going to provide Jesus' followers with their awaited companion, a new law written upon their hearts that will dwell within them, a new covering as part of the new covenant.

> *When the day of Pentecost came, they were all together in one place. Suddenly a sound like the blowing of a violent wind came from heaven and filled the whole house where they were sitting. They saw what seemed to be tongues of fire that separated and came to rest on each of them. All of them were filled with the Holy Spirit and began to speak in other tongues, as the Spirit enabled them.*

The spirit of God, appearing as tongues of fire, descends upon them like a great wind. This is the same wind that hovered over the waters in the beginning.[1] Just like the spirit that once descended upon Jesus at his baptism,[2] this wind will carry them on their way as they move on to proclaim this good news to the nations.

Sure enough, they have their new covering. Clothed with God's spirit, they have what is necessary for the journey. The new temple has arrived. God is making his new home, but instead of within a building it is within a people. The people are the temple. Jesus, a new high priest,[3] has made the necessary sacrifice to cover our sin[4] as required by the law. Now, people can have intimate fellowship again with God. God's presence dwells on earth again in a new way, spreading further and further as more people come to place their faith in Jesus. This is the means through which God will occupy new "territory." As Jesus predicted, through his crucifixion and resurrection, God is bringing about this new temple, and its foundation is Jesus.[5]

---

[1] See chapter 1, Genesis 1:2   [2] See chapter 3, Matthew 3:16-17   [3] Psalm 110:4; Zechariah 6:11-13   [4] Isaiah 53:5,8,10,12; Zechariah 3:8-9   [5] Psalm 118:22-23; Zechariah 4:7-9

THE MOVEMENT SPREADS
Acts 2:41-47

And so the story continues. Commissioned as his witnesses to share the story, that's exactly what the disciples do. His disciples, now known as the Apostles, begin telling the story of what has happened to all of the people who have gathered in Jerusalem for this special festival. Their movement quickly grows from a few hundred to thousands. Echoing the significance of Pentecost, they begin to preach about God's providing in Jesus the parameters of a new relationship in fulfillment of the law given through Moses (the very reason people celebrate Pentecost).

...about three thousand were added to their number that day.

They devoted themselves to the apostles' teaching and to fellowship, to the breaking of bread and to prayer. Everyone was filled with awe at the many wonders and signs performed by the apostles. All the believers were together and had everything in common. They sold property and possessions to give to anyone who had need. Every day they continued to meet together in the temple courts. They broke bread in their homes and ate together with glad and sincere hearts, praising God and enjoying the favor of all the people. And the Lord added to their number daily those who were being saved.

Just as Jesus instructed in the Great Commission, the disciples invite others to repentance and faith in Jesus, and a multitude is baptized. The apostles go on to share Jesus' teachings (referred to above as the "apostles' teaching"), and celebrate the crucifixion and resurrection regularly through "the breaking of bread" (as we saw at the Last Supper). These pillars listed above—fellowship (commonly called church), "the breaking of bread" (commonly called communion, the "Lord's Supper," or the Eucharist), baptism, prayer and "the apostles' teaching" (what we know as the New Testament)—go on to become foundational elements of the Christian movement throughout the ages.

Baptism quickly became central to Christian conversion. As people were dipped, dunked, and kneeled into water, it was understood as the once-and-for-all[1] forgiveness of sins as people were "washed clean" and freed from their "slavery" to sin. The practice was also understood as a rebirth[2] as someone "passed through the waters," a kind of new exodus like the one once experienced by Israel during the exodus as God parted the waters to free them from their enemy.[3] Probably most significant of all, baptism was understood as entering into Jesus' death and resurrection[4] as a person lay down in the waters (like a grave) and rose out of them. As you might remember, Jesus spoke of his death and resurrection as a baptism[5] that his followers would enter,[6] and Christians have similarly done so along with confessions of faith to celebrate their entry into a new covenant relationship with God. In many ways, the practice came to resemble the significance of a wedding and the exchange of vows as people celebrated their new union with God. While there are some variations to the tradition, it's still common to see people practice and speak of baptism in these ways today.

The fellowship, or "church," actually comes from the word for a gathering or assembly. It doesn't refer to a building, but a people. It's like a reunion. In fact, for centuries the first Christians met in homes and didn't even have specially built structures. The church is the community of believers who have similarly formed their identity through Jesus. As I've explained, this is the new temple or the dwelling of God upon the earth.[7] In this way, Christians often speak of the church as the "body of Christ,"[8] a living and organic union of unique parts actively serving in the world and directed by God, the head. The church is also often referred to as the "family of God," people radically devoted to one another who have come to find their identity shared together in the community of God.[9] Even the earliest of Christians became known for referring to each other as "brothers

---

[1] Ephesians 4:4-6   [2] John 3:3-8; Titus 3:4-5; 1 Peter 1:3   [3] Exodus 13:17-14:31
[4] Romans 6:3-11; Colossians 2:11-14; 1 Peter 3:18-22   [5] See chapter 17, John 13:6-8
[6] See chapter 14, Mark 10:37-39   [7] Ephesians 2:19-22; Hebrews 3:4-6
[8] 1 Corinthians 12:12-31; Ephesians 4:15-16; Colossians 3:15   [9] Romans 8:15-16

and sisters"[1] and uniquely welcoming newcomers across all sorts of otherwise rigid social boundaries and classes.[2]

It became a common practice early on for Christians to gather together Sunday mornings around sunrise. It wasn't until a few centuries later when Christianity became the religion of Rome that Sundays were celebrated as a day of rest. This gathering on Sunday mornings was to celebrate Jesus' resurrection (which took place on a Sunday morning) before heading off to work. At these gatherings, people often sang together, prayed, shared the stories and teachings of Jesus, and even recited simple creeds.[3] Treating each other like family, they often gave to meet the needs of others within their community. Christians today still gather like this Sunday mornings to remember and celebrate the resurrection.

One of the other special practices of these communities was what now goes by the name of the Eucharist, the "Lord's Supper," or communion. There's reason to think that this was initially celebrated as a full meal together,[4] though over time logistics and other factors influenced the way it was carried out. Built upon the events surrounding the Last Supper,[5] it consists of bread (Jesus' body) and the "fruit of the vine" (Jesus' blood)[6] to celebrate his death and resurrection.[7] Jesus' body was broken and his blood was poured out for the forgiveness of sins to initiate a new covenant relationship with God. Bread is also a basic food and expresses the way Christ sustains his followers along the journey. Wine marks the bittersweet redemption accomplished through his suffering, which ultimately brought salvation through his resurrection. It's a special time to reflect upon and celebrate both things past and still to come. Now Christians look forward one day to partaking of this great feast[8] with Jesus upon his return.

While the first Christians got to dialogue with Jesus' pupils and other eye-witnesses, those teachings have now been passed on to us

---

[1] One Roman writer humorously misunderstood this to be a sign of rampant incest among Christians! [2] Galatians 3:26-29 [3] One of the earliest creeds we have evidence of, called the "Old Roman Creed," is from the 2nd century and is likely a precursor to the later and lengthier "Apostles' Creed" which is still recited by many churches today. [4] 1 Corinthians 11:20-29; Some other early Christian writers describe a Sunday fellowship feast as well. [5] 1 Corinthians 10:16-17, 11:23-26 [6] John 6:32-59 [7] Another ancient writer humorously mistook Christians for cannibals! [8] Isaiah 25:6-8

in the form of the New Testament scriptures. Completed by the end of the first century, these books (memoirs, essays, and letters) were written by and among the apostles and communicate the heart of the faith. I usually explain these scriptures in a few ways: as testimony, story, and message.[1] They are the testimony and account that reveal who God is and what he has done. They are the story that God has orchestrated through human history to bring about salvation. And they are God's message of good news for the world and his teachings for his people.

Finally, prayer is probably the most basic Christian discipline. It's a focused communication with God that involves both speaking and listening. It's kindling the intimate relationship with God's presence, the Holy Spirit, who is the great counselor, teacher, and guide that Jesus promised to send his followers.[2] Prayer expresses the basic struggle to discern the path of righteousness. It's submitting and aligning oneself with the will of God as Jesus once did as he prayed in Gethsemane.[3] It's open and honest, raw communication that can even be artistic.[4] As Jesus once taught,[5] he couldn't explain everything to his followers during his ministry. While he could leave them some useful rules-of-thumb like the "Golden Rule,"[6] they would need to continue to seek God.[7] Prayer is a basic way to do that. As we saw in "the Lord's Prayer,"[8] it commonly involves humbling oneself before God (think of bowing one's head, a common posture when praying). Like any intimate relationship, it takes time and can't be one-sided. And for Christians throughout the ages, it has included forms of reflection or meditation upon the scriptures as a way to absorb God's truth into one's life. In one sense, a person's life is to be a constant prayer to God as they are constantly being transformed (through death and resurrection).

As this new community takes shape, these elements become distinctive of the Christian faith. While there are some variations here and there when it comes to practice, these common threads are

---

[1] John 5:39; Luke 24:44-45, 2 Peter 1:19-21, 2 Timothy 3:14-17   [2] John 14:15-31, 15:26-16:15   [3] Matthew 26:36-46   [4] The book of Psalms is a collection of all sorts of music and poetry used as prayers to God.   [5] John 16:12-15   [6] Matthew 7:12   [7] Matthew 7:7-11
[8] See chapter 7, Matthew 6:9-13

foundational to the church across different periods of time, locations, and even traditions within Christianity, and are present to this day.

SEASONS CHANGE
Revelation 21:1-4, 22:1-5

In the years that follow the arrival of God's spirit at Pentecost, we see many of the things Jesus predicted transpire. Following in the footsteps of Jesus, the fellowship of believers grows and spreads beyond the land of Palestine. But with this growth comes much conflict. Just as Jesus faced resistance from many of the established religious groups, so do his followers in some of these very same places. Like him, they are dragged before courts, beaten, driven out of towns, betrayed by loved ones, and even killed at the hands of angry mobs and cruel emperors. Yet instead of being eliminated, the church continues to grow. As the Apostles are driven from town to town, new communities form and the message spreads farther and farther among gentile people (non-Jews). Within a few decades, the movement grows from being a small following around Judea and Galilee to a transnational movement of people from all sorts of ethnicities spanning North Africa, the Middle East, Europe, and Asia.

As commissioned, the Apostles travel far and wide retelling these stories for the decades that follow as a testimony to Jesus' life, death and resurrection. At a time when not everyone can read and writing is an expensive and laborious process, their oral society heavily favors this kind of interpersonal dialogue with the eyewitnesses instead of written testimonies. However, as the Apostles become targets and begin getting executed, recording their stories in written form becomes essential. It is around the time of one of these early persecutions in the 60s that the first gospel is written. Sometime between the late 50s and mid-90s, four of these testimonies are written and are included in the Bible today as the gospels of Matthew, Mark, Luke, and John.

With the temple's destruction and the murder of most priests during the Jewish Wars in 66-70 A.D., the Sadducees disappear and Judaism is forced to re-organize. After a second revolt around 130 A.D., a pagan temple is constructed in the place of the temple and messianic hopes diminish severely. The Jewish religion coalesces around something like the rabbinical structure of the Pharisaic movement, with different branches taking shape around different teachers. Meanwhile, Christianity (a movement including Jewish people that embraced Jesus as the Messiah) continues to spread. While flying under the radar initially as a sort of Jewish sect, it is viewed more separately by the Romans after the Jewish Wars, and it struggles for recognition as an allowable religion within the empire. Was this community that claimed a Lord other than Caesar treasonous toward Rome? Wasn't its leader a revolutionary punished with crucifixion? Depending on the sentiments of different rulers, Christians in various places experienced periods of peace as well as times of great persecution.

Toward the end of the first century, during another of these persecutions, the last of the remaining disciples, John, now an old man, received a vision recorded in the scriptures as the book of Revelation. It is the last book of the Bible. Writing from the confines of his imprisonment on the island of Patmos, John addresses his book to churches all over Asia. A difficult book to interpret, it is an example of a unique genre called apocalyptic literature and is full of complicated symbols. Its meaning is still heavily debated, but one thing is quite clear. John is writing to encourage the church during what otherwise seem like dark days. As God's instrument spreading his message to the ends of the earth, they are to remain faithful. The book ends with what sounds like a description of the awaited return of Jesus and the final consummation of God's restored kingdom on earth. Interestingly, the final chapters of the Bible bear striking resemblance to the first few, and we catch a glimpse of the final resolution.

> Then I saw "a new heaven and a new earth," for the first heaven and the first earth passed away, and there was no longer any sea. I saw the Holy City, the new Jerusalem, coming down out of heaven from God, prepared as a bride beautifully dressed for her husband. And I heard a loud voice from the throne saying, "Look! God's dwelling place is now among the people, and he will dwell with them. They will be his people, and God himself will be with them and be their

God. 'He will wipe every tear from their eyes. There will be no more death' or mourning or crying or pain, for the old order of things has passed away. "

Then the angel showed me the river of the water of life, as clear as crystal, flowing from the throne of God and of the Lamb down the middle of the great street of the city. On each side of the river stood the tree of life, bearing twelve crops of fruit, yielding its fruit every month. And the leaves of the tree are for the healing of the nations. No longer will there be any curse. The throne of God and of the Lamb will be in the city, and his servants will serve him. They will see his face, and his name will be on their foreheads. There will be no more night. They will not need the light of a lamp or the light of the sun, for the Lord God will give them light. And they will reign for ever and ever.

The end is like the beginning, but it sounds even better. We see the tree of life again bearing fruit for all people, and the curse has been eliminated. The relationship between God and humanity has been restored and resembles a marriage. There is even mention of a bride and groom! But things are also different. There is a throne and God himself is their light. This is the new creation where a new heaven intersects with a transformed earth. The "first" heaven and earth have passed away, and the division between these two realms has been removed. The fullness of God is present and dwelling with people as never before, and they can flourish under God's guidance forever.

EPILOGUE (Finish Here)

Just as our story has brought us back to the beginning, so has our study. If you'll remember, we began in the prologue discussing what makes something a good story. I talked about the ways that good stories reveal who we are and help us understand the experiences we find ourselves in. I said that if the Bible was a good story, it had to address our most basic human struggles. Along the way, we've walked through how the Bible identifies these struggles, and why Christianity views Jesus as central to the solution. As we've explored these stories together, I've attempted to connect these dots for you, but ultimately the question is now back in your hands. What do you think of all of this? Did you find yourself "humming along to the music"? Did it speak to the experiences and struggles of your own life? And ultimately, does this story matter?

I also understand that I've presented you with a challenge. As we've read these stories, I've explained how they were passed along as real events in human history. This claim is significant. It's one thing to like some things that Jesus has said or done, it's another to believe that he is resurrected and has conquered death. It's one thing to think that Jesus is an intriguing historical figure and another thing to believe that Jesus is fully God and human and has forged the path for this world's redemption. It's one thing to think this is a nice story, but another to believe that it's *the* story of the world and the trajectory of all of human history.

So what kind of story do you believe it to be?

I think back to the story where Jesus asked something along these lines of his own disciples. While there were all sorts of theories floating around about him, he turned to them and asked, "Who do you say I am?" We've already witnessed several responses to this question. Many of these same kinds of opinions still circulate today. Was Jesus an ancient wise man, maybe like Buddha? An unfortunate Jewish rabbi? A prophet of God, as Muslims believe? A lunatic, heretic, and blasphemer? Or, even more scandalous, was he the Messiah? As we come to a close, I guess I'd like to leave you with this same question.

Who do you say Jesus is?

It was in my college years that, like a lot of people, I found myself in the middle of all sorts of uncertainty and returning to this question again and again. I was overwhelmed. I didn't know what to make of miracles, or ancient texts with strange moral codes, let alone the constant cultural tensions surrounding Christianity in my own time, but I was still captivated by Jesus. The way I saw it, rather than wander in and out of the extensive arguments that seemed to exist about everything I could imagine, I'd reduce Christianity to a simple question. Did I believe that Jesus rose from the dead? I knew that answering no meant I didn't need to mess around anymore with everything else because, well, it meant that the foundation of Christianity was an enormous lie without any real hope to offer. While I might like some of the teachings, if it wasn't true, Christianity didn't give a solution to the very real struggles of our world. Yet I also knew that if I said yes I had a foundation to build upon. It would give me a starting place to reconstruct how I understood things like the scriptures, miracles, and ultimately, the way I would live my life. While it wouldn't magically answer every question I had, I knew it would at least give me a place to begin again.

As I continued to explore many of the arguments surrounding the gospel texts and the life of Jesus, I was very fortunate to have people in my life who were patient with my questions and generous toward my curiosity. I hope I've at least been able to be something like that for you, the reader, through this book. When it comes to who you believe Jesus is, I realize that some of you have an answer to that question, and others don't. You might find yourself in a place like I just described above, ready to do some more research into a particular issue or concern. Wherever you might be, I should probably explain a little more about where to go from here.

Christians are basically people who have said, "Yes, this is who I am. This is my story, and Jesus is at its center." Built on the belief that this story is ultimately *the* story of humanity, the reason they are called scriptures, Christians trust that this story explains the basic problem (sin and our need for God's help) and offers a resolution in Jesus' death and resurrection. For people interested in such a journey, I'd point to the basic Christian foundations described above with the story of Pentecost: baptism, a fellowship of believers, the Lord's Supper, the apostles' teachings, and engaging in other practices like prayer. Part of the adventure is also joining the mission of sharing this good news with the world. Like other good stories, that could mean something like sharing a book with someone (wink, wink), or sharing your story with others, but ultimately it means reflecting God's goodness to the world.

Some of you might not be ready for (or interested in) all that. But I would still guess this book has at least stirred all sorts of questions. There are surely places where either the scripture texts or my commentary were immensely confusing, and that's ok. I don't want that to be discouraging. Instead, these questions may be a great place to continue. I don't expect to be able to speak with everyone who reads this book, but you can submit some specific questions online at strangerevolution.com. There I will have a FAQ section with questions related to particular stories organized by chapter. I'll also include some other useful resources there as well. But ultimately, such correspondence is probably far less helpful than a face-to-face conversation with someone. As scary as that might be, it's so important! If you aren't someone who would call yourself a Christian, do you know a Christian that you could talk to? Do you have a friend that you might be able to get together with for dinner or to talk to some other way about some questions? I don't know everyone, but I can tell you that any Christian should welcome such a conversation!

Also, please respect that being a Christian doesn't mean having answers to everything. In fact, it may not even mean being familiar with all the stories we've covered in this book. And it definitely doesn't mean that someone believes they are perfect or "good enough" (as we've talked about before). Being a Christian means acknowledging one's imperfection and trusting God. It means "taking up one's cross" as Jesus once said to his disciples. If you talk to someone, they may not be able to answer your questions, but I'd bet that they can at least listen and help you along the way.

Along these lines, churches are another great resource. If you don't personally know a Christian you can talk to, is there a gathering in town that you know of or are comfortable approaching? Again, most Christians I know would be pretty happy to sit down and talk with someone that had "read a book" and had a bunch of questions. Also, while Christianity might have some different flavors based on different views or traditions here and there, what I've presented in this book, at its core, is common to Christianity across various denominational lines. I'd go so far as to say that if you are finding a "Christian" or "church" significantly at odds with the basics you encountered in this book, you would be better off looking elsewhere.

Another great place to start is actually prayer. Is that a surprise? If you're someone who at least believes in some sort of higher power or a being that can communicate, why not ask that higher power for some help as you try to understand more? If you don't believe in God but are still curious about the possibility, what would it hurt? Heck, you could even ask this God for some help as you pursue your questions.

But, for those of you still shaking your head "no," I hope that you can at least walk away with a better understanding of Christianity, and I hope that you'll keep an open mind in case anything might change down the road.

Well, I think that's all for now. Thanks again for joining me. I hope that you've enjoyed our journey together, and that in some way or another, it's just the beginning!

ACKNOWLEDGMENTS

As a young man, I always had the sense that one day I would write, so this is a bit surreal. It's hard to imagine this book ever coming to be without the influence and contributions of countless people along the way.

To New Beginnings Christian Fellowship in Evansville, IN, you were the first fellowship I was ever comfortable calling a home. I saw the scriptures come to life while I was with you. "Were not our hearts burning within us..." To Mark Whited for giving a young minister the room to grow. I benefitted immensely under your tutelage, and the material in this book was sparked during our time together. To Jim Ware for teaching me most of what I know of the scriptures, really. Your contributions as a teacher, a friend, and more recently as a reader, are all over this book. To Wesley Sam-Bruce and Julie Garbus for your willingness to share your unique gifts and joining me to make this idea a reality.

To my parents and family who have faithfully encouraged me even along less-than-practical paths. I wouldn't be here without you. To my amazing wife, Rachel, whose patience and encouragement have been unending throughout this endeavor. This project surely would have ended if you hadn't believed in me and convinced me that I wasn't an idiot for trying. And finally, to God whose grace and inspiration seem unending. Thine is the kingdom, power, and glory forever. Amen.